Step by Step Spreadsheets

Second Edition

Alan Dillon

Gill & Macmillan

Gill & Macmillan Ltd
Hume Avenue
Park West
Dublin 12
with associated companies throughout the world
www.gillmacmillan.ie

978 07171 4746 5

Design by Mike Connor Design & Illustration
Print origination by Carole Lynch

The paper used in this book is made from the wood pulp of managed forests. For every tree felled, at least one tree is planted, thereby renewing natural resources.

A catalogue record is available for this book from the British Library.

Contents

Chapter 2: Spreadsheet Functions 38

Chapter 3: Linking Data in Worksheets 79

Chapter 4: Spreadsheet Charts 101

Chapter 5: Sorting Spreadsheet Data 142

About This Book

The assignments in this book were written specifically for Microsoft Excel 2007 but can also be completed using Excel 2003. It is a 'learning through practice' book with lots of practical assignments for the student. No previous knowledge of Excel is needed as the assignments start at a very basic level. The book contains three sections:

- Section 1: Beginners' Spreadsheet Assignments
- Section 2: Intermediate and Advanced Spreadsheet Assignments
- Section 3: Project Guidelines and Sample Exams

Students who have no previous spreadsheet experience should start with Section 1. Students already familiar with Microsoft Excel may wish to start with Section 2. However, you may find it beneficial to practise and consolidate your existing spreadsheet skills by completing Section 1.

As you progress through the book, assignments gradually become more complex, with new spreadsheet topics introduced in each chapter. I would encourage students who are already familiar with the SUM function to complete the assignments contained in Chapter 1, which deals with spreadsheet formulas, as this is a very important area often overlooked by students.

Students who are already familiar with Excel will be able to use this book as an independent study guide. However, as it wasn't possible to include certain details relating to formatting and editing spreadsheets, I am leaving this to the teacher.

By completing all the assignments contained in *Step by Step Spreadsheets*, you will have covered all the necessary course material required to successfully complete the FETAC Level 5 Spreadsheet Methods Module.

New versions of Microsoft Excel will be introduced over time. Because the assignments deal more with the principles of spreadsheets than with the features of Microsoft Excel, I am confident that, except for a few minor inconsistencies, the assignments will also be compatible with future versions of Microsoft Excel.

The following symbols are used throughout the book.

Tip	**Note**	**Rule**	**Shortcut**	**Hint**	**Important Point**

Introduction

HISTORY OF THE SPREADSHEET

The spreadsheet was invented in 1978 by Dan Bricklin who, at the time, was a business student attending university in America. As Dan attended lectures in finance, he found that his teachers had to constantly rub out and rewrite numbers on the board as a change in one number, e.g. an interest rate or tax rate, would affect many other numbers. The solution was Visicalc, the first computerised spreadsheet, which was sold with the Apple II computer.

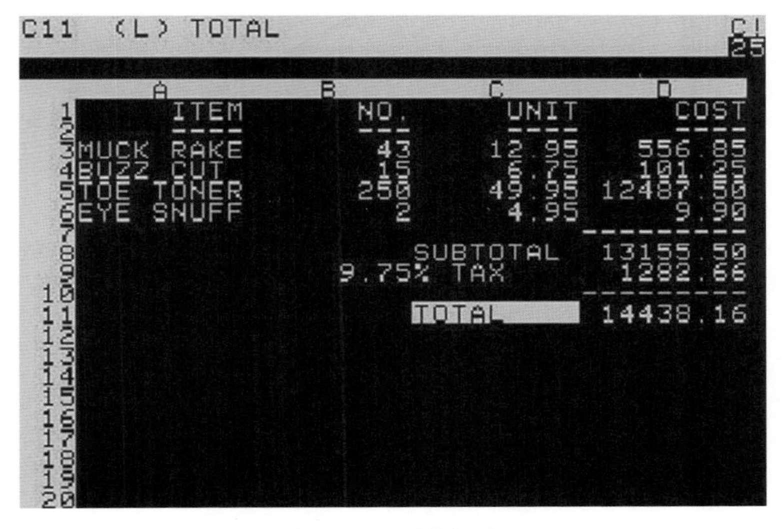

Figure 0.1 Visicalc

In the spreadsheet, the effects of a change in one number could be seen instantly. Visicalc sold over 700,000 copies, but it was quickly overtaken by Lotus 1-2-3 which became the leading spreadsheet package in the 1980s.

Released in 1983, Lotus 1-2-3 was included with the IBM XT PC. It was responsible for a massive increase in sales of the IBM PC mainly because the Lotus 1-2-3 spreadsheet made the IBM PC attractive to the business market. Lotus 1-2-3 included charts which weren't available in Visicalc.

Both Visicalc and Lotus 1-2-3 were written for MS-DOS (*Microsoft Disk Operating System*) so they didn't work with the mouse. There were no menus or toolbar buttons, which made them much more difficult to use than modern spreadsheets. As there was only one worksheet, the spreadsheet user had to scroll vertically or horizontally when the spreadsheet was too big to fit in one screen.

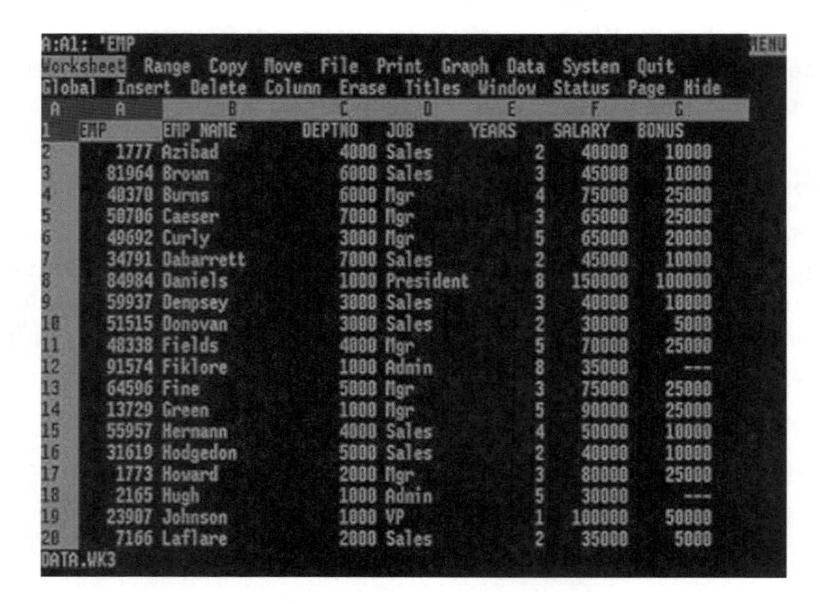

A:A1: 'EMP
Worksheet Range Copy Move File Print Graph Data System Quit
Global Insert Delete Column Erase Titles Window Status Page Hide

	A	B	C	D	E	F	G
1	EMP	EMP_NAME	DEPTNO	JOB	YEARS	SALARY	BONUS
2	1777	Azibad	4000	Sales	2	40000	10000
3	81964	Brown	6000	Sales	3	45000	10000
4	40370	Burns	6000	Mgr	4	75000	25000
5	50706	Caeser	7000	Mgr	3	65000	25000
6	49692	Curly	3000	Mgr	5	65000	20000
7	34791	Dabarrett	7000	Sales	2	45000	10000
8	84984	Daniels	1000	President	8	150000	100000
9	59937	Dempsey	3000	Sales	3	40000	10000
10	51515	Donovan	3000	Sales	2	30000	5000
11	48338	Fields	4000	Mgr	5	70000	25000
12	91574	Fiklore	1000	Admin	8	35000	---
13	64596	Fine	5000	Mgr	3	75000	25000
14	13729	Green	1000	Mgr	5	90000	25000
15	55957	Hermann	4000	Sales	4	50000	10000
16	31619	Hodgedon	5000	Sales	2	40000	10000
17	1773	Howard	2000	Mgr	3	80000	25000
18	2165	Hugh	1000	Admin	5	30000	---
19	23907	Johnson	1000	VP	1	100000	50000
20	7166	Laflare	2000	Sales	2	35000	5000

DATA.WK3

Figure 0.2 Lotus 1-2-3

Microsoft Excel was initially written for the Apple Macintosh in 1984. Excel was the first spreadsheet to use a graphical user interface that worked with the mouse.

Figure 0.3 The first version of Excel for the Apple Macintosh

Spreadsheet users could issue commands to the spreadsheet by selecting menu options or by clicking toolbar buttons with the mouse. This was much easier than the old method of typing sequences of keyboard shortcuts and was an instant hit.

Microsoft launched the Windows operating system in 1987 together with a version of Excel written specifically for the PC. Excel quickly became the spreadsheet of choice and continues to be the market leading spreadsheet package.

WHAT IS A SPREADSHEET?

A spreadsheet is a computer application designed to assist in any type of work involving numbers and calculations. It is made up of rows and columns. Each row is identified by a unique number (1, 2, 3 and so on). Each column is identified by a unique letter (A, B, C and so on). The intersection of a row and a column is called a cell. The current cell is indicated by the cell pointer.

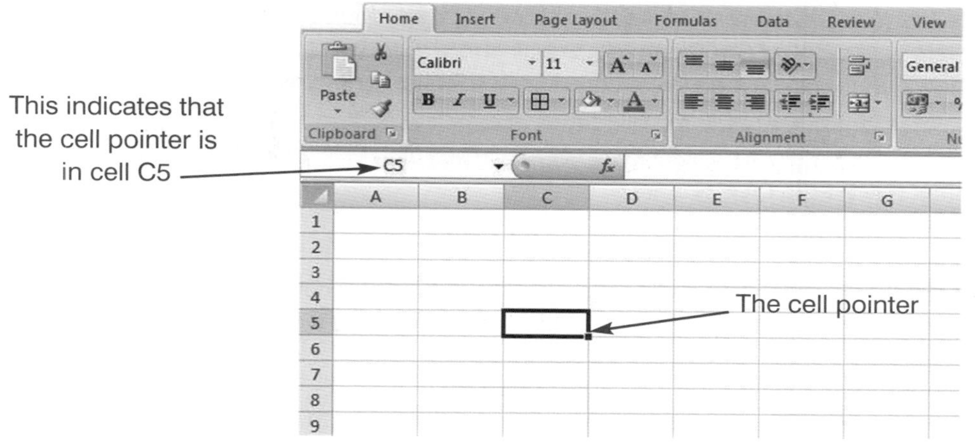

Figure 0.4 A blank Microsoft Excel spreadsheet

In Figure 0.4, the cell pointer is in column C and row 5. This is called cell C5.

WHAT CAN A SPREADSHEET DO FOR YOU?

If you work with numbers regularly, a spreadsheet can save you lots of time. Spreadsheets are great for all types of financial calculation such as budgets, cash-flow statements, profit and loss accounts and travel expenses. Spreadsheets can also be used for statistical analysis with special functions to calculate averages and standard deviations. The spreadsheet's charting facility enables you to present information in a manner that is easy to understand.

Two particular spreadsheet features make them very attractive to people who regularly work with numbers.

1. The ability to copy spreadsheet calculations. For example, a formula to calculate total sales in January can be copied to all of the other months in the year. This is much quicker than having to create a separate formula for each month.

2. The automatic updating of spreadsheet calculations. Because spreadsheet calculations can be linked, changing a single number in a spreadsheet can often cause many other numbers to change. For example, in a monthly profit forecast, changing the tax rate would automatically recalculate the profit figure for each of the 12 months. Doing this without a spreadsheet is very time-consuming.

As Dan Bricklin watched his lecturers laboriously write out the results of calculations on the board, repeating the same calculation for each month of the year, he realised that a computerised spreadsheet would make this process much more efficient. Little did he know that it would become one of the most widely used computer applications in the world!

Many students find it difficult to understand the difference between a database and a spreadsheet. Databases are great for storing large amounts of data and then retrieving that data very quickly. Spreadsheets are all about numbers and calculations. To use an analogy, a database is a bit like a computerised telephone directory and a spreadsheet is like a computerised pocket calculator.

WORKSHEET TABS

Each Excel 2007 spreadsheet consists of three worksheets. This is like having a copy book with three pages. If you fill up the screen with data in the first worksheet, you can enter more data in the second and third worksheets. You can easily switch between worksheets by clicking the worksheet tabs, shown in Figure 0.5. Additional worksheets can be added to the spreadsheet if you need more than three worksheets.

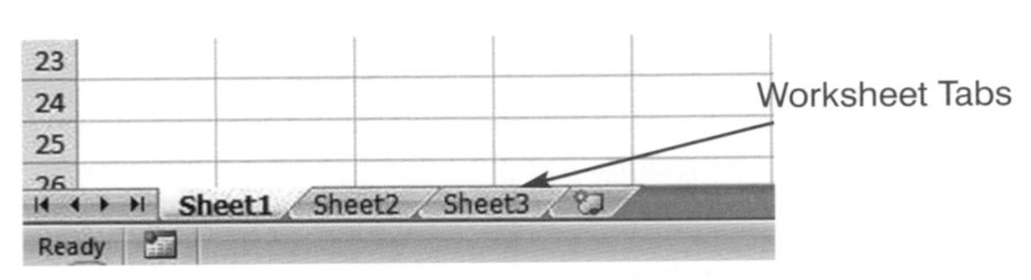

Figure 0.5 By default each Excel spreadsheet contains three worksheets

When data has been entered in more than one worksheet, the worksheets can be linked. For example, Sheet1 could contain data relating to the sales department, Sheet2 could contain data relating to the production department and Sheet3 could summarise data from the sales and production departments.

THE SPREADSHEET WINDOW

The spreadsheet window is the section of the spreadsheet currently visible on the computer screen. The screen is not big enough to display the entire spreadsheet and only a very small percentage of the spreadsheet is visible at any given time.

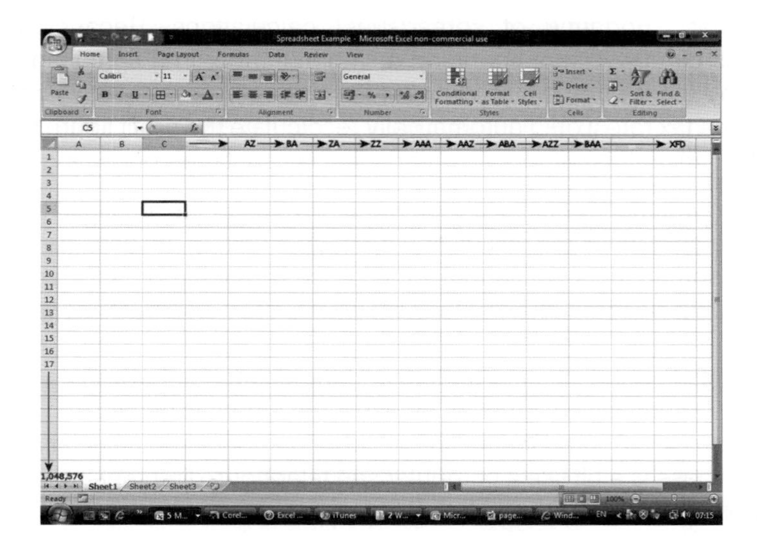

Figure 0.6 The spreadsheet window

Figure 0.6 will give you an idea of the size of an Excel 2007 spreadsheet. It has 1,048,576 rows and 16,384 columns. After column Z, the columns are labelled AA, AB and so on until ZZ. Then the columns are labelled AAA, AAB and so on until the final column, which is XFD.

THE RIBBON

In Excel 2007, the menus and toolbars have been replaced by the Ribbon, which helps you quickly find the commands that you need to complete a task.

Figure 0.7 Commands in the Ribbon are organised into seven groups

Using the Ribbon is very intuitive. Commands in the Ribbon are organised into seven groups; Home, Insert, Page Layout, Formulas, Data, Review and View. A particular section of the Ribbon can be selected by clicking the appropriate tab. Each group in the Ribbon is divided into sections of related buttons. Figure 0.7 displays the commands in the Home section of the Ribbon, which is displayed by default. It contains the Clipboard, Font, Alignment, Number, Styles, Cells and Editing sections. Commands in the Home group can be used for formatting, copying and pasting, inserting and deleting rows or columns as well as sorting data in your spreadsheet.

If you like using shortcut key combinations, you can access Ribbon commands by pressing *ALT* on the keyboard. Once you press *ALT*, letters representing each Ribbon group are displayed together with the letter *F*, which represents the Office button (Figure 0.8). The buttons in the quick access toolbar are represented by numbers.

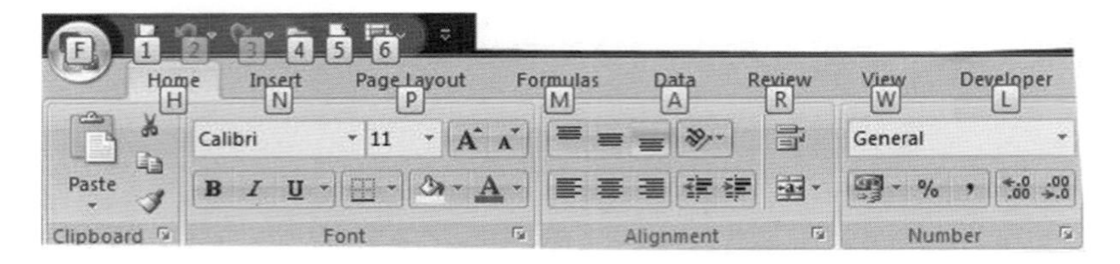

Figure 0.8 Pressing the ALT key displays keyboard shortcuts for the Ribbon

Shortcut key combinations for the commands in a specific Ribbon group can be displayed by typing the appropriate letter on the keyboard. For example, pressing *H* displays the shortcut key combinations for the Home group, as shown in Figure 0.9.

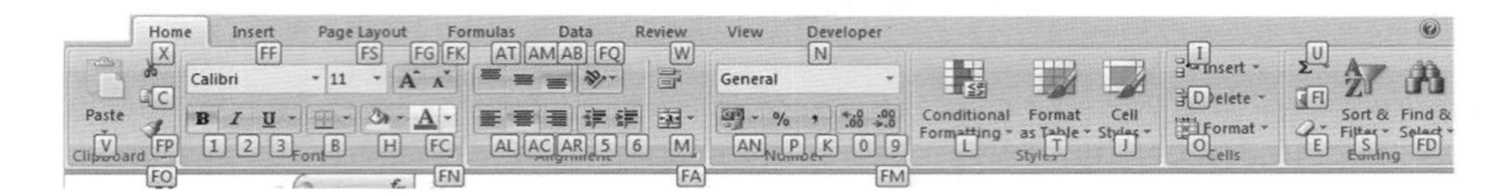

Figure 0.9 Shortcut key combinations in the Home group

In Figure 0.9, the keyboard shortcuts for the Home group are displayed. Each keyboard shortcut can be used to access a specific command or button. For example, typing *1* will format the current cell or selected cells to Bold. The complete sequence of commands is *ALT+H+1*. If you use these keyboard combinations frequently, they can speed up many tasks.

THE OFFICE BUTTON

In Excel 2007 the File menu has been replaced by the Office button. Commands to create, save or print spreadsheet files do not appear in the Ribbon and are accessed by clicking the Office button, as shown in Figure 0.10.

Clicking the Office button also displays a list of recently used files in Excel. Files can be permanently pinned to the list by clicking the pin icon to the right of the file name.

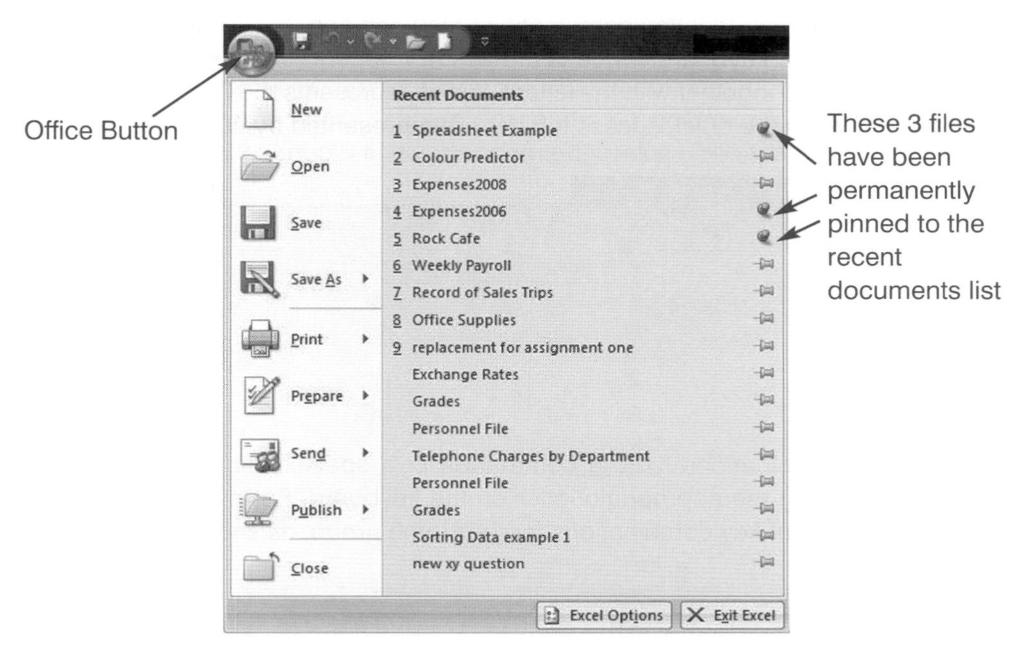

Figure 0.10 Common commands and recent documents are accessed by clicking the Office button

In Office 2010, the Office button has been replaced by the File menu.

QUICK ACCESS TOOLBAR

The Quick Access Toolbar (Figure 0.11) contains frequently used commands. It appears to the right of the Office button and can also be used to open or save a spreadsheet file as well as creating new spreadsheet files. The Undo and Redo buttons also appear in the Quick Access Toolbar.

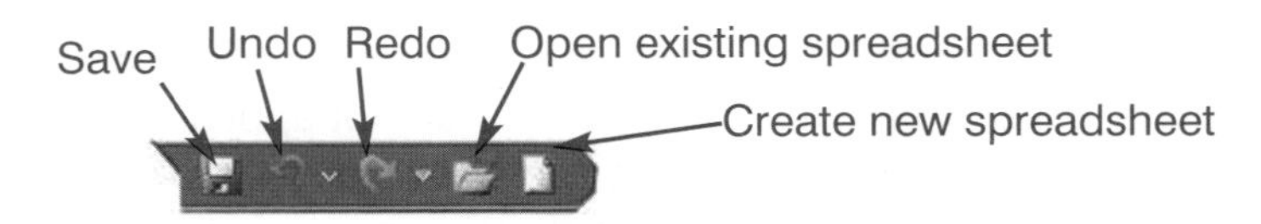

Figure 0.11 The Quick Access Toolbar

Because the Quick Access Toolbar is always visible, adding commands that you frequently use to this toolbar makes the commands readily available.

POP-UP MENUS

Pressing the right mouse button will display a pop-up menu in Excel. Different pop-up menus will appear depending on where the mouse pointer is on the screen. Right clicking a *spreadsheet cell* displays the menu shown in Figure 0.12.

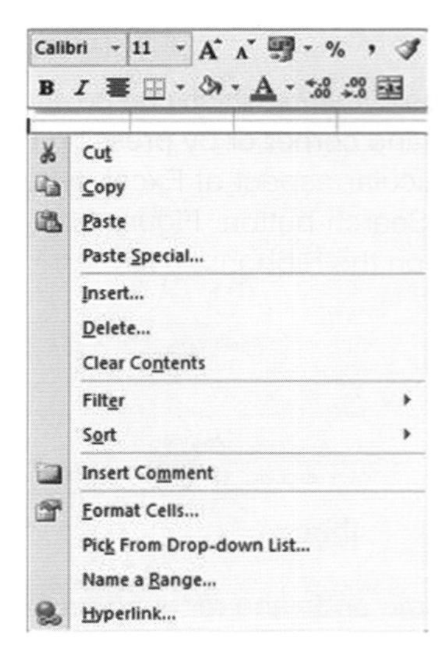

Figure 0.12 This menu is displayed when you right click on a spreadsheet cell

Using the options displayed in Figure 0.12, you can, for example, format, move or copy the data stored in the cell.

Right clicking a *worksheet tab* displays the menu shown in Figure 0.13.

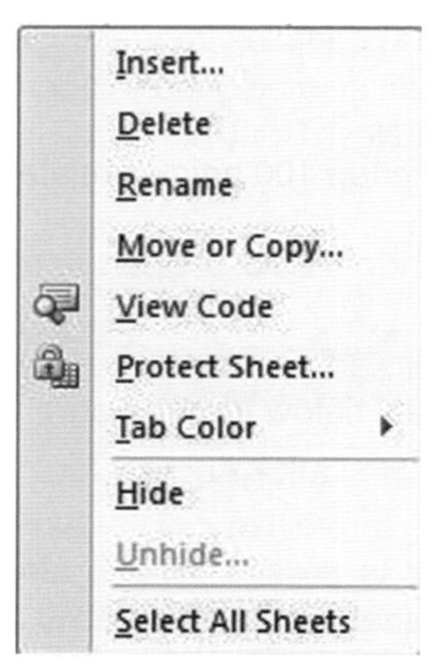

Figure 0.13 This menu is displayed when you right click on a worksheet tab

Using the options displayed in Figure 0.13, you can insert or delete a worksheet, rename a worksheet or change the tab colour of a worksheet as well as move or copy a worksheet.

GETTING HELP IN EXCEL

Excel contains a very powerful help feature which can be accessed either by clicking the question mark in the top right-hand corner or by pressing F1 on the keyboard.

To search for help on a particular aspect of Excel, type your search term into the search box and then click the Search button. Figure 0.14 is an example of using the help feature to find information on the Ribbon.

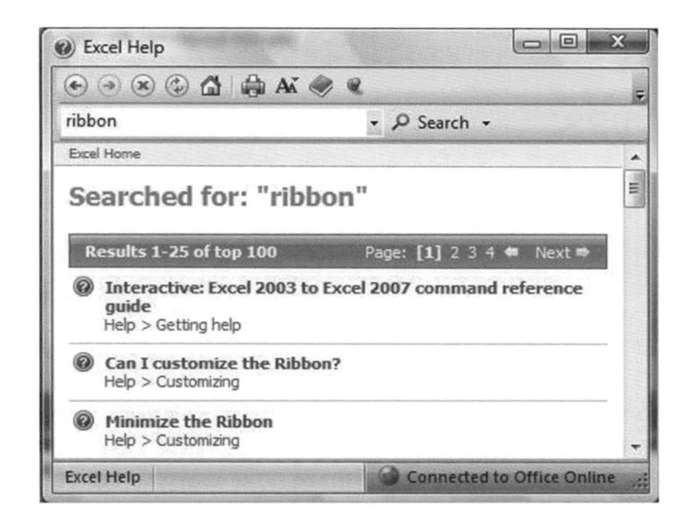

Figure 0.14 An example of searching for help on the Ribbon

In Figure 0.14 Excel is displaying the top 100 articles related to the Ribbon. To read an article, simply click the article's title.

THE FORMULA BAR

The formula bar appears immediately below the Ribbon.

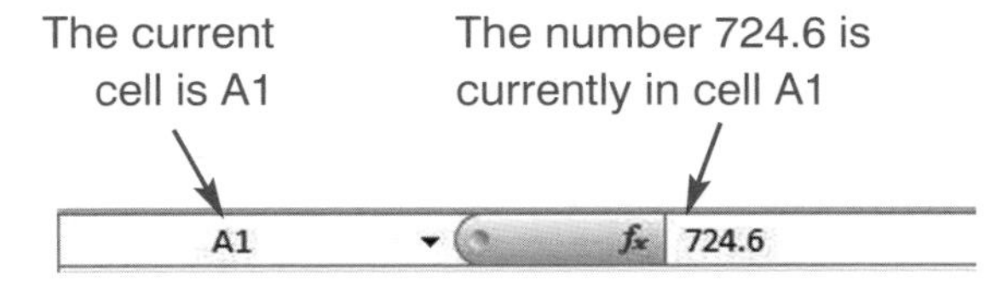

Figure 0.15 The formula bar displaying the contents of cell A1

It provides us with two important pieces of information: the current location of the cell pointer and the contents of the current cell. A cell may contain text, a number or a formula/function. In Figure 0.15, the formula bar is indicating that the cell pointer in is A1 and that 724.6 is stored in this cell.

Figure 0.16 As C1 contains a formula, this formula is displayed in the formula bar

When a cell contains a formula, as shown in Figure 0.16, the result of the formula is displayed in the cell and the formula is displayed in the formula bar. The formula bar is also used for editing individual cell data.

MOUSE POINTERS

As you point at different items on the screen, the mouse pointer takes on different shapes. The shape of the mouse pointer determines what will happen when you click the left or right button of the mouse and also determines what will happen when you click and drag using the left mouse button. Mouse pointers and their functions are summarised in Table 0.1.

Mouse Pointer	Function
	Use this mouse pointer to select a single cell or to highlight a number of cells. It can also be used to select an entire row by clicking a row number or an entire column by clicking a column letter.
	This mouse pointer is used to select commands from the Ribbon. It can also be used to move data in the current cell or a number of highlighted cells by pointing at the edge of the cell or highlighted cells and dragging.
Fill Handle	The mouse pointer takes the shape of a black cross when it is positioned above the Fill Handle, at the bottom right-hand corner of the cell pointer. Holding down the left mouse button and dragging while the mouse pointer has this shape will copy the cell contents.

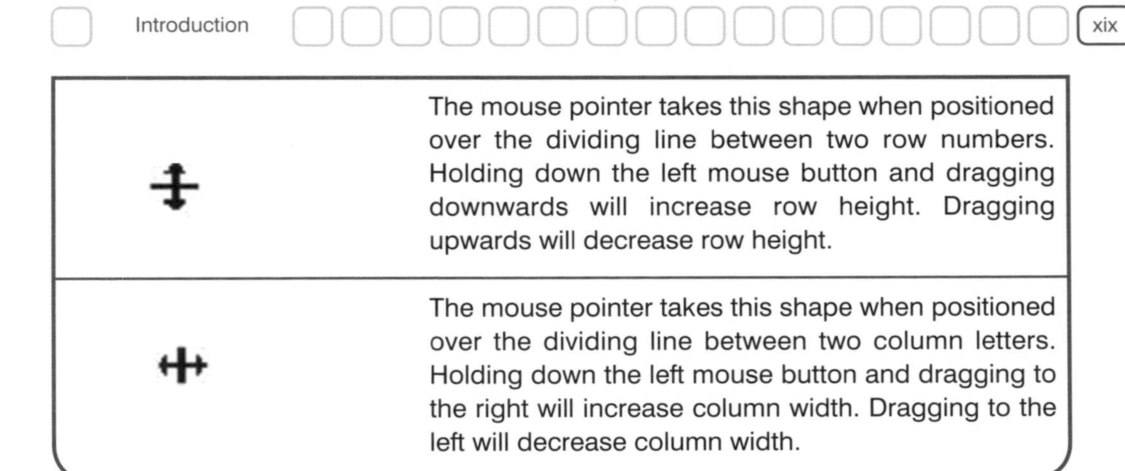

	The mouse pointer takes this shape when positioned over the dividing line between two row numbers. Holding down the left mouse button and dragging downwards will increase row height. Dragging upwards will decrease row height.
	The mouse pointer takes this shape when positioned over the dividing line between two column letters. Holding down the left mouse button and dragging to the right will increase column width. Dragging to the left will decrease column width.

Table 0.1

ENTERING DATA IN A SPREADSHEET

A single item of data is generally entered in each spreadsheet cell. An item of data can be text, a number, a formula or a function.

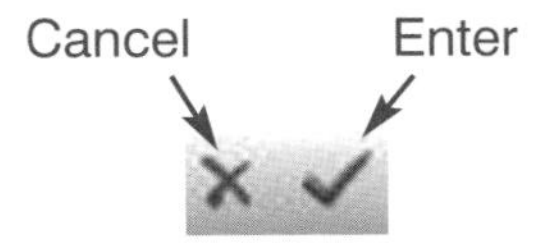

As soon as you type something in a cell, the Cancel and Enter symbols appear in the formula bar.

In Figure 0.17, the cell pointer is in A1 and the spreadsheet user has typed the text 'Month'. This text can be entered in the spreadsheet in a number of ways: by pressing Enter on the keyboard, by pressing the right or down arrow key or by clicking the Enter button in the formula bar.

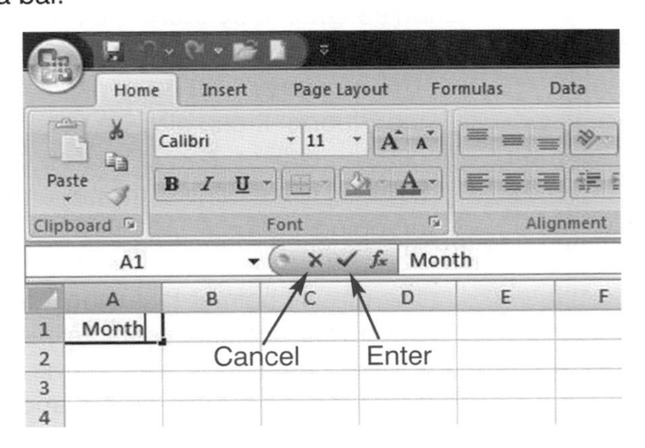

Figure 0.17 Entering data in a spreadsheet cell

To reject what was typed, press *Esc* on the keyboard or click the Cancel button in the formula bar.

WHAT CAN YOU TYPE IN A SPREADSHEET CELL?

Depending on what you type in a spreadsheet cell, it will be interpreted as one of three things: a number, text or a formula/function.

1. A Number

This is anything that begins with a number and doesn't contain any text.

Examples: 3
46
156

But not: 3 cars
46x
room 156

2. Text

This is anything that contains words or letters.

Examples: Monday
09KY2296
10CF

3. Formulas and Functions

All the calculations in a spreadsheet are done by formulas and functions. Each formula or function begins with the equals sign and refers to cell references. Spreadsheet functions have specific names such as SUM or AVERAGE.

Examples:

Formula	**Function**
=A1+A2	=average(B15:B30)

If you don't start a formula or function with an equals sign, Excel will interpret it as text.

A typical spreadsheet will contain all three types of data; numbers, text and formulas/functions, as shown in Figure 0.18.

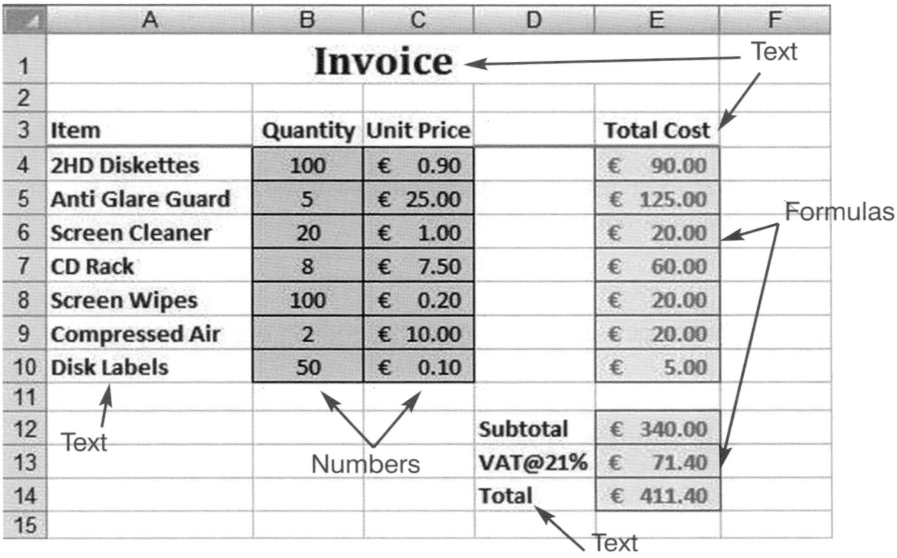

	A	B	C	D	E	F
1			Invoice			
2						
3	Item	Quantity	Unit Price		Total Cost	
4	2HD Diskettes	100	€ 0.90		€ 90.00	
5	Anti Glare Guard	5	€ 25.00		€ 125.00	
6	Screen Cleaner	20	€ 1.00		€ 20.00	
7	CD Rack	8	€ 7.50		€ 60.00	
8	Screen Wipes	100	€ 0.20		€ 20.00	
9	Compressed Air	2	€ 10.00		€ 20.00	
10	Disk Labels	50	€ 0.10		€ 5.00	
11						
12				Subtotal	€ 340.00	
13				VAT@21%	€ 71.40	
14				Total	€ 411.40	
15						

Text, Formulas, Numbers, Text, Text

Figure 0.18

Formulas will be explained in detail in Chapter 1. Functions will be introduced in Chapter 2.

SECTION 1

Beginners' Spreadsheet Assignments

Symbols used in this book:

Tip **Note** **Rule** **Shortcut** **Hint** **Important Point**

1 Spreadsheet Formulas

In Chapter 1, you will learn how to:

- Enter data in a spreadsheet
- Print a spreadsheet
- Create basic spreadsheet formulas using addition, subtraction, multiplication and division
- Copy spreadsheet formulas
- Move and copy spreadsheet data
- Use brackets in a formula
- Use absolute cell references
- Calculate percentages.

Spreadsheets are all about numbers and calculations. Using a spreadsheet will allow you to do your calculations quicker and more accurately. A spreadsheet calculation can be carried out using either a formula or a function. In this chapter you will learn how to create and copy spreadsheet formulas.

CELL REFERENCES

Before you can create a spreadsheet formula, it is important to understand the concept of a cell reference.

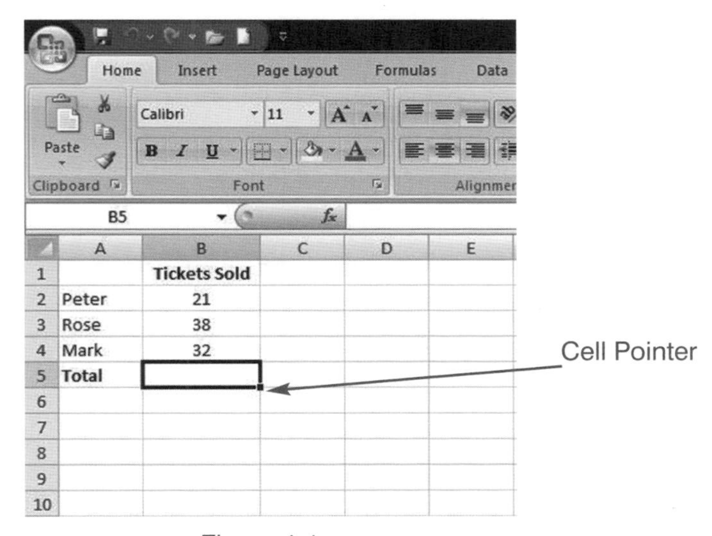

Figure 1.1

A spreadsheet is divided into rows and columns. The rows are identified using numbers 1, 2, 3 and so on. The columns are identified with letters A, B, C and so on. This can be seen in Figure 1.1. The intersection of a row and a column is called a cell. Each cell is rectangular in shape and has a unique name depending on which row it is in and which column it is in. For example, 'Tickets Sold' is in cell B1. 'Total' is in cell A5. In spreadsheet terminology, these cell names are called cell references. When writing a cell reference, the column letter is always written first and this is followed by the row number. The cell pointer allows us to select a particular cell. In Figure 1.1, the cell pointer is in B5.

CREATING A SPREADSHEET FORMULA

Spreadsheet formulas are used for calculations involving plus(+), minus(-), multiply(*) or divide(/). In mathematics, these are called the arithmetic operators. A spreadsheet formula is created by combining cell references with one or more arithmetic operators. Each Excel formula must start with the = sign. In Figure 1.1, we will calculate the Total using an addition formula. Initially, it is a good idea to break down the process of creating a formula into two distinct steps:

Step	Process	Result
1	Think of the formula in numbers	21+38+32
2	Replace each number with its corresponding cell reference. Remember to start the formula with =	=B2+B3+B4

Table 1.1 Calculating total tickets sold

In Figure 1.1 the individual ticket sales of the three sellers are in cells B2, B3 and B4. These three cell references are combined with + to make a spreadsheet formula. Remember that all Excel formulas start with =. The completed formula is

=B2+B3+B4

Before entering the formula, ensure that the cell pointer is in the correct position. Once B5 is selected, the formula can be entered, as seen in Figure 1.2.

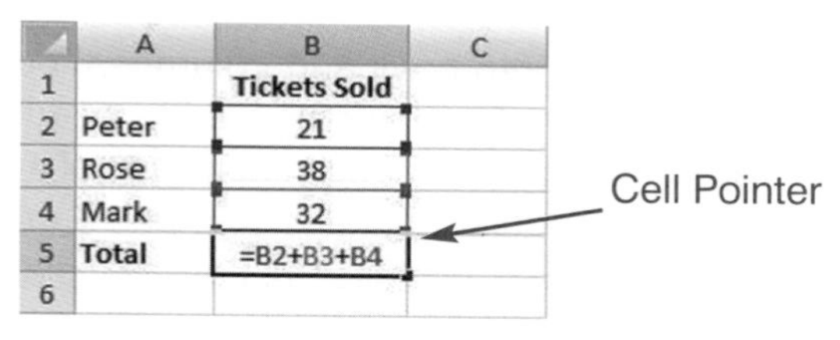

	A	B	C
1		**Tickets Sold**	
2	Peter	21	
3	Rose	38	
4	Mark	32	
5	**Total**	=B2+B3+B4	
6			

Figure 1.2 An addition formula has been entered in B5

When you press Enter, Excel calculates the result, giving *91*. This is shown in Figure 1.3.

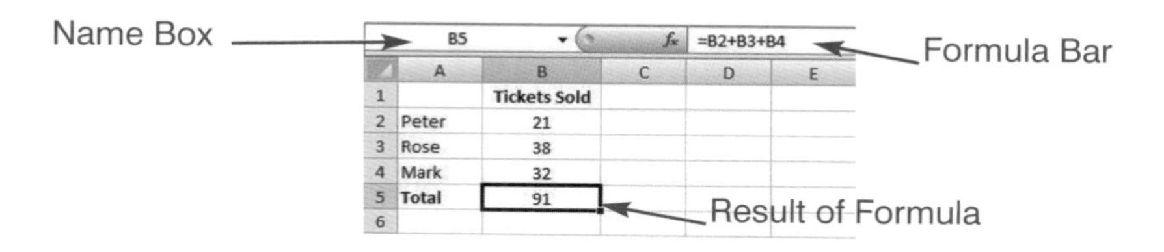

B5 =B2+B3+B4

	A	B	C	D	E
1		Tickets Sold			
2	Peter	21			
3	Rose	38			
4	Mark	32			
5	Total	91			
6					

Figure 1.3 The result of the calculation is displayed in B5.
The formula is displayed in the formula bar.

In Figure 1.3, B5, which is currently selected by the cell pointer, displays the result of the formula. The formula itself is displayed in the Formula Bar. The Name Box tells us that the cell pointer is in B5. The Formula Bar, Name Box and Cell Pointer are important concepts to familiarise yourself with as you will use them in each spreadsheet assignment.

 All spreadsheet formulas start with =

 If you don't start your formula with =, Excel will interpret it as text and will not carry out the calculation.

COPYING A SPREADSHEET FORMULA

One of the major advantages of using a spreadsheet is the ability to copy formulas. This greatly reduces the amount of calculation work. As a formula is copied, it automatically adjusts depending on whether it is being copied across or down.

Fill Right

In Figure 1.4, a formula to calculate total lecture attendance for Monday has been entered in B9. This formula can be seen in the Formula Bar.

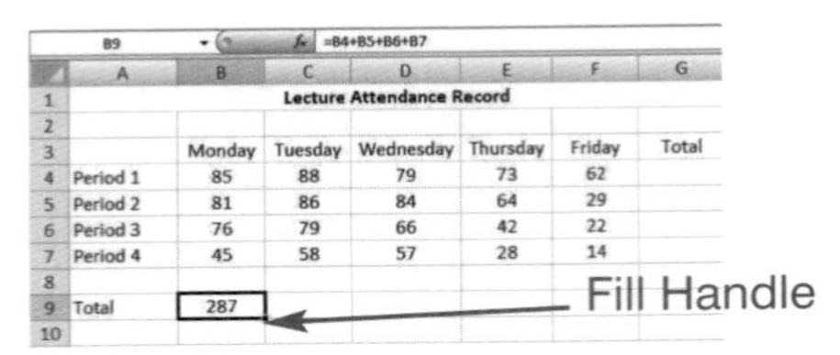
B9 =B4+B5+B6+B7

	A	B	C	D	E	F	G
1		Lecture Attendance Record					
2							
3		Monday	Tuesday	Wednesday	Thursday	Friday	Total
4	Period 1	85	88	79	73	62	
5	Period 2	81	86	84	64	29	
6	Period 3	76	79	66	42	22	
7	Period 4	45	58	57	28	14	
8							
9	Total	287					
10							

Figure 1.4 The Fill Handle is used to copy a spreadsheet formula

We can copy the formula using the Fill Handle, which is a small black square at the bottom right-hand corner of the cell pointer. When the mouse pointer is positioned over the Fill Handle, it changes to a black cross, indicating that the cell contents can be copied.

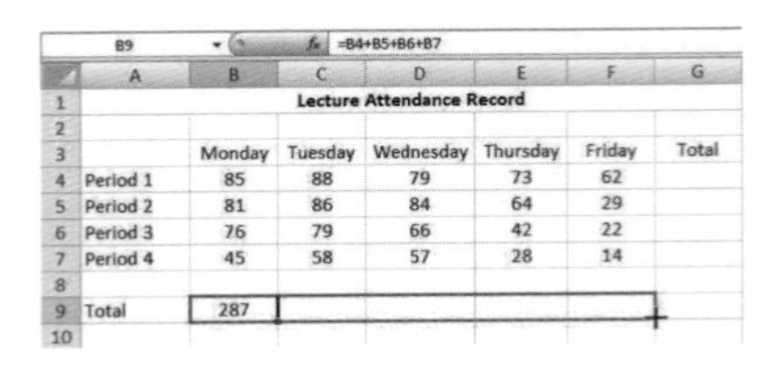
B9 =B4+B5+B6+B7

	A	B	C	D	E	F	G
1		Lecture Attendance Record					
2							
3		Monday	Tuesday	Wednesday	Thursday	Friday	Total
4	Period 1	85	88	79	73	62	
5	Period 2	81	86	84	64	29	
6	Period 3	76	79	66	42	22	
7	Period 4	45	58	57	28	14	
8							
9	Total	287					
10							

Figure 1.5 Copying a formula using Fill Right

The formula is copied by holding down the left mouse button and dragging to the right. In Figure 1.5, the formula in B9 will be copied to C9, D9, E9 and F9. In Excel, copying a formula to the right is called **Fill Right**.

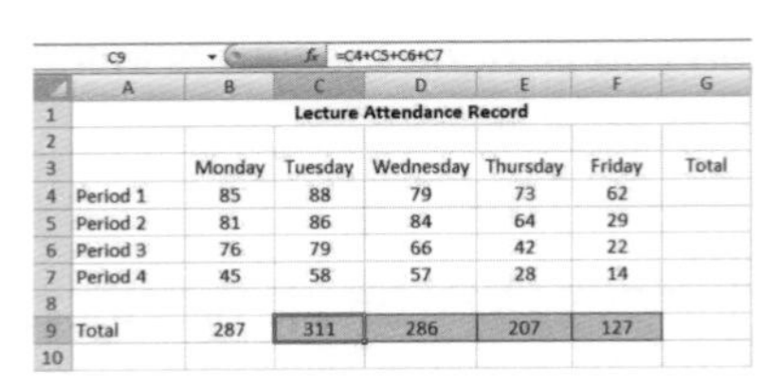
C9 =C4+C5+C6+C7

	A	B	C	D	E	F	G
1		Lecture Attendance Record					
2							
3		Monday	Tuesday	Wednesday	Thursday	Friday	Total
4	Period 1	85	88	79	73	62	
5	Period 2	81	86	84	64	29	
6	Period 3	76	79	66	42	22	
7	Period 4	45	58	57	28	14	
8							
9	Total	287	311	286	207	127	
10							

Figure 1.6 The results of Fill Right

When the left mouse button is released, Excel copies the formula to the selected cells. In Figure 1.6 cells C9 to F9 have been shaded to emphasise the results of the Fill Right process. Notice from the formula bar that the cell references have adjusted. The original formula was

=B4+B5+B6+B7

By copying this formula one column to the right, the letters in the cell references have increased by one, giving

=C4+C5+C6+C7

The formula will continue to self-adjust as it is copied to cells D9, E9 and F9.

Fill Down

G4 =B4+C4+D4+E4+F4

	A	B	C	D	E	F	G	H
1			Lecture Attendance Record					
2								
3		Monday	Tuesday	Wednesday	Thursday	Friday	Total	
4	Period 1	85	88	79	73	62	387	
5	Period 2	81	86	84	64	29		
6	Period 3	76	79	66	42	22		
7	Period 4	45	58	57	28	14		
8								
9	Total	287	311	286	207	127		
10								
11								

Figure 1.7 Copying a formula using Fill Down

In Figure 1.7, the formula *=B4+C4+D4+E4+F4* is being copied down. As before, the mouse pointer is positioned over the Fill Handle. When the mouse pointer changes to a black cross, the formula is copied by dragging downwards while holding down the left mouse button. The results of the copy operation are displayed once the left mouse button is released. The shaded cells in Figure 1.8 show how the formula updates when it is filled down.

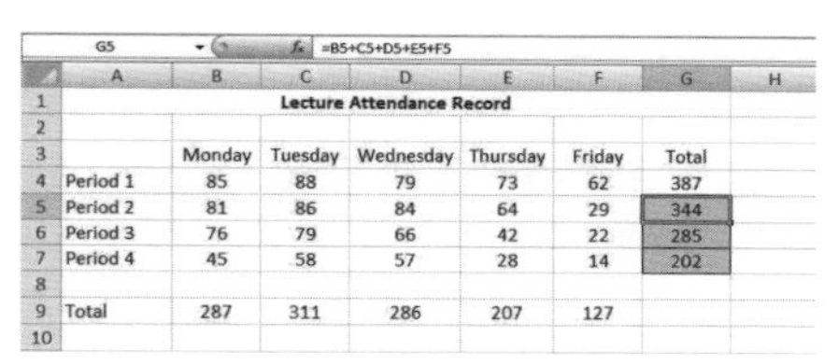

G5 =B5+C5+D5+E5+F5

	A	B	C	D	E	F	G	H
1			Lecture Attendance Record					
2								
3		Monday	Tuesday	Wednesday	Thursday	Friday	Total	
4	Period 1	85	88	79	73	62	387	
5	Period 2	81	86	84	64	29	344	
6	Period 3	76	79	66	42	22	285	
7	Period 4	45	58	57	28	14	202	
8								
9	Total	287	311	286	207	127		
10								

Figure 1.8 The results of Fill Down

In Figure 1.8, the original formula *=B4+C4+D4+E4+F4* has changed to *=B5+C5+D5+E5+F5*. Because we are filling down, the numbers in the cell references have increased by one. When you fill right, the letters in the cell references increase.

HOW DO I START USING EXCEL?

To start Excel, double click the Excel icon on the desktop. Alternatively, click the Start button and select All Programs. Now select Microsoft Office from the list of programs and then select Microsoft Office Excel.

1.  2. All Programs 3. Microsoft Office 4. Microsoft Office Excel

Spreadsheet Formulas Assignment One

Start Excel using one of the methods outlined above. A new spreadsheet workbook is displayed. Enter the data shown in Table 1.2. Enter addition formulas in the shaded cells to complete the spreadsheet.

To wrap text within a cell, click the Wrap Text button in the Home section of the Ribbon. The text will wrap when the column is not wide enough to accommodate the text.

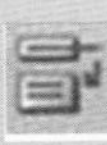

	A	B	C	D	E
1	**Screen on the Green**				
2					
3		**Terminator Salvation**	**Star Trek**	**Angels and Demons**	**Total**
4	Monday	250	185	205	
5	Tuesday	290	190	210	
6	Wednesday	300	120	220	
7	Thursday	260	200	188	
8	Friday	450	208	180	
9					
10	Total				

Table 1.2 Cinema ticket sales

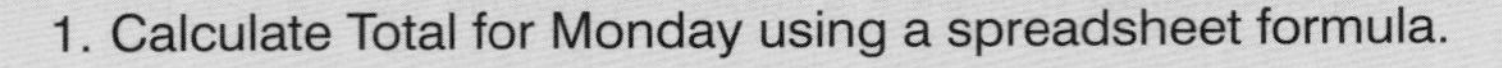

1. Calculate Total for Monday using a spreadsheet formula.
2. Copy this formula using Fill Down (*with the answer to your first formula displayed in the cell pointer, position the mouse pointer over the Fill Handle. When the mouse pointer changes to a black cross, drag downwards to copy the formula*).
3. Create a formula to calculate the total sales for *Terminator Salvation*.
4. Copy this formula using Fill Right.
5. Increase the width of columns A, B and D.
6. Center the data in columns B, C, D and E using the Center button.
7. Format the headings to bold as shown using the Bold button.
8. Click the Office button in the top left hand corner of the screen. Select *Save* from the list of commands and save the spreadsheet as **Screen on the Green**

In Excel 2010, the Office button has been replaced by the File menu.

MOVING AND COPYING SPREADSHEET DATA

Spreadsheet data can be moved or copied using the Cut, Copy and Paste buttons in the Home section of the Ribbon.

Moving Data in a Spreadsheet (Cut and Paste)

Moving data from one location to another in a spreadsheet requires three steps.

1. Highlight the data to be moved either with the mouse or by pressing F8, followed by an arrow key. Data can also be highlighted by pressing an arrow key while holding down the Shift key.
2. Click the Cut button in the Home section of the Ribbon. This copies the highlighted data from its current location and places it in a temporary storage area referred to as the Clipboard. 
3. Position the cell pointer in the new location for the data and click the Paste button. This copies the contents of the Clipboard to the new location and erases the data from its original location. 

To quickly access the Cut command, hold down the *CTRL* key and type *X*. Paste can be accessed by holding down the *CTRL* key and typing *V*.

Copying Data in a Spreadsheet (Copy and Paste)

Copying spreadsheet data also requires three steps:

1. Highlight the data to be copied using any of the three methods already described.
2. Click the Copy button in the Home section of the Ribbon. This copies the highlighted data to the Clipboard. 
3. Position the cell pointer in the new location for the data and click the Paste button. This copies the contents of the Clipboard to the new location. 

To quickly access the Copy command, hold down the *CTRL* key and type *C*.

Multiple Clipboard

Excel 2007 has a multiple clipboard which stores the last 24 items that you have cut or copied. These items can be pasted at a later stage by activating the clipboard task pane.

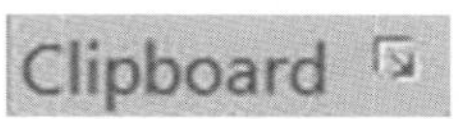

The clipboard task pane is activated by clicking the clipboard button in the Home section of the Ribbon.

In Figure 1.9, the clipboard shows three items which have been copied from three different spreadsheet cells.

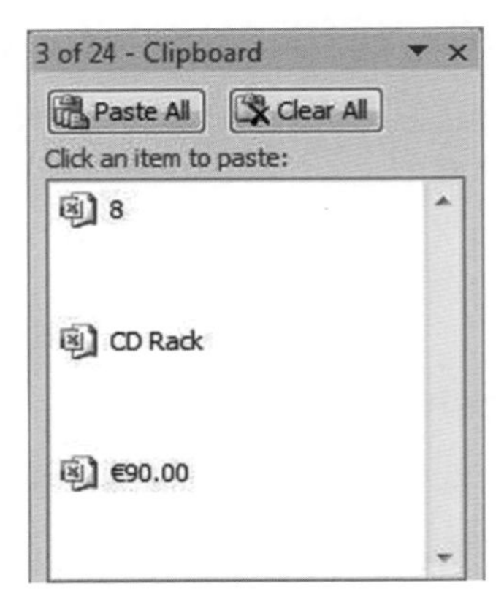

Figure 1.9: Excel's multiple clipboard feature

Each of the three items in the clipboard can be pasted to another cell in the current worksheet or to a cell in a different worksheet simply by clicking the item and selecting Paste from the drop-down list (Figure 1.10).

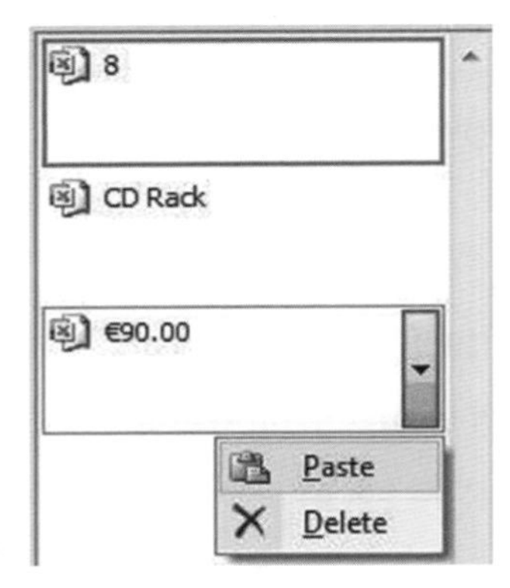

Figure 1.10: Pasting an item from the multiple clipboard

Items can be removed from the multiple clipboard by selecting *Delete* from the drop-down list.

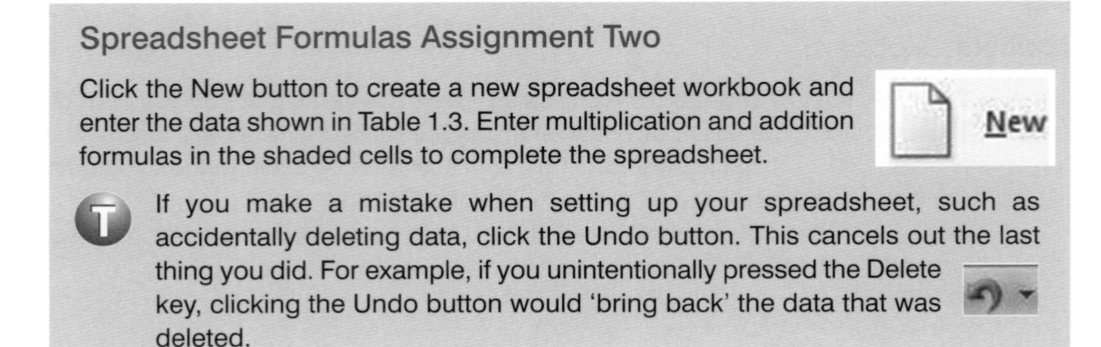

Spreadsheet Formulas Assignment Two

Click the New button to create a new spreadsheet workbook and enter the data shown in Table 1.3. Enter multiplication and addition formulas in the shaded cells to complete the spreadsheet.

If you make a mistake when setting up your spreadsheet, such as accidentally deleting data, click the Undo button. This cancels out the last thing you did. For example, if you unintentionally pressed the Delete key, clicking the Undo button would 'bring back' the data that was deleted.

	A	B	C	D	E
1	**O Sullivan Office Supplies**			Vat Rate:	21%
2					
3	**Item**	**Quantity**	**Unit Price**		**Total Cost**
4	Memory Sticks	25	14.99		
5	Anti Glare Guard	5	25		
6	Screen Cleaner	20	1		
7	CD Rack	8	7.5		
8	Screen Wipes	100	0.2		
9	Compressed Air	2	10		
10	Disk Labels	50	0.1		
11					
12			Subtotal		
13			VAT		
14			Total		

Table 1.3

1. Calculate total cost. Copy this formula using Fill Down.

2. Move the headings Subtotal, VAT and Total to column D. (*Use the cut and paste buttons.)*
3. Calculate Subtotal.
4. Calculate the VAT on the Subtotal using the VAT rate in E1.
5. Calculate Total.

6. Format all money amounts to currency, using the Accounting button.

If a number changes to ##### when you format to currency, this means you need to increase the column width.

In previous versions of Excel, the Accounting button was called the Currency button.

 7. Increase the width of column A.

 8. Center the data in columns B, C and E.

 9. Save the spreadsheet as **O Sullivan Office Supplies**

Always use the Accounting button to insert a euro sign. Typing a euro sign can cause Excel to interpret the cell entry as text, leading to errors in formulas. E.g. type 34.5 and format to currency to get €34.50.

Spreadsheet Formulas Assignment Three

Create a new spreadsheet workbook and enter the data shown in Table 1.4. Enter multiplication, addition and subtraction formulas in the shaded cells to complete the spreadsheet.

	A	B	C	D	E	F	G
1	**Mega Night School**						
2							
3	**Income**	**Class Size**	**Course Fee**	**Total Fees**	**Number of Classes**	**Duration of Class**	**Total Hours**
4	Spreadsheets	25	160		15	2	
5	Database	20	200		20	2	
6	Word Processing	30	130		12	1.5	
7							
8	**Expenditure**	**Hourly Rate**	**Total Wages**	**Profit**			
9	Spreadsheets	34.5					
10	Database	38.5					
11	Word Processing	32.5					

Table 1.4

1. Calculate the total fees (class size multiplied by course fee).
2. Calculate total hours (number of classes multiplied by duration of class).

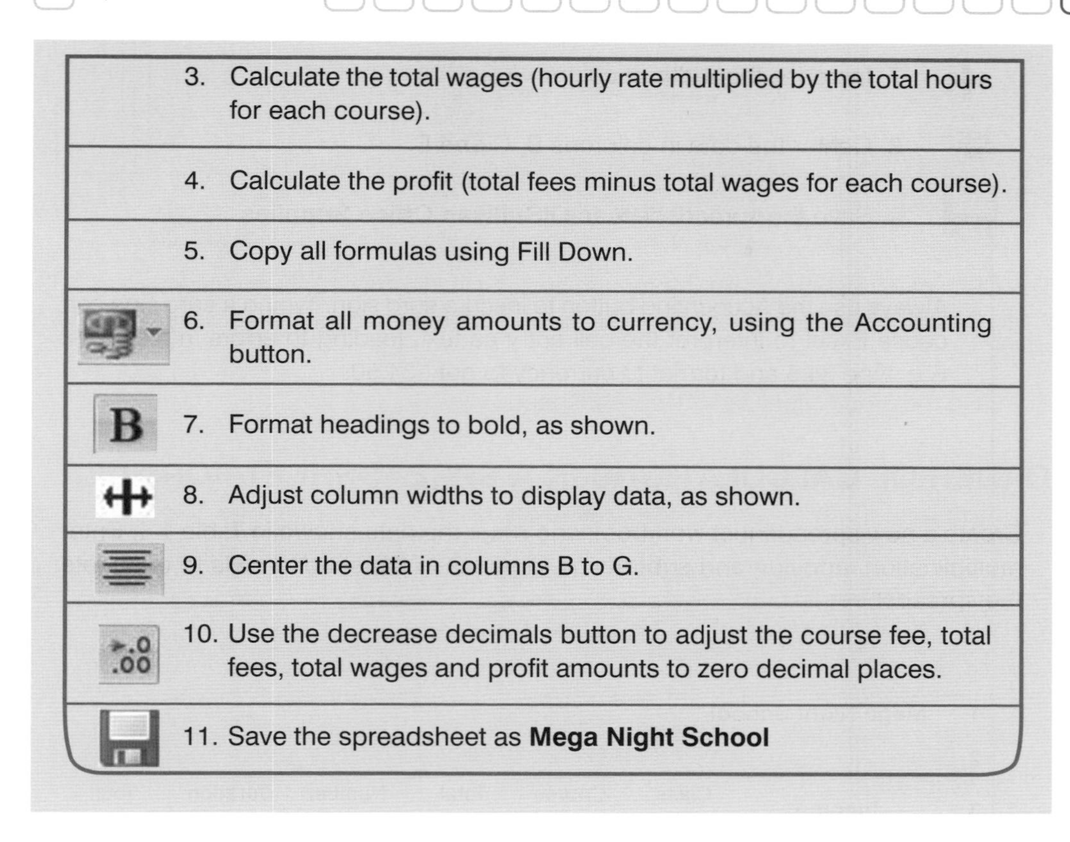

3. Calculate the total wages (hourly rate multiplied by the total hours for each course).
4. Calculate the profit (total fees minus total wages for each course).
5. Copy all formulas using Fill Down.
6. Format all money amounts to currency, using the Accounting button.
7. Format headings to bold, as shown.
8. Adjust column widths to display data, as shown.
9. Center the data in columns B to G.
10. Use the decrease decimals button to adjust the course fee, total fees, total wages and profit amounts to zero decimal places.
11. Save the spreadsheet as **Mega Night School**

CENTERING A SPREADSHEET HEADING – WORKED EXAMPLE

The Merge and Center button can be used to center a heading across a number of columns.

1. Open the *Mega Night School* spreadsheet if it is not already open.

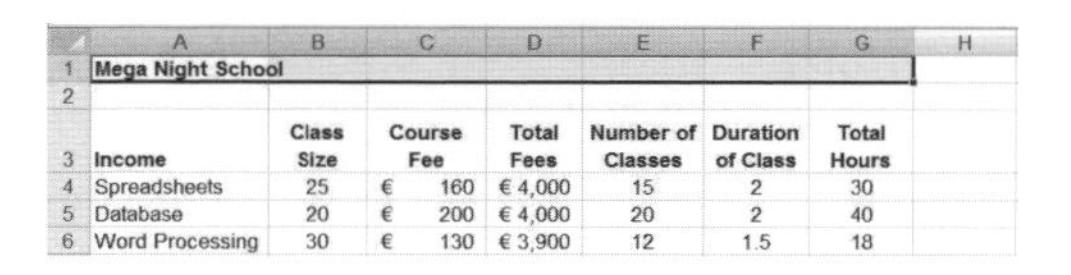

	A	B	C	D	E	F	G	H
1	Mega Night School							
2								
3	Income	Class Size	Course Fee	Total Fees	Number of Classes	Duration of Class	Total Hours	
4	Spreadsheets	25	€ 160	€ 4,000	15	2	30	
5	Database	20	€ 200	€ 4,000	20	2	40	
6	Word Processing	30	€ 130	€ 3,900	12	1.5	18	

Figure 1.11: A1:G1 is highlighted

2. Highlight *A1:G1*, as shown in Figure 1.11.
3. Click the Merge and Center button 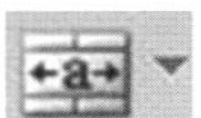

	A	B	C	D	E	F	G	H
1	Mega Night School							
2								
3	**Income**	**Class Size**	**Course Fee**	**Total Fees**	**Number of Classes**	**Duration of Class**	**Total Hours**	
4	Spreadsheets	25	€ 160	€ 4,000	15	2	30	
5	Database	20	€ 200	€ 4,000	20	2	40	
6	Word Processing	30	€ 130	€ 3,900	12	1.5	18	

Figure 1.12: The result of Merge and Center

The effect of using Merge and Center can be seen in Figure 1.12. Excel has merged cells A1 to G1 into a single 'big' cell and has centered the text in that cell, across columns A to G.

4. Save the *Mega Night School* spreadsheet.

ORDER OF CALCULATIONS IN A SPREADSHEET FORMULA

Each spreadsheet formula contains one or more instructions that tell Excel what to do with the numbers in the cells referred to by that formula. The instructions that can be used in a formula are the arithmetic operators: plus (+), minus (-), multiply (*) and divide (/). When formulas have more than one arithmetic operator, Excel uses the BoMDAS mathematical rule to determine the sequence in which the calculations will be carried out. BoMDAS assigns a different level of importance to each arithmetic operator as follows:

1. Brackets
2. Multiplication
3. Division
4. Addition
5. Subtraction

This can be summarised as follows:

Rule 1: Calculations enclosed in brackets will always be carried out first.
Rule 2: Multiplication and Division are always carried out before addition and subtraction.
Rule 3: Addition and Subtraction are always done last.

Example:

	A	B
1	30	
2	10	
3	2	
4		
5	**=A1-A2*A3**	

Table 1.5

Consider the formula displayed in Table 1.5. Our natural reaction when evaluating this formula is to do the subtraction first followed by the multiplication, reading from left to right, giving an answer of 40 *(30-10=20, 20*2=40)*. This is incorrect.

When evaluating this formula, Excel uses the BoMDAS rule. The formula contains a mixture of subtraction and multiplication. Under the BoMDAS rule, multiplication must be done first.

*10*2=20*

Once the multiplication is complete, the subtraction is done.

30–20=10

The correct answer to the formula is 10, not 40.

Brackets can be used to change the natural order of a formula. In Table 1.5, we could force Excel to do the subtraction first by enclosing the subtraction in brackets as follows.
*=(A1-A2)*A3*

The result of this formula is now 40 as the subtraction will be done first.

In any formula that doesn't contain brackets, multiplication and division are always done first.

USING DIVISION IN A SPREADSHEET FORMULA – WORKED EXAMPLE

Create a new spreadsheet workbook and enter the data shown in Table 1.6.

	A	B
1	**College Attendance**	
2		
3		**No. of Students**
4	Monday	583
5	Tuesday	601
6	Wednesday	610
7	Thursday	608
8	Friday	550
9		
10		
11	**Average Daily Attendance**	

Table 1.6

Using Brackets to Change the Natural Order of a Formula

1. In order to calculate average daily attendance in the spreadsheet displayed in Table 1.6, we must first add the attendance for Monday to Friday and then divide by five. Position the cell pointer in B11 and enter the following formula:

   =B4+B5+B6+B7+B8/5

   Press *Enter*. Excel displays the answer 2512. This is incorrect. Because the formula contains both addition and division, Excel uses the BoMDAS rule and carries out the division first – *B8/5=110*, which is then added to the remaining numbers, giving 2512. Brackets are required to force the spreadsheet to add before it divides.

2. Correct the formula by enclosing the addition in brackets as follows:

   =(B4+B5+B6+B7+B8)/5

   The answer to the formula is now 590.4.

3. Save the spreadsheet as **Division Example**

To change the natural order of a formula, use brackets. Calculations enclosed in brackets will be done first.

Spreadsheet Formulas Assignment Four

Create a new spreadsheet workbook and enter the data shown in Table 1.7. Enter formulas in the shaded cells to complete the spreadsheet.

Day and month names can be copied using the Fill Handle. Select A4 and then position the mouse pointer over the Fill Handle. When the mouse pointer changes to a black cross, drag downwards to copy. The days will adjust as they are copied.

	A	B	C	D	E
1	**Maureen's Corner Shop**				
2					
3		**Fruit**	**Drink**	**Hardware**	**Dairy**
4	Monday	100	20	15	150
5	Tuesday	95	15	10	125
6	Wednesday	80	18	8	140
7	Thursday	120	10	12	150
8	Friday	110	50	14	180
9	Saturday	50	70	20	70
10					
11	**Average Daily Sales**				

Table 1.7

	1. Increase the width of column A.
	2. Calculate the average daily sales for fruit. Copy this formula using Fill Right. N *The correct answer is 92.5. If the addition is not enclosed in brackets, the answer will be 513.33.*
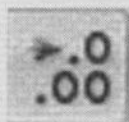	3. Using the decrease decimals button, display all averages with no decimal places.
	4. Using the Merge and Center button, center the heading in row 1 across columns A to E.
	5. Format headings to bold and center data, as shown.
	6. Save the spreadsheet as **Maureen's Corner Shop**

Spreadsheet Formulas Assignment Five

Open the *Screen on the Green* spreadsheet. Enter division formulas in the shaded cells to complete the spreadsheet.

	A	B	C	D	E	F
1	**Screen on the Green**					
2						
3		**Terminator Salvation**	**Star Trek**	**Angels and Demons**	**Total**	**Average**
4	Monday	250	185	205	640	
5	Tuesday	290	190	210	690	
6	Wednesday	300	120	220	640	
7	Thursday	260	200	188	648	
8	Friday	450	208	180	838	
9						
10	**Total**	1550	903	1003		
11	**Average**					

Table 1.8

1. Insert an extra row and column, as shown in Table 1.8.
2. Calculate the average ticket sales by film and by day.
3. Copy all formulas using Fill Down and Fill Right.
4. Use the decrease decimals button so that all averages display no decimal places.
5. Center the heading in row 1 across columns A to F.
6. Format headings to bold and center data, as shown.
7. Save the **Screen on the Green** spreadsheet.

HOW A SPREADSHEET WORKS WITH PERCENTAGES

A percentage is a method of expressing a fraction in relation to the number 100, e.g. $\frac{1}{4}$ is 25% and $\frac{3}{4}$ is 75%. To convert a fraction to a percentage, we multiply by 100, e.g. $\frac{1}{4} \times 100 = 100/4 = 25\%$, or $\frac{3}{4} \times 100 = 300/4 = 75\%$.

In a spreadsheet there is no need to multiply by 100. The spreadsheet does this for you when you click the Percent Style button. %
For example, entering 0.25 and clicking the Percent Style button gives 25%. Entering 0.4 and clicking the Percent Style button gives 40%. Percentages can also be entered directly without using the Percent Style button. Entering 25% in a cell achieves the same result as entering 0.25 and then clicking the Percent Style button.

To get a percentage between 0 and 100 when you click the Percent Style button, the number in the cell must be between zero and one.

PRINTING A SPREADSHEET

It's a good idea to get a preview of what your spreadsheet will look like on a printed page before you actually print it. Previewing the spreadsheet allows you to see if you need to make any adjustments, such as reducing the width of some columns so that the spreadsheet fits on the page. Sometimes you may need to change the page orientation to landscape if the spreadsheet is too wide to fit on a page in portrait orientation.

To preview how the spreadsheet will appear on a printed page, click the Office button and select Print, followed by Print Preview, as shown in Figure 1.13.

In Excel 2010, the Office button has been replaced by the File menu.

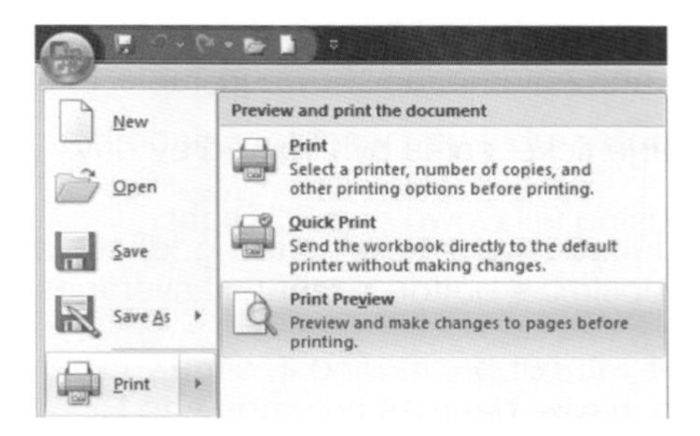

Figure 1.13: How to Print Preview a spreadsheet

When you click the Print Preview button, the Print Preview options are displayed (Figure 1.14).

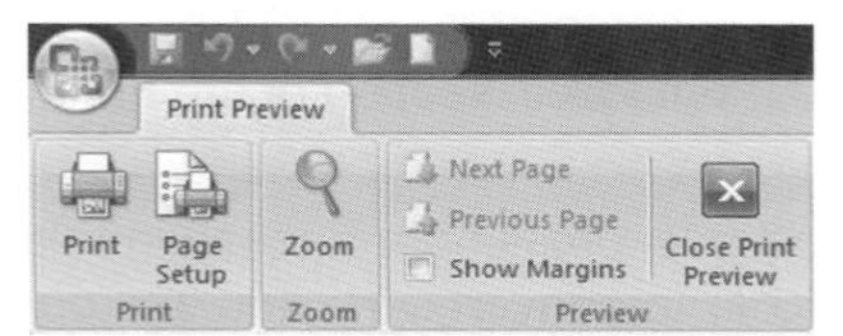

Figure 1.14: Print Preview options in Excel

Click the Page Setup button to make adjustments to your printout.

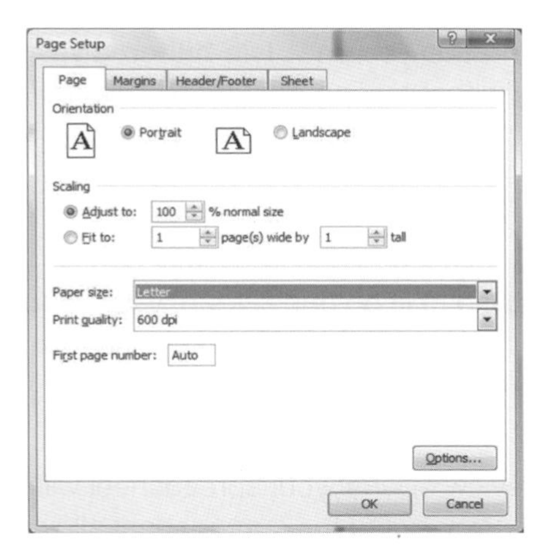

Figure 1.15: The Page Setup dialog box allows you to fine tune your printout

The Page Setup dialog box (Figure 1.15) has four sections, which can be used as follows.

1. Select the **Page** tab if you want to change the orientation of the printed spreadsheet from portrait to landscape. You can also shrink your spreadsheet onto one page by specifying a percentage less than 100% of the normal size. The downside of this is that the print will be smaller.

2. Select the **Margins** tab if you want to adjust the size of one or more of the page margins.
3. Select the **Header/Footer** tab if you want to include headers and/or footers in the printed spreadsheet.
4. Select the **Sheet** tab if you want to print the gridlines and the row and column headings.

To print your spreadsheet without previewing it, simply click the Office button and then select Print

To quickly display a Print Preview of your spreadsheet, hold down the *CTRL* key and press the *F2* function key.

If you only want to print a section of your spreadsheet, highlight the range of cells containing the data you want to print. Select **Print** from the Office menu and then click **Selection** in the 'Print What' section of the Print dialog box.

FREEZE PANES

The Freeze Panes option is accessed from the View section of the Ribbon, as shown in Figure 1.16.

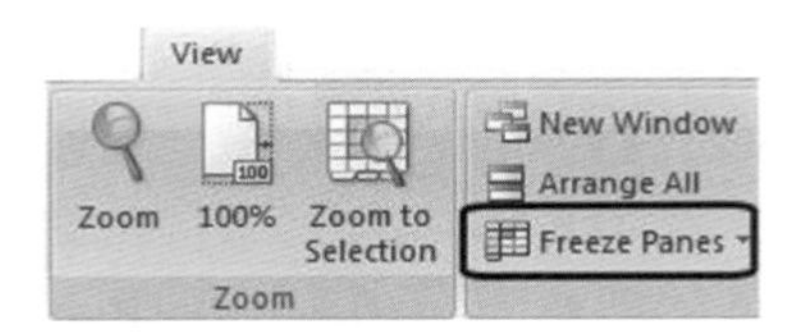

Figure 1.16

When a spreadsheet is too big to fit on one screen, your headings will disappear off the screen as you scroll down or to the right. This can make it difficult to work with your data. The headings can be locked in position using the Freeze Panes option, which is displayed in Figure 1.17.

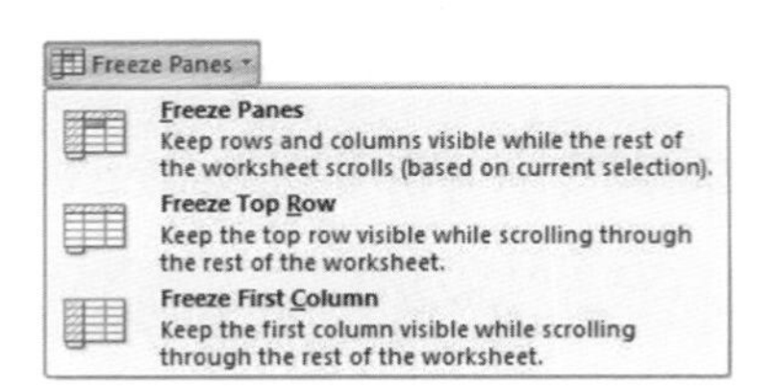

Figure 1.17: Freeze Panes options

Using the Freeze Panes option is useful in assignment six as the spreadsheet may not fit on one screen. How much of the spreadsheet will actually fit on the screen depends on the size of the screen and the screen resolution (which differs from computer to computer).

Spreadsheet Formulas Assignment Six

Create a new spreadsheet workbook and enter the data shown in Table 1.9. Enter formulas in the shaded cells to complete the spreadsheet.

It's a good idea to save your spreadsheet before you complete it and then click the Save button every ten minutes or so. If you get into the habit of doing this you won't lose hours of work if your PC crashes or if you accidentally close your spreadsheet without saving it.

	A	B	C	D	E	F
1	**Household Budget**					
2						
3		**January**	**February**	**March**	**April**	**May**
4	**Opening Balance**	250				
5	Interest Rate	.03	.031	.03	.029	.029
6						
7	**Income**					
8	Deposit Interest					
9	Children's Allowance	166	166	166	166	166
10	Wages	702.5	702.5	702.5	702.5	702.5
11	Night Classes	91.3	91.3	91.3	91.3	91.3
12	**Total Income**					
13						
14	**Expenses**					
15	Mortgage	718.26	718.26	718.26	718.26	718.26
16	Petrol	63	60	59	60	52
17	Food	185.5	179.91	172.65	169.77	183.46
18	Car Insurance	55.7	55.7	55.7	55.7	55.7
19	**Total Expenses**					
20						
21	**Closing Balance**					

Table 1.9

Position the cell pointer in cell B4 and freeze the panes.

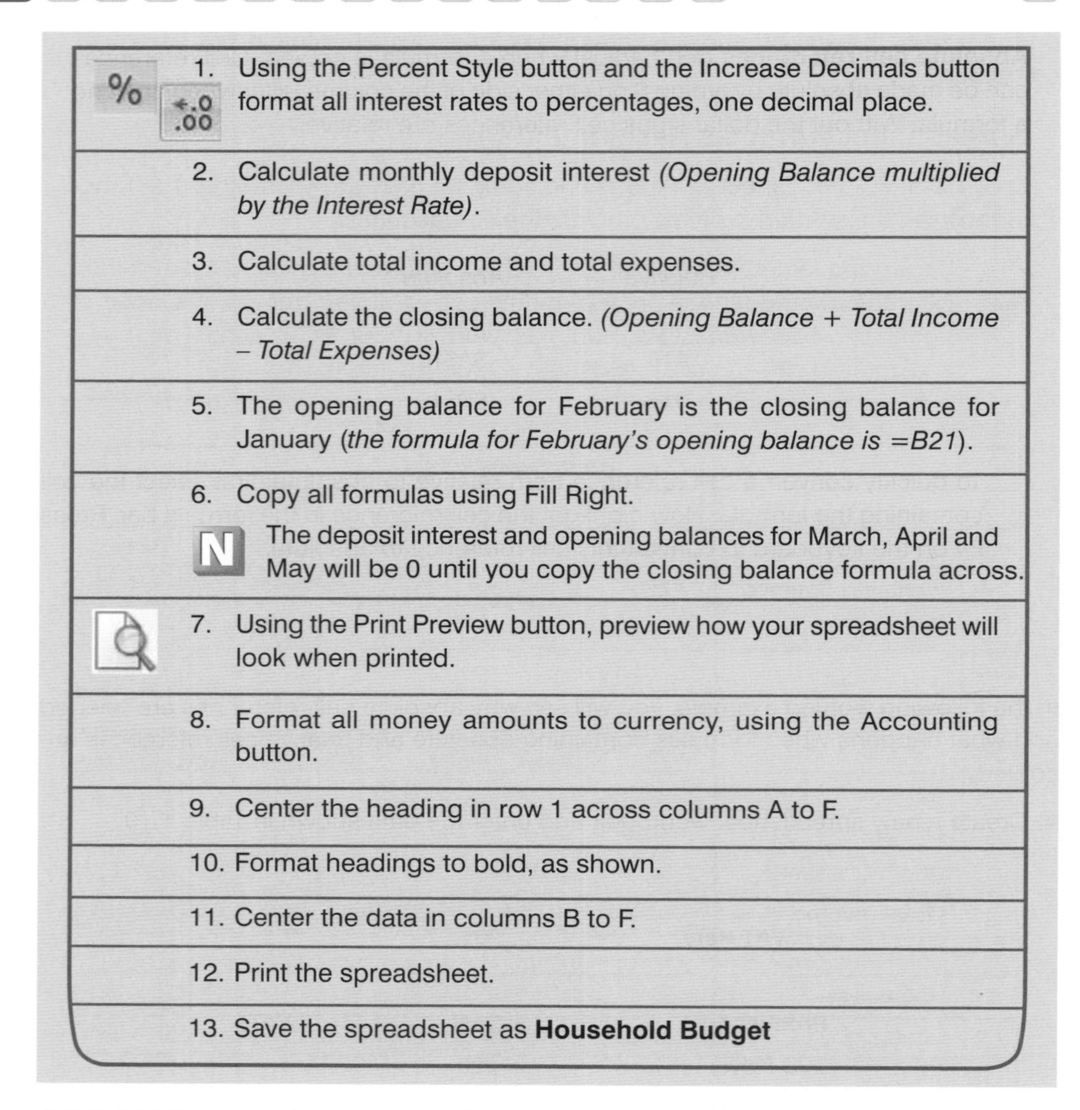

1. Using the Percent Style button and the Increase Decimals button format all interest rates to percentages, one decimal place.
2. Calculate monthly deposit interest *(Opening Balance multiplied by the Interest Rate)*.
3. Calculate total income and total expenses.
4. Calculate the closing balance. *(Opening Balance + Total Income – Total Expenses)*
5. The opening balance for February is the closing balance for January (*the formula for February's opening balance is =B21*).
6. Copy all formulas using Fill Right.

   N The deposit interest and opening balances for March, April and May will be 0 until you copy the closing balance formula across.
7. Using the Print Preview button, preview how your spreadsheet will look when printed.
8. Format all money amounts to currency, using the Accounting button.
9. Center the heading in row 1 across columns A to F.
10. Format headings to bold, as shown.
11. Center the data in columns B to F.
12. Print the spreadsheet.
13. Save the spreadsheet as **Household Budget**

ABSOLUTE AND RELATIVE CELL REFERENCES

Spreadsheet formulas refer to cells. Each reference a formula makes to a cell can be relative or absolute. So far we have only used relative cell references in formulas.

Relative cell references automatically adjust when a formula is copied to other cells. When a formula is copied to the right, the column letters automatically adjust. For example, the formula *=A2+A3* will become *=B2+B3* when it is copied one column to the right. When a formula is copied down, the row numbers automatically adjust. For example, the formula *=B3+C3* will become *=B4+C4* when it is copied down to the next row.

Absolute cell references don't adjust when a formula is copied. Cell references can be made absolute by typing $ on either side of the column letter when creating a formula. Without the dollar signs cell references are relative.

Examples of Relative and Absolute Cell References

Relative	*Absolute*
B1	B1
A10	A10
D15	D15

To quickly convert a cell reference from relative to absolute, first select the cell containing the formula. Now highlight the cell reference in the formula bar. Press *F4* on the keyboard to convert this cell reference to absolute.

Using Absolute and Relative Cell References in a Formula – Worked Example

In the following worked example, you will see why absolute cell references are needed and what happens when formulas containing absolute and relative cell references are copied.

- Create a new spreadsheet workbook and enter the data shown in Table 1.10.

	A	B	C
1	**VAT Rate**	**20%**	
2			
3	**Product**	**Cost**	**VAT**
4	DVD Player	220	
5	Digital Camera	361	
6	Fax Machine	158	
7	Personal Stereo	55	
8	Portable Radio	10	
9	Clock Radio	25	
10	Mini Disc System	140	

Table 1.10

1. Position the cell pointer in C4 and enter the following formula:
   =B4*B1

2. Copy this formula down as far as C10. Table 1.11 displays the results of the VAT calculations and the formula used in each calculation.

	A	B	C
1	**VAT Rate**	**20%**	
2			
3	**Product**	**Cost**	**VAT**
4	DVD Player	220	44 *(=B4*B1)*
5	Digital Camera	361	0 *(=B5*B2)*
6	Fax Machine	158	#VALUE! *(=B6*B3)*
7	Personal Stereo	55	12100 *(=B7*B4)*
8	Portable Radio	10	3610 *(=B8*B5)*
9	Clock Radio	25	3590 *(=B9*B6)*
10	Mini Disc System	140	7700 *(=B10*B7)*

Because this formula contains relative cell references, both cell references change each time the formula is copied down to the next row. This is correct for the part of the formula that refers to the Cost but incorrect for the part of the formula that refers to the VAT rate.

Table 1.11

Because the original formula *=B4*B1* contains relative cell references, both cell references have changed as a result of the copy operation. However, each cost must be multiplied by the VAT rate stored in B1. The formulas in cells C5 to C10 are giving incorrect answers because the reference to B1 has changed to B2, B3, B4, B5, B6 and B7.

To prevent the reference to B1 from changing we need to make it absolute by typing $ on either side of the letter B, giving = *B4*B1*. When this formula is copied, the reference to B1 won't change.

3. Delete the data in cells C4 to C10.

4. Position the cell pointer in C4 and enter the following formula:
   *=B4*B1*

5. Copy this formula down as far as C10. Table 1.12 displays the results of the VAT calculations and the formula used in each calculation.

Adjusted Formulas with Absolute Cell References

	A	B	C
1	**VAT Rate**	**20%**	
2			
3	**Product**	**Cost**	**VAT**
4	DVD Player	220	€44.00 *(=B4*B1)*
5	Digital Camera	361	€72.20 *(=B5*B1)*
6	Fax Machine	158	€31.60 *(=B6*B1)*
7	Personal Stereo	55	€11.00 *(=B7*B1)*
8	Portable Radio	10	€2.00 *(=B8*B1)*
9	Clock Radio	25	€5.00 *(=B9*B1)*
10	Mini Disc System	140	€28.00 *(=B10*B1)*

Table 1.12

6. Save the spreadsheet as **Absolute Cells Example**

Absolute cell references are generally used in multiplication and division formulas. It would be unusual to see an absolute cell reference in an addition or subtraction formula. The most common use of absolute cell references is when applying a single percentage rate, such as a tax rate, to multiple cells.

Spreadsheet Formulas Assignment Seven

Create a new spreadsheet workbook and enter the data shown in Table 1.13. Enter formulas in the shaded cells to complete the spreadsheet, using absolute cell references where appropriate.

	A	B	C	D	E	F
1	**PAYE Rate**	**0.2**	**PRSI Rate**	**0.035**		
2						
3	**Employee Name**	**Gross Pay**	**PAYE**	**PRSI**	**Total**	**Net Pay**
4	John O Neill	601.04				
5	Mary Doyle	553.77				
6	Peter Hennessy	767.43				
7	Sinead Murray	595.83				
8	Noreen Keogh	555.98				
9	Susan Donovan	666.22				
10	Tom Larkin	780.01				

Table 1.13

1. Format the PAYE rate to percentage, zero decimal places and the PRSI rate to percentage, one decimal place.
2. Calculate PAYE.

Highlighting a cell reference in a formula and pressing the *F4* function key converts from relative to absolute.

3. Calculate PRSI.
4. Calculate the total by adding PAYE and PRSI.
5. Net pay is gross pay minus total.
6. Copy all formulas using Fill Down.
7. Format all money amounts to currency, using the Accounting button.
8. Format all headings to bold.
9. Adjust column widths where necessary.
10. Center the data in cells B3 to F10.
11. Print the spreadsheet.
12. Save the spreadsheet as **Weekly Payroll**

ROUNDING ERRORS

In Assignment Seven, we calculated John O Neill's PAYE by multiplying his gross pay by 20%. The result of this calculation is 120.208. When this is formatted as currency, it becomes €120.21. Excel has rounded the number up. It adds 0.002 to 120.208 to give €120.21. The rounded number is technically incorrect. There is a rounding error of +0.002.

When formatting numbers to currency, Excel will always round to two decimal places. It uses the third decimal to decide whether to round up or down.

Rounding Down

When the third number to the right of the decimal point is 4 or less, Excel will round down the number.

50.75**4** becomes €50.75

The rounding error is -0.004.

Rounding Up

When the third number to the right of the decimal point is 5 or greater, Excel will round up the number.

53.48**7** becomes €53.49

The rounding error is +0.003

These rounding up and rounding down rules are universally applied in financial transactions.

Rounding errors will also occur when using the Percent Style button. Numbers will be multiplied by 100 and then rounded to zero decimal places.

Examples:

0.2168 becomes 22% when the Percent Style button is clicked

The rounding error is +0.32.

Clicking the Increase decimals button once changes the percentage to 21.7%
Clicking Increase decimals a second time changes the percentage to 21.68%

0.8647 *becomes* 86% when the Percent Style button is clicked

The rounding error is -0.47.

Clicking the Increase decimals button once changes the percentage to 86.5%
Clicking Increase decimals a second time changes the percentage to 86.47%

In the examples relating to percentages, there is a discrepancy between cell content and cell display. Using the Percent button converts 0.2168 to 22%. Even though the cell display is 22%, 0.2168 is actually stored in the cell.

Spreadsheet Formulas Assignment Eight

Create a new spreadsheet workbook and enter the data shown in Table 1.14. Enter formulas in the shaded cells to complete the spreadsheet.

	A	B	C	D	E	F	G
1				**VAT**	**0.21**		
2							
3	**Car Type**	**Daily Rate**	**Days Hired**	**Discount**	**Subtotal**	**VAT**	**Total**
4	Fiesta	50	5	10			
5	Primera	55.5	2	5			
6	Sunny	52	1	2.5			
7	Fusion	52	3	7.5			
8	Corsa	49.5	7	15			
9	Tigra	60	10	25			
10	Corolla	52	14	30			
11	Focus	52	7	16.5			
12	Ibiza	50	5	10			

Table 1.14

1. Format the VAT rate to percentage, zero decimal places.
2. Calculate the subtotal (daily rate multiplied by the days hired minus the discount). *Remember that multiplication is always done before subtraction in any formula that doesn't contain brackets*.
3. VAT is charged on the subtotal.
4. Calculate total.
5. Copy all formulas using Fill Down.
6. Format all money amounts to currency, using the Accounting button.
7. Format headings to bold, as shown.
8. Center the data in columns B to G.
9. Print the spreadsheet.
10. Save the spreadsheet as **Car Rentals**

Spreadsheet Formulas Assignment Nine

Create a new spreadsheet workbook and enter the data shown in Table 1.15. Enter formulas in the shaded cells to complete the spreadsheet.

N In metre^2, the '2' is called a superscript. In Excel a number can be formatted as a superscript by ticking the Superscript check box in the Format Cells dialog box.

	A	B	C	D	E	F	G	H	I
1	**O Callaghan's Imports**								
2									
3							**Inches to Metres:**		0.0254
4							**Price per metre^2 (Pounds):**		8.50
5							**Exchange Rate:**		0.92
6									
7		**Length (inches)**	**Length (metres)**	**Height (inches)**	**Height (metres)**	**Window Area (metres^2)**			
8	Wall 2 Window	60		40					
9									

(Contd.)

	A	B	C	D	E	F	G	H	I
10		Length (inches)	Length (metres)	Height (inches)	Height (metres)	Wall Area (metres2)	Wall Area minus Window	Wallpaper Cost (Sterling)	Wallpaper Cost (Euro)
11	Wall 1	124		96					
12	Wall 2	148		96					
13	Wall 3	124		96					
14	Wall 4	148		96					
15									
16							Total:		

Table 1.15

Figure 1.18

N Money amounts can be displayed with foreign currency symbols by accessing the Accounting button drop-down list from the Home section of the Ribbon, as shown in Figure 1.18.

1. Convert all lengths in inches to metres using the conversion factor in I3.
2. Calculate Window Area in metres^2.
3. Calculate the area of each wall in metres^2.
4. In column G, subtract the Window Area from the area of wall 2.
5. Calculate the sterling cost of wallpaper for each wall using Price per metre^2 (pounds).
6. Using the exchange rate, calculate the euro cost of wallpaper for each wall.
7. Calculate the total wallpaper cost in sterling and euros.
8. Using the Accounting button drop-down list (Figure 1.18), display the Wallpaper Cost (Sterling) and the Price per metre^2 in British pounds. Display the converted wallpaper costs in euro.
9. Using the Decrease Decimals button, display data relating to metres with 2 places of decimals.

10. Center the heading in row 1 across columns A to I.
11. Format headings to bold, as shown.
12. Save the spreadsheet as **O Callaghan's Imports**

CIRCULAR REFERENCES

A circular reference is where a formula refers to itself.

	A	B
1	Tax Rate	41%
2		
3	Weekly Pay	€720
4	Tax	**=B1*B4**
5		

Table 1.16

In Table 1.16, the formula to calculate tax is incorrect because it refers to itself. The formula is in cell B4 and also refers to cell B4. This is called a circular reference. Excel displays a Circular Reference message in the status bar at the bottom of the screen, as shown in Figure 1.19.

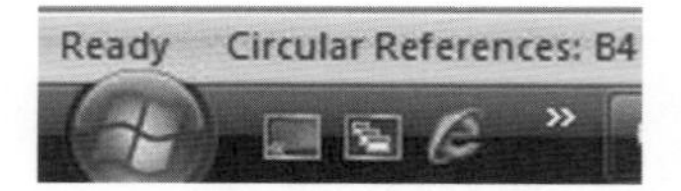

Figure 1.19

To check for circular references in your spreadsheet:

1. Click the **Formulas** tab in the Ribbon.
2. In the **Formula Auditing** section, click the drop-down arrow to expand the **Error Checking** list (Figure 1.20).
3. Select **Circular References** from this list.
4. Excel identifies the cell containing the circular references. Review the formula and remove the circular reference.

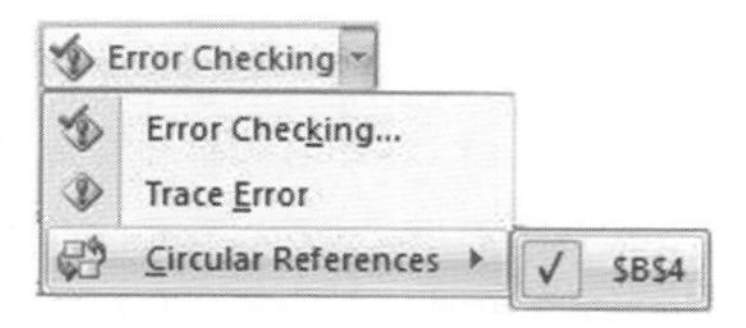

Figure 1.20

In Figure 1.20, Excel has indicated that B4 contains a circular reference. This relates to the formula *=B1*B4* in Table 1.16, which refers to itself. The correct formula is *=B1*B3*.

Spreadsheet Formulas Assignment Ten

Create a new spreadsheet workbook and enter the data shown in Table 1.17. Enter formulas in the shaded cells to complete the spreadsheet.

You can reduce the amount of typing required to set up this spreadsheet by copying the side headings using the Copy and Paste buttons.

	A	B	C	D	E	F
1			**Interest Forecaster**			
2						
3	**Principal**	6000				
4						
5	**Account 1**		**Account 2**		**Account 3**	
6	Interest rate:	0.06	Interest rate:	0.069	Interest rate:	0.065
7	DIRT tax:	0.01	DIRT tax:	0.055	DIRT tax:	0.016
8						
9		**Account 1**	**Account 2**	**Account 3**		
10	Principal year 1					
11	Year 1 interest					
12	Year 1 DIRT tax					
13	Adjusted interest					
14	Principal year 2					
15	Year 2 interest					
16	Year 2 DIRT tax					
17	Adjusted interest					
18	Principal year 3					
19	Year 3 interest					
20	Year 3 DIRT tax					
21	Adjusted interest					
22	Principal year 4					
23	Year 4 interest					
24	Year 4 DIRT tax					
25	Adjusted interest					
26	Four Year Total					

Table 1.17

1. Format all interest rates and DIRT tax rates to percentage, one decimal place.
2. Use a formula to read the contents of *B3* as principal year 1 for each of the three accounts.
3. The interest is calculated by multiplying the principal by the interest rate.
   DIRT tax is calculated by multiplying the interest by the DIRT tax rate.
   H Use absolute cell references when referring to cells containing interest rates.
4. Subtract the DIRT tax from the interest to calculate the adjusted interest.
5. Principal year 2 is calculated by adding the adjusted interest to principal year 1.
6. Use the copy and paste functions to copy the interest, DIRT tax, adjusted interest and principal from year 1 to year 2.
7. Continue using the Paste button to copy the calculations to year 3 and year 4.
   N You only need to click the Copy button once.
8. Print preview the spreadsheet. Click the Setup button and display the gridlines and the row and column headings.
9. Center the heading in row 1 across columns A to F.
10. Format all money amounts to currency, using the Accounting button.
11. Format headings to bold, as shown.
12. Center data as shown.
13. In the Review section of the Ribbon, click the Spelling and Grammar button. Check the spellings in the spreadsheet.

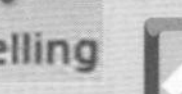

You can quickly check the spelling and grammar in your worksheet using the *ALT+R+S* keyboard combination.

14. Print the spreadsheet.
15. Which account provides the best return on investment?
16. What is the four-year total on accounts 1, 2 and 3 for each of the following investment amounts: €10,000, €20,000, €50,000 and €100,000?
17. Save the spreadsheet as **Interest Forecaster**

CHAPTER 1 SUMMARY

1. Basic Concepts

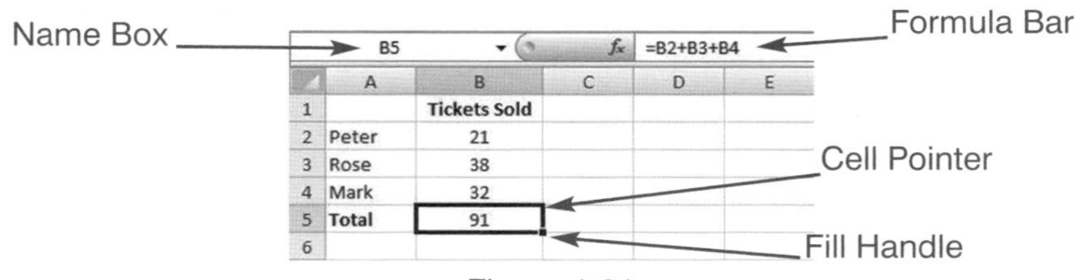

Figure 1.21

- A spreadsheet consists of rows and columns.
- The rows are identified by numbers.
- The columns are identified by letters.
- The intersection of a row and a column is called a cell.
- Each cell has a unique name which refers to the column and row, e.g. B5.
- The Cell Pointer is used to select a specific cell.
- The Fill Handle is used to copy cell data.
- The Formula Bar displays the contents of the current cell.
- The Name Box identifies the current cell by name.

2. Formulas

*=B5*B6*	A spreadsheet formula is a method of calculation that combines cell references with the arithmetic operators plus (+), minus (-), multiply (*) or divide (/).
=F4-C3/C4	When a formula includes more than one calculation, multiplication and division will always be carried out before addition and subtraction.
*=(B10+B11)*B12*	Calculations enclosed in brackets get the highest priority and will be carried out before all other calculations.
Relative: ***D5***	A relative cell reference in a formula will automatically adjust as the formula is copied. When the formula is copied down, the numbers increase, e.g. D5 will become D6. When the formula is copied to the right, the letters increase, e.g. D5 will become E5.
Absolute: ***D5***	An absolute cell reference in a formula remains constant when the formula is copied.
Circular Reference	A circular reference is where a formula refers to itself. If you are typing a formula in B7, you can't refer to B7 in that formula.

3. Formatting

	**Accounting Button** This displays numbers in currency format with two places of decimal. A rounding error may occur when you click the Accounting button, e.g. 50.245 becomes €50.25. The rounding error is +0.005.
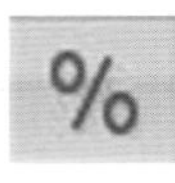	**Percent Button** This displays numbers in percent format. The formatted number is multiplied by 100. E.g. 0.55 becomes 55%.
	**Increase Decimals Button** This increases the numbers to the right of the decimal place by 1 each time it is clicked, e.g. 68 becomes 68.0.
	**Decrease Decimals Button** This reduces the numbers to the right of the decimal place by 1 each time it is clicked. Rounding errors may occur, e.g. 34.24 becomes 34.2. The rounding error is -0.04.

4. Potential Pitfalls

- Formulas aren't always calculated from left to right. Calculations in brackets will be carried out first followed by multiplication and division, even if they are not written first.
- Absolute cell references are rarely used in addition or subtraction formulas.

5. Useful Shortcuts

Keyboard Combination	Action
CTRL + X	Cut
CTRL + C	Copy
CTRL + V	Paste
CTRL + F2	Print Preview
ALT+R+S	Check spelling and grammar
F4	Converts highlighted cell reference in a formula from relative to absolute

Table 1.18

SPREADSHEET FORMULAS REVIEW QUESTIONS

Answers to the review questions are available on www.gillmacmillan.ie

1. In a spreadsheet, each column is identified by a __________. Each row is identified by a __________. The intersection of a row and a column is called a __________.
2. Write down the function of the mouse pointers in the space provided in Table 1.19.

Mouse Pointer	Function
✥	
+	
‡	
↔	

Table 1.19

3. Rearrange the list in Table 1.20 into the correct order of calculation.

		Correct Order
1	Addition	
2	Division	
3	Subtraction	
4	Brackets	
5	Multiplication	

Table 1.20

4. You can prevent your spreadsheet headings scrolling off the screen by selecting ______________________ from the View section of the Ribbon.
5. Table 1.21 displays a number of formulas and a brief explanation of what each formula does. In each formula, one of the cell references must be made absolute so that it can be copied correctly. Rewrite each formula using absolute cell references where appropriate.

	Formula	Explanation	Formula with Absolute Cell Reference
1.	=D1*B4	The PRSI rate in D1 is multiplied by the basic pay in B4.	
2.	=D5*F2	The account balance in D5 is multiplied by the interest rate in F2.	
3.	=D6*F3	The annual interest in D6 is multiplied by the DIRT tax rate in F3.	
4.	=B2*C4	The VRT rate in B2 is multiplied by the value of the car in C4.	
5.	=G2*D8	The discount rate in G2 is multiplied by the total spent in D8.	

Table 1.21

6. Table 1.22 displays classroom attendance over a 5-day period.

	A	B
1		**Total Attendance**
2	Monday	12
3	Tuesday	6
4	Wednesday	9
5	Thursday	10
6	Friday	8
7		
8	**Average**	

Table 1.22

Write down the formula required to calculate the average in Table 1.22.

____

7. The formula *=A3*B3* contains:
   (i) absolute cell references
   (ii) constant cell references

(iii) static cell references

(iv) relative cell references.

8. Table 1.23 displays retail purchase data.

	A	B
1	Price	€100
2	Discount	5%
3	Quantity	6
4		
5	Total	

Table 1.23

Write down the formula to calculate the total in Table 1.23.

____

9. Table 1.24 displays a formula that calculates total tax.

	A	B
1	Total Sales	€43670
2	Sales Tax	5%
3		
4	Total Tax	**=b1*b4**

Table 1.24

What is wrong with the formula displayed in Table 1.24?

____

What name does Excel give to this type of error?

____

10. Round each of the numbers in Table 1.25 to 1 decimal place. Calculate the rounding error in each case.

Number	Rounded to 1 Decimal	Rounding Error
34.46		
300.901		
22.19		
67.95		

Table 1.25

SPREADSHEET FORMULAS REVISION EXERCISE

Create a new spreadsheet workbook and enter the data shown in Table 1.26.

Enter the heading in C1. Create the remaining headings using the fill handle.

	A	B	C	D
1	1		Formula 1	*=A9–A2*A3+A4/2*
2	2		Formula 2	
3	3		Formula 3	
4	4		Formula 4	
5	5		Formula 5	
6	6		Formula 6	
7	7		Formula 7	
8	8		Formula 8	
9	9		Formula 9	
10	10		Formula 10	

Table 1.26

Save this spreadsheet as **Formulas Review**

Ten numeric calculations are listed in Table 1.27. In each case, first work out the answer to the calculation using pen and paper and then check your answer by creating a corresponding formula using cell references in the Formulas Review spreadsheet.

		Write the answer to each formula below
Formula 1	9–2×3+4/2	5
Formula 2	1+2×3–8/2	
Formula 3	8–2×3–8/2	
Formula 4	6+2×3–4/2	
Formula 5	(5–3)× (1+4)/4	
Formula 6	(8–6/2+4×5)–((8–6)/2+4×5)	
Formula 7	3+9/3+9/3	
Formula 8	9–4×2–6/2	
Formula 9	6–4/2–6/2	
Formula 10	(9+1+5)/3	

Table 1.27

Worked Example

9–2×3+4/2: In any formula that doesn't contain brackets, multiplication and division are always done first.

Step One
2×3=6
4/2=2

Step Two
The results of any multiplication and division operations will then replace those calculations in the original formula.

- 6 replaces 2×3
- 2 replaces 4/2
- which results in the following formula:
- 9–6+2
- giving 5 as the answer.

Now check your answer by entering the formula in cell D1 in the spreadsheet (Table 1.26). When we change the numbers to cell references, we get the following spreadsheet formula:

=A9–A2×A3+A4/A2

If your calculations are correct the spreadsheet will give the same answer. Complete formulas 2 to 10 in the same way.

2 Spreadsheet Functions

In Chapter 2, you will learn how to:

- Use the SUM, AVERAGE, MAX, MIN, COUNT and COUNTA functions
- Use advanced functions: POWER, SQRT, DB, SUMIF and COUNTIF
- Assign a name to a single cell
- Assign a name to a range of cells.

WHAT IS A SPREADSHEET FUNCTION?

In Chapter 1, we saw that a formula uses a combination of cell references and arithmetic operators to perform calculations involving plus, minus, multiply or divide. Functions are designed to make calculations easier by taking some of the calculation work away from the spreadsheet user. Each Excel function carries out a very specific task such as calculating the average or finding the highest number in a group of numbers. Excel functions are divided into seven different categories, which are shown in Figure 2.1.

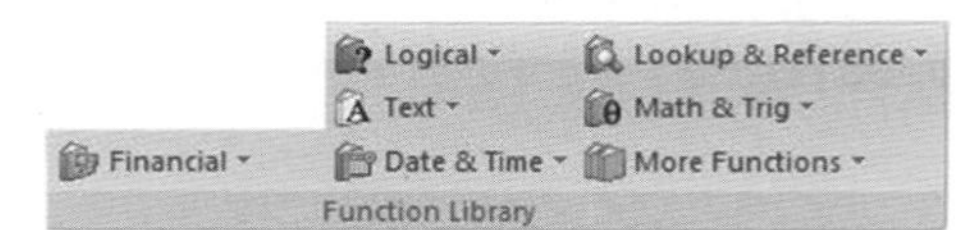

Figure 2.1: Categories of functions available in Excel

The range of functions available in Excel is vast. No one person will use all the functions. Which functions you use depends on your job or area of expertise. For example, an engineer would use the Math and Trigonometry functions. An accountant would use the Financial functions. In this chapter you will learn about some of the most commonly used functions in Excel.

SPREADSHEET RANGES

Because most functions work with spreadsheet ranges, it is important to understand what a spreadsheet range is before you learn about functions. A spreadsheet range can be defined as two or more cells in a spreadsheet that can be highlighted using any one of the following methods.

1. Clicking and dragging with the mouse.
2. Holding down the Shift key and pressing an arrow key (usually either the down or the right arrow key).
3. Pressing F8 followed by an arrow key.

Ranges are described by referring to the first and the last cell in the range. There are four types of spreadsheet range.

1. **Horizontal range.** The range displayed in Figure 2.2 is referred to as *A1:C1*.

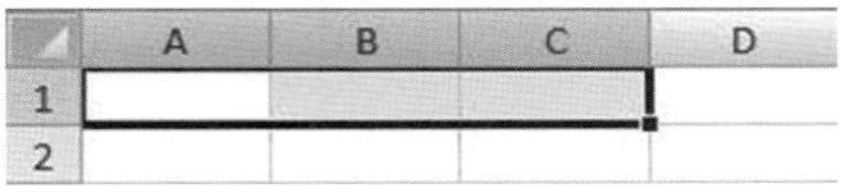

Figure 2.2

2. **Vertical range.** The range displayed in Figure 2.3 is referred to as *A1:A4*.

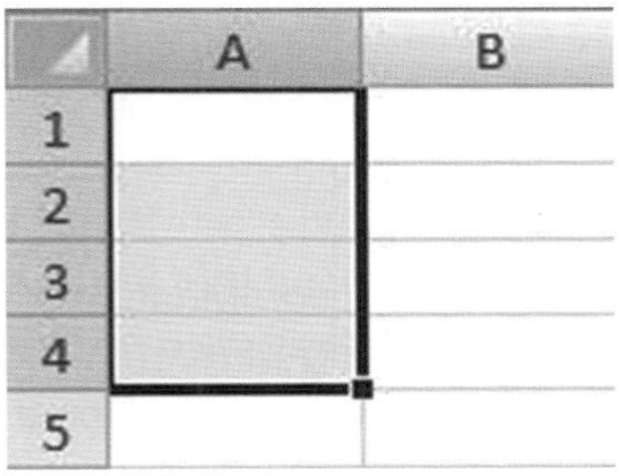

Figure 2.3

3. **Ranges consisting of two or more rows and columns of cells.** The range displayed in Figure 2.4 is referred to as *A1:B5*.

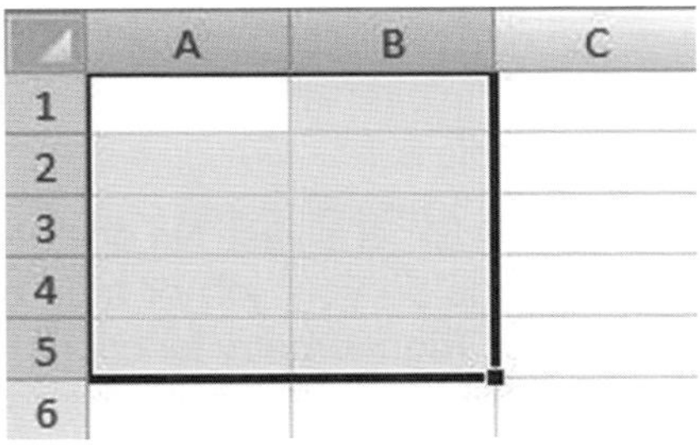

Figure 2.4

N When a single range is highlighted, the first cell in the range is white. All the other cells in the range are shaded.

4. **Ranges consisting of cells or groups of cells in different locations.** The range displayed in Figure 2.5 is referred to as *A1:A5,C1:C5*. To highlight multiple ranges hold down the *CTRL* key when highlighting the second and subsequent ranges.

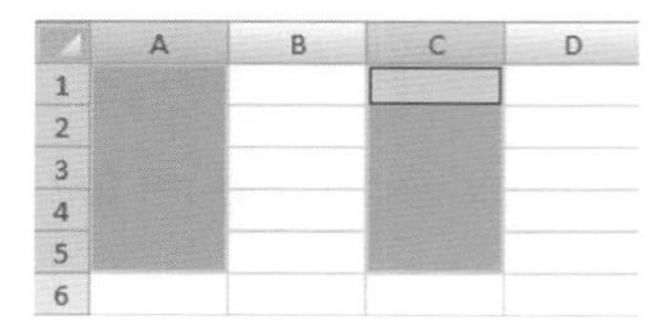

Figure 2.5

Spreadsheet ranges are very important because, as we'll see in the next section, they are used in spreadsheet functions.

WHY SPREADSHEET FUNCTIONS ARE NEEDED

In Chapter 1 we used spreadsheet formulas to do all our calculations. Some of these formulas were quite long and some formulas required correct positioning of brackets. More complicated calculations may require a number of formulas. Fortunately, the people who developed spreadsheets realised that the need to use complex formulas in a spreadsheet would have two major implications.

1. Spreadsheet users would have to spend a lot of time developing formulas.
2. The more complex the formula, the greater the chance of an error being made.

Spreadsheet functions were developed for these reasons. Each function is programmed to carry out a specific task such as adding, calculating averages, finding the highest number in a list or calculating depreciation of an asset. Simply tell the function where the data is and it does all the calculation work for you. In cases where a calculation can be performed using a function or a formula, both methods will give the same result, but the function method is usually quicker and requires less effort. Some of the more popular functions are listed in Table 2.1.

It's worth noting that these functions represent only a small percentage of the full list of functions available in Excel. Specialist functions are available for maths and trigonometry, statistical and financial analysis as well as engineering applications.

Even spreadsheet experts don't know *all* the functions. The functions you will learn and use depend on the type of calculations you're doing with the spreadsheet. The functions listed in Table 2.1 are common to nearly every type of numerical work.

Function name	Action	Example (Single range)	Example (Multiple ranges)
SUM	Adds numbers in a range of cells or multiple ranges	=SUM(B4:B15)	=SUM(B4:B15,E4:E15)
AVERAGE	Calculates the average of numbers in a range of cells or multiple ranges	=AVERAGE(B4:B15)	=AVERAGE(B4:B15,E4:E15)
MAX	Finds the highest number in a range of cells or multiple ranges	=MAX(B4:B15)	=MAX(B4:B15,E4:E15)
MIN	Finds the lowest number in a range of cells or multiple ranges	=MIN(B4:B15)	=MIN(B4:B15,E4:E15)
COUNT	Counts the number of cells containing numbers in a range of cells or multiple ranges	=COUNT(B4:B15)	=COUNT(C4:C15,F4:F15)
COUNTA	Counts the number of cells containing numbers or text in a range of cells or multiple ranges	=COUNTA(A4:A15)	=COUNTA(A4:A15,G4:G15)

Table 2.1

SYNTAX OF A SPREADSHEET FUNCTION

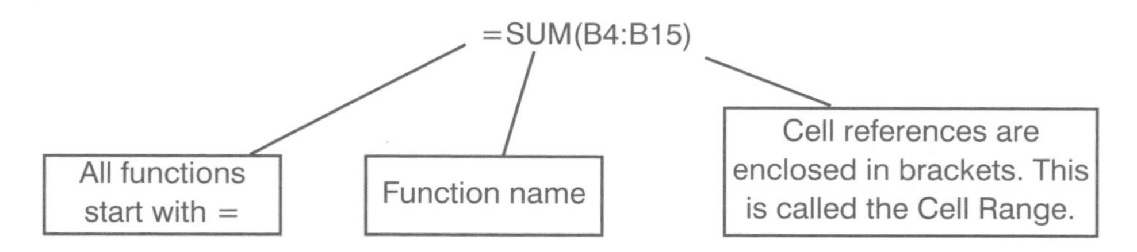

All spreadsheet functions have a similar structure or syntax. A function starts with = and must include a name, such as SUM or AVERAGE. All functions have brackets. The information used by the function to calculate a result is positioned inside the brackets. This information is called an argument. In the example the argument B4:B15 tells the SUM function to add numbers in cells B4 to B15 inclusive. Basic functions like the SUM function have only one argument. We will see later on in this chapter that more advanced functions can have two or more arguments.

FUNCTIONS VS. FORMULAS – WORKED EXAMPLE

In the following worked example we will see how some calculations can be performed using a function or a formula. We will also see that in some cases only a function can be used for a particular calculation.

1. Create a new spreadsheet workbook and enter the data shown in Table 2.2.

	A	B	C	D
1	**Business Travel Analysis**			
2		**2010**		
3		**Distance Travelled**	**Business Trips Abroad**	**Outside EU?**
4	January	1244		
5	February	1450	1	Yes
6	March	1155		
7	April	1632	2	
8	May	1871		
9	June	2193	3	
10	July	2500	2	
11	August	3410		
12	September	3685		
13	October	2177	1	Yes
14	November	2450	2	
15	December	1804	4	
16				
17		**2010**		
18	**Total Distance Travelled**			
19	**Average Distance per Month**			
20	**Highest Monthly Distance Travelled**			
21	**Lowest Monthly Distance Travelled**			
22	**Months with Foreign Travel**			
23	**Trips Outside EU**			

Table 2.2

2. In row 1, center the heading across cells A1 to D1.
3. Format headings to bold and wrap text as shown.

Calculating Total Distance Travelled

Method 1: Formula	Method 2: SUM Function
=B4+B5+B6+B7+B8+B9+B10+ B11+B12+B13+B14+B15	**=SUM(B4:B15)**
Result of formula: **25571**	Result of function: **25571**
In an addition formula we must refer to every cell that we're adding; the more cells that we're adding, the longer the formula becomes. Long formulas cause two problems. First, they take longer to write and second, the longer a formula, the greater the chance you'll make a mistake when writing it.	In the SUM function, instead of referring to every cell that we're adding, we simply refer to the range of cells containing the numbers we're adding. Even though the function is much shorter than the formula it gives the same answer.

Table 2.3

4. In B18, enter the function *=SUM(B4:B15)*

Calculating Average Distance Travelled per Month

Method 1: Formula	Method 2: AVERAGE Function
=(B4+B5+B6+B7+B8+B9+B10+B11+ B12+B13+B14+B15)/12	**=AVERAGE(B4:B15)**
Result of formula: **2130.9**	Result of function: **2130.9**
To get the average, we must first add all the numbers together and then divide by the number of months. Brackets are required to ensure that the addition is carried out before the division.	The AVERAGE function adds all the numbers contained in a range of cells and then divides by the number of numbers in that range. Here, the AVERAGE function adds all the numbers from B4 to B15 inclusive and then divides by 12.

Table 2.4

5. In B19, enter the function *=AVERAGE(B4:B15)*

   There are four remaining calculations in the Business Travel Analysis example.

   - Calculating the highest monthly distance travelled.
   - Calculating the lowest monthly distance travelled.
   - Counting months with foreign travel.
   - Counting trips outside the EU.

All of these calculations require specialist functions. It is not possible to do these calculations using formulas. Explanations of the functions required are given in Table 2.5.

Function	Explanation	Result
=MAX(B4:B15)	The MAX function finds the highest number in a range of cells.	3685
=MIN(B4:B15)	The MIN function finds the lowest number in a range of cells.	1155
=COUNT(C4:C15)	The COUNT function calculates the total number of cells in the specified range that contain numbers. The COUNT function does not count cells containing text.	7
=COUNTA(D4:D15)	The COUNTA function counts the total number of cells in the specified range containing numbers or text.	2

Table 2.5

6. In B20, enter the function *=MAX(B4:B15)*
7. In B21, enter the function *=MIN(B4:B15)*
8. Type the function *=COUNT(C4:C15)* in B22
9. In B23, enter the function *=COUNTA(D4:D15)*
10. Save the spreadsheet as **Business Travel Analysis**

USING FUNCTIONS WITH MULTIPLE RANGES – WORKED EXAMPLE

1. Open the *Business Travel Analysis* spreadsheet if it is not already open.
2. Enter the data for 2011, as shown in Table 2.6.
3. Calculate the following for 2011 using appropriate functions in cells C18 to C23.
   - Total distance travelled.
   - Average distance per month.
   - Highest monthly distance travelled.
   - Lowest monthly distance travelled.
   - Months with foreign travel.
   - Trips outside EU.

You can copy the functions from 2010!

4. We will use functions with multiple ranges to carry out the two-year analysis. When referring to more than one range in a function, ranges must be separated with commas. Enter the following function in E18.

   =SUM(B4:B15,E4:E15)

This function calculates the total distance travelled over two years by adding numbers in column B and column E.

5. Enter the AVERAGE, MAX, MIN, COUNT and COUNTA functions in cells E19 to E23, as shown in Table 2.6.
6. Save the *Business Travel Analysis* spreadsheet.

	A	B	C	D	E	F	G
1	Business Travel Analysis						
2		2010			2011		
3		Distance Travelled	Business Trips Abroad	Outside EU?	Distance Travelled	Business Trips Abroad	Outside EU?
4	January	1244			1066	2	
5	February	1450	1	Yes	1522	1	Yes
6	March	1155			1716		
7	April	1632	2		1088	2	
8	May	1871			2044		
9	June	2193	3		1989	2	
10	July	2500	2		2750	2	
11	August	3410			3400	1	Yes
12	September	3685			3890	2	
13	October	2177	1	Yes	2544	1	Yes
14	November	2450	2		2525	2	
15	December	1804	4		1800	2	
16							
17		2010	2011		2 Year Analysis		
18	**Total Distance Travelled**	25571			=SUM(B4:B15,E4:E15)		
19	**Average Distance per Month**	2130.9			=AVERAGE(B4:B15,E4:E15)		
20	**Highest Monthly Distance Travelled**	3685			=MAX(B4:B15,E4:E15)		
21	**Lowest Monthly Distance Travelled**	1155			=MIN(B4:B15,E4:E15)		
22	**Months with Foreign Travel**	7			=COUNT(C4:C15,F4:F15)		
23	**Trips Outside EU**	2			=COUNTA(D4:D15,G4:G15)		

Table 2.6

Each function does calculations based on 2 ranges of numbers, which are highlighted above

Explanations of functions with multiple ranges are given in Table 2.7.

Function	Explanation	Result	Alternative Method
=SUM(B4:B15,E4:E15)	Calculates the total distance travelled over two years by adding numbers in columns B and E.	51905	=SUM(B4:B15) + SUM(E4:E15)
=AVERAGE(B4:B15,E4:E15)	Calculates the average distance travelled per month in 2010 and 2011.	2162.7	=(B19+C19)/2 or =D18/24
=MAX(B4:B15,E4:E15)	Displays the highest distance travelled in a single month during the two-year period.	3890	—
=MIN(B4:B15,E4:E15)	Displays the lowest distance travelled in a single month during the two-year period.	1066	—
=COUNT(C4:C15,F4:F15)	Counts the number of months with foreign travel during the two-year period	17	=COUNT(C4:C15) + COUNT(F4:F15)
=COUNTA(D4:D15,G4:G15)	Counts the number of months with trips outside the EU during the two-year period	5	=COUNTA(D4:D15) + COUNTA(G4:G15)

Table 2.7 Using multiple ranges in functions

From Table 2.7 it can be seen that there are often a number of ways of carrying out a particular calculation: a formula, a function or a combination of both. It's good spreadsheet practice to use a mixture of formulas and functions in your calculations.

Spreadsheet Functions Assignment One

Create a new spreadsheet workbook and enter the data shown in Table 2.8. Enter functions in the shaded cells to complete the spreadsheet.

The match names can be copied using the Fill Handle.

1. Wrap text within cells in row 3, as shown.

With the cell pointer in a cell where the text has been wrapped, click the Format Painter button and then highlight any other cells where you want to wrap the text.

2. Calculate total attempts on goal using the SUM function.
3. Calculate average attempts on goal using the AVERAGE function.

	A	B	C	D	E	F	G	H
1	**United Football Club**							
2								
3		**Attempts on Goal**	**Wides**	**Fouls**	**Goals Scored**	**Goals Conceded**	**Corners**	**Free Kicks**
4	Match 1	5	4	15	1	2	2	5
5	Match 2	7	3	20	2	1	1	6
6	Match 3	6	6	22	0	0	4	3
7	Match 4	10	5	11	2	1	3	5
8	Match 5	4	2	17	2	3	5	4
9	Match 6	5	4	9	1	2	0	2
10	Match 7	9	3	18	3	2	1	8
11	Match 8	6	2	14	0	1	3	7
12	Match 9	5	3	10	1	2	1	6
13	Match 10	8	5	17	2	3	2	10
14								
15	Total							
16	Average							
17	Highest							
18	Lowest							

Table 2.8

4. Calculate highest number of attempts on goal using the MAX function.
5. Calculate lowest number of attempts on goal using the MIN function.
6. Copy all functions using Fill Right.

Highlight *B15:B18* first. Next, copy all functions using the Fill Handle. Remember, it's a white cross for highlighting and a black cross for copying.

7. Center the heading in row 1 across columns A to H.

The Merge and Center button can be used to center a heading within a range of selected cells.

8. Format headings in bold, as shown.
9. Center the data in columns B to H.
10. Save the spreadsheet as **United Football Club**

Spreadsheet Functions – Worked Example

Create a new spreadsheet workbook and enter the data shown in Table 2.9. Functions will be created in the shaded cells to complete the spreadsheet.

	A	B	C	D	E
1	**Rainfall (mm) Analysis**				
2		Roches Point	Valentia	Loop Head	Erris Head
3	Monday	0	5	3	2.5
4	Tuesday	10	12	11	8
5	Wednesday	0	0	0	0
6	Thursday	5	8	7	6
7	Friday	0	0	0	0
8	Saturday	0	0	0	5
9	Sunday	14	12	10	6
10					
11	**South/West Weekly Rainfall Summary**				
12	Total (mm)				
13	Average (mm)				
14	Highest Daily Amount (mm)				
15	Lowest Daily Amount (mm)				

Table 2.9

In this example we will use functions to do calculations on all the rainfall data. Each function will refer to ranges consisting of multiple rows and columns of cells.

1. In B12, enter the function *=SUM(B3:E9).* This adds all the numbers in columns B to E.
2. In B13, enter the function *=AVERAGE(B3:E9).* This calculates the average of the numbers in columns B to E.
3. Format Average (mm) to 2 decimal places.
4. In B14, display the highest daily rainfall amount using an appropriate function.
5. In B15, display the lowest daily rainfall amount using an appropriate function.
6. Save the spreadsheet as **Rainfall Analysis**

Spreadsheet Functions Assignment Two

Create a new spreadsheet workbook and enter the data shown in Table 2.10. Enter functions in the shaded cells to complete the spreadsheet.

To quickly create a new Excel workbook, hold down the *CTRL* key and type *N*

	A	B	C	D	E	F	G
1	**Western Area Sales**					**Date**	
2							
3		**JAN**	**FEB**	**MAR**	**APR**	**MAY**	**JUN**
4	Unit 1	2076	2971	2241	2503	2418	2063
5	Unit 2	3510	2085	3394	2957	2048	2279
6	Unit 3	1866	1600	1750	1780	1800	1975
7	Unit 4	1200	1341	1200	1453	1098	1255
8							
9	**Monthly Unit Sales Analysis**						
10	**Total Sales**						
11	**Average Sales**						
12	**Highest Sales Achieved**						
13	**Lowest Sales Achieved**						
14							
15			**Western Area Six Month Totals**				
16			**Total Western Area Sales**				
17			**Average Western Area Sales**				
18			**Six-Month Sales High**				
19			**Six-Month Sales Low**				

Table 2.10

1. Enter today's date in G1 (*typing =today() inserts the date from the computer clock*).
2. Calculate total sales, average sales, highest sales achieved and lowest sales achieved for each month. Copy these functions using Fill Right.

When creating functions, type the function name followed by an open bracket and then highlight the range of cells. When you do this, Excel types the cell range for you. For example, to add numbers in the range A2:A10, first type *=SUM* followed by an open bracket. Next, highlight from A2 to A10 and close the bracket. Creating functions using this method reduces the chances of making a mistake.

3. Calculate total western area sales, average western area sales, six-month sales high and six-month sales low (*these calculations are based on sales figures for units one to four over six months*).
4. Format all averages to zero decimal places.
5. Center the heading in row 1 across columns A to E.
6. Format headings to bold and center data, as shown.
7. Save the spreadsheet as **Western Area Sales**

A SUMMARY OF THE DIFFERENCES BETWEEN FORMULAS AND FUNCTIONS

The SUM function is the most commonly used function in Excel. It is frequently used incorrectly by students new to Excel and sometimes even by experienced Excel users. SUM is only used for addition. It should not be used for subtraction, multiplication or division. Table 2.11 summarises the differences between formulas and functions.

Formula	Function
The calculation work carried out by a formula depends on how big the formula is. Longer formulas do more work but take longer to write.	Functions are programmed to carry out specific tasks, some of which can be quite complex. Although the function itself may be very easy and quick to create it may do a huge amount of calculation work in the background, which is not seen by the spreadsheet user.
Each formula combines plus (+), minus (-), multiply (*) or divide (/) with two or more cell references. Example: *=B6+C4-C5*	The information used by a function is called an argument. This is usually a range of cells. Example: *=SUM(B2:B20)* This is much quicker than writing a long formula to add up the numbers in cells B2 to B20. More advanced functions have more than one argument. Example: *=COUNTIF(B2:B20,">20")*
The order of calculation in a formula is determined by the BoMDAS rule. 1. Brackets 2. Multiplication 3. Division 4. Addition 5. Subtraction	Once the correct data are supplied to the function it will look after the method of calculation.

Formula	Function
Brackets change the order of calculation in a formula. Example: =*G8+F8/E8* In this formula, division is done first even though it is written second. We can force Excel to do the addition first by enclosing the addition in brackets as follows: *=(G8+F8)/E8*	The brackets have no specific function other than to act as a container for the arguments of the function.
Not all formulas have brackets. All functions have brackets. Never use **:** in a formula. *=C4:C5* has no effect	Never use **+**, **-**, ***** or / in a function. *=SUM(D2+D20)* adds D2 and D20 and ignores all the numbers in between
The following calculations cannot be completed using a formula: • Finding the highest number • Finding the lowest number • Counting numbers or text	There is no function for subtraction or division. The following functions are incorrect: *=SUM(D3-D4)* *=SUM(F8/A2)* 1. The SUM function is designed specifically for addition. It should not be used for subtraction, multiplication or division. 2. Minus (-), multiply (*) and divide (/) should not be used inside a function.

Table 2.11 A summary of the differences between formulas and functions

Spreadsheet Functions Assignment Three

Create a new spreadsheet workbook and enter the data shown in Table 2.12. Use a combination of formulas and functions to complete the spreadsheet.

A date can be entered in shortened form, e.g. type 8/9/10 and press Enter. The date will be displayed as 08/09/2010 or 08/09/10 depending on how your spreadsheet is set up.

	A	B	C	D	E	F	G	H	I	J
1					**Rock Café**				**Date**	
2										
3								**Stalls**	**300**	
4								**Circle**	**350**	
5								**Balcony**	**250**	
6										
7	**Artist**	**Date**	**Stalls**	**%Full**	**Circle**	**%Full**	**Balcony**	**%Full**	**Total Tickets**	**%Full**
8	The Blizzards	08/09/10	150		300		220			
9	U2	10/09/10	276		245		141			
10	Mundy	11/09/10	290		307		209			
11	Duffy	14/09/10	250		312		196			
12	Arcade Fire	18/09/10	300		350		250			
13	Kings of Leon	19/09/10	100		267		233			
14	Mick Flannery	20/09/10	180		255		200			
15										
16	**Total Sales**									
17	**Average Sales**									
18	**Highest Sales**									
19	**Lowest Sales**									
20	**Number of Performances**									

Table 2.12

1. Insert the date using the Today function (*typing =today() inserts the date from the computer clock*).
2. Calculate the percentage of the stalls that was full, the percentage of the circle that was full, and the percentage of the balcony that was full for each performance. Format these cells using the Percent Style button.
3. Calculate the total tickets sold for each performance.
4. Calculate the percentage of the venue that was full for each performance. Format these cells using the Percent Style button.
5. Calculate the total sales, average sales, highest sales, lowest sales and number of performances in the stalls. Use Copy and Paste to copy the functions that calculate the total, average, highest and lowest sales to the circle and the balcony.

In this case, the Fill Handle can't be used to copy the functions because this would also copy functions to columns D and E where they are not required.

6. Center the heading in row 1 across columns A to H.
7. Format headings to bold, as shown.
8. Print the spreadsheet with gridlines and row and column headings displayed.
9. Save the spreadsheet as **Rock Café**

WHEN SHOULD YOU USE A FUNCTION?

Usually you can get the answer with a function more quickly than if you used a formula, but this doesn't mean that you should always use functions. An experienced spreadsheet user will use a combination of formulas and functions as the need arises. New spreadsheet users often forget about formulas once they learn how to create functions. It's good spreadsheet practice to use a combination of formulas and functions. As a general rule, if a formula is long and complicated, consider using a function. Most basic calculations can be performed using formulas.

Sometimes it will be more appropriate to use a formula, as outlined in Table 2.13.

	A	B	C	D	E	F	G	H	I
7	**Artist**	**Date**	**Stalls**	**%Full**	**Circle**	**%Full**	**Balcony**	**%Full**	**Total Tickets**
8	The Blizzards	08/09/10	150	50%	300	85.7%	220	88%	

Table 2.13

To calculate the total tickets for the Blizzards, we must add 150, 300 and 220. In this case we should use the formula =C8+E8+G8, giving 670 as the total tickets. Using the SUM function =sum(C8:G8) would add the percentages as well as the ticket sales, incorrectly giving 671.357 as the total tickets.

ADVANCED FUNCTIONS

The POWER Function

The POWER function calculates the result of a number raised to a power (where you multiply a number by itself a number of times). For example, 2×2 is 2^2 or 2 to the power of 2; $2 \times 2 \times 2$ is 2^3 or 2 to the power of 3; $2 \times 2 \times 2 \times 2$ is 2^4 or 2 to the power of 4, and so on. In Excel, we can use the POWER function to do these calculations for us. Examples of the POWER function are shown in Table 2.14.

	A	B	Explanation
1	2	=POWER(A1,2)	2 to the power of 2 = 4
2	3	=POWER(A2,3)	3 to the power of 3 = 27
3	4	=POWER(A3,2)	4 to the power of 2 = 16
4	5	=POWER(A4,3)	5 to the power of 3 = 125

Table 2.14

A common use of this would be where we're calculating the area of a circle. To calculate the area of a circle, we must square the radius and multiply the result by Pi (3.14). In Table 2.15 a circle radius of five has been entered in A2, the square of the circle radius is calculated using *=POWER(A2,2)*. The square is multiplied by 3.14, giving 78.5 as the circle area.

Example One: Calculating the Area of a Circle Using the POWER Function

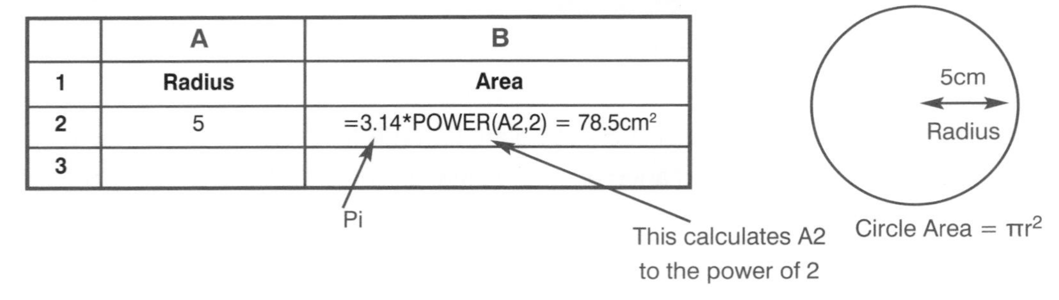

	A	B
1	**Radius**	**Area**
2	5	=3.14*POWER(A2,2) = 78.5cm^2
3		

Table 2.15

In Table 2.15, the POWER function squares the radius of the circle. This is multiplied by 3.14 (the mathematical number called Pi) to give a circle area of 78.5cm^2.

Example Two: Calculating the Number of Bytes Using the POWER Function

Another application of the POWER function is in the conversion of kilobytes, megabytes, gigabytes and terabytes into bytes. A kilobyte is equal to 2^{10} bytes. A megabyte is equal to 2^{20} bytes. A gigabyte is equal to 2^{30} bytes. A terabyte is 2^{40} bytes. Power functions that calculate the number of bytes in a kilobyte, megabyte, gigabyte and terabyte are shown in Table 2.16.

	A	B	C	D
1	1	kilobyte equals	**=POWER(2,10)** = 1024	bytes
2	1	megabyte equals	**=POWER(2,20)** = 1,048,576	bytes
3	1	gigabyte equals	**=POWER(2,30)** = 1073,741,824	bytes
4	1	terabyte equals	**=POWER(2,40)** = 1,099,511,627,776	bytes

Table 2.16

Spreadsheet Functions Assignment Four

Create a new spreadsheet workbook and enter the data shown in Table 2.17. Enter functions in the shaded cells to complete the spreadsheet.

	A	B	C
1	**Circle Radius (cm)**	**Area**	
2	25		
3	15		
4	31		
5	59		
6	12		

Table 2.17

1. Calculate the area of each circle using the POWER function.
2. Format headings to bold and center the data, as shown.
3. Save the spreadsheet as **Circle Area Calculator**

 To save an Excel workbook, hold down the *CTRL* key and type *S*.

Spreadsheet Functions Assignment Five

Create a new spreadsheet workbook and enter the data shown in Table 2.18. Enter functions in the shaded cells to complete the spreadsheet.

	A	B	C	D
1	**Byte Converter**			
2				
3	512	**Kilobyte Cache =**		**Bytes**
4	4	**Gigabytes of RAM =**		**Bytes**
5	256	**Megabytes Video Memory =**		**Bytes**
6	2	**Terabyte Hard Disk =**		**Bytes**

Table 2.18

1. Enter functions in the shaded cells to complete the spreadsheet. (*Multiply by 2^{10} to convert from kilobytes to bytes, by 2^{20} to convert from megabytes to bytes, by 2^{30} to convert from gigabytes to bytes and by 2^{40} to convert from terabytes to bytes.*)
2. Center the heading in row 1 across columns A to D.
3. Format data as shown in Table 2.18.

If you want to use a number in a formula or function, always enter that number in a separate cell. Table 2.19 is correct because the number and the text were entered in separate cells.

	A	B
1	512	Kilobyte Cache =

Table 2.19

Table 2.20 is incorrect because the number and the text were entered in the same cell. We would be unable to use 512 in a calculation because the spreadsheet interprets A1 as text and not as a number. The #VALUE error message will be displayed if A1 is referred to by a formula or a function.

	A
1	512 Kilobyte Cache =

Table 2.20

Calculating the Volume of a Cylinder

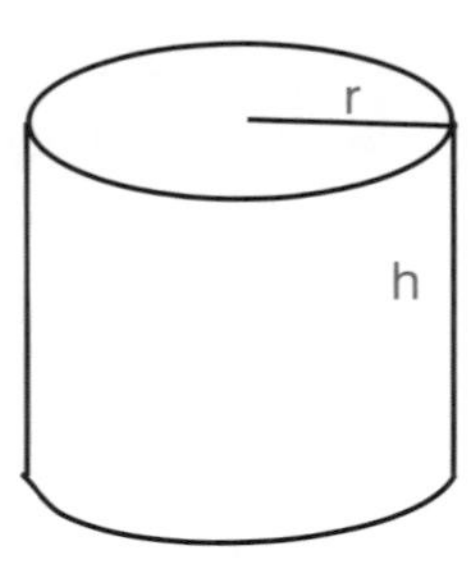

The mathematical formula to calculate the volume of a cylinder is:

$$\pi r^2 h$$

where **r** = radius and **h** = height of the cylinder.

Spreadsheet Functions Assignment Six

Create a new spreadsheet workbook and enter the data shown in Table 2.21. Enter formulas and functions in the shaded cells to complete the spreadsheet.

	A	B	C	D	E	F
1	**Cosy Oil Deliveries**					
2	**Price per litre**	**0.3965**				
3						
4						
5	**Delivery Date**	**Tank Radius (metres)**	**Tank Height (metres)**	**Tank Volume (m^3)**	**Tank Volume (litres)**	**Total Cost**
6	01/04/2010	0.75	2			
7	01/04/2010	0.6	1.8			
8	01/04/2010	0.65	1.75			
9	02/04/2010	0.8	1.85			
10	02/04/2010	0.6	1.6			
11	02/04/2010	0.65	1.75			

Table 2.21

1. Calculate the volume of the oil tank in metres cubed using the mathematical formula $\pi r^2 h$. *($\pi = 3.14$)*
2. Multiply tank volume (m^3) by 1000 to convert it to tank volume (litres).
3. Calculate the total cost for each fill.
4. Center the heading in row 1 across columns A to F.
5. Format headings to bold, as shown.
6. Format all money amounts to currency.
7. Save the spreadsheet as **Cosy Oil**

The SQRT Function

The SQRT function calculates the square root of a number. A common use of this would be where we know the area of a circle and we want to calculate the radius.

Circle Area = *3.14*r²*

$$r = \sqrt{\frac{Area}{3.14}}$$

From the above it can be seen that the radius of a circle is calculated by getting the square root of the area divided by 3.14.

Example Three: Calculating the Radius of a Circle Using the SQRT Function

	A	B
1	**Circle Area**	**Radius**
2	78.5	*=SQRT(A2/3.14)*
3		

Table 2.22

In Table 2.22, a circle area of 78.5 has been entered in A2. The radius of the circle is calculated using *=SQRT(A2/3.14)*, which gives 5 as the radius.

Spreadsheet Functions Assignment Seven

Create a new spreadsheet workbook and enter the data shown in Table 2.23. Enter functions in the shaded cells to complete the spreadsheet.

	A	B	C
1	**Circle Radius Calculator**		
2			
3	**Circle Area**	**Radius**	
4	314		
5	1256		
6	2826		
7	5024		
8	7850		

Table 2.23

1. Calculate the radius using an appropriate function.
2. Center the heading in row 1 across columns A to C.
3. Format data as shown.
4. Save the spreadsheet as **Circle Radius Calculator**

The DB Function (Declining Balance)

The DB function calculates the depreciation of an asset over a number of years, using the declining balance method. The DB function requires four items of data, referred to as arguments, in order to calculate depreciation. These are as follows.

- Purchase price or initial value of the asset.
- Disposal value of the asset after the depreciation period.
- Number of years over which to depreciate the asset.
- Year number.

Example Four: Calculating Annual Depreciation Using the DB Function

Table 2.24 demonstrates how the DB function calculates the depreciation on a company van over 5 years. The DB function is programmed to calculate higher levels of depreciation in the earlier years, as this is when an asset loses most of its value.

	A	B	C	D	E
1	**Asset**	**Company Van**		**Purchase Price**	**€20,000**
2				**Disposal Price**	**€5,000**
3				**Expected Life (years):**	**5**
4					
5	**Year 1 depreciation**	=DB(E1,E2,E3,1) gives *€4840*			
6	**Year 2 depreciation**	=DB(E1,E2,E3,2) gives *€3668.72*			
7	**Year 3 depreciation**	=DB(E1,E2,E3,3) gives *€2780.89*			
8	**Year 4 depreciation**	=DB(E1,E2,E3,4) gives *€2107.91*			
9	**Year 5 depreciation**	=DB(E1,E2,E3,5) gives *€1597.80*			

Purchase Price (€20000) — Disposal Value (€5000) — Number of years over which the asset is depreciated (5) — Year Number

Table 2.24

Spreadsheet Functions Assignment Eight

Create a new spreadsheet workbook and enter the data shown in Table 2.25. Enter functions in the shaded cells to complete the spreadsheet.

	A	B	C	D	E
1	**Depreciation Schedule**				
2					
3	**Asset**	**Company Car**	**Machinery**	**Computer**	**Truck**
4	**Purchase Price**	34500	120000	900	42800
5	**Disposal Value**	8500	20000	300	12500
6	**Expected Life (years)**	5	8	4	6
7					
8	Year 1 depreciation				
9	Year 2 depreciation				
10	Year 3 depreciation				
11	Year 4 depreciation				
12	Year 5 depreciation				
13	Year 6 depreciation				
14	Year 7 depreciation				
15	Year 8 depreciation				

Table 2.25

1. Calculate depreciation for each asset.

   H The functions for years one to four can be copied using Fill Right if you use absolute cell references.
2. Format all money amounts to currency.
3. Center the heading in row 1 across columns A to E.
4. Format headings to bold and center data, as shown.
5. Save the spreadsheet as **Depreciation Schedule**

The SUMIF Function

The SUMIF function adds cell values in a range if they satisfy a given condition. This is very useful if there are values relating to different items in the same row or column and these values are in random order. In Table 2.26, sales values relating to apples, bananas and pears have been entered in column C. The SUMIF function can be used to calculate total sales for each of the three products.

Example: Calculating Sales by Product Using the SUMIF Function

	A	B	C	D	E
1	**Monday Sales**				
2					
3	**Customer**	**Product**	**Amount**		
4	Tony Leahy	Apples	250		
5	Sinead Donovan	Bananas	100		
6	Peter Smith	Apples	300		
7	Stephen Connors	Pears	75		
8	Seamus O Neill	Bananas	80		
9	Gary Jennings	Bananas	150		
10	Mike Healy	Apples	200		
11	Eileen Carr	Pears	300		
12	Christine Flynn	Apples	50		
13					
14	Total Sales of Apples	=SUMIF(B4:B12,“Apples”,C4:C12) *gives 800*			
15	Total Sales of Bananas	=SUMIF(B4:B12,“Bananas”,C4:C12) *gives 330*			
16	Total Sales of Pears	=SUMIF(B4:B12,“Pears”,C4:C12) *gives 375*			

Range of cells to be evaluated

Which cells in the range B4:B12 contain the word “Pears”

Only add numbers from this range which satisfy the condition, i.e. numbers relating to Pears

Table 2.26

Logical operators can be added to the SUMIF function to refine its calculations. Examples of this are shown in Table 2.27 and Table 2.28.

	A	B
1	**Units Sold**	**Bonus**
2	565	€400
3	191	€150
4	854	€600
5	904	€1000
6	227	€200
7	601	€450

Table 2.27

Example	Explanation
=SUMIF(A2:A7, ">300",B2:B7)	Adds the bonus amounts where the number of units sold is greater than 300.
=SUMIF(A2:A7, "<=300",B2:B7)	Adds the bonus amounts where the number of units sold is 300 or less.

Table 2.28

The SUMIF function will not work if >*300* is not enclosed in double quotes.

Spreadsheet Functions Assignment Nine

Create a new spreadsheet workbook and enter the data shown in Table 2.29. Enter functions in the shaded cells to complete the spreadsheet.

	A	B	C	D
1	**Main Street Car Repairs**			
2				
3	**Date**	**Description**	**Mechanic**	**Hours**
4	02/06/10	Standard Service	Pat	1.5
5	02/06/10	Clutch	Dave	4
6	02/06/10	Gearbox	Pat	6
7	02/06/10	Standard Service	Dave	2
8	02/06/10	Puncture	Dave	0.2
9	03/06/10	Puncture	Pat	0.2
10	03/06/10	Puncture	Pat	0.2
11	03/06/10	Clutch	Dave	3
12	03/06/10	Gearbox	Dave	6
13	03/06/10	Timing Belt	Pat	4
14				
15	**Mechanic**	**Total Hours**	**Hourly Rate**	**Total Pay**
16	Pat		25.5	
17	Dave		25.5	

Table 2.29

1. Calculate the total hours worked by each mechanic using the SUMIF function.
2. Calculate total pay using a formula.
3. Format all numbers relating to hours worked to one decimal place.

4. Center the heading in row 1 across columns A to D.
5. Format all money amounts to currency.
6. Format headings to bold and align data as shown.
7. Save the spreadsheet as **Main Street Car Repairs**

The COUNTIF Function

The COUNTIF function counts the number of cells in a range containing specific data or satisfying a given condition.

	A	B	C	D
1	**Maintenance Department Work Log**			
2				
3	**Month**	**Work Done**	**Department**	
4	June	Painting	Finance	
5	June	Cleaning	Sales	
6	July	Install new PCs	Computer	
7	July	Service alarm	Sales	
8	July	Painting	Finance	
9	July	Service alarm	Finance	
10	August	Cleaning	Sales	
11	August	Painting	Computer	
12				
13	**Analysis of Jobs by Department**		**Monthly Job Count**	
14	Finance	=COUNTIF(C4:C11,A14) *gives 3*	June	=COUNTIF(A4:A11,C14) *gives 2*
15	Sales	=COUNTIF(C4:C11,A15) *gives 3*	July	=COUNTIF(A4:A11,C15) *gives 4*
16	Computer	=COUNTIF(C4:C11,A16) *gives 2*	August	=COUNTIF(A4:A11,C16) *gives 2*
17				

Range of cells to be evaluated

Count the number of cells in the range C4:C11 which contain the text "Computer" which is stored in A16

Range of cells to be evaluated

Count the number of cells in the range A4:A11 which contain the text "August" which is stored in C16

Table 2.30

Example: Analysis of Jobs by Department and Month Using the COUNTIF Function

=COUNTIF(C4:C11,A16)

In Table 2.30, this COUNTIF function checks to see how many cells in the range C4:C11 match what's stored in A16, i.e. how many cells in the range C4:C11 contain the text *Computer*. The function gives *2* as the answer.

The COUNTIF function can also count numbers. Logical operators can be included to specify that COUNTIF only counts numbers matching a certain condition; e.g. only count numbers that are greater than 10. Examples of COUNTIF functions are shown in Table 2.31.

Example	Explanation
=COUNTIF(G2:G20,"Overdue")	Count the number of cells in the range G2:G20 containing the text "Overdue".
=COUNTIF(D4:D12,100)	Count the number of cells in the range D4:D12 containing the number 100.
=COUNTIF(F2:F25,">25")	Count the number of numbers in the range F2:F25 that are greater than 25.
=COUNTIF(A2:A20,B2)	Count the number of cells in the range A2:A20 that exactly match the data entered in cell B2.

Table 2.31

When counting numbers, double quotes are optional. =COUNTIF(D4:D12,100) gives the same answer as =COUNTIF(D4:D12,"100"). However, if you use a logical operator, such as >, double quotes are required; e.g. =COUNTIF(D2:D12,">200")

Spreadsheet Functions Assignment Ten

Create a new spreadsheet workbook and enter the data shown in Table 2.32. Enter functions in the shaded cells to complete the spreadsheet.

Using absolute cell references in the functions in this assignment will help you to copy the functions more efficiently.

1. Calculate the total number of bookshelves, desks, etc.
2. Calculate the total value of each item.
3. Calculate the number of items in room 12 and room 14.
4. Calculate the total value of items in room 12 and room 14.
5. Center the heading in row 1 across columns A to D.
6. Format all money amounts to currency.

7. Format headings to bold, as shown.
8. Save the spreadsheet as **Classroom Equipment List**

	A	B	C	D
1	**Classroom Equipment List**			
2				
3	**Item**	**Location**	**Category**	**Value**
4	Filing Cabinet	Room 12	Office Equipment	450
5	Desk	Room 14	Office Furniture	300
6	PC	Room 12	Computer Equipment	850
7	Bookshelf	Room 12	Office Furniture	400
8	PC	Room 14	Computer Equipment	700
9	Desk	Room 12	Office Furniture	250
10	Filing Cabinet	Room 12	Office Furniture	550
11	Laptop	Room 14	Computer Equipment	990
12	Laser Printer	Room 12	Computer Equipment	165
13	Deskjet Printer	Room 14	Computer Equipment	105
14	Bookshelf	Room 14	Office Furniture	240
15	Laptop	Room 12	Computer Equipment	900
16				
17	**Item**	**Number**	**Total Value**	
18	Bookshelf			
19	Desk			
20	Deskjet Printer			
21	Filing Cabinet			
22	Laptop			
23	Laser Printer			
24	PC			
25				
26		**Items**	**Total Value**	
27	Room 12			
28	Room 14			

Table 2.32

Spreadsheet Functions Assignment Eleven

Create a new spreadsheet workbook and enter the data shown in Table 2.33. Enter functions in the shaded cells to complete the spreadsheet.

	A	B	C	D	E
1	**Tech Support Call Analysis**				
2					
3	**Referred By**	**Date**	**Problem**	**Total Problems Referred By**	
4	Afsoon Sahar	02/09/10	Hard Disk	Evelyn Smith	
5	Evelyn Smith	03/09/10	Operating System	Tom O Donoghue	
6	Tom O Donoghue	03/09/10	Printer	Afsoon Sahar	
7	Joan Donovan	03/09/10	Word 2007	Peter Jones	
8	Joan Donovan	06/09/10	Word 2007	Joan Donovan	
9	Tom O Donoghue	06/09/10	Windows 7		
10	Joan Donovan	07/09/10	Word 2007	**Type of Problem**	
11	Evelyn Smith	07/09/10	Excel 2007	Floppy Disk	
12	Joan Donovan	07/09/10	Windows 7	Hard Disk	
13	Peter Jones	07/09/10	Floppy Disk	Operating System	
14	Afsoon Sahar	07/09/10	Hard Disk	Printer	
15	Tom O Donoghue	08/09/10	Printer	Word 2007	
16	Peter Jones	08/09/10	Windows 7	Excel 2007	
17	Evelyn Smith	08/09/10	Excel 2007	Windows 7	

Table 2.33

1. Calculate the number of problems reported by each employee.
2. Calculate the number of times each problem occurred.
3. Copy both functions using Fill Down.

H You'll get incorrect results if you don't use absolute cell references.

4. Format the data as shown in Table 2.33.
5. Save the spreadsheet as **Tech Support**

The SUMIF and COUNTIF functions will only give a result if exact matches are found. For example, there were two hard disk problems. If a spelling error is made and 'Hard Dosk' is incorrectly entered in C14, the COUNTIF function will not include this in its count. Unnecessary use of the spacebar also leads to problems here. Hard Disk, typed with no space after the letter 'k', is not the same as Hard Disk typed with a space after the letter 'k'. Remember, SUMIF and COUNTIF must find an exact match.

Spreadsheet Functions Assignment Twelve

Create a new spreadsheet workbook and enter the data shown in Table 2.34. Enter functions in the shaded cells to complete the spreadsheet.

	A	B	C	D	E	F
1	**Penalty Points Analysis**					
2						
3	**Driver Name**	**Province**	**Penalty Points**		**Province**	**Drivers**
4	Joe Carey	Munster	10		Leinster	
5	Michelle Murphy	Leinster	13		Munster	
6	Lisa O Neill	Leinster	9		Connaught	
7	Maya Vandana	Munster	14			
8	Paul Tolan	Connaught	8		**Points**	**Drivers**
9	Peter Ahearne	Leinster	13		12 or more	
10	Niall Tobin	Connaught	12		10 or more	
11	Martin Hanson	Munster	8		8 or more	
12	Thomas Conway	Leinster	13			

Table 2.34

1. Calculate the number of drivers from Leinster, Munster and Connaught.
2. Calculate the number of drivers with 12 or more points, 10 or more points and 8 or more points.
3. Format the data as shown in Table 2.34.
4. Save the spreadsheet as **Penalty Points**

Spreadsheet Functions Assignment Thirteen

Create a new spreadsheet workbook and enter the data shown in Table 2.35. Enter functions in the shaded cells to complete the spreadsheet.

The exam numbers can be copied using Fill Series. Enter the first exam number in A4. Next, highlight A4:A15, using the white cross mouse pointer. In the Home section of the Ribbon, click the Fill button which is located in the Editing group. Select Series from the drop-down list. Click OK.

	A	B	C	D
1	Galway Examining Board			
2				
3	**Exam Number**	**Centre**	**Marker**	**Result**
4	102511	Castlebar	Brian Williams	Pass
5	102512	Sligo	Marina Milyukov	Fail
6	102513	Galway	Susan Kinsella	Merit
7	102514	Sligo	Brian Williams	Merit
8	102515	Sligo	Brian Williams	Distinction
9	102516	Sligo	Marina Milyukov	Fail
10	102517	Galway	Marina Milyukov	Distinction
11	102518	Galway	Susan Kinsella	Pass
12	102519	Castlebar	Brian Williams	Pass
13	102520	Galway	Susan Kinsella	Fail
14	102521	Sligo	Brian Williams	Fail
15	102522	Castlebar	Susan Kinsella	Merit
16				
17	**Exam Centre**	**Number of Students Examined**	**Marker**	**Number of Exams Corrected**
18	Galway		Susan Kinsella	
19	Sligo		Brian Williams	
20	Castlebar		Marina Milyukov	

Table 2.35

1. Calculate the number of students examined in each centre.
2. Calculate the number of exams corrected by each examiner.
3. Format the data as shown in Table 2.35.
4. Save the spreadsheet as **Galway Examining Board**

NAMING A SPREADSHEET CELL – WORKED EXAMPLE

A name can be assigned to an individual cell or range of cells. Using cell or range names in formulas and functions makes them easier to understand and remember. It's a good idea to name a cell if that cell is frequently referred to by formulas or functions.

1. Create a new spreadsheet workbook and enter the data shown in Table 2.36.

	A	B	C	D	E	F	G
1	**Building Supplies Invoice**						
2							
3						**Discount Rate**	**5%**
4							
5	**Product Code**	**Description**	**Quantity**	**Price**	**Total**	**Discount**	
6	200	Sandpaper	20	0.19	**= C6*D6**	**= E6*G3**	
7	305	Wood Filler	2	6.34	**= C7*D7**	**= E7*G3**	
8	307	Filling Knife	1	7.22	**= C8*D8**	**= E8*G3**	
9	451	Pine Cornice	3	8.38	**= C9*D9**	**= E9*G3**	
10	178	Matt Varnish	1	15.99	**= C10*D10**	**= E10*G3**	

Table 2.36

2. Enter formulas, as shown in E6 and F6.
3. Copy these formulas using Fill Down.
4. Format all money amounts to currency.

In Table 2.36, calculating the discount for each product requires the use of an absolute cell reference. The reference to G3 (the cell containing the discount rate) is absolute so that when the formula *=E6*G3* is copied to calculate discounts for the remaining products, the reference to G3 doesn't change. Formulas using absolute references can be quite difficult to write, especially if you have to scroll vertically or horizontally to determine what the absolute cell reference should be. Absolute cell references are also difficult to remember. You may find yourself asking, *Was that number in A10 or B10?* and then moving to that area of the spreadsheet just to check. This is time-consuming and can also lead to errors in formulas. The solution is to name the cell and then refer to the cell name in the formula instead of using an absolute cell reference.

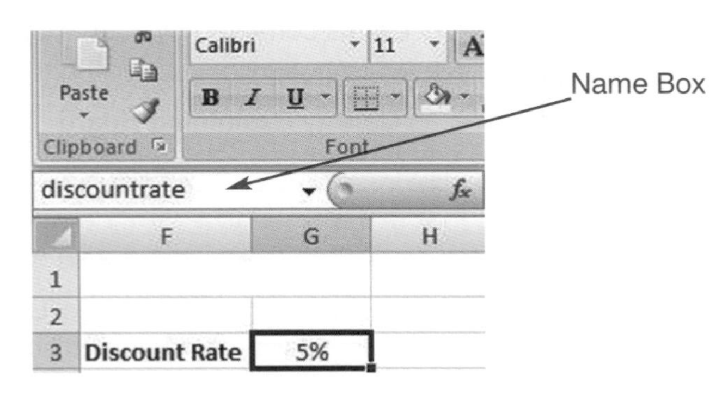

Figure 2.6

5. Select G3 and type *discountrate* in the Name Box, as shown in Figure 2.6.
6. Press Enter to assign this name to G3.

N The name will not be accepted unless you press Enter. Clicking the left mouse button does not work when naming a cell.

N Excel will not accept a cell or range name containing a space.

7. Edit the formulas in column F, replacing each absolute cell reference with the *discountrate* cell name. The edited formulas are shown in Table 2.37.

T You can edit the first formula and then copy it.

	A	B	C	D	E	F	G
1	**Building Supplies Invoice**						
2							
3						**Discount Rate**	**5%**
4							
5	**Product Code**	**Description**	**Quantity**	**Price**	**Total**	**Discount**	
6	200	Sandpaper	20	0.19	**= C6*D6**	**=E6*discountrate**	
7	305	Wood Filler	2	6.34	**= C7*D7**	**=E7*discountrate**	
8	307	Filling Knife	1	7.22	**= C8*D8**	**=E8*discountrate**	
9	451	Pine Cornice	3	8.38	**= C9*D9**	**=E9*discountrate**	
10	178	Matt Varnish	1	15.99	**= C10*D10**	**=E10*discountrate**	

Table 2.37

8. Save the spreadsheet as **Building Supplies Invoice**

NAMING A SPREADSHEET RANGE

Formulas that refer to cell names are much easier to understand. Cell names are absolute and can be used to refer to cells in other worksheets within the workbook.

Names can also be assigned to spreadsheet ranges. This is useful if you frequently refer to a particular range of cells in calculations and also when there are so many cells in the range that it's too big to fit in the spreadsheet window.

In Table 2.38, we need to refer to the range B4:B11 with a number of functions to calculate average, highest and lowest marks as well as number of exams.

	A	B
1	**Analysis of Exam Results**	
2		
3		**Maths**
4	Tom Boyle	89
5	Mick Gavin	44
6	William Treacy	53
7	Sharon Byrne	70
8	Jaki McKay	66
9	Derek McCormack	30
10	Eileen Nolan	24
11	Margaret O Connell	59
12		
13	**Average Mark**	
14	**Highest Mark**	
15	**Lowest Mark**	
16	**Number of Exams**	

Table 2.38

To make the functions easier to understand and use, we'll assign the name *mathsresults* to the range B4:B11.

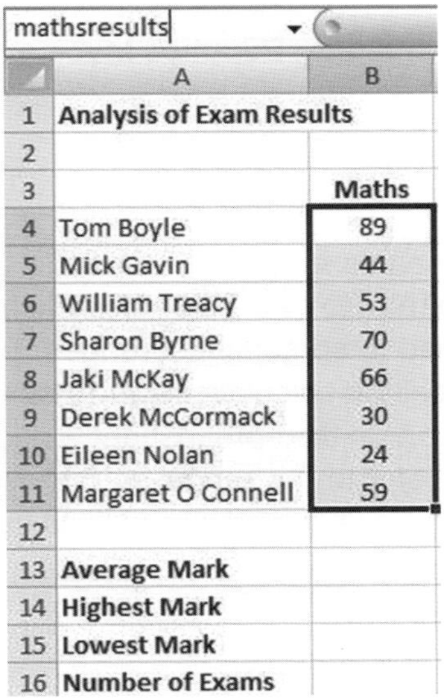

mathsresults

	A	B
1	**Analysis of Exam Results**	
2		
3		**Maths**
4	Tom Boyle	89
5	Mick Gavin	44
6	William Treacy	53
7	Sharon Byrne	70
8	Jaki McKay	66
9	Derek McCormack	30
10	Eileen Nolan	24
11	Margaret O Connell	59
12		
13	**Average Mark**	
14	**Highest Mark**	
15	**Lowest Mark**	
16	**Number of Exams**	

Figure 2.7

This is done by highlighting the range, as shown in Figure 2.7, typing *mathsresults* in the name box and pressing Enter. We can now use *mathsresults* instead of B4:B11 in all functions, as shown in Table 2.39.

	Function (Cell Refs)	Function (Range Name)
Average Mark	=AVERAGE(B4:B11)	=AVERAGE(mathsresults)
Highest Mark	=MAX(B4:B11)	=MAX(mathsresults)
Lowest Mark	=MIN(B4:B11)	=MIN(mathsresults)
Number of Exams	=COUNT(B4:B11)	=COUNT(mathsresults)

Table 2.39

Spreadsheet Functions Assignment Fourteen

Create a new spreadsheet workbook and enter the data shown in Table 2.40. Enter functions in the shaded cells to complete the spreadsheet.

	A	B	C	D
1	**Analysis of Exam Results**			
2				
3		**Maths**	**Chemistry**	**English**
4	Tom Boyle	89	58	60
5	Mick Gavin	44	62	n.a.
6	William Treacy	53	73	88
7	Sharon Byrne	70	n.a.	43
8	Jaki McKay	66	n.a.	75
9	Derek McCormack	30	77	78
10	Eileen Nolan	24	68	62
11	Margaret O Connell	59	91	68
12				
13	**Average Mark**			
14	**Highest Mark**			
15	**Lowest Mark**			
16	**Number of Exams**			

Table 2.40

1. Assign the names **mathsresults** to B4:B11, **chemresults** to C4:C11 and **engresults** to D4:D11.

Excel doesn't allow spaces in cell names or range names.

2. Calculate average, highest and lowest mark and number of exams using functions and range names.

When writing a formula or function that refers to named cells or ranges, press **F3** to display a list of all cell and range names in your spreadsheet.

3. Format the averages to display zero decimal places.
4. Format headings to bold and align data as shown in Table 2.40.
5. Save the spreadsheet as **Analysis of Exam Results**

CHAPTER 2 SUMMARY

1. Basic Concepts

Range Two or more cells that can be highlighted in a spreadsheet. E.g. *B2:B10*. Most functions refer to ranges, e.g. *=SUM(B2:B10)*

Argument The information required by a specific function. Basic functions require only one argument, which is usually a spreadsheet range, e.g. *=COUNT(D6:D20)*.

Advanced functions will have more than one argument, e.g. *=SUMIF(F2:F30,"Sales",H2:H30)*

Cell Name If you frequently refer to a specific cell in a formula or a function, it is worthwhile assigning a special name to that cell, using the Name Box. The formula *=F18*taxrate* contains the cell name 'taxrate'. Spaces are not allowed in cell names. Using a cell name can make a formula easier to create and understand

Range Name This is a name assigned to a range of cells. For example, we could assign the name *julysales* to the range *G2:G40*. This range name can then be referred to by functions, e.g. *=SUM(julysales)*. Using a range name can make a function easier to understand. When creating formulas or functions, press F3 to display a list of cell and range names. As cell and range names are absolute, you don't have to enclose column letters in dollar signs before copying a function.

2. Functions Introduced in Chapter 2

Function Name	Purpose	Example
SUM	Adding	=SUM(B4:B15)
AVERAGE	Calculates average	=AVERAGE(B4:B15)
MAX	Finds highest number	=MAX(B4:B15)
MIN	Finds lowest number	=MIN(B4:B15)
COUNT	Counts cells containing numbers	=COUNT(B4:B15)
COUNTA	Counts cells containing numbers or text	=COUNTA(A4:A15)
POWER	Raises a number to a power	=POWER(A2,10)
SQRT	Calculates square root	=SQRT(A2)
DB	Calculates depreciation using the declining balance method	=DB(E1,E2,E3,1)
SUMIF	Adds cell values in a range if they satisfy a given condition	=SUMIF(B4:B12,"Apples", E4:E12)
COUNTIF	Counts the number of cells in a range that contain specific data or satisfy a given condition	=COUNTIF(C4:C11,A14)
TODAY	Retrieves the date from the computer clock and displays it in the spreadsheet cell	=TODAY()

Table 2.41

3. Potential Pitfalls

- Plus (+), minus (-), multiply (*) and divide (/) should not be used in a function.
- The SUM function should not be used for subtraction, multiplication or division.

4. Formatting

Format Painter
Copies formatting from one cell to another.

5. Useful Shortcuts

Keyboard Combination	Action
CTRL + N	Create a new Excel workbook.
CTRL + S	Save the current workbook.
F3	Pressing F3 while writing a function displays a list of cell and range names in your workbook. Select the appropriate name and click OK to paste it into the function.

Table 2.42

SPREADSHEET FUNCTIONS REVIEW QUESTIONS

Answers to the review questions are available on www.gillmacmillan.ie

1. Two or more highlighted cells in a spreadsheet are referred to as a __________.
2. Information between the brackets of a function is called an __________.
3. (i) Write down the name of this button.

   ____

   (ii) Briefly describe the function of this button.

   ____

4. Write down the name of the function required to carry out each of the tasks listed in Table 2.43.

	Task	Function Required
(i)	Determining the number of months with sales greater than 3000.	
(ii)	Calculating depreciation on computer equipment	
(iii)	Finding the highest number	
(iv)	Determining from a daily list of restaurant sales how much money was spent on different categories, e.g. coffee, tea, toasted sandwich, etc.	
(v)	Determining the number of guest names in a wedding list	

Table 2.43

5. Each of the functions listed in Table 2.44 has been written incorrectly. Write each function correctly in the space provided.

	Incorrect Function	Corrected Function
(i)	=SUM(C2+C15)	
(ii)	=COUNTIF(D4:D20,>150)	
(iii)	=AVG(F6:F18)	
(iv)	=SUMIF(A2:A100“Computer”D2:D100)	
(v)	=COUNT(B6B20)	

Table 2.44

6. Table 2.45 displays the cost of ski lessons for a holiday group.

	A	B
1		**Ski Lessons**
2	Peter Gallagher	€85
3	Cameron Chou	€250
4	Nick Sheehan	—
5	Martha O Neill	€150
6	Carol Looney	€105
7	Valerie Stephens	€150

Table 2.45

Write down the functions to calculate:

(i) Total cost of ski lessons ______________________________

(ii) Average cost of ski lessons ______________________________

(iii) Most expensive ski lesson ______________________________

(iv) Cheapest ski lesson ___________________________

(v) Number of people taking lessons ______________________________

7. Table 2.46 displays the sales results of Tom Maher and Susan Flynn.

	A	B	C	D
1	**Month**	**County**	**Salesperson**	**Units Sold**
2	July	Dublin	Tom Maher	1050
3	July	Wicklow	Susan Flynn	987
4	July	Dublin	Tom Maher	1215
5	July	Wicklow	Susan Flynn	2055
6	July	Wicklow	Tom Maher	1985
7	August	Dublin	Susan Flynn	1545
8	August	Wicklow	Susan Flynn	1645
9	August	Dublin	Tom Maher	950
10	August	Dublin	Susan Flynn	825
11	August	Wicklow	Tom Maher	705

Table 2.46

Write down the functions to calculate:

(i) Total units sold by Tom Maher ____________________

(ii) Total units sold by Susan Flynn ____________________

(iii) Total units sold in July ____________________

(iv) Total units sold in August ____________________

(v) Total units sold in Dublin ____________________

(vi) Total units sold in Wicklow ____________________

8. Table 2.47 shows the results of a college entrance exam.

	A	B	C
1	**Student**	**Maths Grade**	**Aptitude Score**
2	Brian Ahearne	B1	75
3	Cyryl Pawlak	A2	71
4	Peter Lohan	A1	68
5	Mark Winters	B1	70
6	Tina Lowe	A1	95
7	Vivian Murphy	A2	93
8	Farid Rajavi	B1	90
9	Tony Sheehan	B2	75
10	Sinead Tobin	A2	88

Table 2.47

Write down the functions to calculate:

(i) Number of students whose grade is A1 ____________________

(ii) Number of students whose grade is A2 ____________________

(iii) Number of students whose grade is B1 ____________________

(iv) Number of students whose aptitude score is 80 or higher ____________________

9. Table 2.48 displays the radius of a circular restaurant.

	A	B
1	Room radius (cm)	300
2	Room area (cm^2)	
3	Price per cm^2	€0.02
4	Total cost	

Table 2.48

(i) Write down the function to calculate:
Room area (cm^2) ______________________________

(ii) Write down the formula to calculate:
Total cost __________________________

10. Table 2.49 displays details relating to recently purchased computer equipment.

	A	B
1		**Computer Equipment**
2	Purchase Price	€45,500
3	Disposal Value	€5000
4	Expected Life (years)	3
5		
6	Year 1 Depreciation	
7	Year 2 Depreciation	
8	Year 3 Depreciation	

Table 2.49

Write down the functions to calculate:
Year 1 depreciation ______________________________
Year 2 depreciation ______________________________
Year 3 depreciation ______________________________

3 Linking Data in Worksheets

In Chapter 3, you will learn how to:

- Name and copy worksheets
- Create formulas to read data from multiple worksheets
- Create formulas linked to cells in multiple worksheets
- Apply cell styles.

WORKBOOKS AND WORKSHEETS

An Excel spreadsheet file is referred to as a workbook. By default, each Excel workbook consists of 3 worksheets. A workbook is equivalent to a copybook used for writing. A worksheet is equivalent to a specific page in the copybook. When writing in a copybook, we go on to a new page when we fill up a page. In an Excel workbook, we generally go on to a new worksheet when we fill up the screen with data. When data has been entered in more than one worksheet, we can read data from multiple worksheets using formulas.

NAMING AND INSERTING WORKSHEETS

To rename Sheet1, point at the worksheet tab for Sheet1 with the mouse and then right click (Figure 3.1).

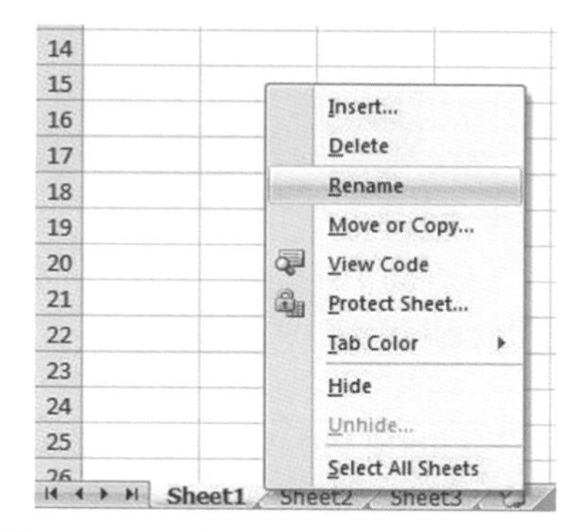

Figure 3.1 Renaming a worksheet

Select Rename from the pop-up menu.

In Excel 2003, each new spreadsheet workbook consists of 16 worksheets, by default.

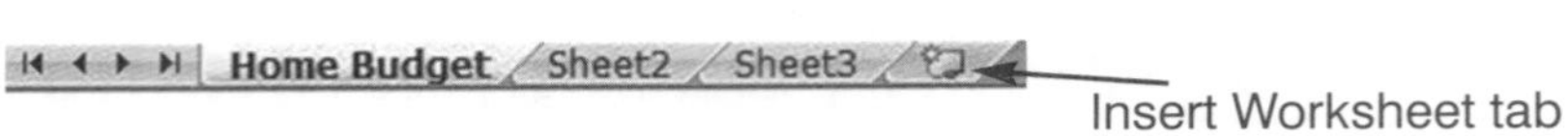

Figure 3.2 Sheet1 has been renamed as Home Budget

Type in the new name (in this case, *Home Budget*) for Sheet1 and press Enter. The name of Sheet1 changes to *Home Budget*, as shown in Figure 3.2.

Additional worksheets can be added by right clicking any worksheet tab and then selecting Insert from the pop-up menu. You can also add a new worksheet by clicking the Insert Worksheet tab (Figure 3.2).

Use the Shift + F11 keyboard combination to quickly insert a new worksheet.

In Excel 2007, there is no limit to the number of worksheets that you can have in a workbook. You can continue to insert new worksheets until your PC runs out of memory.

CHANGING THE WORKSHEET TAB COLOUR

A useful feature in Excel is the ability to change the colour of a worksheet tab. This can be used to emphasise a specific worksheet. It can also be used to colour code worksheets. For example, in a spreadsheet detailing sales by region, each region's worksheet tab could be assigned a different colour.

To change the worksheet tab colour, right click the worksheet tab and select *Tab Color* from the pop-up menu, as shown in Figure 3.3.

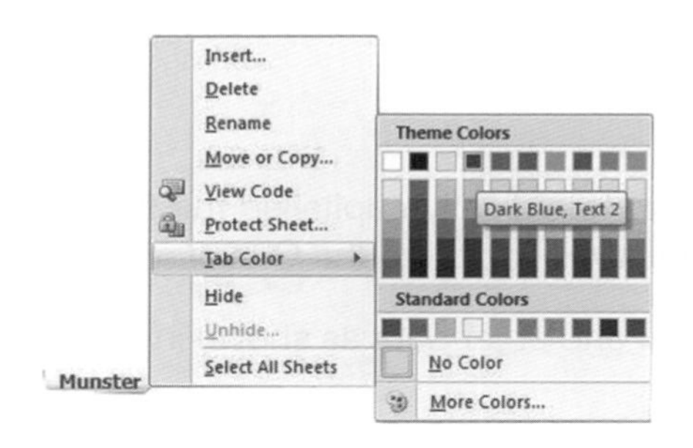

Figure 3.3 Setting the worksheet tab colour

In Figure 3.3, a worksheet tab colour of Dark Blue has been selected for the Munster worksheet.

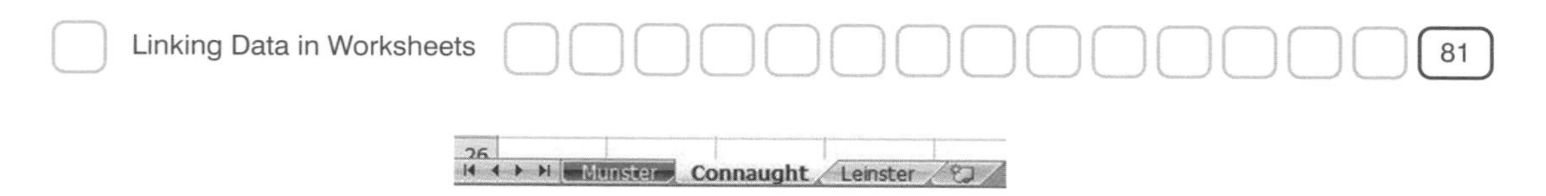

Figure 3.4 The colour of the Munster worksheet tab has been changed

Figure 3.4 shows the resulting Munster worksheet tab with white text on a blue background.

LINKING WORKSHEETS IN A WORKBOOK

Organising data in different worksheets, instead of having a lot of data in a single worksheet, can make a spreadsheet easier to use and easier to understand. In practice, it is best to go on to a new worksheet once you have filled the computer screen with data. In the following worked example, we will see how data relating to the sale of raffle tickets stored in three separate worksheets can be summarised in a fourth worksheet. There are three ticket sellers: Jaki, Ian and Geraldine. A separate worksheet is used to record each ticket seller's sales.

Worked Example

1. Create a new spreadsheet workbook and rename Sheet1 as *Jaki*.
2. Enter data in the worksheet named *Jaki*, as shown in Figure 3.5.

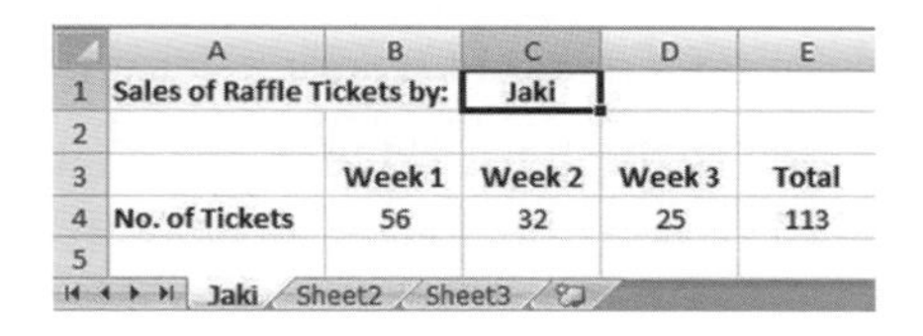

	A	B	C	D	E
1	Sales of Raffle Tickets by:		Jaki		
2					
3		Week 1	Week 2	Week 3	Total
4	No. of Tickets	56	32	25	113
5					

Figure 3.5

Excel is set up to automatically capitalise the first letter of sentences. As *No.* contains a full stop, it will capitalize the O in *of*.

3. Rename Sheet2 as *Ian* and enter data as shown in Figure 3.6.

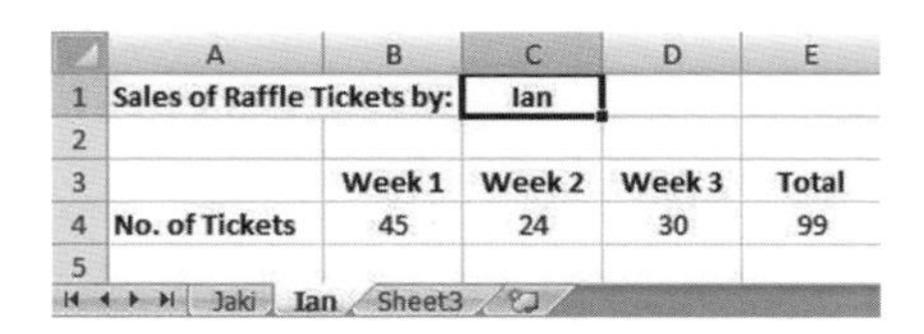

	A	B	C	D	E
1	Sales of Raffle Tickets by:		Ian		
2					
3		Week 1	Week 2	Week 3	Total
4	No. of Tickets	45	24	30	99
5					

Figure 3.6

4. Rename Sheet3 as *Geraldine* and enter data as shown in Figure 3.7.

	A	B	C	D	E
1	Sales of Raffle Tickets by:		Geraldine		
2					
3		Week 1	Week 2	Week 3	Total
4	No. of Tickets	70	41	38	149
5					

Jaki / Ian / Geraldine

Figure 3.7

5. Create a fourth summary worksheet by clicking the *Insert Worksheet* button. *(This appears immediately to the right of the Geraldine worksheet tab.)* Rename this worksheet as *Summary*.

6. Enter data in the worksheet named *Summary*, as shown in Figure 3.8.

	A	B	C	D	E
1	Total Sales of Raffle Tickets				
2					
3	Ticket Sellers:				
4					
5					
6					
7		Week 1	Week 2	Week 3	
8	No. of Tickets:				
9					

Jaki / Ian / Geraldine / Summary

Figure 3.8

7. Position the cell pointer in B3. Type = and then click Jaki's Sheet tab. Now select C1 in Jaki's worksheet. Complete the linking formula by pressing Enter. (***N.b.:*** *Do not click back into the Summary worksheet.*) Figure 3.9 shows the linking formula displayed in the formula bar. The formula refers firstly to the worksheet name and then to a specific cell in that worksheet; **=Jaki!C1** means 'display the data stored in C1 in the worksheet named *Jaki*.'

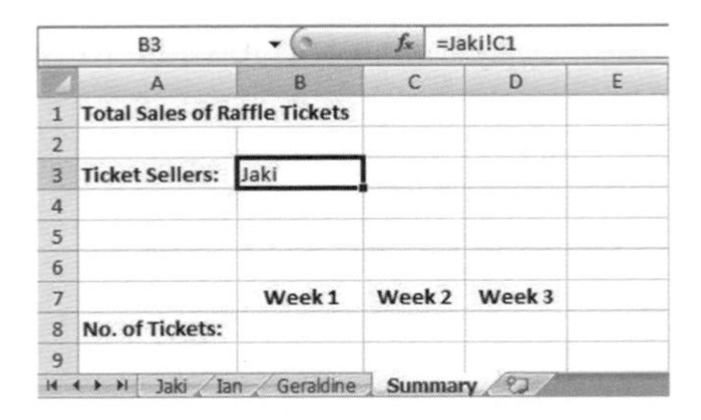

B3 =Jaki!C1

	A	B	C	D	E
1	Total Sales of Raffle Tickets				
2					
3	Ticket Sellers:	Jaki			
4					
5					
6					
7		Week 1	Week 2	Week 3	
8	No. of Tickets:				
9					

Jaki / Ian / Geraldine / Summary

Figure 3.9

8. In the *Summary* worksheet, create linking formulas to link to cell C1 in Ian's worksheet and cell C1 in Geraldine's worksheet, as shown in Figure 3.10.

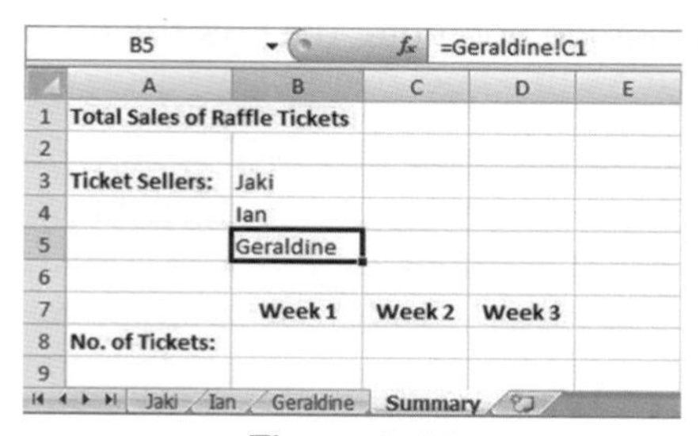

B5 =Geraldine!C1

	A	B	C	D	E
1	Total Sales of Raffle Tickets				
2					
3	Ticket Sellers:	Jaki			
4		Ian			
5		Geraldine			
6					
7		Week 1	Week 2	Week 3	
8	No. of Tickets:				
9					

Jaki / Ian / Geraldine / Summary

Figure 3.10

9. In the *Summary* worksheet, position the cell pointer in B8.
   - Type =, click the worksheet named Jaki, then select B4
   - Type +, click the worksheet named Ian, then select B4
   - Type +, click the worksheet named Geraldine, then select B4
   - Press Enter (**n.b.:** *don't click the worksheet named Summary at this point*).

The resulting linking formula, which adds data across three worksheets, is displayed in Figure 3.11.

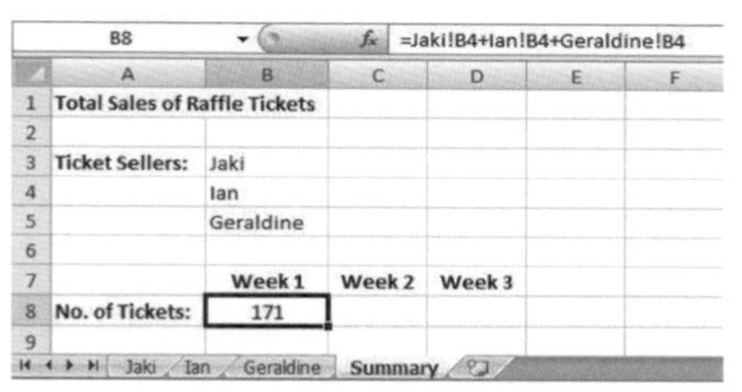

B8 =Jaki!B4+Ian!B4+Geraldine!B4

	A	B	C	D	E	F
1	Total Sales of Raffle Tickets					
2						
3	Ticket Sellers:	Jaki				
4		Ian				
5		Geraldine				
6						
7		Week 1	Week 2	Week 3		
8	No. of Tickets:	171				
9						

Jaki / Ian / Geraldine / Summary

Figure 3.11

N This formula can also be typed directly into the spreadsheet. At this stage it's easier to create the formula by selecting cells in different worksheets.

10. In the *Summary* worksheet, copy the linking formula to week 2 and week 3 (Figure 3.12).

	A	B	C	D	E
1	Total Sales of Raffle Tickets				
2					
3	Ticket Sellers:	Jaki			
4		Ian			
5		Geraldine			
6					
7		Week 1	Week 2	Week 3	
8	No. of Tickets:	171	97	93	
9					

Jaki / Ian / Geraldine / Summary

Figure 3.12

11. Save the spreadsheet as **Raffle Ticket Sales**

As well as referring to cells, the formula in Figure 3.11 also refers to worksheets. =Jaki!B4 means cell B4 in the worksheet named *Jaki*. Notice how each worksheet name is followed by an exclamation mark.

If the name of the worksheet you are linking to includes spaces, Excel will include apostrophes in the linking formula. *Example:* ='Week 1 Sales'!C9 links to cell C9 in the worksheet named *Week 1 Sales*. Apostrophes are not required in the linking formula when the worksheet name doesn't include spaces. *Example:* =Monday!F6 links to cell F6 in the worksheet named *Monday*.

Copying Worksheets

In a workbook containing many worksheets that are similar in structure, copying and then editing an existing worksheet is often quicker than creating a new worksheet from scratch. To copy a worksheet, right click the worksheet name, as shown in Figure 3.13.

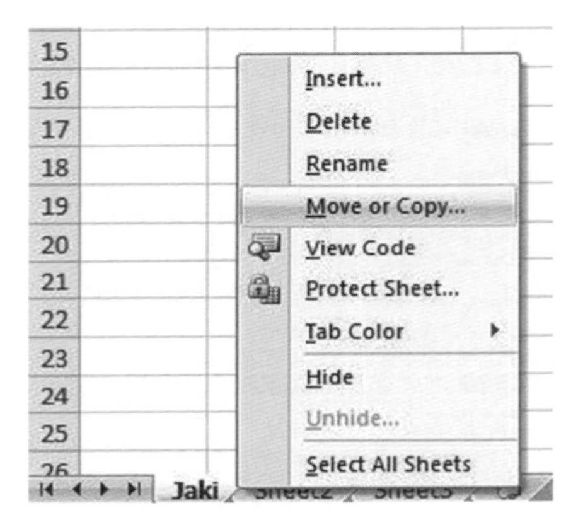

Figure 3.13

1. Select Move or Copy from the pop-up menu. The Move or Copy dialog box is displayed (Figure 3.14).

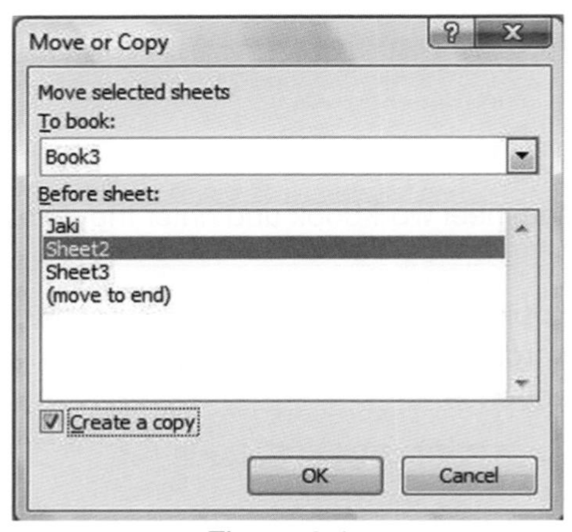

Figure 3.14

2. Click Create a copy and select *Sheet2*. This means that a copy of the worksheet named *Jaki* will be inserted before *Sheet2*. Excel assigns the name *Jaki(2)* to this worksheet. It can be renamed by right clicking the worksheet name and selecting Rename from the pop-up menu.

You can also copy a worksheet by dragging its sheet tab and dropping it on another sheet tab while holding down the *CTRL* key.

FORMATTING WITH CELL STYLES

Excel has a number of pre-defined cell styles. Using cell styles allows you to apply a number of formats in one step as well as ensuring consistent formatting throughout your spreadsheet. Clicking the Cell Styles button in the Home section of the Ribbon displays Excel's pre-defined cell styles, shown in Figure 3.15.

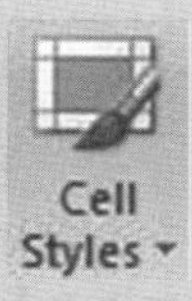

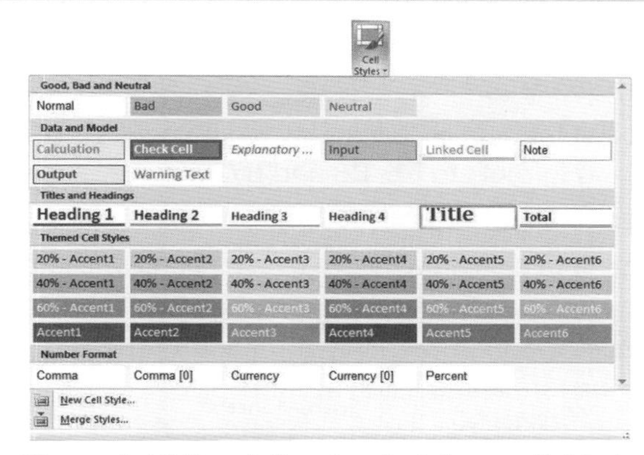

Figure 3.15 Pre-defined cell styles available in Excel

When applying styles, it is best to select styles from the same column. The assignments in this chapter will be formatted using the Accent1 styles.

Linking Data in Worksheets Assignment One

Part 1: Create Joe Murphy's worksheet

1. Create a new spreadsheet workbook and enter the data shown in Table 3.1 in Sheet1.

Dates can be copied using the Fill Handle. Enter 04/10/10 and drag the Fill Handle downwards to enter the remaining dates. This only works when the dates are in sequence.

	A	B	C	D	E	F
1	Travel Expenses		Joe Murphy			
2	Date	Kilometres a.m.	Kilometres p.m.	Distance Travelled	Rate per Kilometre	Total Due
3	04/10/10	25109	25271		0.85	
4	05/10/10		25388		0.85	
5	06/10/10		25529		0.85	
6	07/10/10		25701		0.85	
7	08/10/10		25853		0.85	
8						
9			Total			

Table 3.1

2. Rename Sheet1 as *Joe Murphy.*
3. In B4 enter the linking formula =*C3* to read the kilometres p.m. of the previous day. Copy this linking formula to B5, B6 and B7.
4. Calculate the distance travelled and the total due.
5. Use the SUM function to calculate the total distance travelled and overall total due.
6. Click the Cell Styles button in the Home section of the Ribbon and apply the formatting listed in Table 3.2.

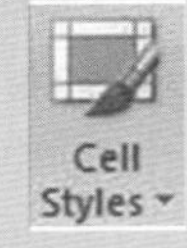

Range of Cells	Cell Style
A1:C1	60% Accent1
A2:F2, C9	Accent1
A3:F7, D9, F9	20% Accent1

Table 3.2

Part 2: Create Sile O Shea's worksheet

1. Rename Sheet2 as *Sile O Shea*
2. Enter the data shown in Table 3.3 in the worksheet named *Sile O Shea*

Copy Joe Murphy's worksheet and then change the employee name and the kilometres a.m. and p.m. figures.

3. Apply styles as in John Murphy's worksheet. (This is not necessary if you created Sile O Shea's worksheet using the *copy* method.)

	A	B	C	D	E	F
1	Travel Expenses		Sile O Shea			
2	Date	Kilometres a.m.	Kilometres p.m.	Distance Travelled	Rate per Kilometre	Total Due
3	04/10/10	73109	73215		0.85	
4	05/10/10		73399		0.85	
5	06/10/10		73501		0.85	
6	07/10/10		73546		0.85	
7	08/10/10		73722		0.85	
8						
9			Total			

Table 3.3

4. Calculate kilometres a.m., distance travelled and total due for Sile O Shea.

Part 3: Create Tom Doyle's worksheet

1. Rename an empty worksheet as *Tom Doyle*
2. Enter the data shown in Table 3.4 in the worksheet named *Tom Doyle* (*or copy and edit an existing worksheet*).
3. Apply styles as in John Murphy's worksheet. (This is not necessary if you created Tom Doyle's worksheet using the *copy* method.)

	A	B	C	D	E	F
1	Travel Expenses		Tom Doyle			
2	Date	Kilometres a.m.	Kilometres p.m.	Distance Travelled	Rate per Kilometre	Total Due
3	04/10/10	59115	59209		0.85	
4	05/10/10		59356		0.85	
5	06/10/10		59592		0.85	
6	07/10/10		59771		0.85	
7	08/10/10		59920		0.85	
8						
9			Total			

Table 3.4

4. Calculate kilometres a.m., distance travelled and total due for Tom Doyle.

Part 4: Create the Summary worksheet

1. Rename an empty worksheet as *Travel Summary* or insert a new worksheet if necessary.
2. Enter the data shown in Table 3.5 in the worksheet named *Travel Summary*.

	A	B	C
1	Summary of Travel Expenses		
2			
3	Employee Name	Distance Travelled	Total Due
4			
5			
6			

Table 3.5

3. Enter linking formulas in the shaded cells to read the employee name, distance travelled and total due from each of the three employee worksheets.
4. Click the Cell Styles button in the Home section of the Ribbon and apply the formatting listed in Table 3.6.

Range of Cells	Cell Style
A1	60% Accent1
A3:C3	Accent1
A4:C6	20% Accent1

Table 3.6

5. Highlight A1:C1. Merge the *Summary of Travel Expenses* heading across cells A1:C1 using the Merge and Center button.
6. Format money amounts to currency in all worksheets.
7. Adjust column widths where necessary.
8. Delete all unused worksheets.
9. Print the *Summary* worksheet.
10. Save the spreadsheet as **Travel Expenses**

Linking Data in Worksheets Assignment Two

Part 1: Create the Spreadsheets worksheet

1. Create a new spreadsheet workbook and enter the data shown in Table 3.7 in Sheet1.

Ensure that AutoComplete is turned on to speed up the entering of results. Click the Microsoft Office button and then click Excel Options. Select Advanced from the list of Excel options and ensure that the *Enable AutoComplete for Cell Values* checkbox is ticked. When AutoComplete is on Excel will suggest the remaining letters of a particular result as soon as you type the first letter, as long as that result has already been previously entered. For example, when entering the second result, simply type *M*. Excel displays *Merit* in the current cell. Press Enter to accept Excel's suggestion.

N In Excel 2010, the Office button has been replaced by the File menu.

	A	B	C	D	E
1	**Spreadsheets Results**				
2					
3	**Student Name**	**Result**		**No of Distinctions**	
4	Tom Boyle	Merit		**No of Merits**	
5	Naresh Jeeri	Merit		**No of Passes**	
6	William Treacy	Pass		**No of Fails**	
7	Sharon Byrne	Merit		**Total Students**	
8	Jaki McKay	Distinction			
9	Derek McCormack	Fail			
10	Eileen Nolan	Merit			
11	Margaret O Connell	Distinction			
12	Dermot Rogers	Pass			
13	John Keegan	Merit			
14	Mary Hamilton	Merit			
15	Abasiama Omotoso	Merit			
16	Joe Dalton	Distinction			

Table 3.7

2. Rename Sheet1 as *Spreadsheets Results*.
3. Assign the name **ssresults** to the range *B4:B16*.
4. Assign the name **ssstudents** to the range *A4:A16*.

Holding down SHIFT and then pressing an arrow key is another way of highlighting cells in a spreadsheet. This is particularly useful when the highlighted range extends beyond one screen.

5. Use the COUNTIF function, together with the range name *ssresults*, to count the number of distinctions, merits, passes and fails.

Use F3 to paste the cell name into the function.

6. Use the COUNTA function, together with the range name *ssstudents,* to count the number of students.
7. Apply the cell styles listed in Table 3.8.

Range of Cells	Cell Style
A1	Title
A3:B3, D3:D7	Accent1
A4:B16, E3:E7	20% Accent1

Table 3.8

Part 2: Create the Databases Results worksheet

1. Rename Sheet2 as *Database Results*

	A	B	C	D	E
1	Database Results				
2					
3	**Student Name**	**Result**		**No of Distinctions**	
4	Tom Boyle	Pass		**No of Merits**	
5	Naresh Jeeri	Fail		**No of Passes**	
6	William Treacy	Distinction		**No of Fails**	
7	Sharon Byrne	Merit		**Total Students**	
8	Jaki McKay	Merit			
9	Derek McCormack	Pass			
10	Eileen Nolan	Distinction			
11	Margaret O Connell	Distinction			
12	Dermot Rogers	Merit			
13	John Keegan	Fail			
14	Mary Hamilton	Merit			
15	Abasiama Omotoso	Pass			
16	Joe Dalton	Merit			

Table 3.9

2. Enter the data shown in Table 3.9 in the worksheet named *Database Results*.

   Copy the student names from the Spreadsheet Results worksheet.

3. Assign the name **dbresults** to the range *B4:B16*.
4. Assign the name **dbstudents** to the range *A4:A16*.
5. Use the COUNTIF function, together with the range name *dbresults*, to count the number of distinctions, merits, passes and fails.
6. Use the COUNTA function, together with the range name *dbstudents*, to count the number of students.
7. Apply the cell styles listed in Table 3.10.

Range of Cells	Cell Style
A1	Title
A3:B3, D3:D7	Accent1
A4:B16, E3:E7	20% Accent1

Table 3.10

Part 3: Create the Word Processing Results worksheet

1. Rename an empty worksheet as *Word Processing Results*

	A	B	C	D	E
1	**Word Processing Results**				
2					
3	**Student Name**	**Result**		**No of Distinctions**	
4	Tom Boyle	Distinction		**No of Merits**	
5	Naresh Jeeri	Merit		**No of Passes**	
6	William Treacy	Merit		**No of Fails**	
7	Sharon Byrne	Pass		**Total Students**	
8	Jaki McKay	Merit			
9	Derek McCormack	Merit			
10	Eileen Nolan	Distinction			
11	Margaret O Connell	Pass			
12	Dermot Rogers	Merit			
13	John Keegan	Merit			
14	Mary Hamilton	Merit			
15	Abasiama Omotoso	Merit			
16	Joe Dalton	Distinction			

Table 3.11

2. Enter the data shown in Table 3.11 in the worksheet named *Word Processing Results* (or copy and edit the *Database Results* worksheet).
3. Assign the name **wpresults** to the range *B4:B16*.
4. Assign the name **wpstudents** to the range *A4:A16*.
5. Use the COUNTIF function, together with the range name *wpresults*, to count the number of distinctions, merits, passes and fails.
6. Use the COUNTA function, together with the range name *wpstudents*, to count the number of students.
7. Apply the cell styles listed in Table 3.12.

Range of Cells	Cell Style
A1	Title
A3:B3, D3:D7	Accent1
A4:B16, E3:E7	20% Accent1

Table 3.12

Part 4: Create the Summary worksheet

1. Rename an empty worksheet as *Summary*. *(Insert a new worksheet, if necessary.)*
2. Enter the data shown in Table 3.13 in the worksheet named *Summary*.

	A	B	C	D
1	**Exam Report**			
2				
3		**Spreadsheets**	**Database**	**Word Processing**
4	Distinction			
5	Merit			
6	Pass			
7	Fail			
8	Total Students			

Table 3.13

3. Enter formulas to link to the relevant cells in the *Spreadsheet Results*, *Database Results* and *Word Processing Results* worksheets.
4. Apply the cell styles listed in Table 3.14.

Range of Cells	Cell Style
A1	Title
B3:D3, A8:D8	Accent1
A4:D7	20% Accent1

Table 3.14

5. Save the spreadsheet as **Computer Applications Results**

Linking Data in Worksheets Assignment Three

Part 1: Create the 0745 worksheet

1. Create a new spreadsheet workbook and enter the data shown in Table 3.15 in Sheet1.

Weekdays can be copied using the Fill Handle. Enter Monday and drag the Fill Handle downwards to enter the remaining days. This only works when the days are in sequence.

	A	B	C	D	E	F	G	H
1	**Week 1 Ticket Sales**							
2	**Galway–Dublin departing 07:45**							
3								
4		**Galway**	**Athenry**	**Ballinasloe**	**Athlone**	**Tullamore**	**Portarlington**	**Kildare**
5	Monday	233	48	64	104	96	71	180
6	Tuesday	172	23	39	81	95	57	148
7	Wednesday	130	18	36	72	81	59	137
8	Thursday	163	18	35	71	80	47	152
9	Friday	220	21	51	81	100	75	180
10								
11	**Total Ticket Sales**							
12								
13	**Grand Total**							

Table 3.15

2. Rename Sheet1 as *0745*

3. Calculate total ticket sales at each station.
4. Calculate the grand total for ticket sales.
5. Apply the cell styles listed in Table 3.16.

Range of Cells	Cell Style
A1	Title
A2	Explanatory
A4:H4, A11, A13	Accent1
A5:H9, B11:H11, B13	20% Accent1

Table 3.16

Part 2: Create the 1100 worksheet

1. Rename Sheet2 as *1100*
2. Enter the data shown in Table 3.17 in the worksheet named *1100* (or copy and edit the *0745* worksheet).

	A	B	C	D	E	F	G	H
1	**Week 1 Ticket Sales**							
2	**Galway–Dublin departing 11:00**							
3								
4		**Galway**	**Athenry**	**Ballinasloe**	**Athlone**	**Tullamore**	**Portarlington**	**Kildare**
5	Monday	65	12	20	34	28	20	45
6	Tuesday	49	6	18	28	30	18	31
7	Wednesday	34	4	13	22	25	16	30
8	Thursday	42	5	10	18	23	18	34
9	Friday	81	4	13	23	29	19	40
10								
11	**Total Ticket Sales**							
12								
13	**Grand Total**							

Table 3.17

3. Calculate total ticket sales and grand total as before.
4. Apply the cell styles listed in Table 3.18.

Range of Cells	Cell Style
A1	Title
A2	Explanatory
A4:H4, A11, A13	Accent1
A5:H9, B11:H11, B13	20% Accent1

Table 3.18

Part 3: Create the 1510 worksheet

1. Rename an empty worksheet as *1510*
2. Enter the data shown in Table 3.19 in the worksheet named *1510* (or copy and edit the *1100* worksheet).

	A	B	C	D	E	F	G	H
1	**Week 1 Ticket Sales**							
2	**Galway–Dublin departing 15:10**							
3								
4		**Galway**	**Athenry**	**Ballinasloe**	**Athlone**	**Tullamore**	**Portarlington**	**Kildare**
5	Monday	56	15	12	15	28	25	50
6	Tuesday	43	5	6	10	30	20	45
7	Wednesday	31	6	2	12	25	22	37
8	Thursday	25	8	8	8	23	15	42
9	Friday	34	10	10	20	29	35	67
10								
11	**Total Ticket Sales**							
12								
13	**Grand Total**							

Table 3.19

3. Calculate total ticket sales and grand total as before.
4. Apply the cell styles listed in Table 3.20.

Range of Cells	Cell Style
A1	Title
A2	Explanatory
A4:H4, A11, A13	Accent1
A5:H9, B11:H11, B13	20% Accent1

Table 3.20

Part 4: Create the Summary worksheet

1. Rename an empty worksheet as *Weekly Ticket Sales*. *(Insert a new worksheet if necessary.)*
2. Enter the data shown in Table 3.21 in the worksheet named *Weekly Ticket Sales*.

	A	B	C	D	E	F	G	H
1	**Week 1 Ticket Sales Summary**							
2	**07:45, 11:00 and 15:10 Trains**							
3								
4		**Galway**	**Athenry**	**Ballinasloe**	**Athlone**	**Tullamore**	**Portarlington**	**Kildare**
5	Monday							
6	Tuesday							
7	Wednesday							
8	Thursday							
9	Friday							
10								
11	**Total Ticket Sales**							
12								
13	**Grand Total**							

Table 3.21

3. Calculate total weekly ticket sales for each day at each station using linking formulas to add data from the *0745*, *1100* and *1510* worksheets.
4. Calculate total ticket sales and grand total as before.
5. Apply the cell styles listed in Table 3.22.

Range of Cells	Cell Style
A1	Title
A2	Explanatory
A4:H4, A11, A13	Accent1
A5:H9, B11:H11, B13	20% Accent1

Table 3.22

6. Save the spreadsheet as **Ticket Sales Galway–Dublin Route**

CHAPTER 3 SUMMARY

1. Basic Concepts

Workbook An Excel spreadsheet file is called a workbook.

Worksheet By default, each Excel workbook consists of three worksheets. A worksheet is similar to a page in a copybook. Typically, you would go on to a new worksheet once you have filled up the screen with data in the first worksheet. If you run out of worksheets, more worksheets can easily be added to the workbook.

Linking Formula When data has been entered in multiple worksheets, linking formulas can be used to read data from other worksheets (e.g. *=Sales!D9*) or to perform calculations across multiple worksheets (e.g. *=Sales!F20 – Costs!H32*). As well as referring to cells, linking formulas also refer to worksheet names.

Formatting

Cell Styles The Cells Styles option allows you to apply consistent formatting throughout your worksheets.

Merge and Center Merges highlighted cells into one big cell and centers the data in this cell.

2. Potential Pitfalls

- When creating a linking formula that calculates across multiple worksheets, always press Enter to complete the formula. Students often click back into the worksheet containing the linking formula instead of pressing Enter. This causes an error in the linking formula.

3. Useful Shortcut

Keyboard Combination	Action
SHIFT + F11	Inserts a new worksheet.

Table 3.23

LINKING DATA IN WORKSHEETS REVIEW QUESTIONS

Answers to the review questions are available on www.gillmacmillan.ie

1. By default, each spreadsheet ______________ consists of 3 _________________.

2. Identify the errors in the following linking formula.

   =StockC20 + PurchasesD15

   ____

3. Figures 3.16, 3.17 and 3.18 display total sales data from Munster, Connaught and Leinster.

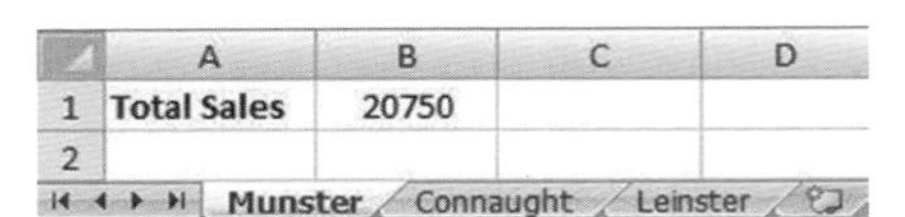

Figure 3.16

	A	B	C	D
1	Total Sales	15825		
2				

Munster | Connaught | Leinster

Figure 3.17

	A	B	C	D	E
1	Total Sales	32780			
2					

Munster | Connaught | Leinster

Figure 3.18

   Write down the linking formula that will add total sales across the three worksheets.

   ____

4. The maximum number of worksheets in an Excel workbook is limited by

   ____

5. What is wrong with the following linking formula? *=Sales!B4!*

6. Describe two methods of adding a new worksheet to an Excel workbook.

   (i)

   (ii)

7. Describe the method for changing the tab colour of a worksheet tab.

8. Figures 3.19, 3.20 and 3.21 display the difference between target and actual sales in Munster, Connaught and Leinster.

	A	B	C	D
1	Munster Sales Forecast			
2				
3	Target	Actual	Difference	
4	€ 100,000	€ 92,500	-€ 7,500	
5				

Figure 3.19

	A	B	C	D
1	Connaught Sales Forecast			
2				
3	Target	Actual	Difference	
4	€ 85,000	€ 89,450	€ 4,450	
5				

Munster Connaught Leinster

Figure 3.20

	A	B	C	D
1	Leinster Sales Forecast			
2				
3	Target	Actual	Difference	
4	€ 150,000	€152,500	€ 2,500	
5				

Figure 3.21

Write down the formula to calculate the total difference for all three provinces.

9. Describe two methods of renaming a worksheet.

   (i) ____________________

   (ii) ____________________

10. Figures 3.22 and 3.23 display the training completed by a long-distance runner.

	A	B	C	D
1		**Distance (km)**		
2	Monday	5		
3	Wednesday	30		
4	Friday	15		
5	Saturday	10		
6	Sunday	8		
7				

Week 1 training | Week 2 training

Figure 3.22

	A	B	C	D
1		**Distance (km)**		
2	Tuesday	10		
3	Wednesday	5		
4	Friday	20		
5	Saturday	10		
6	Sunday	5		
7				

Week 1 training | **Week 2 training**

Figure 3.23

(i) Write down the function or the formula/function combination that calculates the total distance run over the two weeks.

____

(ii) Write down the formula/function combination that adds the longest distance run in week 1 to the longest distance run in week 2.

____

(iii) Write down the function that calculates the average distance run over the two weeks.

____

4 Spreadsheet Charts

In Chapter 4, you will learn how to:

- Create column charts, bar charts, line charts, pie charts and scatter charts
- Modify existing charts to include new data.

USING CHARTS IN A SPREADSHEET

Presenting information in a chart helps us to quickly grasp the meaning of the information as well as making it easier to remember. It's difficult to figure out the trends by looking at the information contained in Table 4.1. Representing this information in an Excel chart makes it much easier to understand.

	A	B	C	D	E	F	G
1	**Employee Travel Record**						
2		**Jan**	**Feb**	**Mar**	**Apr**	**May**	**Jun**
3	Jim	1175	1298	875	901	809	900
4	Tom	2012	1899	790	855	750	800
5	Eileen	500	560	555	1990	2025	2117
6	Karen	408	459	501	2339	2450	2098

Table 4.1

The chart in Figure 4.1 is a graphical representation of the data in Table 4.1. Looking at the chart, we can instantly see that Eileen and Karen do most of their travelling in April, May and June. Tom does most of his travelling in January and February and Jim's travel is more or less constant. Essentially, the chart tells the story of the numbers in a picture.

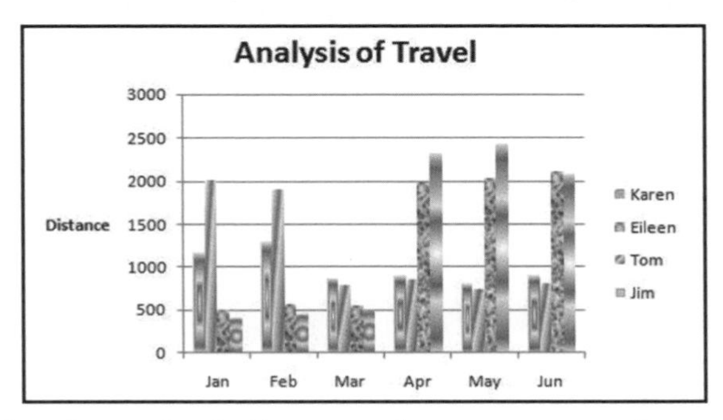

Figure 4.1 A column chart allows you to compare numbers at a glance

There is a wide range of chart types available in Excel. The most popular chart types are column, bar, line, pie and scatter. Column, bar, line and pie charts will be illustrated using the information in Table 4.1 relating to employee travel. The scatter chart type will be illustrated using test results from a speed experiment.

TYPES OF SPREADSHEET CHART

Column Chart (Single Series)

In a column chart, each number is represented by a vertical column. The higher the number, the taller the column. Each set of numbers represented in the chart is called a data series.

	A	B	C	D	E	F	G
1	Employee Travel Record						
2		Jan	Feb	Mar	Apr	May	Jun
3	Jim	1175	1298	875	901	809	900

Table 4.2

In Table 4.2 there is only one set of numbers so the chart displayed in Figure 4.2 has a single column for each month.

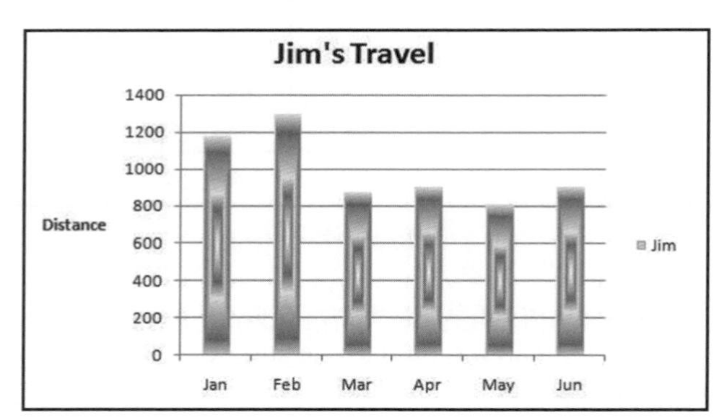

Figure 4.2 Single series column chart

From the chart in Figure 4.2, we can quickly see that February was Jim's busiest month for travelling.

Column Chart (Multiple Series)

A multiple series column chart shows the relationship between different sets of numbers.

	A	B	C	D	E	F	G
1	**Employee Travel Record**						
2		**Jan**	**Feb**	**Mar**	**Apr**	**May**	**Jun**
3	Jim	1175	1298	875	901	809	900
4	Tom	2012	1899	790	855	750	800
5	Eileen	500	560	555	1990	2025	2117
6	Karen	408	459	501	2339	2450	2098

Table 4.3

In Figure 4.3, the chart is representing four sets of numbers, or data series (Jim's travel, Tom's travel, Eileen's travel and Karen's travel). This is why each month in the chart has four columns. Excel automatically assigns a different colour to each employee's column.

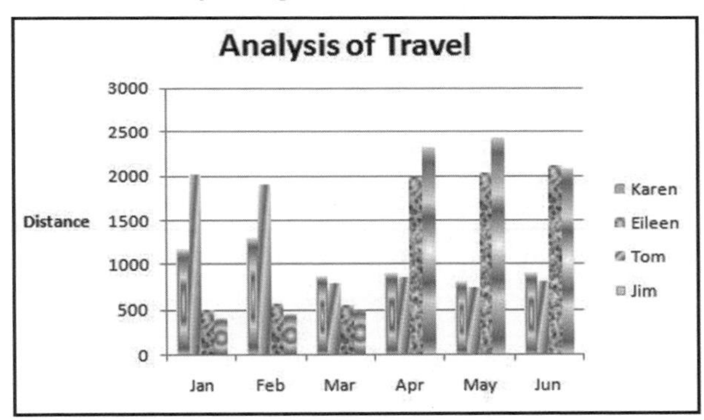

Figure 4.3 Multiple series column chart

With a multiple series column chart, we can make comparisons between distances travelled by employees in a given month, as well as seeing the trend of each employee's travel over the six-month period.

Stacked Column Chart

In a stacked column chart, distances travelled by Karen, Eileen, Tom and Jim make up one column for each month (Figure 4.4). This makes it easier to see how the total travel is divided between the four employees in each month.

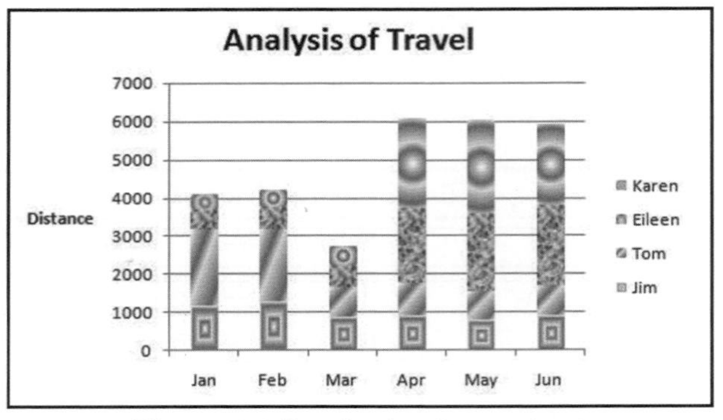

Figure 4.4 Stacked column chart

Bar Chart

In a bar chart, each number is represented by a horizontal bar. This places more emphasis on values and less emphasis on time, as seen in Figure 4.5.

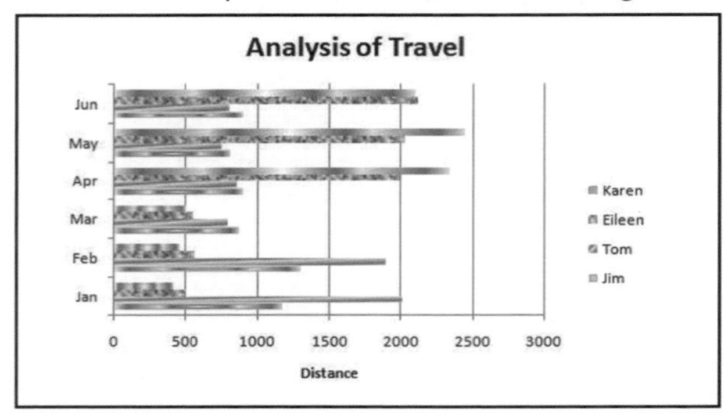

Figure 4.5 Bar chart

Stacked Bar Chart

A stacked bar chart allows us to see at a glance what portion of the total monthly travel each employee accounted for.

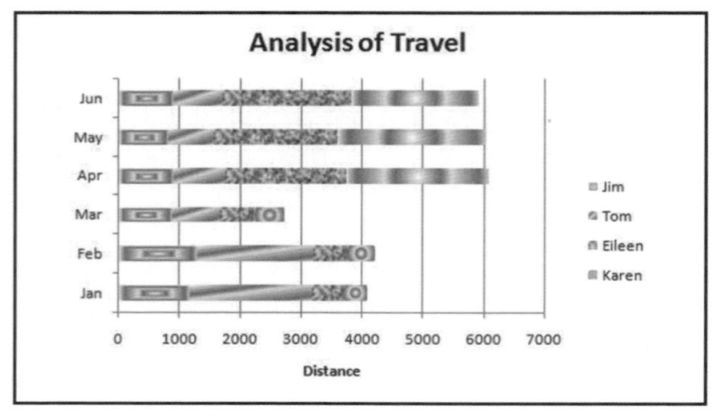

Figure 4.6 Stacked bar chart

From the chart in Figure 4.6, we quickly see that Karen accounted for a small portion of the total travel in January, February and March but accounted for a much higher portion in April, May and June.

Line Chart

In a line chart, each number in a data series is represented by a dot. The higher the number, the higher the dot will be above the baseline. The dots are joined to form a line.

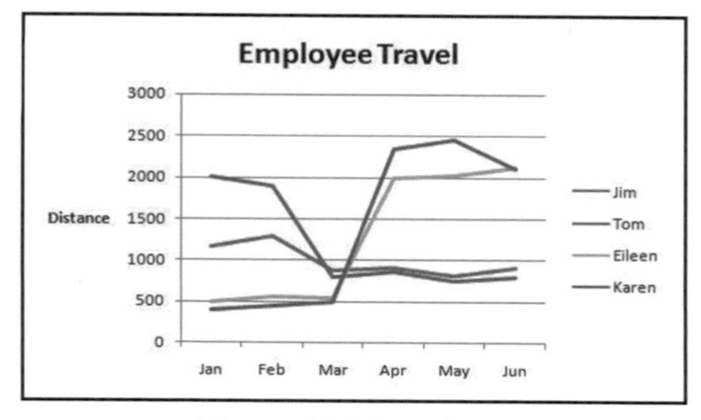

Figure 4.7 Line chart

In the employee travel example in Figure 4.7, an upward slanting line indicates that the distance travelled is increasing. A downward sloping line indicates that the distance travelled is decreasing. Each employee has a different coloured line. Line charts are useful if you want to see trends in the data.

Pie Chart

A pie chart shows only one data series or set of numbers. Pie charts are useful when we want to see how a specific item (e.g. Karen's travel) consists of different categories (Figure 4.8).

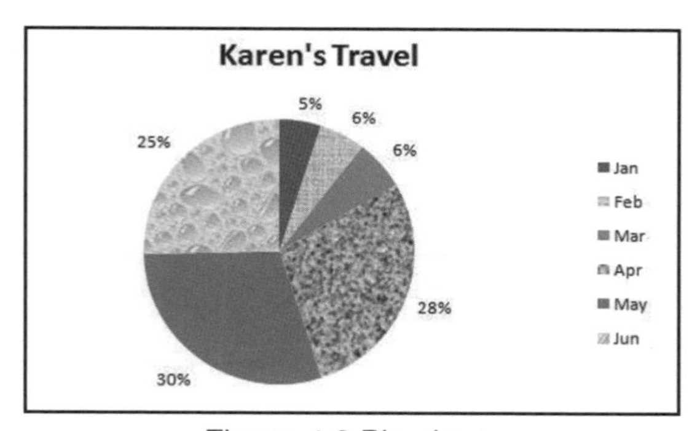

Figure 4.8 Pie chart

The pie chart allows us to see which months Karen did most of her travelling in and which months were the quietest. The pie chart also calculates the percentage of the total made up by each slice of the pie. Separate pie charts could also be created for Jim, Tom and Eileen.

Scatter Chart

A scatter chart shows the relationship between two variables. The example in Figure 4.9 shows the relationship between speed and braking distance. At higher speeds, a greater distance is travelled before a car stops completely. Scatter charts are commonly used to show the results of scientific tests.

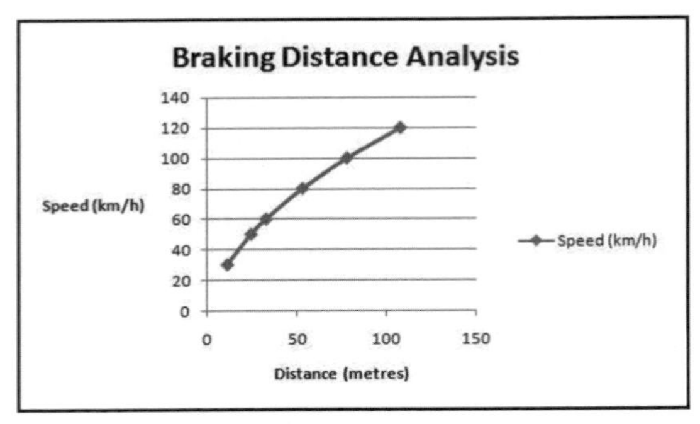

Figure 4.9 Scatter chart

HOW TO CREATE A CHART

Worked Example

In Excel 2007, there are two distinct stages to creating a chart.
Stage 1: Create a basic chart.
Stage 2: Customise the chart.

- Create a new spreadsheet workbook and enter the data shown in Table 4.4.

	A	B	C	D	E
1	**Yearly Sales**				
2		**2007**	**2008**	**2009**	**2010**
3	West Region	100000	125000	65000	72000
4	South Region	80000	85000	42000	47000
5	East Region	112000	100000	53000	63000

Table 4.4

Stage 1: Create a basic chart

1. Select A2:E5, as shown in Figure 4.10. This range contains the data that will appear in the chart.

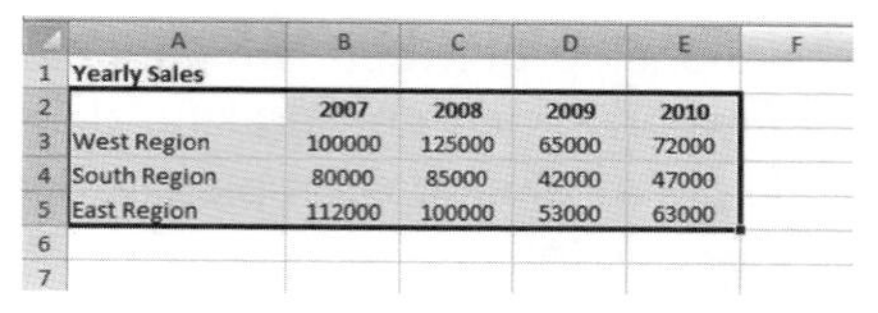

	A	B	C	D	E	F
1	Yearly Sales					
2		2007	2008	2009	2010	
3	West Region	100000	125000	65000	72000	
4	South Region	80000	85000	42000	47000	
5	East Region	112000	100000	53000	63000	
6						
7						

Figure 4.10 Selecting data to create a chart

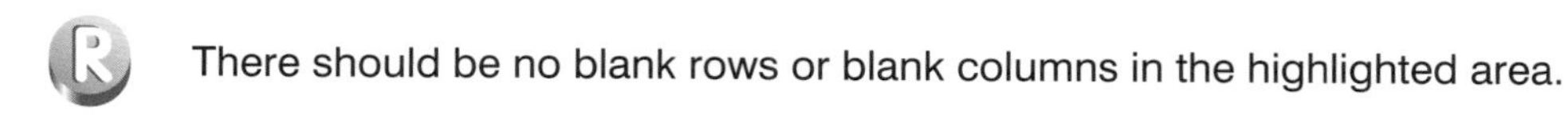

There should be no blank rows or blank columns in the highlighted area.

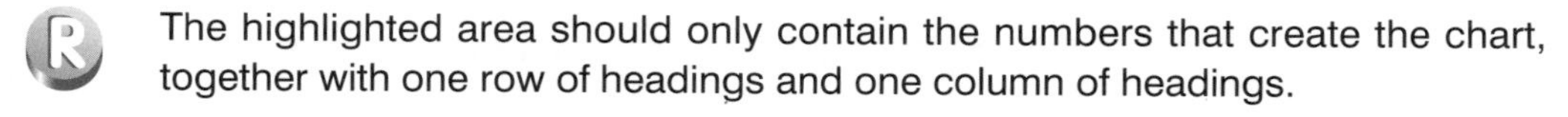

The highlighted area should only contain the numbers that create the chart, together with one row of headings and one column of headings.

2. To see the range of charts available in Excel, click the Insert tab in the Home section of the Ribbon.

The Insert section of the Ribbon can be accessed using the *ALT+N* key combination.

Figure 4.11 The Charts group is in the Insert section of the Ribbon

3. The Charts group, shown in Figure 4.11, contains buttons to create the most popular Excel charts. Click the Column button.

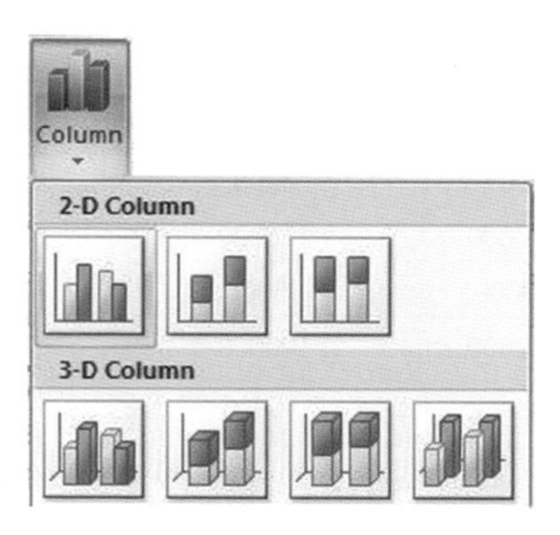

Figure 4.12 The range of column charts available

4. Select the first of the 2-D column options, as shown in Figure 4.12. Excel calls this a Clustered Column chart. The resulting chart is displayed in your spreadsheet (Figure 4.13).

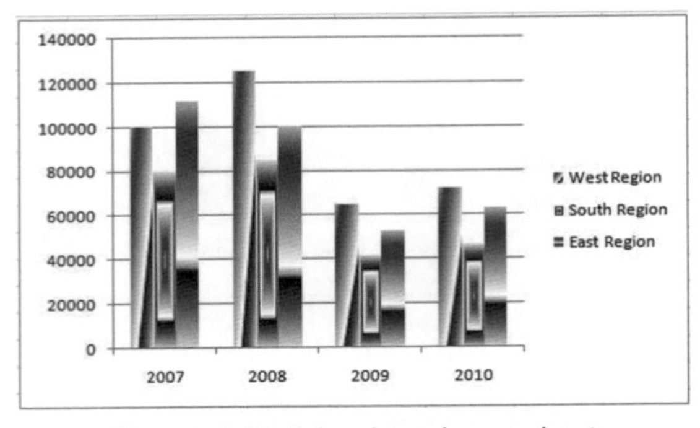

Figure 4.13 A basic column chart

Stage 2: Customise the Chart

1. First we will add a title to the chart. With the chart selected, click the **Layout** tab on the Ribbon. Click the **Chart Title** button and then select **Above Chart** from the drop-down list, as shown in Figure 4.14.

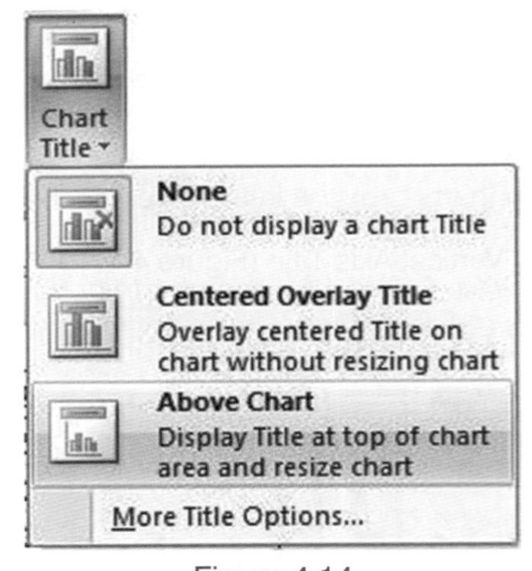

Figure 4.14

You can quickly access the *Chart Title* options using the *ALT+JA+T* keyboard combination.

2. Type the Chart Title, as shown in Figure 4.15.

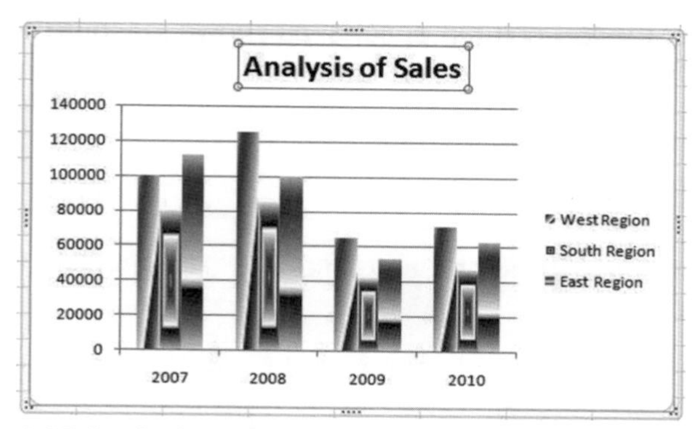

Figure 4.15 Analysis of Sales has been added as the chart title

3. To add a title for the vertical axis, ensure that the Layout section of the Ribbon is still selected and then click the **Axis Titles** button. Select **Primary Vertical Axis Title** and then select **Horizontal Title** from the drop-down list, as shown in Figure 4.16.

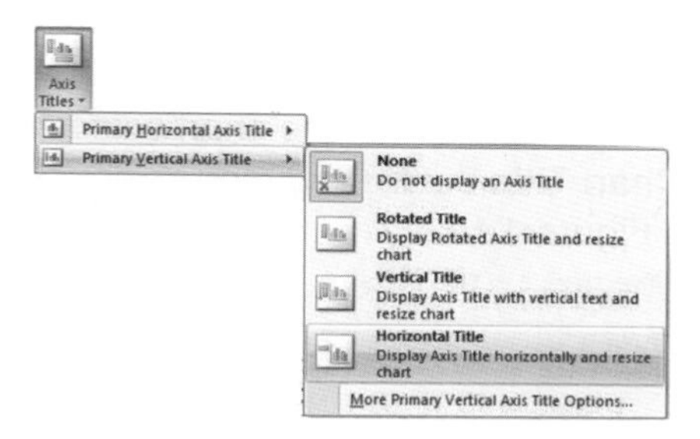

Figure 4.16 Adding a Vertical Axis Title to the chart

4. Type *Units Sold* as the Vertical Axis Title (Figure 4.17).

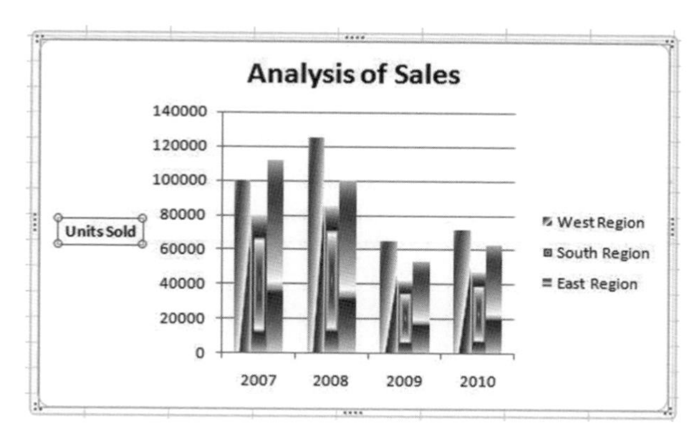

Figure 4.17 Units Sold has been added as the Vertical Axis Title

DISPLAYING A CHART ON A SEPARATE SHEET

Once the chart has been created, you can change its location to a Chart Sheet, where it will be separate from the data. One of the benefits of this is that the chart will be bigger.

1. With the chart selected, click the **Design** tab in the Ribbon and then click the **Move Chart Location** button.

You can quickly access the *Move Chart* dialog box using the *ALT+JC+M* keyboard combination.

2. In the Move Chart dialog box, enter the name of the new sheet, as shown in Figure 4.18. Excel will create a separate chart sheet, named *Sales Chart*, that will store the chart separately from the data.

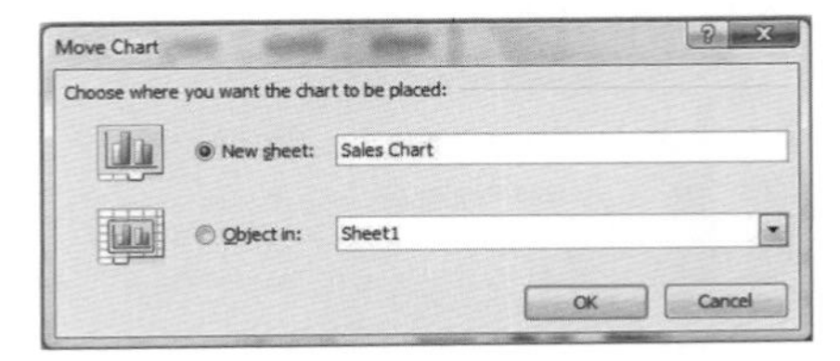

Figure 4.18 Creating a chart sheet

A sheet that displays a chart is called a chart sheet. Although the chart sheet is linked to a worksheet, you can't enter data in a chart sheet.

3. Click OK to create the new chart sheet.
4. Save the spreadsheet as **Regional Sales**

You can quickly create a column chart by highlighting the data and then pressing the F11 key. When you create a column chart using this method, it is always created on a separate chart sheet.

CHARTS – IMPORTANT TERMS

1. Data Series

The data series is the set of numbers Excel needs to create the chart. A chart can have one or many data series. In the example in Figure 4.19, there are three data series; West Region, South Region and East Region.

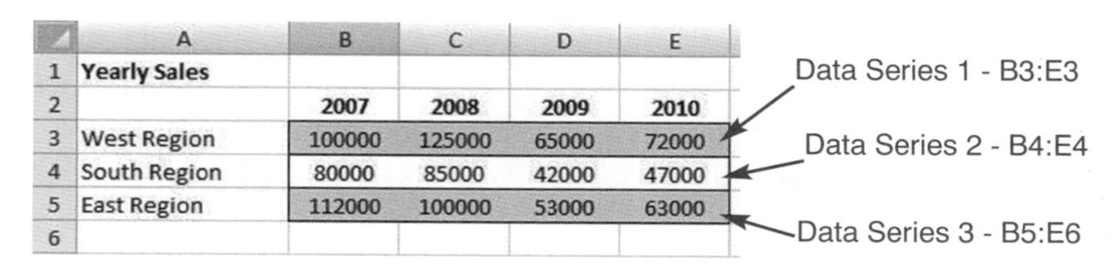

	A	B	C	D	E
1	Yearly Sales				
2		2007	2008	2009	2010
3	West Region	100000	125000	65000	72000
4	South Region	80000	85000	42000	47000
5	East Region	112000	100000	53000	63000
6					

Figure 4.19

Excel always assumes that your data series are set up in rows and creates the chart accordingly. Figure 4.20 shows how Excel converts each data series into a set of vertical columns.

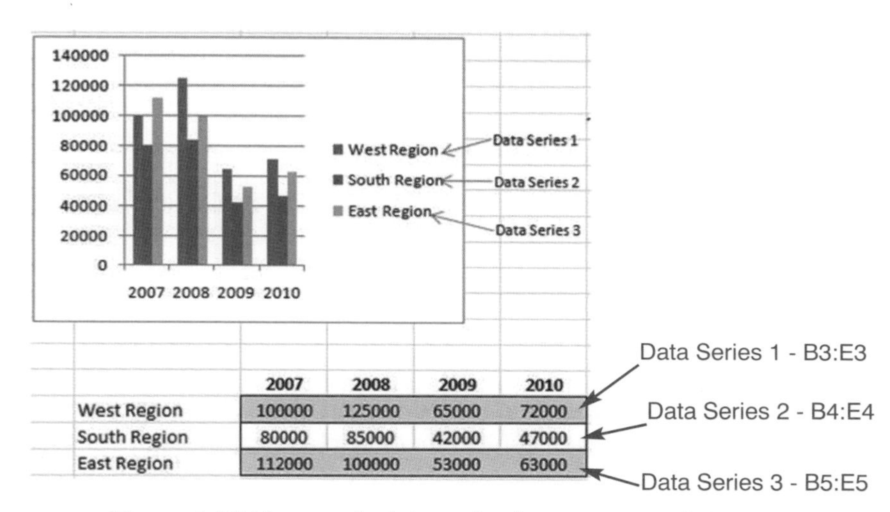

	2007	2008	2009	2010
West Region	100000	125000	65000	72000
South Region	80000	85000	42000	47000
East Region	112000	100000	53000	63000

Figure 4.20 How each data series becomes a column

In Figure 4.20, each data series is represented by four columns as there are four numbers in each row.

Viewing Data Series in Columns

Switch Row/Column

Clicking the **Switch Row/Column** button causes Excel to view the data series in columns instead of rows. This changes the focus of the chart, as shown in Figure 4.21.

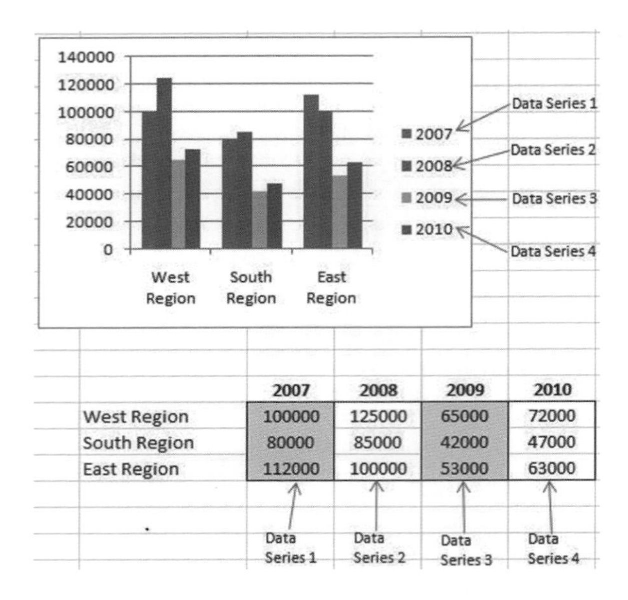

Figure 4.21 The result of clicking the Switch Row/Column button

There is now an extra data series as the chart range has four columns. Notice how the legend now refers to years whereas previously it referred to regions.

2. Legend

The Legend is the key to understanding the message conveyed by a chart, as it identifies the colour of each column. The first step in creating a chart is to highlight the cells containing data to be displayed in the chart. Excel assumes that the first column of the highlighted range of cells contains descriptions. It uses these descriptions to create the chart legend, as shown in Figure 4.22.

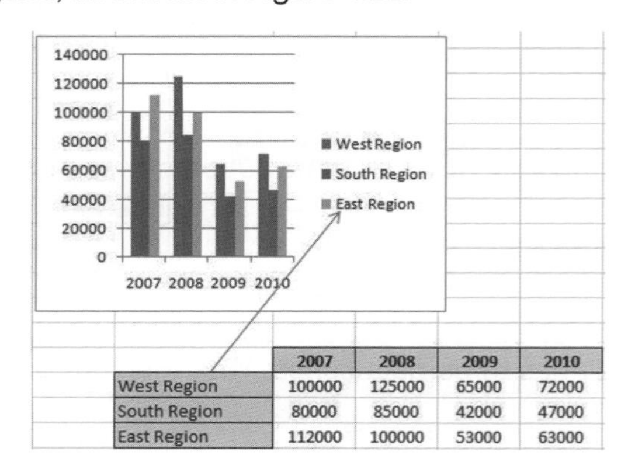

Figure 4.22 How Excel creates a chart legend

3. Horizontal Axis Titles

Excel uses data in the top row of the highlighted range to create horizontal axis titles. This is shown in Figure 4.23.

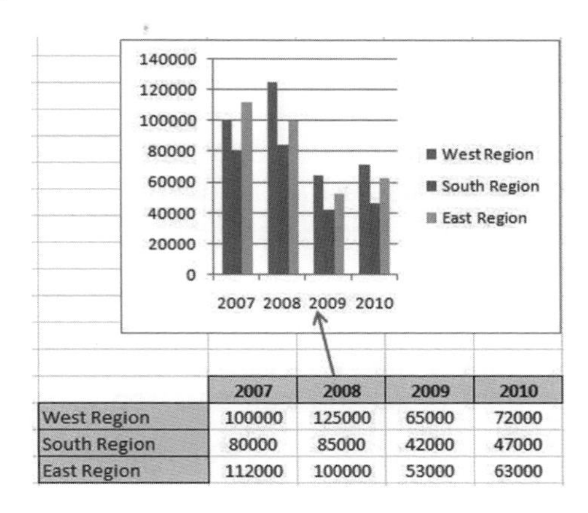

	2007	2008	2009	2010
West Region	100000	125000	65000	72000
South Region	80000	85000	42000	47000
East Region	112000	100000	53000	63000

Figure 4.23 How Excel creates horizontal axis titles

It is best when setting up your chart data to ensure that you have a row of descriptive headings in the top row together with descriptive text to the left of the data. This allows Excel to set up the horizontal axis titles and the chart legend correctly.

Figure 4.24 shows where the chart title, vertical axis title, horizontal axis title and legend are positioned in a column chart.

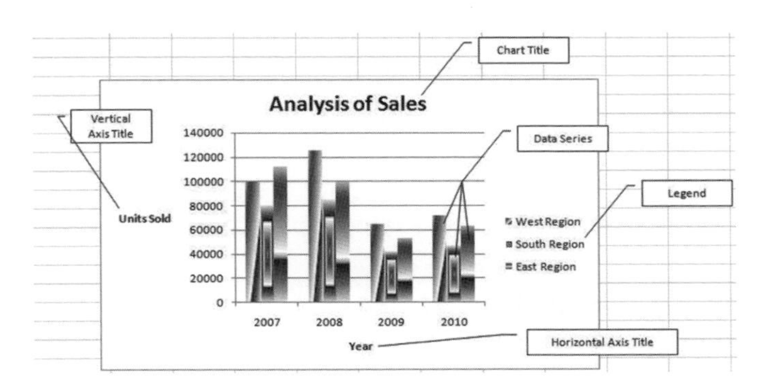

Figure 4.24

The chart in Figure 4.24 has three data series: West Region, South Region and East Region.

4. Data Labels

This option allows you to display the numbers associated with each column or bar in a chart. In a line chart, numbers can be positioned next to each dot. In a pie chart, numbers or percentages can be displayed for each slice of the pie.

5. Chart Sheet

A chart sheet is a separate sheet within a workbook that displays a chart but doesn't store any data. Chart sheets are very useful if you require a greater level of detail in your chart or if you don't have enough room to include your chart in the worksheet containing the source data.

6. Data Table

Data Table

When you create a data table, the numbers represented by the chart are attached to the bottom of the chart.

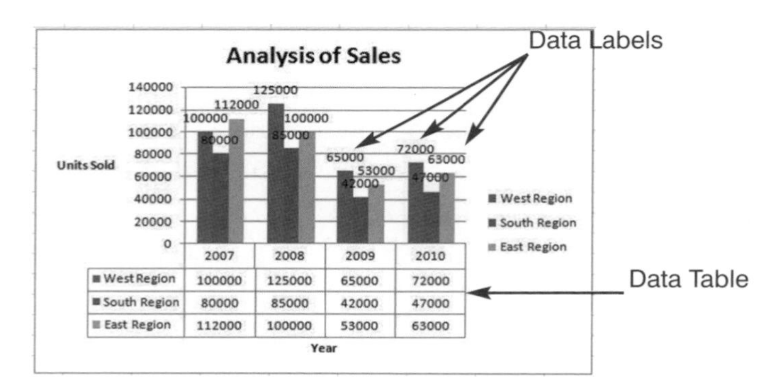

Figure 4.25 A column chart with a data table attached

To attach a data table to your chart, simply click the Data Table button in the Layout section of the Ribbon. Figure 4.25 is an example of a chart with a data table attached.

FORMATTING A CHART

Design Layout Format

When you select your chart in Excel, three new tabs become available in the Ribbon – the Design tab, the Layout tab and the Format tab. Each of these tabs has options specifically designed to help you fine tune the appearance of the chart.

1. The Design Tab

Using the Design tab, you can:

- Change the chart type, e.g. to Bar instead of Column
- Create a custom chart format that can be applied to future charts
- Change the focus of the chart from rows of data to columns of data
- Add new data to the chart
- Change the layout of the chart by selecting from a list of 12 pre-formatted layouts
- Select one of 5 basic chart colour schemes
- Move the chart to a separate Chart Sheet.

Design tab options are explained in Figure 4.26 and Figure 4.27.

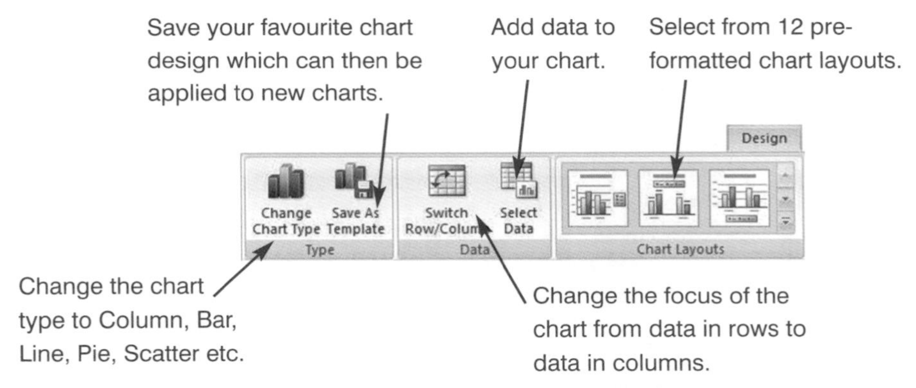

Figure 4.26 The Design tab (part 1)

Figure 4.27: The Design tab (part 2)

2. The Layout Tab

Using the Layout tab, you can:

- Select a specific section of the chart and apply formatting to that section
- Add a chart title as well as titles for the horizontal and vertical axes

- Display a legend explaining the colours used in the chart
- Attach numbers to the chart
- Modify the chart gridlines
- Format the chart background.

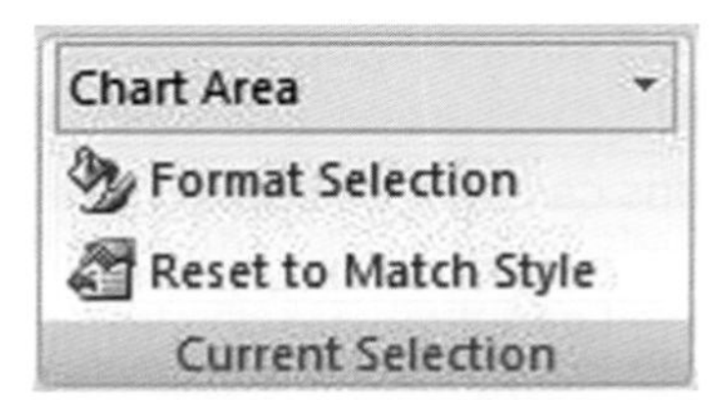

Figure 4.28 The Layout tab (part 1)

The first section of the Layout tab, displayed in Figure 4.28, allows you to select a specific section of the chart and then apply formatting to that chart section.

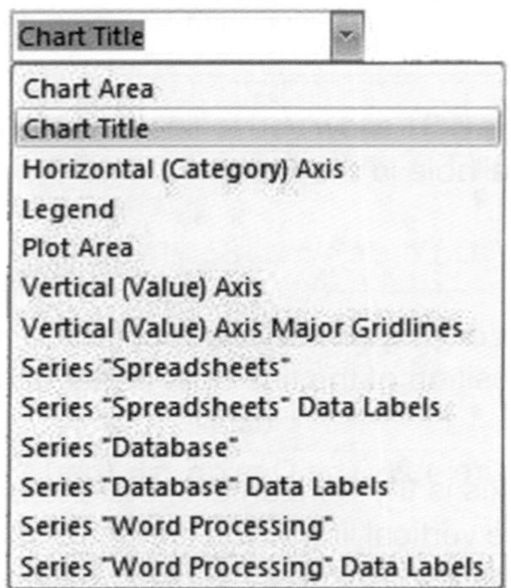

Figure 4.29 Using the Layout tab to select a specific chart item

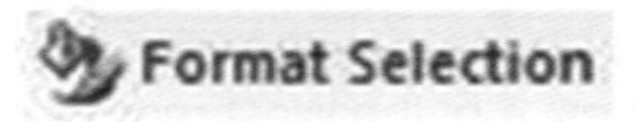

In Figure 4.29 the chart title has been selected for formatting. Once selected, the chart title can be formatted by clicking the Format Selection option which in turn displays the Format Chart Title dialog box (Figure 4.30).

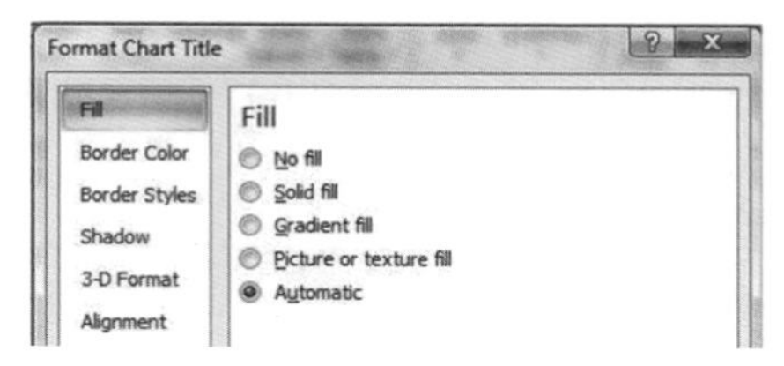

Figure 4.30 Format Chart Title dialog box

A selection of formatting options can now be applied to the chart title using the Format Chart Title dialog box.

Other options available in the Layout tab are displayed in Figure 4.31.

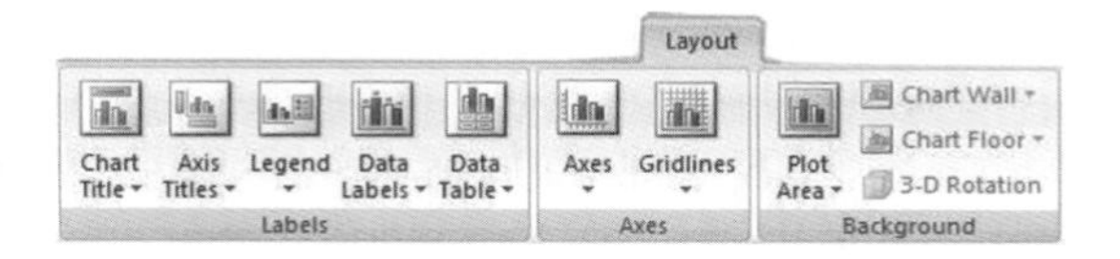

Figure 4.31 Layout Tab (part 2): Formatting Options

The options displayed in Figure 4.31 allow you to fine tune the appearance of your chart. The Layout tab will not be available in the Ribbon unless the chart is selected.

Summary of Options Available in the Layout Section of the Ribbon

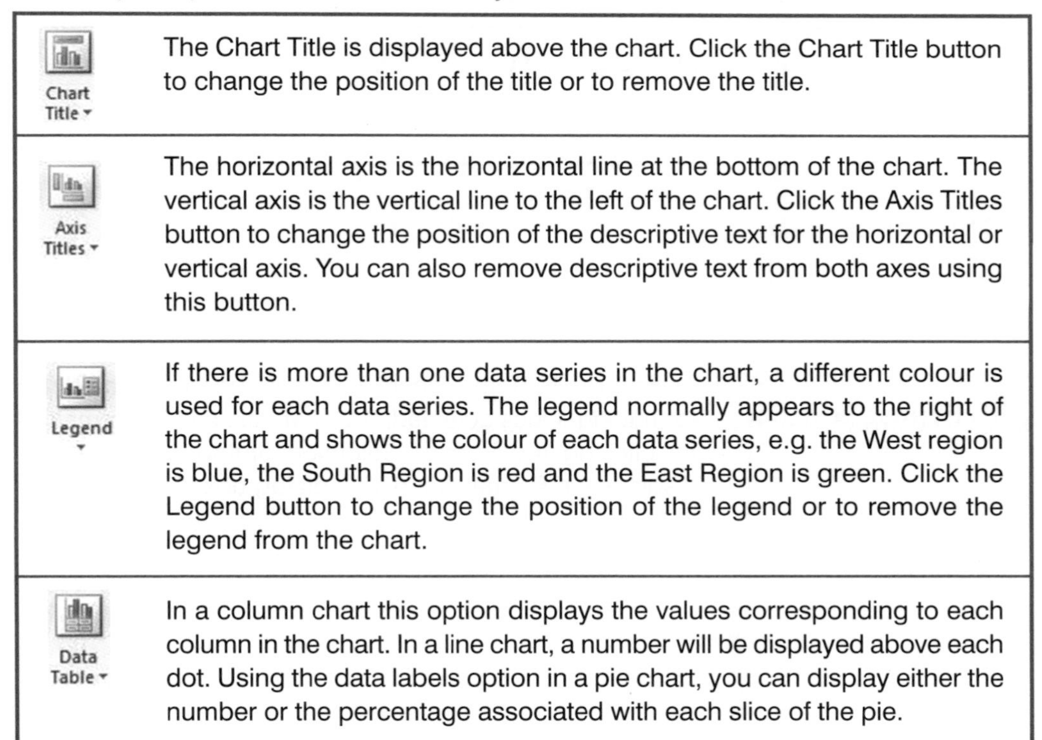

Chart Title	The Chart Title is displayed above the chart. Click the Chart Title button to change the position of the title or to remove the title.
Axis Titles	The horizontal axis is the horizontal line at the bottom of the chart. The vertical axis is the vertical line to the left of the chart. Click the Axis Titles button to change the position of the descriptive text for the horizontal or vertical axis. You can also remove descriptive text from both axes using this button.
Legend	If there is more than one data series in the chart, a different colour is used for each data series. The legend normally appears to the right of the chart and shows the colour of each data series, e.g. the West region is blue, the South Region is red and the East Region is green. Click the Legend button to change the position of the legend or to remove the legend from the chart.
Data Table	In a column chart this option displays the values corresponding to each column in the chart. In a line chart, a number will be displayed above each dot. Using the data labels option in a pie chart, you can display either the number or the percentage associated with each slice of the pie.

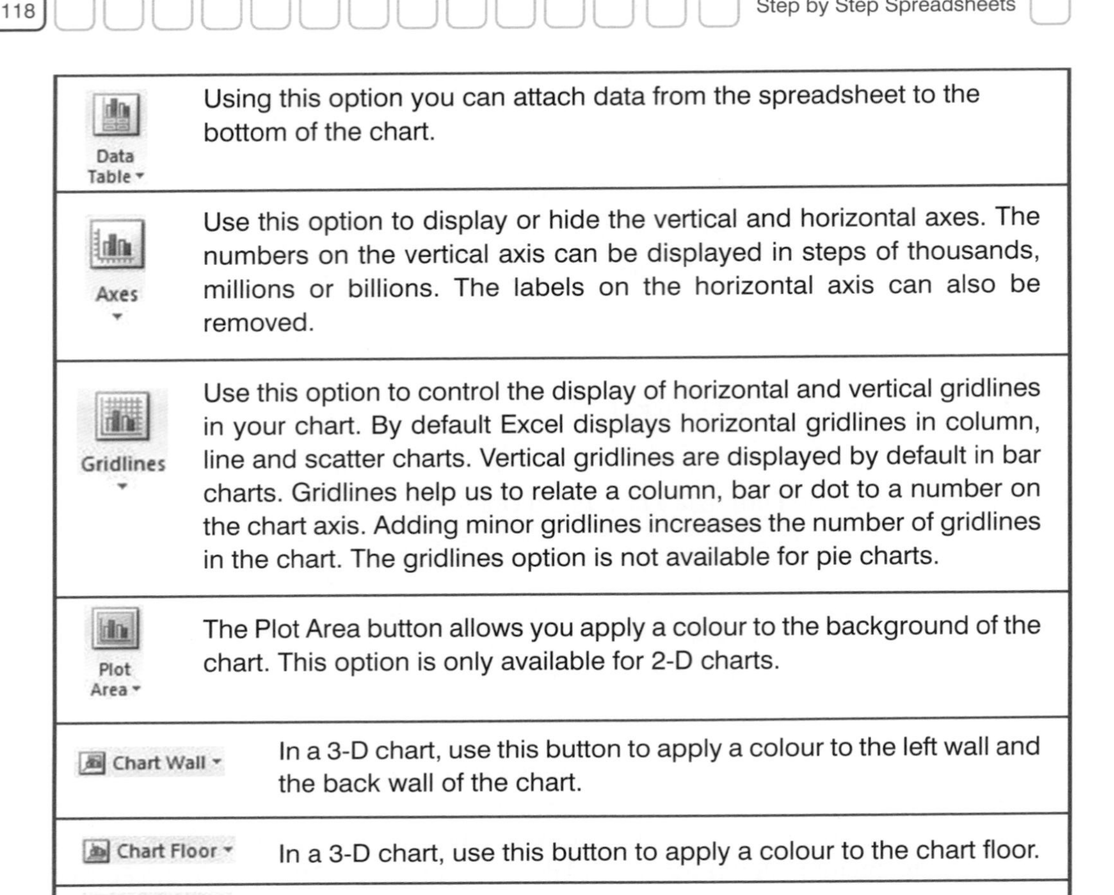

Button	Description
Data Table	Using this option you can attach data from the spreadsheet to the bottom of the chart.
Axes	Use this option to display or hide the vertical and horizontal axes. The numbers on the vertical axis can be displayed in steps of thousands, millions or billions. The labels on the horizontal axis can also be removed.
Gridlines	Use this option to control the display of horizontal and vertical gridlines in your chart. By default Excel displays horizontal gridlines in column, line and scatter charts. Vertical gridlines are displayed by default in bar charts. Gridlines help us to relate a column, bar or dot to a number on the chart axis. Adding minor gridlines increases the number of gridlines in the chart. The gridlines option is not available for pie charts.
Plot Area	The Plot Area button allows you apply a colour to the background of the chart. This option is only available for 2-D charts.
Chart Wall	In a 3-D chart, use this button to apply a colour to the left wall and the back wall of the chart.
Chart Floor	In a 3-D chart, use this button to apply a colour to the chart floor.
3-D Rotation	Use this button to rotate your 3-D chart.

3. The Format Tab

Using the Format tab you can:

- Apply a range of outlines and background fills to your chart
- Format columns and bars using a variety of fill effects
- Apply WordArt effects to the chart title and axis titles.

Format tab options are explained in Figure 4.32.

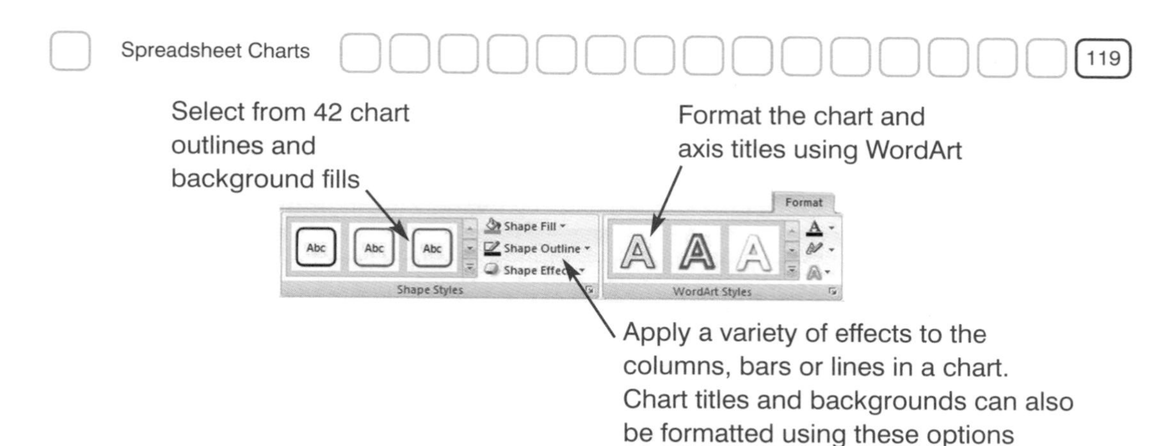

Figure 4.32 The Format tab

Like the Layout tab, the Format tab also has a Chart Area section (Figure 4.33).

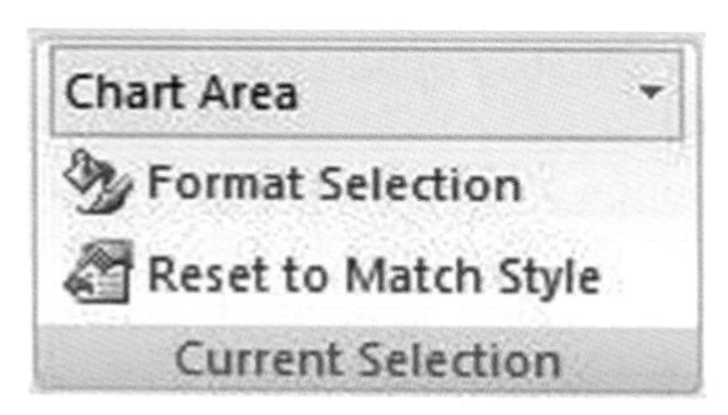

Figure 4.33

Use the Chart Area option to select a specific chart item. Once that chart item is selected, it can be formatted using the Shape Styles and WordArt Styles in the Format tab. Figure 4.34 shows a chart that has been formatted using the options in the Format tab.

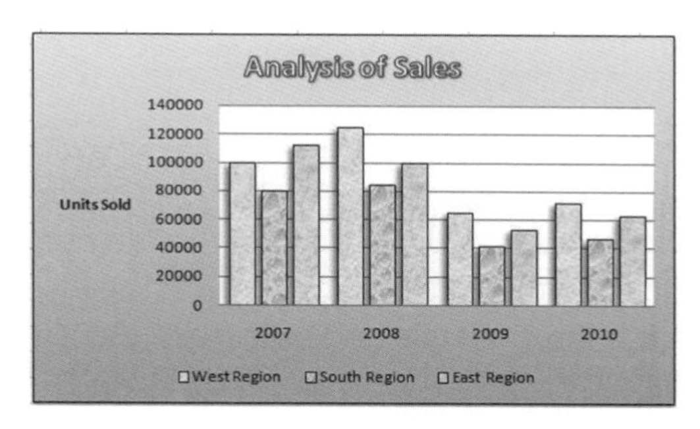

Figure 4.34 Formatting options have been applied using the Format tab

In Figure 4.34, a background fill has been applied to the chart. The chart title has been formatted using WordArt. The chart columns have been formatted using fill effects.

PIE CHARTS

The purpose of a pie chart is to show how an overall total is divided into different categories. By looking at a pie chart we can see the how the individual categories relate to each other.

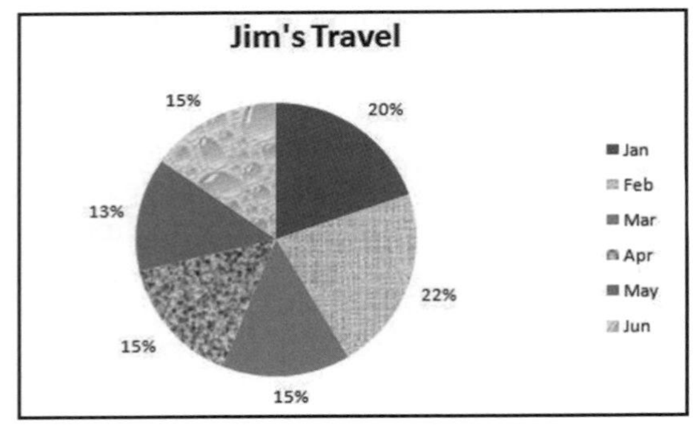

Figure 4.35

The pie chart in Figure 4.35 divides Jim's total travel into six slices; one for each month he travelled. This enables us to see at a glance how each month's travel compares to the other months. It also allows us to see in which months he did the most travelling. Larger pie slices mean greater distances travelled.

A pie chart can only display one data series. Because of this, only one row of data should be highlighted each time you create a pie chart. The row containing the headings should also be highlighted as the headings will be used to create the legend.

	A	B	C	D	E	F	G	H
1	Employee Travel Record							
2								
3		Jan	Feb	Mar	Apr	May	Jun	
4	Jim	1175	1298	875	901	809	900	
5	Tom	2012	1899	790	855	750	800	
6	Eileen	500	560	555	1990	2025	2117	
7	Karen	408	459	501	2339	2450	2098	
8								

Figure 4.36 Required range to create Jim's travel pie chart

This is straightforward in the case of Jim's pie chart as the headings and the data are next to each other, as shown in Figure 4.36.

Where the headings and data aren't in adjacent rows we need to highlight separate ranges, as shown in Figure 4.37. This is done by highlighting the headings, then holding down the *CTRL* key and highlighting the data.

	A	B	C	D	E	F	G	H
1	Employee Travel Record							
2								
3		Jan	Feb	Mar	Apr	May	Jun	
4	Jim	1175	1298	875	901	809	900	
5	Tom	2012	1899	790	855	750	800	
6	Eileen	500	560	555	1990	2025	2117	
7	Karen	408	459	501	2339	2450	2098	
8								

Figure 4.37 Two separate ranges are highlighted to create Tom's pie chart

To create Tom's travel pie chart, first highlight *A3:G3*, then release the left mouse button. Now highlight *A5:G5* while holding down the *CTRL* key.

Both highlighted areas must contain the same number of cells. For this reason, A3 must be included in the first highlighted range even though it doesn't contain any data. The pie chart will be incorrect if both highlighted ranges don't contain the same number of cells.

A word of warning: if A3:G5 is highlighted when creating Tom's pie chart, as shown in Figure 4.38, the numbers in the first series (i.e. Jim's travel) will be used to create the chart.

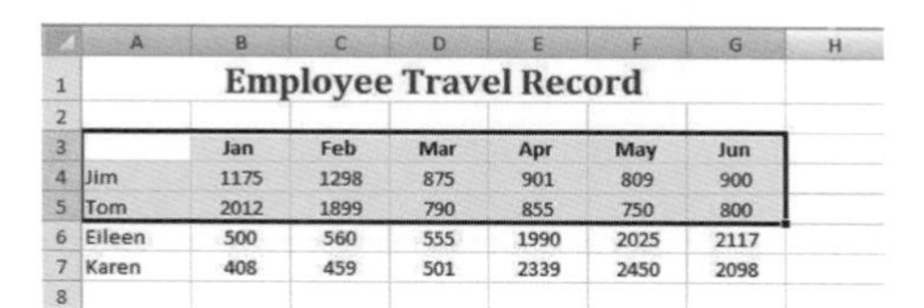

	A	B	C	D	E	F	G	H
1	Employee Travel Record							
2								
3		Jan	Feb	Mar	Apr	May	Jun	
4	Jim	1175	1298	875	901	809	900	
5	Tom	2012	1899	790	855	750	800	
6	Eileen	500	560	555	1990	2025	2117	
7	Karen	408	459	501	2339	2450	2098	
8								

Figure 4.38 Incorrectly highlighted range leads to unexpected results in your pie chart!

A pie chart created from the range highlighted in Figure 4.38 will be based on Jim's travel and not on Tom's travel.

INCORPORATING ADDITIONAL DATA IN A CHART

Worked Example

If you add data to your spreadsheet after the chart has been created, this can be included in the chart by adjusting the source data of the chart.

1. Open the *Regional Sales* spreadsheet.
2. Enter data for the North Region, shown in Figure 4.39. The new data relating to the North Region must be incorporated into any existing charts.

	A	B	C	D	E
1	Yearly Sales				
2		2007	2008	2009	2010
3	West Region	100000	125000	65000	72000
4	South Region	80000	85000	42000	47000
5	East Region	112000	100000	53000	63000
6	North Region	90000	85000	62000	65000
7					

Figure 4.39 Additional data has been added to the spreadsheet

3. Select the chart sheet named *Sales Chart*.
4. In the Ribbon, click the **Design** tab and then click the **Select Data** button.
5. The Select Data Source dialog box is displayed. (Figure 4.40)

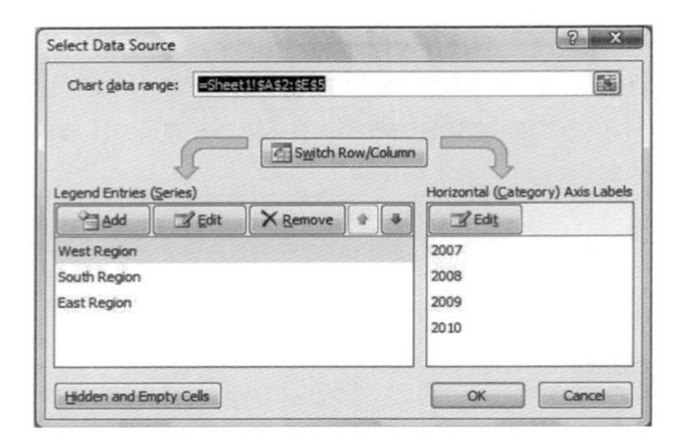

Figure 4.40 Specify the location of the new chart data using the Select Data Source dialog box

We can use the Select Data Source dialog box to add the North Region, which is a new data series, to the chart. In the Legend Entries section, click the Add button. The Edit Series dialog box is displayed (Figure 4.41).

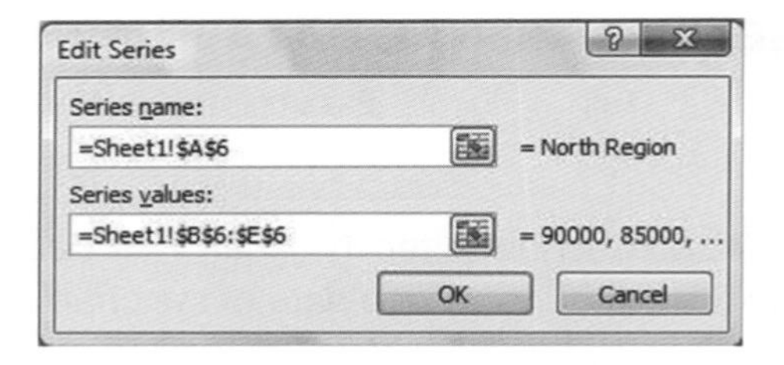

Figure 4.41 Identify the name and location of new chart data using the Edit Series dialog box

6. With the mouse pointer in the Series name box, click cell A6 in the spreadsheet. This identifies 'North Region' as the series name.
7. With the mouse pointer in the Series values box, highlight cells B6:E6, identifying these cells as the data series for the North Region.
8. Click OK twice to add the North Region data series to the column chart.

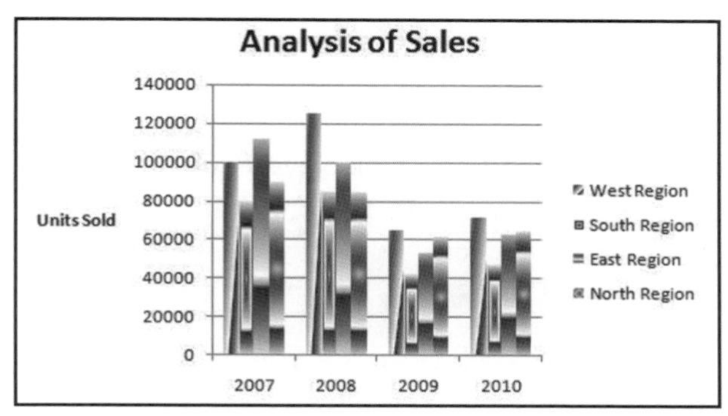

Figure 4.42 North Region has been added to the chart

The edited chart, including North Region, is displayed in Figure 4.42.

9. Save the *Regional Sales* spreadsheet.

Spreadsheet Charts Assignment One

- Create a new spreadsheet workbook and enter the data shown in Table 4.5 in Sheet 1.
- Rename Sheet1 as *Exam Data*

	A	B	C	D	E
1	**Summer Test Results**				
2		**Fail**	**Pass**	**Merit**	**Distinction**
3	Spreadsheets	2	5	25	8
4	Database	1	2	15	20
5	Word Processing	0	6	30	20

Table 4.5

Chart 1

Display the exam results using a column chart. Information relating to chart setup is displayed in Table 4.6.

Chart Type	2-D Clustered Column
Vertical Axis Title	Number of Students
Chart Location	*Exam Data* worksheet
Chart Position	Below the data

Table 4.6

- Click the Switch/Row column button to view the chart from the perspective of exam results.
- Select Style 3 as the chart style.
- Apply the *Colored Outline – Accent1* Shape Style.

Chart 2

Display the Spreadsheet results on a separate chart sheet using a pie chart. Information relating to chart setup is displayed in Table 4.7.

Chart Type	2-D Pie
Chart Title	Spreadsheets – Breakdown of Grades
Data Labels	Percentage – Outside End position
Chart Location	Separate chart sheet named *Spreadsheet Grades*

Table 4.7

Chart 3

Display the Database results on a separate chart sheet using a pie chart. Information relating to chart setup is displayed in Table 4.8.

You'll have to highlight two separate ranges to do this.

Chart Type	2-D Pie
Chart Title	Database – Breakdown of Grades
Data Labels	Percentage – Outside End position
Chart Location	Separate chart sheet named *Database Grades*

Table 4.8

You can select multiple spreadsheet ranges by highlighting the first range as normal and then holding down *CTRL* and dragging with the mouse to highlight subsequent ranges.

Chart 4

Display the Word Processing results on a separate chart sheet using a pie chart. Information relating to chart setup is displayed in Table 4.9.

Chart Type	2-D Pie
Chart Title	Word Processing – Breakdown of Grades
Data Labels	Percentage – Outside End position
Chart Location	Separate chart sheet named *Word Processing Grades*

Table 4.9

Update Chart Data

- In the *Exam Data* worksheet, change the number of students who failed Database from 1 to 6.
- Verify that this change has been reflected in:
  - the column chart in the *Exam Data* worksheet
  - the pie chart in the *Database Grades* chart sheet (the pie slice for database should now be 14%).
- Save the spreadsheet as **Summer Test Results**

Spreadsheet Charts Assignment Two

- Create a new spreadsheet workbook and enter the data shown in Table 4.10 in Sheet 1.
- Rename Sheet1 as *Race Data*

	A	B	C
1		**Formula One Results**	
2			
3	**Driver**	**Top Speed**	**Fastest Lap**
4	Jenson Button	340	1.55
5	Rubens Barrichello	339	1.49
6	Jarno Trulli	335	1.62
7	Timo Glock	332	1.48
8	Fernando Alonso	325	1.54
9	Nico Rosberg	320	1.59
10	Sebastien Buemi	329	1.56
11	Toro Rosso	312	1.58
12			

Table 4.10

Chart 1

Display the top speeds using a bar chart. Information relating to chart setup is displayed in Table 4.11

Chart Type	2-D Clustered Bar
Chart Title	Driver Top Speeds
Horizontal Axis Title	Speed (kph)
Chart Location	*Race Data* worksheet
Chart Position	Below the data

Table 4.11

- Apply Style 27 to the chart.
- Move the chart to a separate chart sheet named *Top Speeds*
- Change the chart type to Clustered Bar in 3-D.
- Apply a Shape Fill to the Chart Side Wall using *White, Background 1, Darker 15%.*
- Apply a Shape Fill to the Chart Floor using *White, Background 1, Darker 35%.*

Chart 2

Display the fastest laps using a bar chart. Information relating to chart setup is displayed in Table 4.12.

Chart Type	2-D Clustered Bar
Chart Title	Fastest Lap by Driver
Horizontal Axis Title	Time (minutes)
Bar Colour	Red
Chart Location	*Race Data* worksheet
Chart Position	Below chart 1

Table 4.12

- Apply Style 28 to the chart.
- Move the chart to a separate chart sheet named *Fastest Laps*
- Change the chart type to Clustered Bar in 3-D.
- Apply a Shape Fill to the Chart Side Wall using *Blue, Accent1, Lighter 80%.*
- Apply a Shape Fill to the Chart Floor using *Blue, Accent1, Lighter 60%.*

Update Chart Data

- In the *Race Data* worksheet, change Jensen Button's top speed to 310.
- Verify that the driver top speeds chart has updated to reflect this change.
- In the *Race Data* worksheet, change Timo Glock's fastest lap to 1.64.
- Verify that the fastest lap by driver chart has updated to reflect this change.
- Save the spreadsheet as **Formula 1**

Spreadsheet Charts Assignment Three

- Create a new spreadsheet workbook and enter the data shown in Table 4.13 in Sheet 1.
- Rename Sheet1 as *European Election Results*

	A	B	C	D
1	**European Elections**			
2				
3	**Party**	**Votes 2004**	**Votes 2010**	**Percentage Gain/Loss**
4	Democrats	75309	125539	
5	Republicans	63581	118937	
6	Greens	138933	88127	
7	Liberals	81243	73131	
8	Socialists	30107	34938	
9	Independents	15668	20511	
10				

Table 4.13

- Calculate Percentage Gain/Loss.

Chart 1

Display Votes 2004 using a pie chart. Information relating to chart setup is displayed in Table 4.14.

Chart Type	2-D Pie
Chart Title	Election Results 2004
Data Labels	Percentage – Outside End position
Chart Location	*European Election Results* worksheet
Chart Position	Below the data

Table 4.14

- Apply the *Subtle Effect – Dark 1* Shape Style.

Chart 2

Display Votes 2010 using a pie chart. Information relating to chart setup is displayed in Table 4.15.

Chart Type	2-D Pie
Chart Title	Election Results 2010
Data Labels	Percentage – Outside End position
Chart Location	*European Election Results* worksheet
Chart Position	Below the 2004 pie chart

Table 4.15

- Apply the *Subtle Effect – Dark 1* Shape Style.

Chart 3

Display Votes 2004 and Votes 2010 on a separate chart sheet using a bar chart. Information relating to chart setup is displayed in Table 4.16.

Chart Type	2-D Clustered Bar
Chart Title	Analysis of Voting Patterns
Data Labels	Value – Outside End position
Chart Location	Separate chart sheet named *Analysis by Year*

Table 4.16

- Apply a Shape Outline of Black to the bars in the chart.

Chart 4

Display Percentage Gain/Loss by party on a separate chart sheet using a column chart. Attach a data table to the chart. Information relating to chart setup is displayed in Table 4.17.

Chart Type	2-D Clustered Column
Chart Title	Shift in Voting Patterns
Data Labels	Value – Outside End position
Data Table	Display without legend keys
Chart Location	Separate chart sheet named *Voting Patterns*

Table 4.17

- Apply *Style 34* to the chart.

Update Chart Data

- In the *European Election Results* worksheet, change Votes 2010 for Independents to 28907.
- Check your charts for the following changes:
  - in the Election Results 2010 pie chart, Independents have increased from 4% to 6%
  - in the Analysis of Voting Patterns bar chart, Independents' vote for 2010 has increased to 28907
  - in the Shift in Voting Patterns column chart, Independents' percentage gain has increased to 84%.
- Save the spreadsheet as **European Elections**

Spreadsheet Charts Assignment Four

- Create a new spreadsheet workbook and enter the data shown in Table 4.18 in Sheet 1.
- Rename Sheet1 as *Diving Tables*

	A	B	C
1		**Pressure Predictor**	
2			
3	**Depth (metres)**	**Pressure**	
4	0	1	
5	10	2	
6	20	3	
7	30	4	
8	40	5	
9	50	6	
10			

Table 4.18

Display the depth and pressure data using a scatter chart. Information relating to chart setup is displayed in Table 4.19.

Chart Type	Scatter with smooth lines and markers
Chart Title	Depth/Pressure Relationship
Horizontal Axis Title	Depth (metres)
Vertical Axis Title	Atmospheres
Chart Location	*Diving Tables* worksheet
Chart Position	Below the data

Table 4.19

- Select *Style 48* as the chart style.
- Save the spreadsheet as **Pressure Predictor**

Spreadsheet Charts Assignment Five

- Create a new spreadsheet workbook and enter the data shown in Table 4.20 in Sheet 1.
- Rename Sheet1 as *Opinion Poll Data*

	A	B	C	D	E	F	G
1	**Results of Party Satisfaction Poll**						
2							
3		**Jan**	**Feb**	**Mar**	**Apr**	**May**	**June**
4	Democrats	40%	42%	48%	31%	51%	55%
5	Socialists	56%	38%	43%	55%	53%	63%
6	Republicans	55%	51%	31%	49%	35%	45%
7							

Table 4.20

Chart 1

Display the Democrats' poll results using a line chart. Information relating to chart setup is displayed in Table 4.21.

Chart Type	Line with markers
Chart Title	Democrats – Voter Satisfaction
Vertical Axis Title	% Satisfied
Chart Location	*Opinion Poll Data* worksheet
Chart Position	Below the data

Table 4.21

- Apply a colour of blue to the Democrats series.

Chart 2

Display the Socialists' poll results using a line chart. Information relating to chart setup is displayed in Table 4.22.

You will need to highlight two separate ranges.

Chart Type	Line with markers
Chart Title	Socialists – Voter Satisfaction
Vertical Axis Title	% Satisfied
Chart Location	*Opinion Poll Data* worksheet
Chart Position	Below the Democrats chart

Table 4.22

- Apply a colour of red to the Socialists series.

Chart 3

Display the Republicans' poll results using a line chart. Information relating to chart setup is displayed in Table 4.23.

Chart Type	Line with markers
Chart Title	Republicans – Voter Satisfaction
Vertical Axis Title	% Satisfied
Chart Location	*Opinion Poll Data* worksheet
Chart Position	Below the Socialists chart

Table 4.23

- Apply a colour of green to the Republicans series.

Update Chart Data

- In the *Opinion Poll Data* worksheet, change the Socialists' April satisfaction rating to 33%.
- Verify that the Socialist voter satisfaction chart has updated to reflect this change.
- Save the spreadsheet as **Voter Satisfaction**

Spreadsheet Charts Assignment Six

- Create a new spreadsheet workbook and enter the data shown in Table 4.24 in Sheet1.
- Rename Sheet1 as *Passenger Data*

	A	B	C	D
1	**Passenger Numbers**			
2		**Stranraer**	**Holyhead**	**Le Havre**
3	Monday	290	450	280
4	Tuesday	250	400	220
5	Wednesday	295	310	350
6	Thursday	300	490	210
7	Friday	400	550	450
8	Saturday	525	550	500
9	Sunday	480	400	520

Table 4.24

Chart 1

Display the data using a line chart. Information relating to chart setup is displayed in Table 4.25.

Chart Type	Line with markers
Chart Title	Analysis of Passenger Numbers
Vertical Axis Title	No of passengers
Chart Location	Separate chart sheet named *Travel Chart*

Table 4.25

- Apply the *Gradient Fill – Accent6, Inner Shadow* style to the chart title.

Update Chart Data

- Add the data for the Cairnryan route, as shown in Table 4.26, in column E of the *Passenger Data* worksheet. Include this new data in the chart by adjusting the cell references of the source data.

E
Cairnryan
320
250
300
320
350
450
450

Table 4.26

- In the *Passenger Data* worksheet, change the number of passengers on the Thursday Le Havre sailing to 560.
- Verify that the travel chart has updated to reflect this change.
- Save the spreadsheet as **Passenger Ferries**

CREATING A COLUMN CHART BASED ON MULTIPLE RANGES

When you're creating a chart, the data will sometimes be in a number of non-adjacent ranges. To select multiple ranges, select the first range as normal with the mouse. To select additional ranges, hold down the *CTRL* key while dragging with the mouse.

Worked Example

1. Open the spreadsheet named *Rock Café* (created in Chapter 2).
2. Select four separate ranges, as shown in Figure 4.43.

6										
7	Artist	Date	Stalls	%Full	Circle	%Full	Balcony	%Full	Total Tickets	%Full
8	The Blizzards	08/09/2010	150	50%	300	86%	220	88%	670	74%
9	U2	10/09/2010	276	92%	245	70%	141	56%	662	74%
10	Mundy	11/09/2010	290	97%	307	88%	209	84%	806	90%
11	Duffy	14/09/2010	250	83%	312	89%	196	78%	758	84%
12	Arcade Fire	18/09/2010	300	100%	350	100%	250	100%	900	100%
13	Kings of Leon	19/09/2010	100	33%	267	76%	233	93%	600	67%
14	Mick Flannery	20/09/2010	180	60%	255	73%	200	80%	635	71%
15										

Figure 4.43 Four separate ranges have been selected for the chart

3. Display the concert ticket sales using a column chart. Information relating to chart setup is displayed in Table 4.27.

Chart Type	2-D Clustered Column
Chart Title	Ticket Sales Analysis
Vertical Axis Title	Tickets Sold
Chart Location	Separate chart sheet named *Sales Chart*

Table 4.27

4. Click the Save button to save the spreadsheet.

 Important Points Relating to Charts Based on Multiple Ranges

1. There should be a heading in the top cell of each range selected. Each heading should occupy a single cell.
2. All selected ranges should contain the same number of cells. In the example in Figure 4.44, there would be an error in the chart because an extra blank cell has been incorrectly highlighted in the Stalls and Balcony columns.

6										
7	Artist	Date	Stalls	%Full	Circle	%Full	Balcony	%Full	Total Tickets	%Full
8	The Blizzards	08/09/2010	150	50%	300	86%	220	88%	670	74%
9	U2	10/09/2010	276	92%	245	70%	141	56%	662	74%
10	Mundy	11/09/2010	290	97%	307	88%	209	84%	806	90%
11	Duffy	14/09/2010	250	83%	312	89%	196	78%	758	84%
12	Arcade Fire	18/09/2010	300	100%	350	100%	250	100%	900	100%
13	Kings of Leon	19/09/2010	100	33%	267	76%	233	93%	600	67%
14	Mick Flannery	20/09/2010	180	60%	255	73%	200	80%	635	71%
15										

Figure 4.44 Incorrectly selected chart ranges in the Stalls and Balcony columns

3. The first range selected should contain headings or descriptions. Here, the first range selected contains the artists' names. These will be inserted either in the legend or below the horizontal axis depending on whether 'Series in rows' or 'Series in columns' is selected.

CHAPTER 4 SUMMARY

1. Basic Concepts

- A spreadsheet chart allows us to present numeric data visually.
- A chart conveys the story of the numbers, allowing us to see trends in the numbers much more easily.
- The main chart types are Column, Bar, Line, Pie and Scatter.
- Each set of numbers represented in the chart is called a data series.
- A chart can be positioned on the same worksheet as the data or on a separate chart sheet.

- Excel views chart data in rows by default. Clicking the Switch Row/Column button changes the focus of the chart to *data in columns.*

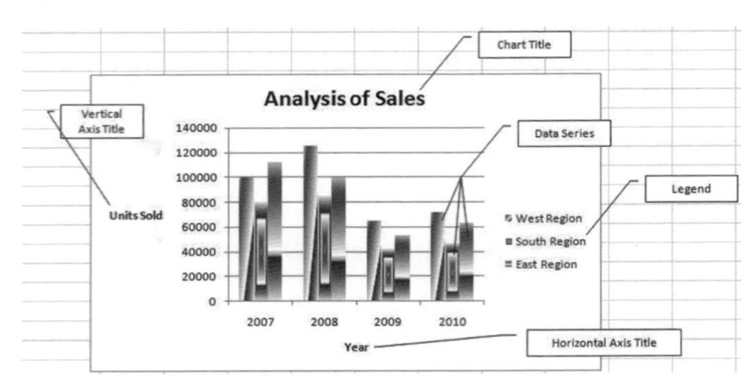

Figure 4.45

2. Formatting

Excel charts are formatted using the Design, Layout and Formatting sections of the Ribbon.

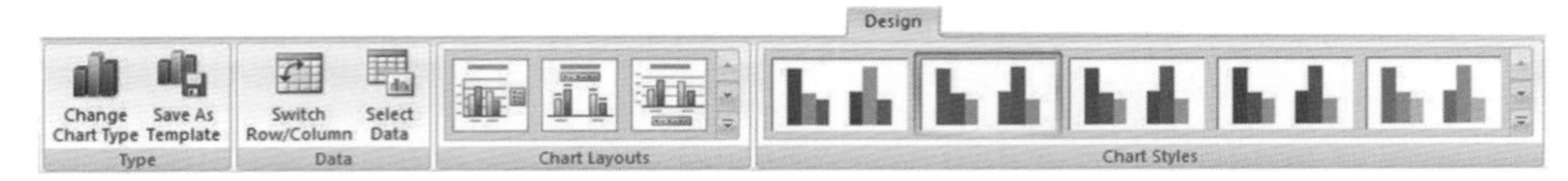

Figure 4.46 Design section of the Ribbon

Using the Design section of the Ribbon (Figure 4.46) you can change the chart type or source data as well as selecting from a range of chart layouts and colour schemes.

Figure 4.47 Layout section of the Ribbon

The Layout section of the Ribbon (Figure 4.47) contains a number of formatting options which can be used to change the appearance of a chart.

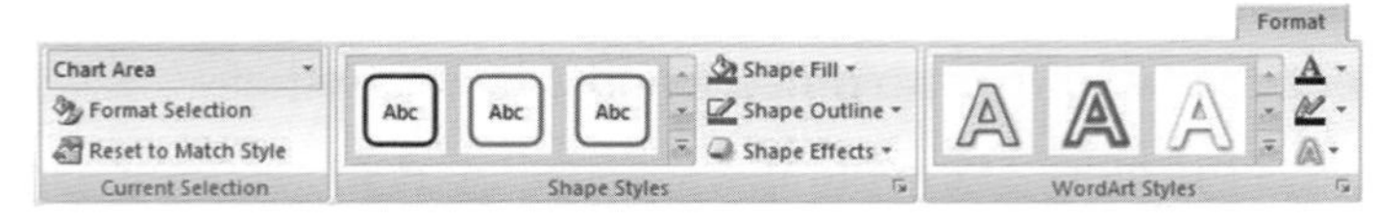

Figure 4.48 Format section of the Ribbon

The Format section of the Ribbon (Figure 4.48) is used to apply colour and fill effects to the chart background as well as the columns, bars, lines or pie segments in a chart. WordArt styles can also be applied to the chart and axes titles.

3. Potential Pitfalls

- When highlighting data for a chart, always ensure that the first row of the highlighted range contains headings and that the first column contains descriptions.
- There should be no blank rows or columns in the source data of the chart. A blank row or column will cause an error in the chart.
- When creating a pie chart, highlight only one row of headings and one row of data. Ensure that both highlighted rows contain the same number of cells. If the headings and the data are not adjacent to each other, highlight the headings separately and then hold down the *CTRL* key while highlighting the data.
- If you highlight more than one row of data for a pie chart, Excel will use the numbers in the row immediately below the headings and ignore any other rows.

4. Useful Shortcuts

Keystroke	Action
F11	Creates a column chart in a separate chart sheet based on the selected cells.
ALT+N	Displays the Insert group in the Ribbon.
ALT+JA	Displays the Layout group in the Ribbon.
ALT+JC	Displays the Design group in the Ribbon.

Table 4.28

SPREADSHEET CHARTS REVIEW QUESTIONS

Answers to the review questions are available on www.gillmacmillan.ie

	A	B	C	D	E
1		**2007**	**2008**	**2009**	**2010**
2	West Region	100000	125000	112000	130000 ←
3	South Region	80000	85000	90000	70000 ←
4	East Region	112000	100000	120000	114000 ←

Table 4.29

1. A chart has been created using the data in Table 4.29. What is the name that Excel gives to the 3 individual rows of data in the chart (indicated by arrows above)?

   ____

2. Write down the names of the chart types displayed below:

(i)

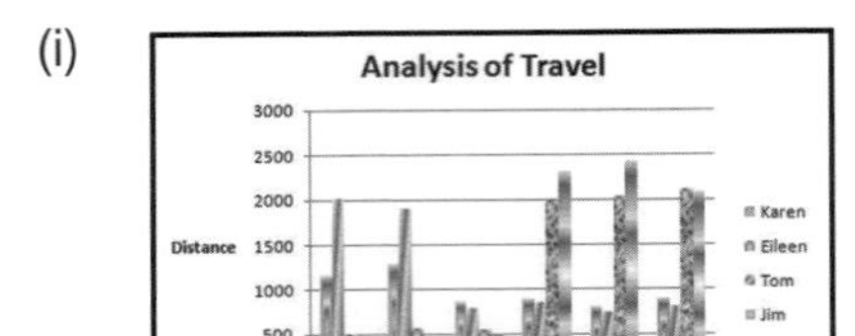

____

(ii)

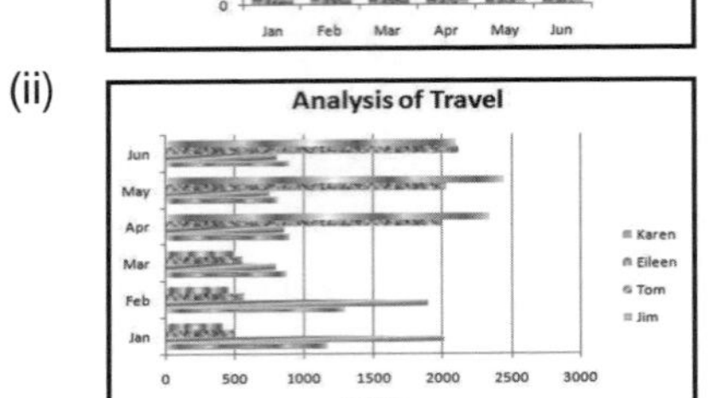

____

(iii)

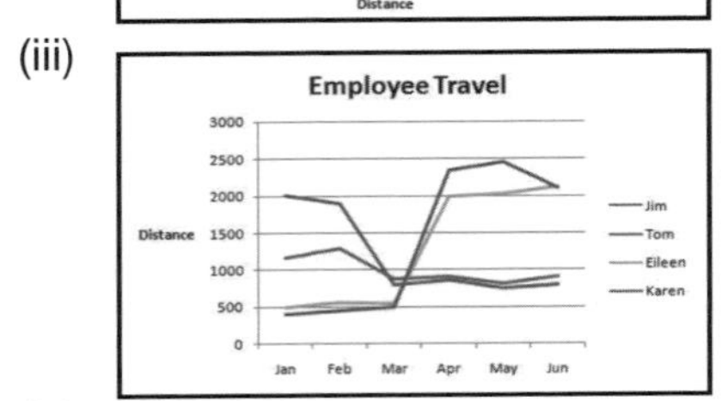

____

(iv)

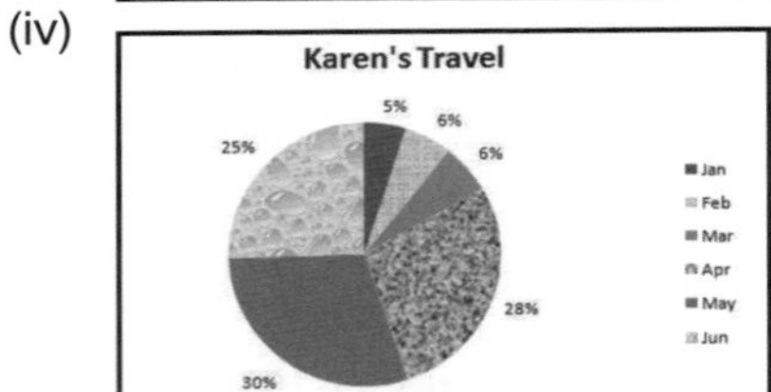

____

(v)

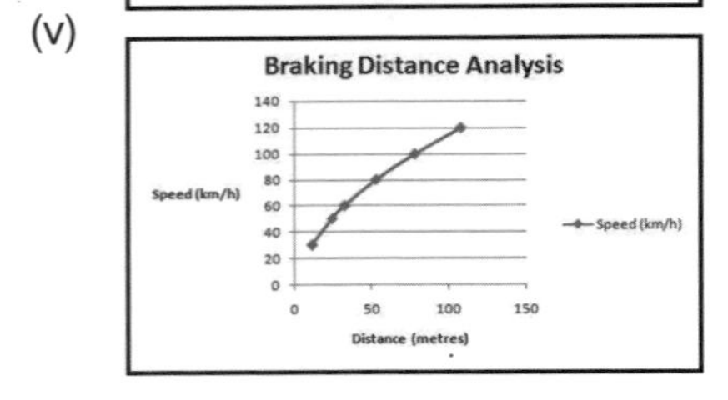

____

3. Write down the names of the items labelled in Figure 4.49.

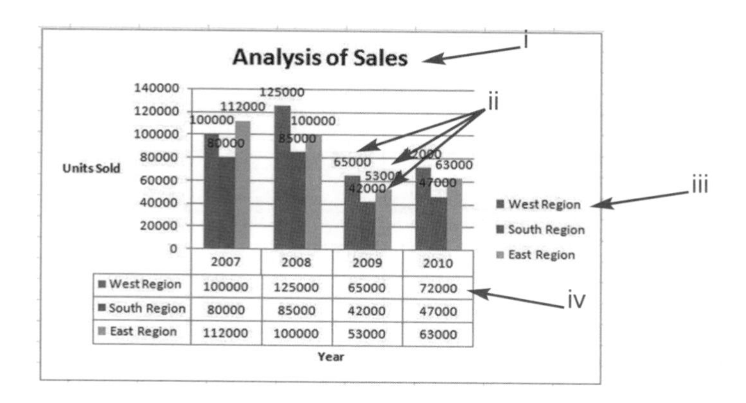

Figure 4.49

(i) ______________________________

(ii) ______________________________

(iii) ______________________________

(iv) ______________________________

4. Write down the most appropriate chart type for each of the objectives listed in Table 4.30.

	Objective	Most Suitable Chart Type
(i)	Show the trend in petrol prices over the last five years.	
(ii)	Compare student numbers in Engineering, Marketing and Maths over the last three years.	
(iii)	Display the percentage of votes obtained by Fianna Fáil, Fine Gael, Labour, Green, Sinn Féin and Other in the last election.	
(iv)	Graph the results of an experiment displaying the relationship between pressure and temperature.	
(v)	Show how interest rates have changed over the last 12 months.	

Table 4.30

5. Click the ____________________ button to colour in the background of a 2-D chart.

6. In Figure 4.50, a range of cells has been highlighted for a standard column chart.

	A	B	C	D	E	F
1		IT	Programming	Finance	Admin	
2	Spreadsheet Methods	26	23	32	14	
3	Database Methods	34	38	8	22	
4	Web Design	12	44	3	1	
5						

Figure 4.50

(i) Which range of cells will Excel use for the Horizontal Axis Titles?

____

(ii) Which range of cells will be used for the Legend? ____________________

(iii) Which range of cells will be used to create the columns in the chart?

____

(iv) How many data series will be in this chart? ____________________

7. In Figure 4.51, an extra row of data has been added to the spreadsheet referred to in question 6. Briefly explain how to include this new data in the column chart.

	A	B	C	D	E
1		IT	Programming	Finance	Admin
2	Spreadsheet Methods	26	23	32	14
3	Database Methods	34	38	8	22
4	Web Design	12	44	3	1
5	Word Processing	8	6	25	38
6					

Figure 4.51

____

____

8. Figure 4.52 displays cells highlighted for a pie chart. When the pie chart button was clicked the chart appeared as in Figure 4.53.

	A	B	C	D	E	F
1		IT	Programming	Finance	Admin	
2	Spreadsheet Methods	26	23	32	14	
3	Database Methods	34	38	8	22	
4	Web Design	12	44	3	1	
5	Word Processing	8	6	25	38	
6						

Figure 4.52

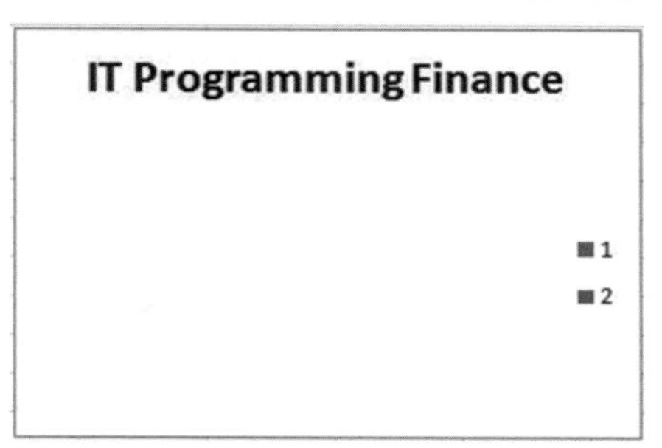

Figure 4.53

What caused this error? ______________________________

____

9. To switch the data series from rows to columns, click the ______________ button.

10. Figure 4.54 displays data highlighted for a column chart. When the chart was created it appeared like Figure 4.55.

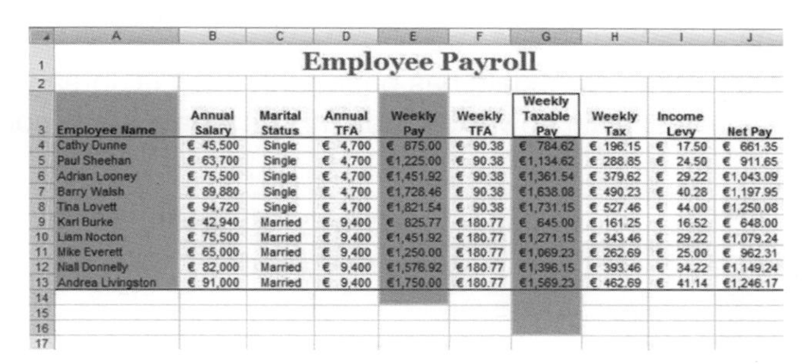

Employee Payroll

Employee Name	Annual Salary	Marital Status	Annual TFA	Weekly Pay	Weekly TFA	Weekly Taxable Pay	Weekly Tax	Income Levy	Net Pay
Cathy Dunne	€ 45,500	Single	€ 4,700	€ 875.00	€ 90.38	€ 784.62	€ 196.15	€ 17.50	€ 661.35
Paul Sheehan	€ 63,700	Single	€ 4,700	€1,225.00	€ 90.38	€1,134.62	€ 288.85	€ 24.50	€ 911.65
Adrian Looney	€ 75,500	Single	€ 4,700	€1,451.92	€ 90.38	€1,361.54	€ 379.62	€ 29.22	€1,043.09
Barry Walsh	€ 89,880	Single	€ 4,700	€1,728.46	€ 90.38	€1,638.08	€ 490.23	€ 40.28	€1,197.95
Tina Lovett	€ 94,720	Single	€ 4,700	€1,821.54	€ 90.38	€1,731.15	€ 527.46	€ 44.00	€1,250.08
Karl Burke	€ 42,940	Married	€ 9,400	€ 825.77	€ 180.77	€ 645.00	€ 161.25	€ 16.52	€ 648.00
Liam Nocton	€ 75,500	Married	€ 9,400	€1,451.92	€ 180.77	€1,271.15	€ 343.46	€ 29.22	€1,079.24
Mike Everett	€ 65,000	Married	€ 9,400	€1,250.00	€ 180.77	€1,069.23	€ 262.69	€ 25.00	€ 962.31
Niall Donnelly	€ 82,000	Married	€ 9,400	€1,576.92	€ 180.77	€1,396.15	€ 393.46	€ 34.22	€1,149.24
Andrea Livingston	€ 91,000	Married	€ 9,400	€1,750.00	€ 180.77	€1,569.23	€ 462.69	€ 41.14	€1,246.17

Figure 4.54

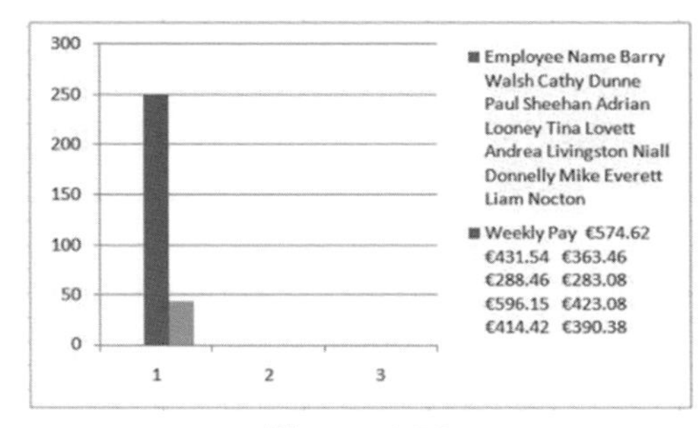

Figure 4.55

Briefly describe what caused this error.

____

____

5 Sorting Spreadsheet Data

In Chapter 5 you will learn how to:

- Sort spreadsheet data in ascending and descending order
- Use a custom sort for weekdays and month names
- Create your own custom sort
- Modify an existing cell style.

FOUR METHODS OF SORTING SPREADSHEET DATA

Data such as customer transactions is often entered in a spreadsheet in the order in which it naturally occurs. For example, sales data is usually entered as each transaction is completed. You'll often want to view that data in a different order, such as in ascending order of customer name or descending order of amount owed.

There are four methods of sorting data in a spreadsheet. These are outlined below.

1. Numerical sort

Numbers in a particular row or column can be rearranged in ascending *(from the smallest to the largest number)* or descending *(from the largest to the smallest number)* numerical order.

Sort Smallest to Largest
Sort Largest to Smallest

2. Alphabetical sort

Text, such as customer names, can be rearranged in ascending *(starting with names that begin with a, b, c and ending with names that begin with x, y, z)* or descending *(starting with names that begin with z, y, x and ending with names that begin with c, b, a)* alphabetical order.

Sort A to Z
Sort Z to A

3. Filter sort

A Filter Sort is a more powerful type of sort that allows you to hide specific items in a sorted list.

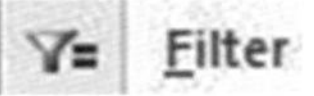

4. Custom sort

A custom sort is used to sort data by two or more columns or rows. Excel also has a number of pre-programmed custom sorts which can be used when the data you are sorting does not follow a natural sort order. For example, if we were to sort the days of the week alphabetically, we would get Friday, Monday, Saturday, Sunday, Thursday, Tuesday, Wednesday. Custom sorts are available for day and month names.

Custom Sort...

To select one of the four sorting options, click the Sort & Filter button in the Home section of the Ribbon.

Sort & Filter

SINGLE-COLUMN SORT

Worked Example

Create a new spreadsheet workbook and enter the data shown in Table 5.1 in Sheet1.

	A	B	C
1	**Formula 1 Drivers Championship**		
2			
3	**Driver Name**	**Team**	**Points**
4	Jarno Trulli	Toyota	17
5	Nick Heidfeld	BMW Sauber	9
6	Timo Glock	Toyota	8
7	Sebastien Bourdais	STR-Ferrari	5
8	Robert Kubica	BMW Sauber	1
9	Kazuki Nakajima	Williams-Toyota	2
10	Jenson Button	Brawn-Mercedes	34
11	Nico Rosberg	Williams-Toyota	12
12	Sebastien Buemi	STR-Ferrari	7
13	Nelson Piquet	Renault	1
14	Rubens Barrichello	Brawn-Mercedes	10
15	Fernando Alonso	Renault	12

Table 5.1

The data in Table 5.1 isn't in any particular order. We will sort this data in descending order of points. This means that the driver with the most points will be at the top of the list and the driver with the least points will be at the bottom of the list.

1. Position the cell pointer in any cell containing data in column C *(any cell in the range C4:C15)*.

2. In the Home section of the Ribbon, click the **Sort & Filter** button.

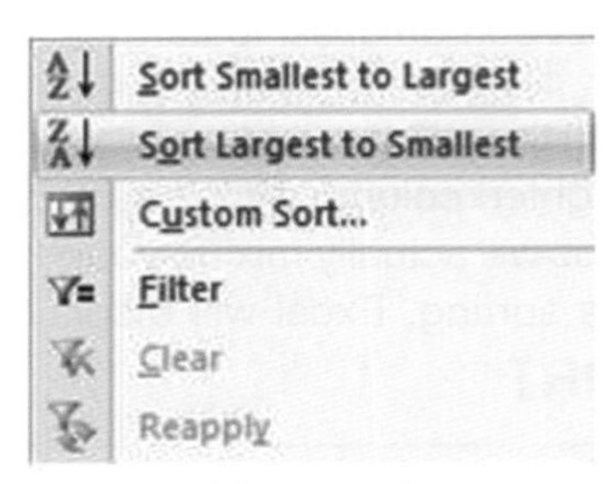

Figure 5.1

3. Select **Sort Largest to Smallest** from the drop-down list (Figure 5.1). The data is now in descending order of points, as displayed in Table 5.2.

	A	B	C
1	**Formula 1 Drivers Championship**		
2			
3	**Driver Name**	**Team**	**Points**
4	Jenson Button	Brawn-Mercedes	34
5	Jarno Trulli	Toyota	17
6	Fernando Alonso	Renault	12
7	Nico Rosberg	Williams-Toyota	12
8	Rubens Barrichello	Brawn-Mercedes	10
9	Nick Heidfeld	BMW Sauber	9
10	Timo Glock	Toyota	8
11	Sebastien Buemi	STR-Ferrari	7
12	Sebastien Bourdais	STR-Ferrari	5
13	Kazuki Nakajima	Williams-Toyota	2
14	Nelson Piquet	RBR-Renault	1
15	Robert Kubica	BMW Sauber	1

Table 5.2

4. Save the spreadsheet as **Formula 1 Championship**

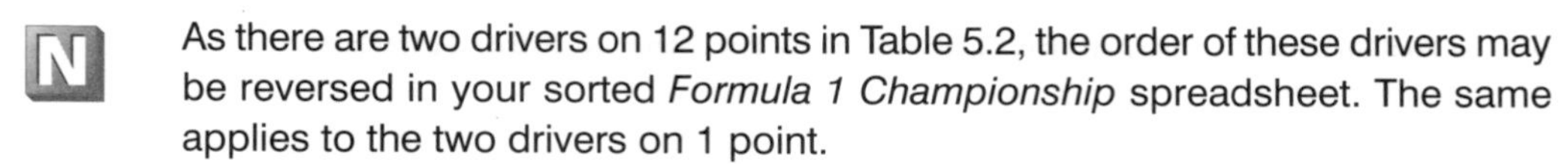

As there are two drivers on 12 points in Table 5.2, the order of these drivers may be reversed in your sorted *Formula 1 Championship* spreadsheet. The same applies to the two drivers on 1 point.

To see the data in ascending order of points, simply click the Sort & Filter button and then select *Sort Smallest to Largest* from the list.

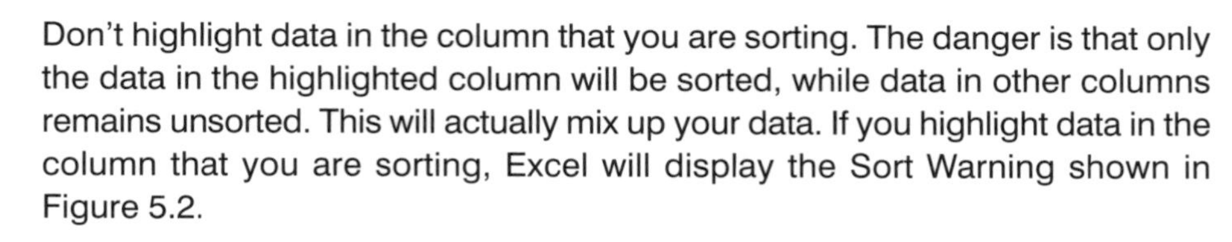

Don't highlight data in the column that you are sorting. The danger is that only the data in the highlighted column will be sorted, while data in other columns remains unsorted. This will actually mix up your data. If you highlight data in the column that you are sorting, Excel will display the Sort Warning shown in Figure 5.2.

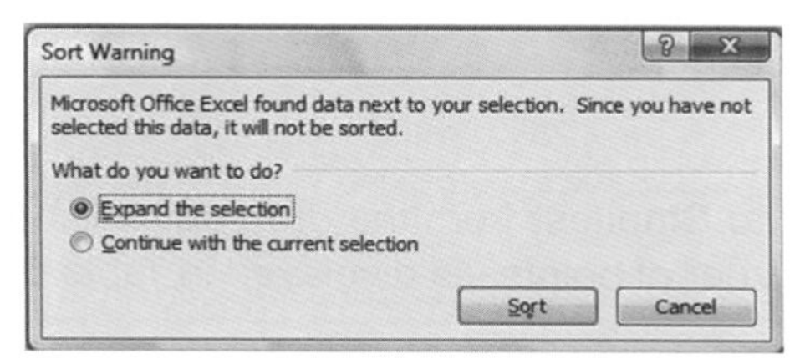

Figure 5.2 Warning displayed by Excel if you highlight the column you are sorting

If this happens, select the *Expand the selection* option to ensure that data in all columns is included in the sort.

MULTIPLE-COLUMN SORT

Worked Example

We have already sorted the Formula 1 Drivers Championship data by a single column – descending order of points. In Excel, you can also sort your data by two or more columns. The drivers championship data can be sorted firstly in ascending order of team so that BMW Sauber is at the top of the list and Williams-Toyota is at the bottom of the list. Because each Formula 1 team has two drivers, the data can then be sorted in descending order of points so that, of the two BMW Sauber drivers, Nick Heidfeld will be higher up in the list with 9 points; and, of the two Williams-Toyota drivers, Nico Rosberg will be higher up in the list with 12 points.

A Custom Sort is required to sort by multiple columns.

1. Open the *Formula 1 Championship* spreadsheet if it is not already open.
2. Click in any cell in the data you are sorting (any cell in the range A4:C15) – *see Table 5.2.*
3. In the Home section of the Ribbon, click the **Sort & Filter** button and select Custom Sort from the list of options. Excel highlights the data automatically.

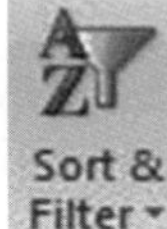

4. In the Sort dialog box, select *Team* from the *Sort by* drop-down list and ensure that the Order is A to Z, as shown in Figure 5.3.

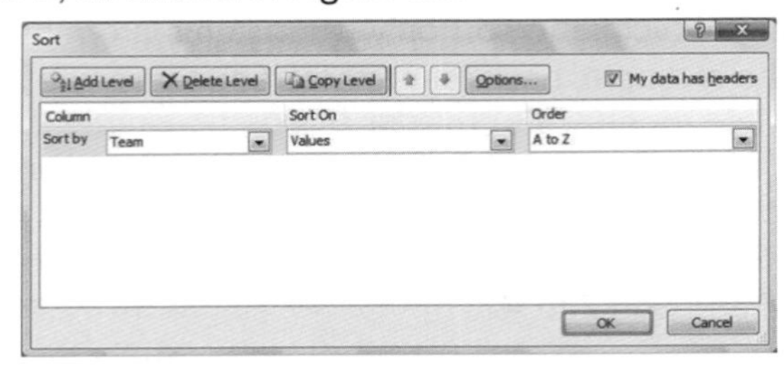

Figure 5.3: Team has been specified as the first-level sort

5. Click the Add Level button and select Points as the second-level sort. Ensure that the Order is Largest to Smallest (Figure 5.4).

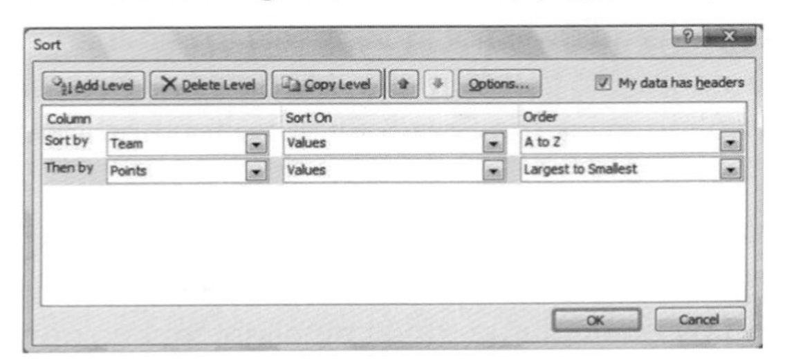

Figure 5.4 Points has been added as the second-level sort

6. Click OK to apply the sort. The resulting Formula 1 Drivers Table is displayed in Table 5.3.

	A	B	C
1	**Formula 1 Drivers Championship**		
2			
3	**Driver Name**	**Team**	**Points**
4	Nick Heidfeld	BMW Sauber	9
5	Robert Kubica	BMW Sauber	1
6	Jenson Button	Brawn-Mercedes	34
7	Rubens Barrichello	Brawn-Mercedes	10
8	Fernando Alonso	Renault	12
9	Nelsinho Piquet	Renault	1
10	Sebastien Buemi	STR-Ferrari	7
11	Sebastien Bourdais	STR-Ferrari	5
12	Jarno Trulli	Toyota	17
13	Timo Glock	Toyota	8
14	Nico Rosberg	Williams-Toyota	12
15	Kazuki Nakajima	Williams-Toyota	2

Table 5.3

7. Save the *Formula 1 Championship* spreadsheet.

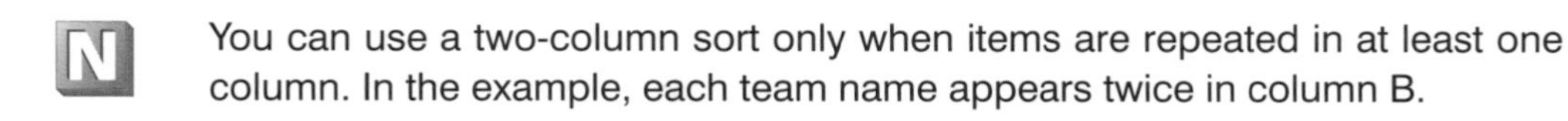

You can use a two-column sort only when items are repeated in at least one column. In the example, each team name appears twice in column B.

The options in the Sort & Filter drop-down list reflect the type of data that is being sorted. When a number is selected, the options are *Sort Smallest to Largest* and *Sort Largest to Smallest*. When text is selected, the options change to *Sort A to Z* and *Sort Z to A*.

SORTING SPREADSHEET DATA – IMPORTANT POINTS

1. Excel assumes that the first row of the data you are sorting contains headings and will not include this row in the sort unless you remove the tick from the '*My data has headers*' check box. To access this option, click the Sort & Filter button and then select Custom Sort.
2. Don't include blank rows or columns in the range you're sorting. Excel won't include all of the data in the sort if this is the case.
3. When sorting by one column, don't highlight that column. Simply select any cell in that column.
4. Each heading should occupy one cell only. This is because Excel assumes that the first row of the highlighted range contains headings. If headings are entered in two rows, the second row of headings will be sorted with the data.
5. It is good practice to emphasise your column headings using formatting (e.g. bold). This will ensure that the headings are not sorted with the rest of the data.

Sorting Spreadsheet Data Assignment One

Create a new spreadsheet workbook and enter the data shown in Table 5.4 in Sheet1. Enter formulas in the shaded cells to complete the spreadsheet.

1. The adjusted score is the score minus handicap.
2. Under/over par is the adjusted score minus course par.

   Assign the name coursepar to cell B3 and then use this name in the formula.

3. Sort the data in ascending order of under/over par.
4. Print the spreadsheet.
5. Save the spreadsheet as **Leader Board**

	A	B	C	D	E
1	**Leader Board**				
2					
3	**Course Par**	72			
4					
5	**Name**	**Handicap**	**Score**	**Adjusted Score**	**Under/ Over Par**
6	Paul Casey	6	76		
7	Henrik Stenson	10	85		
8	Lee Westwood	7	76		
9	Ernie Els	10	84		
10	Rory McIlroy	7	71		
11	Padraig Harrington	8	81		
12	Justin Rose	7	72		
13	Sergio Garcia	11	78		
14	Luke Donald	9	79		
15	Fredrik Jacobson	12	82		

Table 5.4

MODIFYING AN EXISTING CELL STYLE

In Chapter 3, we formatted our spreadsheets using the Cell Styles available in Excel. These styles can be customised to suit your own needs.

1. Open the *Leader Board* spreadsheet if it is not already open.
2. In the Home section of the Ribbon, click the Cell Styles button.
3. Right click Heading 2 and then select Modify from the pop-up menu, as shown in Figure 5.5.

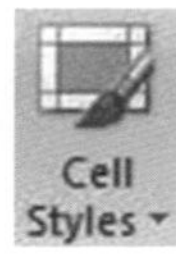

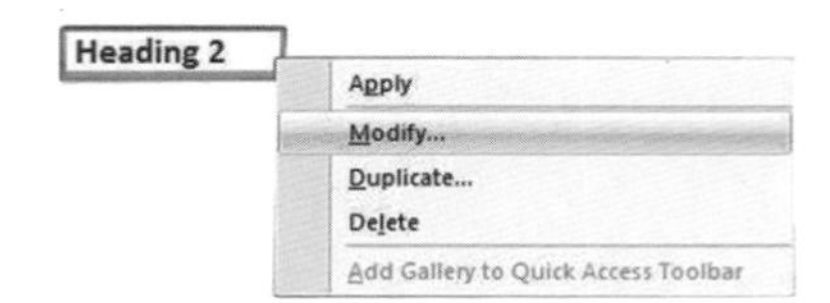

Figure 5.5: Modifying the Heading 2 cell style

4. In the Style dialog box, click the Format button.

Format...

5. In the Format Cells dialog box, select the formatting characteristics listed in Table 5.5.

Style Name	Heading 2
Font	Arial
Font Style	Bold
Size	16
Font Colour	Red, Accent2

Table 5.5

6. Click OK twice to apply these formatting characteristics to the Heading2 style.
7. Modify the Accent2 style to include the formatting characteristics listed in Table 5.6.

Style Name	Accent2
Font	Calibri
Font Style	Bold
Size	12

Table 5.6

8. Apply an outline border to the 20% Accent2 style.
9. Format the *Leader Board* spreadsheet using the styles listed in Table 5.7.

Range of Cells	Cell Style
A1	Heading 2
A3, A5:E5	Accent2
B3, A6:E15	20% – Accent2

Table 5.7

10. Save the *Leader Board* spreadsheet.

Sorting Spreadsheet Data Assignment Two

Create a new spreadsheet workbook and enter the data shown in Table 5.8 in Sheet1. Enter formulas in the shaded cells to complete the spreadsheet.

	A	B	C	D	E
1	**Telephone Charges by Department**				
2					
3	**Name**	**Department**	**Local Calls**	**International Calls**	**Total**
4	Nadeja Chlebowski	Sales	46.85	103.47	
5	Paul Harris	Admin	38.21	0	
6	Jessica Dunne	Sales	29.09	89.83	
7	Aidan Murphy	Finance	54.88	0	
8	Donal Nesdale	Sales	37.36	0	
9	Paula Clane	Admin	61.22	0	
10	Stephan Sobczak	Admin	50.84	0	
11	Joan Langton	Finance	46.04	0	
12	Maeve Rochford	Admin	33.97	0	
13	Mary Dunne	Finance	37.19	0	

Table 5.8

1. Calculate the total.
2. Sort the data first in ascending order of department and then in descending order of total.
3. Format all money amounts to currency.
4. Save the spreadsheet as **Telephone Charges by Department**
5. Rather than modifying the styles in the *Telephone Charges by Department* spreadsheet, we will link to the styles that we created in the *Leader Board* spreadsheet. Open the *Leader Board* spreadsheet.
6. In the *Telephone Charges by Department* spreadsheet, click the Cell Styles button in the Home section of the Ribbon

   Cell Styles

7. Click the Merge Styles button. Merge Styles...
8. In the Merge Styles dialog box, select *Leader Board.xlsx*. Click *Yes* to confirm that you want to merge styles that have the same name. This copies the styles from the *Leader Board* spreadsheet to the *Telephone Charges by Department* spreadsheet.

   Merge styles from: Leader Board.xlsx

9. Format data in the *Telephone Charges by Department* spreadsheet using the styles listed in Table 5.9.

Range of Cells	Cell Style
A1	Heading 1
A3:E3	Accent2
A4:E13	20% – Accent2

Table 5.9

10. Save the *Telephone Charges by Department* spreadsheet.

CUSTOM SORT ORDERS

Although the majority of sorts follow the natural order of the alphabet, there are some exceptions. Consider the days of the week. If we were to sort these alphabetically the resulting order would be Friday, Monday, Saturday, Sunday, Thursday, Tuesday and Wednesday. Sorting by months is another example where data doesn't follow the A to Z sort order (April would be the first month). Excel has a special Custom List facility to overcome this problem.

Worked Example One

Create a new spreadsheet workbook and enter the data shown in Table 5.10 in Sheet1.

	A	B	C
1		**Employee Details**	
2			
3	**Name**	**Department**	**Started**
4	Niamh O Leary	Sales	March
5	Martin Hegarty	Computer	January
6	Liz Hartnett	Admin	May
7	Colin Dunne	Production	March
8	Liam O Looney	Production	February
9	Eileen Flaherty	Sales	April
10	Eamonn Dineen	Admin	March
11	Siobhan Tully	Computer	January
12	Adriana Popescu	Production	April
13	Tom Evans	Computer	February
14	Sarah Mooney	Admin	March
15	Samantha Burke	Computer	May

Table 5.10

1. Select any cell in the range A4:C15.
2. Click the Sort & Filter button and select *Custom Sort* from the list.
3. Select *Started* from the *Sort by* drop-down list and then select *Custom List* from the *Order* drop-down list, as shown in Figure 5.6.

Figure 5.6 Custom Lists are used to sort by weekday or month names

4. Now select 'January, February, March, April' from the available custom lists (Figure 5.7).

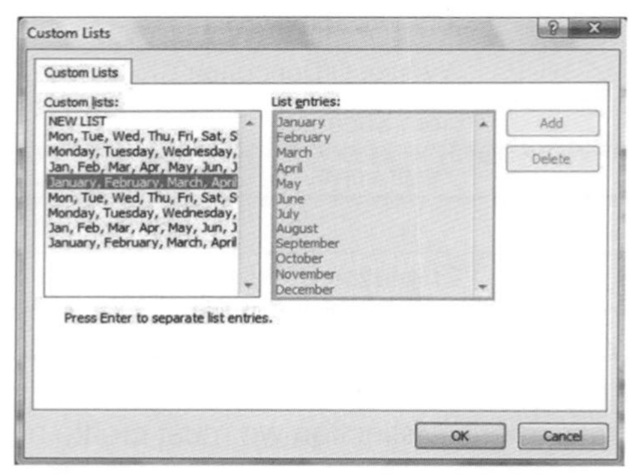

Figure 5.7 Excel's custom lists for sorting days and months

5. Click OK to apply the custom sort.
6. Merge styles from the *Leader Board* spreadsheet.
7. Format the data using the styles listed in Table 5.11.

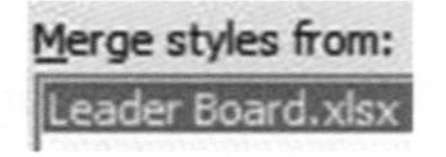

Range of Cells	Cell Style
A1	Heading 1
A3:C3	Accent2
A4:C15	20% – Accent2

Table 5.11

8. Save the spreadsheet as **Personnel File**

Worked Example Two

When we need to sort data in an order that isn't numerical or alphabetical and is not based on days of the week or months of the year, we must create our own custom sort order.

Create a new spreadsheet workbook and enter the data shown in Table 5.12 in Sheet1.

	A	B	C
1		**Web Design Results**	
2			
3	**Student Number**	**Student Name**	**Grade**
4	1	Paul Thornton	Merit
5	2	Avril Green	Distinction
6	3	Enrique Rivera	Fail
7	4	Cathy O Neill	Pass
8	5	Pauline Meehan	Merit
9	6	John Gallagher	Distinction
10	7	Bernard Tompkins	Merit
11	8	Yvonne O Donoghue	Merit
12	9	Tom Sheehan	Pass
13	10	Peter Ferns	Distinction

Table 5.12

If we sort the grades in ascending alphabetical order, they will appear as distinction, fail, merit, pass. If we sort them in descending alphabetical order they will appear as pass, merit, fail, distinction. To sort the data so that it appears in order of distinction, merit, pass, fail or fail, pass, merit, distinction we must create a custom sort order.

1. Select any cell in the range A4:C13.
2. Click the Sort & Filter button and select *Custom Sort* from the list.
3. Select *Grade* from the Sort by list and then select *Custom List.*
4. In the Custom Lists dialog box, type the new list in the *List entries* section, pressing Enter after each entry, and then click the Add button (Figure 5.8).

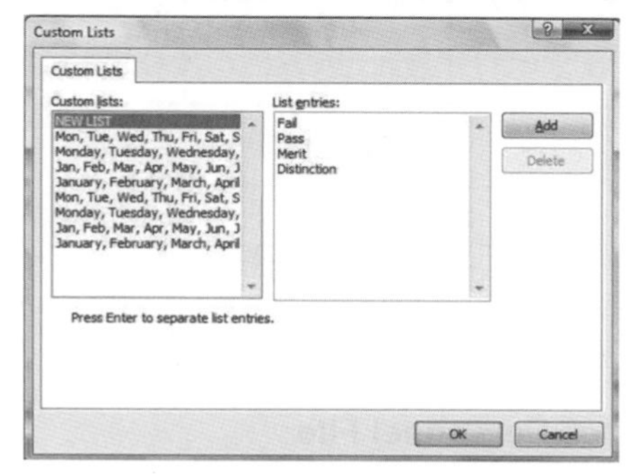

Figure 5.8 Creating your own custom sort

5. Click OK twice to implement the custom sort.
6. Merge styles from the *Leader Board* spreadsheet.
7. Format the data using the styles listed in Table 5.13.

Merge styles from:
Leader Board.xlsx

Range of Cells	Cell Style
A1	Heading 1
A3:C3	Accent2
A4:C13	20% – Accent2

Table 5.13

8. Save the spreadsheet as **Web Design Results**

Sorting Spreadsheet Data Assignment Three

Create a new spreadsheet workbook and enter the data shown in Table 5.14 in Sheet1.

	A	B	C	D
1	**Into the West Adventures**			
2				
3	**Province**	**Product**	**Customer**	**Quantity**
4	Munster	Kayak	Exo Ltd	5
5	Connaught	Tent	Outdoor Action	8
6	Leinster	Paddle	Green Sports	20
7	Connaught	Buoyancy Aid	Green Sports	30
8	Ulster	Wind Jacket	Outdoor Action	25
9	Leinster	Tent	Exo Ltd	7
10	Ulster	Sleeping Bag	Exo Ltd	30
11	Munster	Boots	Westward Bound	20
12	Leinster	Kayak	Green Sports	2
13	Munster	Tent	Westward Bound	6
14	Leinster	Wind Jacket	Outdoor Action	17

Table 5.14

1. Create a custom sort in the following order: Leinster, Ulster, Munster, Connaught.
2. Sort the data using this custom sort.

3. Merge styles from the *Leader Board* spreadsheet.
4. Format the data using the styles listed in Table 5.15.

Merge styles from:
Leader Board.xlsx

Range of Cells	Cell Style
A1	Heading 1
A3:D3	Accent2
A4:D14	20% – Accent2

Table 5.15

5. Save the spreadsheet as **Into the West Adventures**

FILTER SORTS

Filtering data allows you to display data matching certain conditions and to hide data that doesn't meet these conditions. This allows you to focus on specific data in your spreadsheet. For example, you could filter out everything except sales in the Dublin region using a Filter Sort.

Worked Example

1. Open the *Telephone Charges by Department* spreadsheet.
2. Select any cell in the range *A4:E13*.
3. Click the Sort & Filter button and select *Filter* from the list. A drop-down arrow appears to the right of each column heading.
4. Click the drop-down arrow in the Department column. Remove the tick from the Finance check-box.
5. Click OK. The Finance department has been filtered out of the list.
6. Click the drop-down arrow in the Local Calls column and select Number Filters from the list.
7. Select *Greater Than* from the list of number filters.

Filter

(Select All)
Admin
Finance
Sales

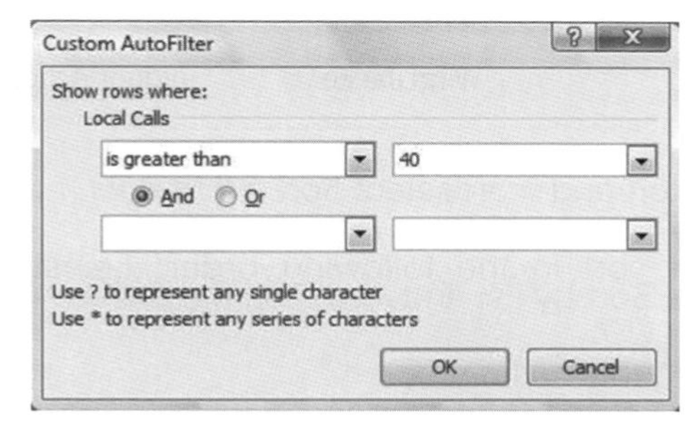

Figure 5.9 Filtering out any local calls costing less than €40

8. Enter *40*, as shown in Figure 5.9, and then click OK to apply the filter. Local calls costing €40 or less are no longer displayed.
9. Save the *Telephone Charges by Department* spreadsheet.

Sorting Data by Columns – Worked Example

By default, Excel sorts data row by row. In some cases, you may need to sort data by columns.

Create a new spreadsheet workbook and enter the data shown in Table 5.16 in Sheet1.

	A	B	C	D	E	F	G	H
1	**Euro Conversion Rates**							
2								
3	**Country**	USA	Japan	Britain	Canada	Norway	South Africa	Russia
4	**Currency**	Dollar	Yen	Pound	Dollar	Kroner	Rand	Rouble
5	**Rate**	1.3891	134.351	0.8452	1.562	8.9223	11.115	43.383
6								

Table 5.16

1. Format all rates so that they display three places of decimals.
2. Highlight B3:H5.
3. Click the Sort & Filter button and select *Custom Sort* from the list.

Figure 5.10

4. Click the Options button and then select *Sort left to right*, as shown in Figure 5.10. Click OK.
5. Select *Row 3* from the Sort by list and *A to Z* as the order.
6. Click OK to implement the sort.
7. Merge styles from the *Leader Board* spreadsheet.

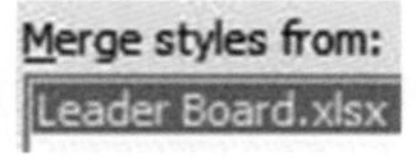

8. Format the data using the styles listed in Table 5.17.

Range of Cells	Cell Style
A1	Heading 1
A3:A5	Accent2
B3:H5	20% – Accent2

Table 5.17

9. Save the spreadsheet as **Exchange Rates**

N When sorting by columns, don't highlight the row headings. In the Exchange Rates spreadsheet *Country*, *Currency* and *Rate* should not be highlighted.

Sorting Spreadsheet Data Assignment Four

Create a new spreadsheet workbook and enter the data shown in Table 5.18 in Sheet1.

	A	B	C	D	E	F
1	**Seasonal Sales Data**					
2						
3		M208	X609	A236	W991	B101
4	**Summer**	1057	3068	2249	109	3695
5	**Winter**	2598	512	3077	5028	1012
6						

Table 5.18

1. Sort the data in ascending order of row 3 from left to right.

T When sorting data by columns don't include the descriptions in the column to the left of the data that you're sorting.

2. Merge styles from the *Leader Board* spreadsheet.
3. Format the data using the styles listed in Table 5.19.

Range of Cells	Cell Style
A1	Heading 1
B3:F3	Accent2
A4:F5	20% – Accent2

Table 5.19

4. Save the spreadsheet as **Seasonal Sales Data**

CHAPTER 5 SUMMARY

1. Basic Concepts

Alphabetical Sort	Text is rearranged in ascending (A to Z) or descending (Z to A) order.
Numerical Sort	Numbers are rearranged in ascending (Smallest to Largest) or descending (Largest to Smallest) order.
Custom Sort	Where data doesn't follow a natural sort order, such as weekday names, a custom sort can be used.
Filter Sort	This allows you to focus on specific data in your spreadsheet by hiding the data you are not currently interested in.

2. Potential Pitfalls

- If you are sorting by one column, don't highlight that column as this may result in a sorting error.
- Don't include blank rows or columns in the data you are sorting as this may cause some data to be omitted from the sort.
- Emphasise your column headings in bold print to ensure they are not included in the sort.

SORTING SPREADSHEET DATA REVIEW QUESTIONS

Answers to the review questions are available on www.gillmacmillan.ie

1. Write down the four types of sort that are available in Excel.
   (i) ______________________________
   (ii) ______________________________
   (iii) ______________________________
   (iv) ______________________________
2. If the list 'Monday, Tuesday, Wednesday, Thursday, Friday' is sorted in ascending order, what will the resulting order be?
   ____
3. In the Sort dialog box, you can add a secondary sort by clicking the ______________ button.
4. Ticking the ____________________ check box ensures that Excel will not include column headings in a sort.

5. A ______________ enables you to hide data you are not currently interested in.
6. To display numbers within a specific range, select the ________________ option from the Filter drop-down list.
7. If you include blank _______ or _________ in your data, Excel may not include all the data in the sort.
8. Rearrange the following list of names in ascending alphabetical order.

   Alex Smith

   Adriana Vega

   Alan Dunne

   Alison Evans

   Adam Murphy

   Alicia Bernard

   Alan Smith
9. Give two examples of sorts which do not follow a natural alphabetical order.

   (i) ____

   (ii) ____
10. When sorting by columns instead of rows, you should never highlight the

    ____

SECTION 2

Intermediate and Advanced Spreadsheet Assignments

Symbols used in this book:

Tip

Note

Rule

Shortcut

Hint

Important Point

6 Spreadsheet Protection and Macros

In Chapter 6, you will learn how to:
- Restrict access to specific cells in a worksheet
- Prevent formulas and functions from being displayed in the formula bar
- Prevent users from deleting, renaming, moving, hiding or unhiding worksheets
- Automate repetitive tasks with macros
- Run macros from shortcut keys and command buttons.

WHAT IS SPREADSHEET PROTECTION?

Each spreadsheet workbook consists of a number of worksheets. You can safeguard your spreadsheet data by protecting the workbook as well as the individual worksheets contained within the workbook.

1. Protecting the workbook prevents people deleting, renaming, moving, hiding or unhiding worksheets contained within the workbook.
2. Protecting individual worksheets prevents people deleting important data such as formulas, functions and headings stored in the worksheet.

In order to understand how worksheet protection works we will divide the cells in a worksheet into four categories:

1. Cells where data is entered
2. Cells containing formulas/functions
3. Cells containing headings or numbers that rarely change
4. Cells where no data entry occurs.

The example in Table 6.1 is the spreadsheet named *Rock Café*, which was created in Chapter 2.

1. Data entry occurs in the shaded cells.
2. Formulas/functions are stored in cells as displayed
3. Headings have been entered in cells with a heavy border. The capacities of the Stalls, Circle and Balcony have also been entered in cells with a heavy border. Once entered in the worksheet, these numbers remain fixed.
4. All of the remaining cells are unused. No data entry occurs in these cells.

	A	B	C	D	E	F	G	H	I	J
1	Rock Café								Date	=today()
2										
3								Stalls	300	
4								Circle	350	
5								Balcony	250	
6										
7	Artist	Date	Stalls	%Full	Circle	%Full	Balcony	% Full	Total Tickets	%Full
8	The Blizzards	08/09/2010	150	=c8/i3	300	=e8/i4	220	=g8/i5	=c8+e8+g8	=i8/sum(i3:i5)
9	U2	10/09/2010	276	=c9/i3	245	=e9/i4	141	=g9/i5	=c9+e9+g9	=i9/sum(i3:i5)
10	Mundy	11/09/2010	290	=c10/i3	307	=e10/i4	209	=g10/i5	=c10+e10+g10	=i10/sum(i3:i5)
11	Duffy	14/09/2010	250	=c11/i3	312	=e11/i4	196	=g11/i5	=c11+e11+g11	=i11/sum(i3:i5)
12	Arcade Fire	18/09/2010	300	=c12/i3	350	=e12/i4	250	=g12/i5	=c12+e12+g12	=i12/sum(i3:i5)
13	Kings of Leon	19/09/2010	100	=c13/i3	267	=e13/i4	233	=g13/i5	=c13+e13+g13	=i13/sum(i3:i5)
14	Mick Flannery	20/09/2010	180	=c14/i3	255	=e14/i4	200	=g14/i5	=c14+e14+g14	=i14/sum(i3:i5)
15										
16	Total Sales		=sum(c8:c14)		=sum(e8:e14)		=sum(g8:g14)			
17	Average Sales		=average(c8:c14)		=average(e8:e14)		=average(g8:g14)			
18	Highest Sales		=max(c8:c14)		=max(e8:e14)		=max(g8:g14)			
19	Lowest Sales		=min(c8:c14)		=min(e8:e14)		=min(g8:g14)			
20	Number of Performances		=count(c8:c14)							

Table 6.1

In the *Rock Cafe* spreadsheet, the objective of worksheet protection is to allow the spreadsheet user to enter data in the shaded cells and to prevent the spreadsheet user entering data in all other cells. Using worksheet protection we can also hide the formulas and functions so that they don't appear in the formula bar.

PURPOSE OF WORKSHEET PROTECTION

The main reasons for protecting an Excel worksheet are summarised below.

- To restrict spreadsheet users to accessing a limited part of the worksheet where data entry occurs. This helps to prevent people typing data into the wrong cells or deleting formulas/functions or headings.
- To prevent spreadsheet users changing the way the worksheet is formatted.
- To prevent spreadsheet users from adding new rows or columns to the worksheet.
- To hide formulas and functions so that they are not visible to the spreadsheet user.

LOCKED AND UNLOCKED CELLS

Before protecting a worksheet, it is important to understand the concept of locked cells and unlocked cells. Each time you create a new Excel workbook, the default setting is that all cells in all worksheets are locked. Whether a cell is locked or unlocked doesn't actually have any effect until a particular worksheet is protected. Once that worksheet is protected, data can no longer be entered in locked cells. Before turning on spreadsheet protection, it is important to unlock any cells where data entry occurs.

If you don't protect your spreadsheet, the fact that the cells are locked makes no difference to the functionality of the spreadsheet. It's only when you turn on spreadsheet protection that the difference between locked and unlocked cells has an effect. This is summarised in Table 6.2.

	Effect of Locked Cells	**Effect of Unlocked Cells**
Spreadsheet Protection **OFF**	None	None
Spreadsheet Protection **ON**	Data entry not permitted	Data entry permitted

Table 6.2

Important Points

1. All cells in a worksheet are locked by default.
2. When a worksheet is protected, the spreadsheet user will not be able to type data into locked cells.
3. Before protecting a worksheet, unlock any cells you want the spreadsheet user to have access to, leaving all other cells locked. Protecting a worksheet without unlocking cells means that you won't be able to enter any data in that worksheet.
4. The fact that cells are locked or unlocked doesn't affect the spreadsheet user in any way until spreadsheet protection is turned on. Once the spreadsheet is protected, the spreadsheet user will only have access to cells that have been unlocked.

Figure 6.1 displays the *Weekly Payroll* spreadsheet created in Chapter 1.

	A	B	C	D	E	F
1	PAYE Rate	20%	PRSI Rate	3.5%		
2						
3	Employee Name	Gross Pay	PAYE	PRSI	TOTAL	Net Pay
4	John O Neill	€ 601.04	€ 120.21	€ 21.04	€ 141.24	€ 459.80
5	Mary Doyle	€ 553.77	€ 110.75	€ 19.38	€ 130.14	€ 423.63
6	Peter Hennessy	€ 767.43	€ 153.49	€ 26.86	€ 180.35	€ 587.08
7	Sinead Murray	€ 595.83	€ 119.17	€ 20.85	€ 140.02	€ 455.81
8	Noreen Keogh	€ 555.98	€ 111.20	€ 19.46	€ 130.66	€ 425.32
9	Susan Donovan	€ 666.22	€ 133.24	€ 23.32	€ 156.56	€ 509.66
10	Tom Larkin	€ 780.01	€ 156.00	€ 27.30	€ 183.30	€ 596.71
11						

Figure 6.1 Weekly Payroll spreadsheet from Chapter 1

In Figure 6.1, we want to set up spreadsheet protection so that the spreadsheet user can type data into the range *A4:B10* but is prevented from typing data anywhere else. This is to facilitate the updating of employee data as new employees join the company as well as the updating of gross pay when wage rates change. To allow access to the range *A4:B10*, these cells must be unlocked. All the other cells in the worksheet remain locked (*remember, all cells are locked by default when you create a new spreadsheet*). Once spreadsheet protection is turned on, data can only be entered in the unlocked cells *(A4:B10)* and cannot be entered in any other cells.

HIDDEN CELLS

When a spreadsheet cell contains a formula or a function, the formula or function is displayed in the formula bar when the cell is selected.

C4 | fx | =B4*B1

	A	B	C	D	E	F
1	PAYE Rate	20%	PRSI Rate	3.5%		
2						
3	Employee Name	Gross Pay	PAYE	PRSI	TOTAL	Net Pay
4	John O Neill	€ 301.04	€ 60.21	€ 10.54	€ 70.74	€ 230.30
5	Mary Doyle	€ 253.77	€ 50.75	€ 8.88	€ 59.64	€ 194.13
6	Peter Hennessy	€ 267.43	€ 53.49	€ 9.36	€ 62.85	€ 204.58
7	Sinead Murray	€ 195.83	€ 39.17	€ 6.85	€ 46.02	€ 149.81
8	Noreen Keogh	€ 155.98	€ 31.20	€ 5.46	€ 36.66	€ 119.32
9	Susan Donovan	€ 266.22	€ 53.24	€ 9.32	€ 62.56	€ 203.66
10	Tom Larkin	€ 180.01	€ 36.00	€ 6.30	€ 42.30	€ 137.71
11						

Figure 6.2 The formula bar displays the formula stored in the selected cell

In Figure 6.2, C4 is selected. The formula =B4*B1, which is stored in C4, is automatically displayed in the formula bar. Spreadsheet protection can be used to hide formulas and functions so that they don't appear in the formula bar and are no longer visible to the spreadsheet user. We can prevent formulas and functions being displayed in the formula bar in two steps:

1. Select all cells containing formulas and functions and turn on the Hidden property.
2. Protect the worksheet.

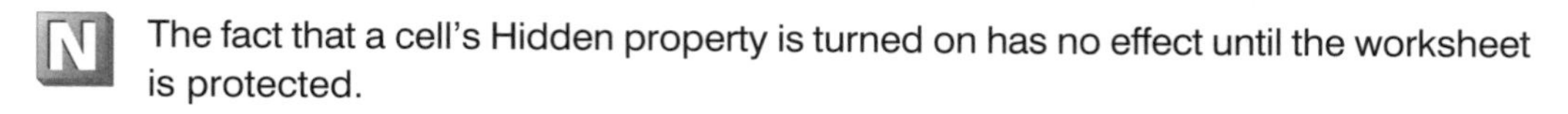

The fact that a cell's Hidden property is turned on has no effect until the worksheet is protected.

C4 fx

	A	B	C	D	E	F
1	PAYE Rate	20%	PRSI Rate	3.5%		
2						
3	Employee Name	Gross Pay	PAYE	PRSI	TOTAL	Net Pay
4	John O Neill	€ 301.04	€ 60.21	€ 10.54	€ 70.74	€ 230.30
5	Mary Doyle	€ 253.77	€ 50.75	€ 8.88	€ 59.64	€ 194.13
6	Peter Hennessy	€ 267.43	€ 53.49	€ 9.36	€ 62.85	€ 204.58
7	Sinead Murray	€ 195.83	€ 39.17	€ 6.85	€ 46.02	€ 149.81
8	Noreen Keogh	€ 155.98	€ 31.20	€ 5.46	€ 36.66	€ 119.32
9	Susan Donovan	€ 266.22	€ 53.24	€ 9.32	€ 62.56	€ 203.66
10	Tom Larkin	€ 180.01	€ 36.00	€ 6.30	€ 42.30	€ 137.71
11						

Figure 6.3 The formula in C4 is no longer displayed in the formula bar

In Figure 6.3, the Hidden property for cells containing formulas has been turned on and the worksheet has been protected. Notice that the formula *=B4*B1*, which calculates John O Neill's PAYE, is no longer displayed.

PROTECTING A WORKSHEET

Worked example

Protecting a worksheet requires three steps:

- Unlock cells where data entry is permitted.
- Turn on the Hidden property for all cells containing formulas or functions.
- Turn on worksheet protection.

Open the *Rock Café* spreadsheet (created in Chapter 2 and modified in Chapter 4).

Stage 1: Unlock Cells

1. Highlight all cells where data will be entered, as shown in Figure 6.4.

Multiple ranges can be selected by holding down the *CTRL* key while dragging with the mouse.

	A	B	C	D	E	F	G	H	I	J
1				Rock Café					Date	05/09/2010
2										
3								Stalls	300	
4								Circle	350	
5								Balcony	250	
6										
7	Artist	Date	Stalls	%Full	Circle	%Full	Balcony	%Full	Total Tickets	%Full
8	The Blizzards	08/09/2010	150	50%	300	86%	220	88%	670	74%
9	U2	10/09/2010	276	92%	245	70%	141	56%	662	74%
10	Mundy	11/09/2010	290	97%	307	88%	209	84%	806	90%
11	Duffy	14/09/2010	250	83%	312	89%	196	78%	758	84%
12	Arcade Fire	18/09/2010	300	100%	350	100%	250	100%	900	100%
13	Kings of Leon	19/09/2010	100	33%	267	76%	233	93%	600	67%
14	Mick Flannery	20/09/2010	180	60%	255	73%	200	80%	635	71%
15										
16	Total Sales		1546		2036		1449			
17	Average Sales		221		291		207			
18	Highest Sales		300		350		250			
19	Lowest Sales		100		245		141			
20	Number of Performances		7							
21										

Figure 6.4 The selected cells must be unlocked before protecting the worksheet

2. In the Home section of the Ribbon, select **Format Cells** from the Format drop-down menu.
3. Click the Protection tab and unlock the selected cells by unticking the *Locked* check box (Figure 6.5).

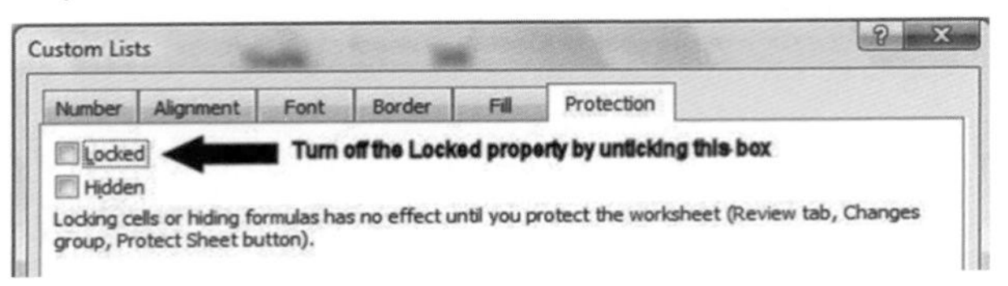

Figure 6.5 Unlock the selected cells by removing the tick from the Locked check box

Stage 2: Turn on the Hidden Property for Cells Containing Formulas or Functions

1. Highlight all cells containing formulas or functions, as shown in Figure 6.6.

	A	B	C	D	E	F	G	H	I	J
1				Rock Café					Date	05/09/2010
2										
3								Stalls	300	
4								Circle	350	
5								Balcony	250	
6										
7	Artist	Date	Stalls	%Full	Circle	%Full	Balcony	%Full	Total Tickets	%Full
8	The Blizzards	08/09/2010	150	50%	300	86%	220	88%	670	74%
9	U2	10/09/2010	276	92%	245	70%	141	56%	662	74%
10	Mundy	11/09/2010	290	97%	307	88%	209	84%	806	90%
11	Duffy	14/09/2010	250	83%	312	89%	196	78%	758	84%
12	Arcade Fire	18/09/2010	300	100%	350	100%	250	100%	900	100%
13	Kings of Leon	19/09/2010	100	33%	267	76%	233	93%	600	67%
14	Mick Flannery	20/09/2010	180	60%	255	73%	200	80%	635	71%
15										
16	Total Sales		1546		2036		1449			
17	Average Sales		221		291		207			
18	Highest Sales		300		350		250			
19	Lowest Sales		100		245		141			
20	Number of Performances		7							
21										

Figure 6.6 Cells containing formulas or functions have been highlighted

2. In the Home section of the Ribbon, select **Format Cells** from the Format drop-down menu.
3. Click the Protection tab and turn on the Hidden property for the selected cells by ticking the *Hidden* check box (Figure 6.7).

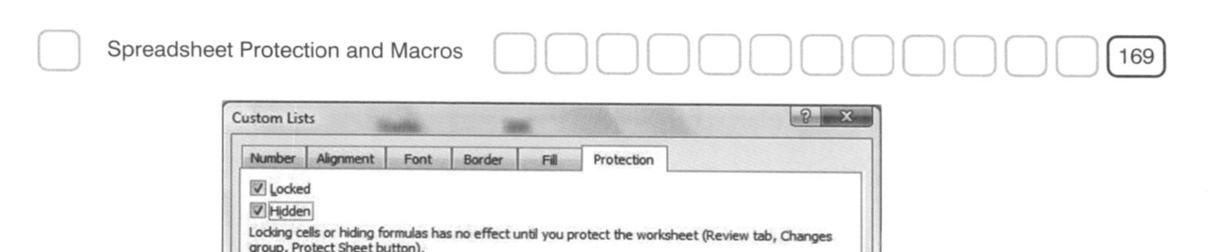

Figure 6.7 Formulas and functions can be hidden by turning on the Hidden property

N These cells should remain locked as they are not data entry cells.

Stage 3: Turn on Worksheet Protection

1. In the Home section of the Ribbon, select **Protect Sheet** from the Format drop-down menu. The Protect Sheet dialog box is displayed (Figure 6.8).

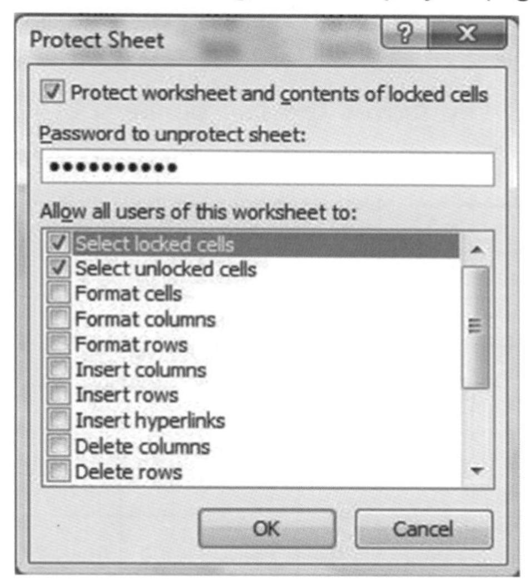

Figure 6.8 The Protect Sheet dialog box allows you to specify what sections of the worksheet can be accessed after the worksheet is protected

2. Enter your own password and then re-enter it to confirm the password. Click OK to protect the worksheet.
3. Save the *Rock Café* spreadsheet.

Using a password prevents someone turning off worksheet protection which would then give them full access to your worksheet. Note that the default setting for protection in Excel is to allow the spreadsheet user to select locked cells. However, the spreadsheet user will only be able to enter data in the unlocked cells.

N You can also protect the worksheet by clicking the Protect Sheet button in the Review section of the Ribbon.

Test your Spreadsheet Protection

1. Open the *Rock Café* spreadsheet if it is not already open.
2. Highlight the column headings (*A7:J7*) and press Delete. Excel will not allow you to delete data from these cells because they are locked.
3. Select cell I8. Although this cell contains a formula, it is no longer displayed in the formula bar.
4. Select cell A1. Change the font style to Verdana and the font size to 48. This has no effect. Notice also that most of the buttons in the Home section of the Ribbon have been dimmed out.
5. Highlight *A8:C14* and press Delete. Excel allows you to delete data from these cells because they have been unlocked.
6. Delete data in E8:E14 and G8:G14. Enter new data displayed in bold print in Table 6.3.

Pressing the TAB key moves the cell pointer between unlocked cells in a protected worksheet.

	A	B	C	D	E	F	G	H	I	J
1	Rock Cafe								Date	
2										
3								Stalls	300	
4								Circle	350	
5								Balcony	250	
6										
7	Artist	Date	Stalls	%Full	Circle	%Full	Balcony	% Full	Total Tickets	%Full
8	**Coldplay**	**03/10/2010**	**288**		**306**		**244**			
9	**Gomez**	**05/10/2010**	**275**		**323**		**239**			
10	**James Blunt**	**06/10/2010**	**280**		**344**		**231**			
11	**Alicia Keys**	**08/10/2010**	**298**		**350**		**247**			
12	**Bell X1**	**09/10/2010**	**249**		**298**		**132**			
13	**MGMT**	**10/10/2010**	**300**		**350**		**250**			
14	**Nelly Furtado**	**12/10/2010**	**280**		**325**		**250**			

Table 6.3

If you need to increase the width of a column so that new data is displayed fully, you will have to unprotect the worksheet, adjust column width and then re-protect the worksheet.

7. Check the Sales Chart to see that it reflects the new data.
8. Save the *Rock Café* spreadsheet.

PROTECTING THE WORKBOOK

By turning on worksheet protection, you are protecting the data stored in the worksheet. However, you are not protecting the worksheet itself. It's a bit like turning on the house alarm but leaving the front door wide open. Although data in locked cells can't be deleted and the formulas and functions are hidden, it is still possible to delete, rename, move or hide the worksheet itself. These options, displayed in Figure 6.9, can be accessed by right clicking the worksheet tab.

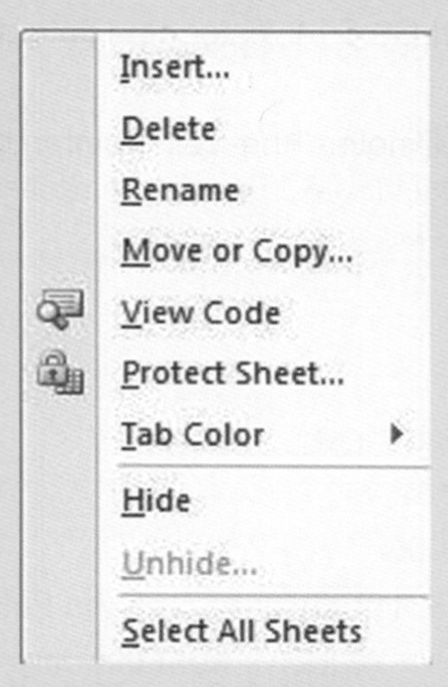

Figure 6.9 Although data in the worksheet is protected, it's still possible to delete the worksheet

From Figure 6.9, it is clear that it is still possible to delete, move, copy or hide the worksheet or insert a new worksheet as all of these options are still available in the pop-up menu. To restrict what the spreadsheet user can select from this pop-up menu you should always protect the workbook after you have protected the worksheet. Once the workbook is protected these options will no longer be available, as shown in Figure 6.10.

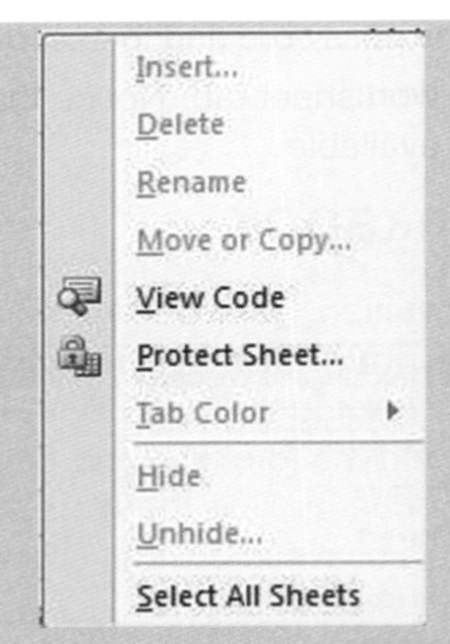

Figure 6.10 Once the workbook is protected, most options are no longer available

In Figure 6.10, the Insert, Delete, Rename, Move or Copy, Tab Color, Hide and Unhide options are not available. This is because the workbook has been protected.

Worked Example

1. Open the *Rock Café* spreadsheet.
2. Rename Sheet1 as *Ticket Sales*
3. Delete all unused worksheets.
4. Click the Review tab in the Ribbon, then click the Protect Workbook button.
5. Select *Protect Structure and Windows* from the drop-down menu. The *Protect Structure and Windows* dialog box is displayed (Figure 6.11).

You can quickly access the *Protect Structure and Windows* settings using the *ALT+R+PW+W* keyboard combination.

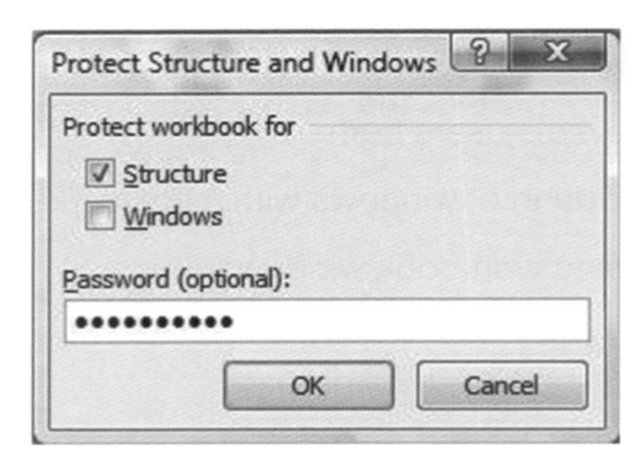

Figure 6.11

6. Enter a password. Confirm the password and then click OK to protect the workbook.
7. Right click the *Ticket Sales* worksheet tab. Notice that most of the options in the pop-up menu are no longer available.

Protecting Workbooks – Additional Points

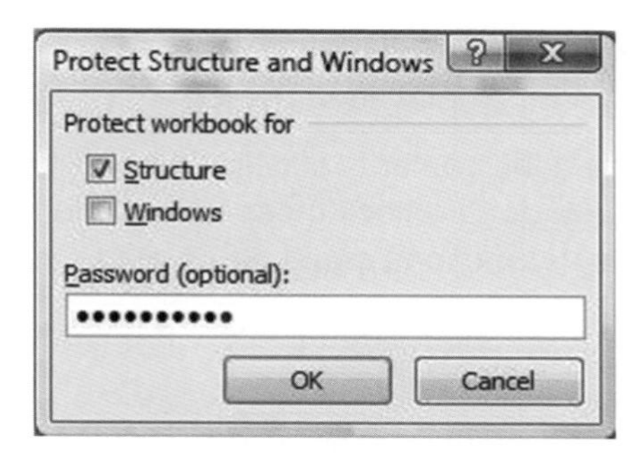

Figure 6.12

The Protect Structure and Windows dialog box (Figure 6.12) offers two levels of protection for a spreadsheet workbook.

Structure

The Structure check box is ticked by default. When a worksheet is protected for structure, users are prevented from:

- Viewing worksheets that you have hidden
- Moving, deleting, hiding or renaming worksheets
- Inserting new worksheets or chart sheets
- Moving or copying worksheets to another workbook
- Recording new macros.

Windows

Ticking this check box prevents users from:

- Changing the size or position of windows within the workbook
- Moving, resizing or closing workbook windows.

Spreadsheet Protection Assignment One

1. Open the spreadsheet named *Ticket Sales Galway–Dublin Route* (created in Chapter 3).
2. Implement worksheet protection so that data can only be entered in cell A1 and in the range B5:H9 in the *0745*, *1100* and *1510* worksheets. No data entry is permitted in the *Weekly Ticket Sales* worksheet.
3. Formulas should not be displayed in the formula bar of any worksheet.

T When you're hiding the contents of cells that contain formulas or functions, make sure that you don't unlock these cells. Unlocking them would mean that the formulas or functions could be deleted.

4. Delete any unused worksheets and protect the workbook for structure and windows.
5. Erase data from unlocked cells in the *0745*, *1100* and *1510* sheets.

N At this point you shouldn't be able to delete formulas, functions or headings.

6. Enter the data displayed in bold print in Table 6.4 in the *0745* worksheet.

	A	B	C	D	E	F	G	H
1	**Week 2 Ticket Sales**							
2	Galway–Dublin departing 07:45							
3								
4		Galway	Athenry	Ballinasloe	Athlone	Tullamore	Portarlington	Kildare
5	Monday	**241**	**40**	**61**	**100**	**89**	**76**	**172**
6	Tuesday	**168**	**25**	**42**	**89**	**90**	**54**	**145**
7	Wednesday	**145**	**20**	**38**	**70**	**87**	**53**	**140**
8	Thursday	**159**	**23**	**39**	**75**	**82**	**49**	**155**
9	Friday	**221**	**25**	**45**	**88**	**106**	**82**	**195**

Table 6.4

7. Enter the data displayed in bold print in Table 6.5 in the *1100* worksheet.

	A	B	C	D	E	F	G	H
1	**Week 2 Ticket Sales**							
2	Galway–Dublin departing 11:00							
3								
4		Galway	Athenry	Ballinasloe	Athlone	Tullamore	Portarlington	Kildare
5	Monday	**61**	**12**	**24**	**37**	**21**	**25**	**44**
6	Tuesday	**45**	**5**	**19**	**25**	**31**	**12**	**36**
7	Wednesday	**31**	**2**	**10**	**32**	**26**	**14**	**23**
8	Thursday	**34**	**1**	**10**	**23**	**33**	**17**	**29**
9	Friday	**76**	**6**	**22**	**28**	**31**	**21**	**38**

Table 6.5

8. Enter the data displayed in bold print in Table 6.6 in the *1510* worksheet.

	A	B	C	D	E	F	G	H
1	**Week 2 Ticket Sales**							
2	Galway–Dublin departing 15:10							
3								
4		Galway	Athenry	Ballinasloe	Athlone	Tullamore	Portarlington	Kildare
5	Monday	**47**	**12**	**14**	**23**	**24**	**28**	**45**
6	Tuesday	**39**	**6**	**1**	**12**	**25**	**21**	**36**
7	Wednesday	**30**	**8**	**4**	**8**	**10**	**19**	**42**
8	Thursday	**22**	**8**	**8**	**13**	**19**	**23**	**44**
9	Friday	**36**	**12**	**20**	**31**	**36**	**29**	**60**

Table 6.6

9. Turn off both workbook and worksheet protection. Select the *Weekly Ticket Sales* worksheet and create a column chart using data in the range A4:H9. Information relating to chart setup is displayed in Table 6.7.

Chart Type	3-D Clustered Column
Chart Title	Weekly Ticket Sales by Station
Vertical Axis Title	Tickets Sold
Chart Position	Separate chart sheet named *Sales Chart*

Table 6.7

10. Re-protect the *Weekly Ticket Sales* worksheet and the workbook. Click the Save button to save the changes.

SPREADSHEET MACROS

What is a Macro?

Did you ever record yourself using a tape recorder, digital dictaphone or other recording device? If you did, you would have started by pressing the record button. Any sounds made were recorded until you pressed the stop button. When the recording is played back the sounds are recreated exactly as they occurred during recording.

A macro works in the same way, the only difference being that instead of recording and playing back sounds, a macro records and plays back spreadsheet tasks such as formatting and copying. When a macro is played back, all the tasks that were recorded are carried out in an instant. This is where macros are really useful – they can greatly reduce the amount of time spent on mundane and repetitive spreadsheet tasks by automating tasks that are frequently carried out.

MACROS – SECURITY ISSUES

Macros can contain viruses. If you create a macro on your own PC, you can be certain that the macro doesn't contain a virus. However, if you open an Excel spreadsheet containing a macro that was created by somebody else on a different PC, there is a possibility that this macro may contain a virus. Because macros can contain viruses Excel has a number of security levels dealing specifically with macros. These are displayed in Figure 6.13.

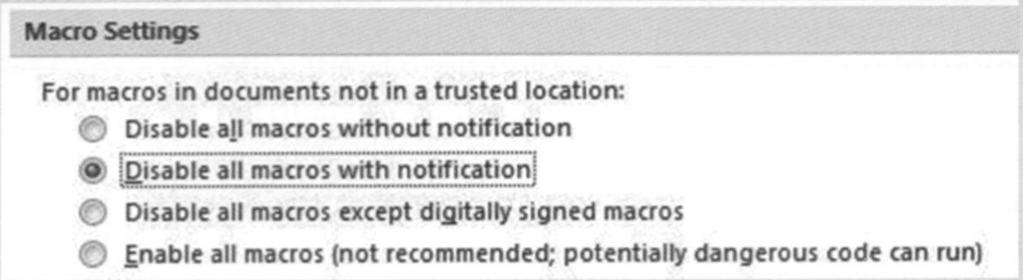

Macro Settings

For macros in documents not in a trusted location:

- ○ Disable all macros without notification
- ● Disable all macros with notification
- ○ Disable all macros except digitally signed macros
- ○ Enable all macros (not recommended; potentially dangerous code can run)

Figure 6.13 Macro security settings in Excel

The default macro setting is *Disable all macros with notification*. This means that macros are prevented from running and that Excel will give you a security warning if it finds a macro in a workbook created by someone else. You can choose which macros to enable on a case by case basis. It is okay to allow a macro to run as long as you are absolutely sure the macro came from a trusted source. If you make a mistake here, your PC could be infected with a virus.

The macro settings are accessed by clicking the Developer tab in the Ribbon. The Developer tab is not displayed in the Ribbon by default.

To display the Developer tab, click the Microsoft Office button and select Excel Options.

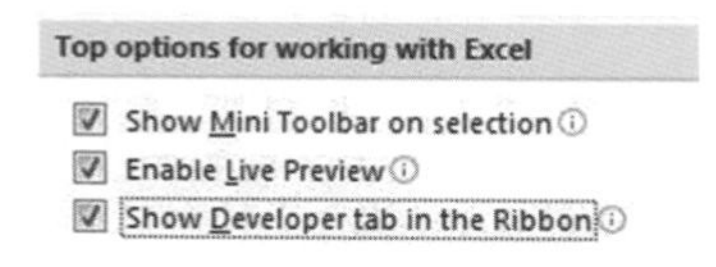

Figure 6.14: Displaying the Developer tab

In Excel 2010, the Office button has been replaced by the File menu.

In the Excel Options dialog box, tick the *Show Developer tab in the Ribbon* check box, as shown in Figure 6.14.

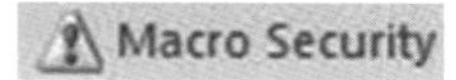

In the Developer section of the Ribbon, click the Macro Security button. The Macro Settings (Figure 6.13) are displayed.

DIGITAL SIGNATURES

In Excel 2007, you can digitally sign a workbook or a macro. If you receive a workbook or a macro with a digital signature, you are guaranteed that it originated from the signer and that it hasn't been altered since the digital signature was created. Before you can digitally sign Excel workbooks, you must obtain a digital certificate from a specialist company, such as Avoco or secure2trust. You will be charged a fee for this service. The majority of home Excel users do not use digital signatures, as they are expensive.

To find out more about companies providing digital certificates, select the Insert tab from the Ribbon and click the *Signature Line* icon. Select *Add Signature Services* from the list. This will automatically display a web page listing companies providing digital certificates.

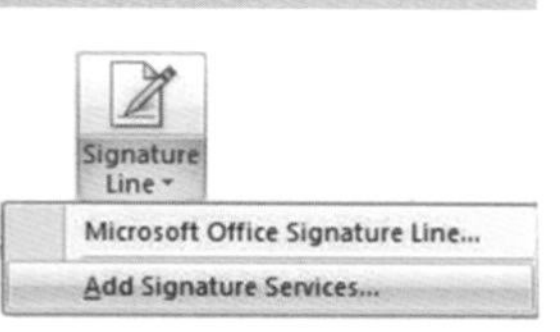

You can quickly access the *Add Signature Services* options using the *ALT+N+G+A* keyboard combination.

Creating a Macro – Worked Example

In the following example we'll create a macro that will generate an invoice heading for a computer supplies company.

1. Create a new spreadsheet workbook.
2. In the Developer section of the Ribbon, click the Macro Security button. Select the Enable all macros setting.

You can quickly access the *Macro Security* settings using the *ALT+L+AS* keyboard combination.

3. Select cell A2.
4. To start recording a new macro, click the View tab in the Ribbon and then click the drop-down arrow of the Macros button. Select **Record Macro** from the drop-down list. *(From this point on each keyboard and mouse action will be recorded by Excel in a Visual Basic program. The recording will continue until you click the Stop Recording button.)*

You can quickly access the *Record Macro* dialog box using the *ALT+W+M+R* keyboard combination.

5. Enter *invoiceheader* as the name of the macro.
6. Enter the letter *e* as the shortcut key (this means that once the macro is recorded, it can be played back by holding down the *CTRL* key and typing e).

Excel will not allow you to include a space in a macro name.

7. Click OK to start recording the macro. The Stop Recording button appears in the taskbar at the bottom left of the screen.
8. Select cell A1. Type Computer Suppliers Ltd and press Enter.
9. With the cell pointer in A1, increase the font size to 16 and change the font colour to blue. Click the Bold button.
10. Highlight from A1 to J1 and then click the Merge and Center button.
11. Type Invoice in A2 and press Enter.
12. With the cell pointer in A2, increase the font size to 14.
13. Highlight from A2 to J2 and then click the Merge and Center button.
14. Click the Stop Recording button in the taskbar at the bottom left of the screen.

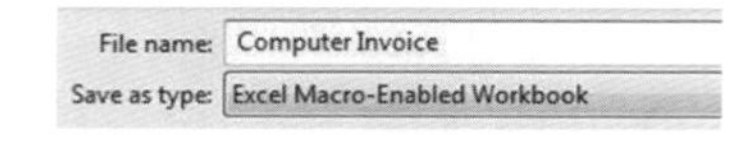

Figure 6.15: Saving an Excel workbook that includes a macro

15. Click the Save button and enter **Computer Invoice** as the file name. Select *Excel Macro-Enabled Workbook* from the Save as type drop-down list (Figure 6.15).

Excel will not let you save a spreadsheet workbook containing a macro unless you change the Save as type from *Excel Workbook* to *Excel Macro-Enabled Workbook*.

The resulting spreadsheet should look something like Figure 6.16.

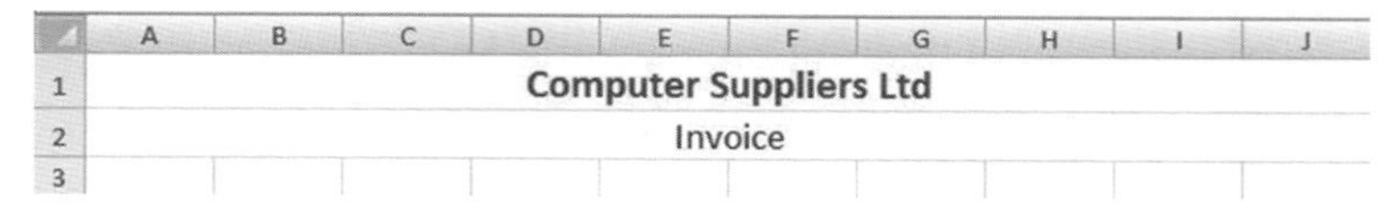

Figure 6.16

Testing the Macro

1. In *Sheet2*, position the cell pointer in any cell except A1.
2. Hold down the *CTRL* key and type *e*.

When you play back a macro, all the steps carried out during recording are executed in one step at high speed. Macros can also be played back by clicking the Macros button in the View section of the Ribbon. In the Macro dialog box, select the *invoiceheader* macro and click Run.

The *invoiceheader* macro can be run in any other worksheet in the Computer Invoice spreadsheet. It can also be run in any other spreadsheet workbook as long as the Computer Invoice spreadsheet is open. Once the Computer Invoice spreadsheet is closed, the *invoiceheader* macro is no longer available to any other spreadsheet workbooks.

Using key combinations to run macros may cause problems. For example, if you regularly use *CTRL* + *S* to save your spreadsheet workbooks, you should not assign *S* as a shortcut key to a macro. The *CTRL* + *S* key combination **will not** save your spreadsheet as long as the spreadsheet containing a macro with a *CTRL* + *S* key combination is open. In Excel, the only letters that haven't been assigned to keyboard shortcuts are *E, J, L, M* and *Q*.

Spreadsheet Macros Assignment One

1. Open the spreadsheet named *Travel Expenses* (created in Chapter 3) and select any cell in the *Summary* worksheet.
2. Record a new macro named *erasedata* that performs the following tasks:
   - Select the worksheet named *Joe Murphy*.
   - Erase data from A3:A7, B3, C3:C7.
   - Select the worksheet named *Sile O Shea*.
   - Erase data from A3:A7, B3, C3:C7.

- Select the worksheet named *Tom Doyle*.
- Erase data from A3:A7, B3, C3:C7.
- Position the cell pointer in A3 in Joe Murphy's worksheet.

3. Click the *Summary* worksheet tab. In the Insert section of the Ribbon click the Shapes button. Select the Rounded Rectangle shape and then drag to draw a rectangle to the right of the data.

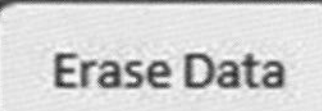

4. Type the text *Erase Data* inside the rectangle. In the Format section of the Ribbon, click the Shape Fill button and set the background colour of the rectangle to *White, Background 1, Darker 5%*. Click the Shape Outline button and set the outline colour to blue.
5. Right click the Erase Data rectangle and select *Assign Macro* from the list. In the Assign Macro dialog box, select the *erasedata* macro. Click OK to assign this macro to the rounded rectangle shape.
6. Click the Save button to save the spreadsheet. The result should look something like Figure 6.17.

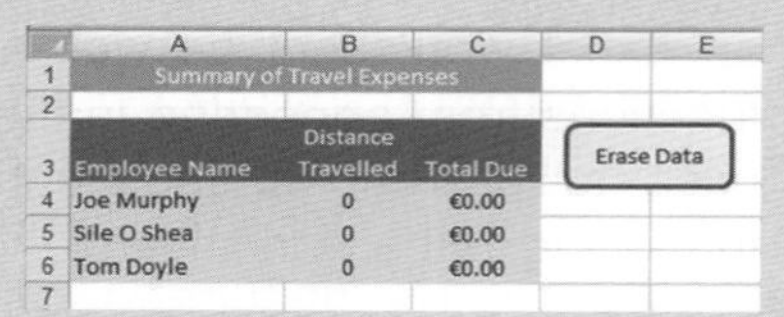

	A	B	C	D	E
1	Summary of Travel Expenses				
2					
3	Employee Name	Distance Travelled	Total Due		
4	Joe Murphy	0	€0.00		
5	Sile O Shea	0	€0.00		
6	Tom Doyle	0	€0.00		
7					

Figure 6.17 The macro can be run by clicking the rounded rectangle

7. Test the macro by entering new dates and distances travelled in Joe Murphy's, Sile O Shea's and Tom Doyle's worksheets. Run the macro from the *Erase Data* button.
8. Save the *Travel Expenses* spreadsheet as an Excel Macro-Enabled Workbook.

Holding down *ALT* and pressing the *F8* key displays a list of all macros in the workbook.

Spreadsheet Macros Assignment Two

1. Open the spreadsheet named *Ticket Sales Galway–Dublin* Route (created in Chapter 3). Select cell A1 in the *Weekly Ticket Sales* worksheet.
2. Record a new macro, named *newweek*, that performs the following tasks:
   - Deletes the contents of A1 and B5:H9 in the worksheet named *0745*.
   - Deletes the contents of A1 and B5:H9 in the worksheet named *1100.*
   - Deletes the contents of A1 and B5:H9 in the worksheet named *1510*.
   - Positions the cell pointer in B5 in the worksheet named *0745*.

3. Select the *Weekly Ticket Sales* worksheet and turn off worksheet protection.
4. Using the Insert section of the Ribbon, draw a rounded rectangle to the right of the data. Type the text *Clear All* inside the rectangle. Link the rounded rectangle to the *newweek* macro.
5. Re-protect the *Weekly Ticket Sales* worksheet.
6. Test the macro by entering dummy ticket sales and then clicking the button.
7. Save the spreadsheet as an Excel Macro-Enabled Workbook.

N When you have completed the assignments in this chapter, ensure that the macro settings are reset to the default setting of *Disable all macros with notification*.

CHAPTER 6 SUMMARY

1. Basic Concepts

Worksheet Protection Worksheet Protection restricts data entry to specific cells in an Excel worksheet as well as preventing formulas and functions from appearing in the formula bar. It can also be used to prevent spreadsheet users from changing the formatting in the worksheet.

Workbook Protection Workbook Protection is used to prevent spreadsheet users deleting individual worksheets in an Excel workbook. When the workbook is protected spreadsheet users are also prevented from moving, copying, hiding or inserting worksheets.

Locked and Unlocked Cells All cells in an Excel worksheet are locked by default. It is important to unlock the cells that you want to have access to before you protect the worksheet. Once a worksheet is protected, you will be unable to enter data in locked cells.

Hidden Property The Hidden property is used to prevent formulas and functions from being displayed in the formula bar. It doesn't have any effect unless the worksheet is protected.

Macro A macro is a computer program generated by Excel based on keystrokes made, options selected from the Ribbon, buttons clicked and data entered while the macro is being recorded by the spreadsheet user. Macros can be used to automate repetitive tasks.

Macro Security Macros stored in Excel workbooks created by other spreadsheet users can contain viruses. Excel will warn you when it finds macros in a workbook created by someone else.

2. Potential Pitfalls

- If you protect a worksheet without unlocking cells, you will not be able to enter data anywhere in that worksheet.
- When protecting a worksheet you must identify the cells where data entry is permitted rather than identifying the cells that you want to protect.
- Locking cells and turning on the Hidden property has no effect unless you protect the worksheet.
- Your spreadsheet is not completely protected unless you protect both the worksheet and the workbook.
- As macros from unknown sources can contain viruses, be careful when opening Excel spreadsheets containing macros.

3. Useful Shortcuts

Keyboard Combination	Action
ALT + F8	Displays a list of macros in the current workbook
ALT + R	Displays the Review group in the Ribbon
ALT+N	Displays the Insert group in the Ribbon
ALT+L	Displays the Developer group in the Ribbon
ALT+W	Displays the View group in the Ribbon
ALT+R+PW+W	Diplays the *Protect Structure and Windows* settings
ALT+N+G+A	Displayes the *Add Signature Services* options
ALT+L+AS	Displays the *Macro Security* settings
ALT+W+M+R	Displays the *Record Macro* dialog box

Table 6.8

SPREADSHEET PROTECTION AND MACROS REVIEW QUESTIONS

Answers to the review questions are available on www.gillmacmillan.ie

1. By default all cells in a worksheet are ____________. When the worksheet is protected, data can only be entered in ____________ cells.
2. To prevent formulas and functions from being displayed in the formula bar, turn on the ____________________ property for any cells containing formulas or functions and then protect the worksheet.

3. All cells where data entry is permitted should be ____________ before protecting the worksheet.

4. The spreadsheet displayed in Table 6.9 calculates the sale price and profit for a computer parts retailer.

	A	B	C	D	E	F
1	**Item**	**Cost Price**	**Markup**	**Sale Price**	**Quantity Sold**	**Profit**
2	640Gb Hard Disk	€48.50	50%	€72.75	15	€363.75
3	512Mb Graphics Card	€25.99	100%	€51.98	22	€571.78
4	1GHz Motherboard	€58.70	35%	€79.25	37	€760.17
5	8x Blu-ray drive	€26.85	120%	€59.07	6	€193.32
6	Wireless Network Card	€9.55	20%	€11.46	48	€91.68

Table 6.9

(i) Which cells in the worksheet should be unlocked before turning on worksheet protection?

____

(ii) For which cells should the Hidden property be turned on before protecting the worksheet?

____

5. Figure 6.18 displays the Protect Sheet dialog box.

Figure 6.18

By default, which options in the Protect Sheet dialog box are pre-selected by Excel?

(i) ______________________________

(ii) ______________________________

6. To prevented worksheets from being deleted, you should protect the workbook for ______________________.

7. The spreadsheet displayed in Table 6.10 calculates travel expenses for employees.

	A	B	C	D
1	**Name**	**Kilometres Travelled**	**Rate per Kilometre**	**Amount**
2	John O Shea	124	€0.95	€117.80
3	Mary Dillon	289	€0.95	€274.55
4	Neill O Donnell	57	€0.95	€54.15
5	Karl Quinn	88	€0.95	€83.60
6	Evelien Urbain	71	€0.95	€67.45
7				
8	**Total:**			**€597.55**

Table 6.10

(i) Which cells in the worksheet should be unlocked before turning on worksheet protection? ______________________

(ii) For which cells should the Hidden property be turned on before protecting the worksheet? ______________________

8. The exclamation mark in the Excel icon indicates that the Travel Expenses Travel Expenses workbook:
   (i) Is infected with a virus.
   (ii) Is read only.
   (iii) Has been enabled for macros.
   (iv) Contains a macro.

9. A macro is a computer ________________ written by Excel based on actions taken by the spreadsheet user while the macro is being ________________.

10. Which of the following is the default security setting for Macros in Excel?
   (i) Disable all macros without notification.
   (ii) Disable all macros with notification.
   (iii) Disable all macros except digitally signed macros.
   (iv) Enable all macros.

7 IF Functions

In Chapter 7, you will:

- Learn about the logic used in IF functions
- Automate decision making using simple and complex IF functions
- Test conditions using AND functions and OR functions
- Use conditional formatting to emphasise specific data.

WHAT IS AN IF FUNCTION?

An IF function is a special type of function that can make an automated decision based on information supplied to it by the spreadsheet user.

We will learn about IF functions by designing a spreadsheet for the OnLine Insurance Company. This spreadsheet will contain IF functions that will make a number of decisions as part of the process of calculating the premium for each OnLine Insurance customer. Because OnLine Insurance deals with hundreds of customers every day, the spreadsheet will greatly reduce the workload of its sales representatives by automating this decision-making with IF functions.

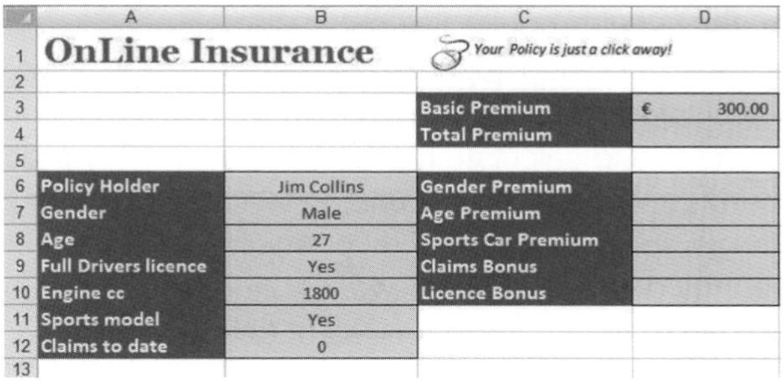

	A	B	C	D
1	OnLine Insurance		Your Policy is just a click away!	
2				
3			Basic Premium	€ 300.00
4			Total Premium	
5				
6	Policy Holder	Jim Collins	Gender Premium	
7	Gender	Male	Age Premium	
8	Age	27	Sports Car Premium	
9	Full Drivers licence	Yes	Claims Bonus	
10	Engine cc	1800	Licence Bonus	
11	Sports model	Yes		
12	Claims to date	0		
13				

Figure 7.1 The OnLine Insurance spreadsheet

OnLine Insurance specialises in motor insurance. They charge a basic premium of €300 and then add to this amount as follows.

Gender premium: Male drivers are charged 20% extra on the basic premium.

Age premium:

- For drivers aged 18 or under, there is an extra charge of 60% of the basic premium.
- For drivers aged between 19 and 21 inclusive, there is an extra charge of 40% of the basic premium.
- For drivers aged between 22 and 25 inclusive, there is an extra charge of 20% of the basic premium.
- For drivers older than 25, there is an extra charge of 10% of the basic premium.

Performance premium: Drivers with sports cars that have an engine capacity above 1600cc are charged 40% extra on the basic premium.

Claims bonus: Drivers who are either over 30 or who have no previous claims are entitled to a reduction of 5% off the basic premium.

Licence bonus:

- Full licence holders aged 18 or under get a reduction of 1% of the basic premium.
- Full licence holders aged between 19 and 21 inclusive get a reduction of 2% of the basic premium.
- Full licence holders aged between 22 and 25 inclusive get a reduction of 3% of the basic premium.
- Full licence holders aged between 26 and 70 inclusive get a reduction of 5% of the basic premium.
- No reduction is given to drivers who don't hold a full licence or to drivers aged 71 or older.

From the above information it can be seen that the total premium for each customer depends on five factors: gender, age, performance of the car, previous claims and licence. It would be very difficult for the sales representatives to calculate premiums manually because each quotation would require five separate decisions as well as five separate calculations. To make each decision correctly, the sales representative would have to refer to documentation detailing rules and premiums and, having calculated the individual premiums, would then have to calculate the total premium. This process would be very slow and with so many customers, errors would inevitably be made. Newer staff would take considerably longer to calculate the total premium until they were properly trained. IF functions take all this decision-making work away from the sales representatives, allowing them to give accurate quotes in an instant to potential customers.

As you work through this chapter you will learn how to automate the decisions in the OnLine Insurance example using IF functions.

Each of the premiums and bonuses listed above requires a separate IF function to automatically decide on the level of the charge or bonus. We will see that there are four different types of IF function. These are as follows:

1. Simple IF function
2. Nested simple IF function
3. Compound IF function
4. Nested compound IF function.

Which IF function you use depends on the nature and complexity of the decision. When you have completed the chapter, the OnLine Insurance spreadsheet will automatically calculate the total premium based on data entered relating to gender, age, performance of the car, previous claims and licence type. The task of decision-making will be taken over by the IF functions in the spreadsheet, allowing the sales representatives to provide quick and accurate quotations. They will no longer have to refer to the rules governing the premiums since these rules will be stored in the IF functions themselves.

STRUCTURE OF AN IF FUNCTION

Each IF function consists of a condition, a true action and a false action. Later in this chapter we will see that more complex IF functions can have more than one condition and more than two actions.

	A	B	C	D
1	**Special Offer: Spend any amount and get a 5% discount! Spend more than €200 and get a 15% discount!**			
2	**Bar Code**	**Product**	**Price**	**Discount**
3	450-1021	iPod 240Gb	€220	

Table 7.1

We will use the example displayed in Table 7.1 to explain how an IF function works. Remember, the main task of an IF function is to reduce your workload by automating decisions. In Table 7.1, the IF function must decide whether to give a 5% discount or a 15% discount. We could represent this decision using the flow chart shown in Figure 7.2

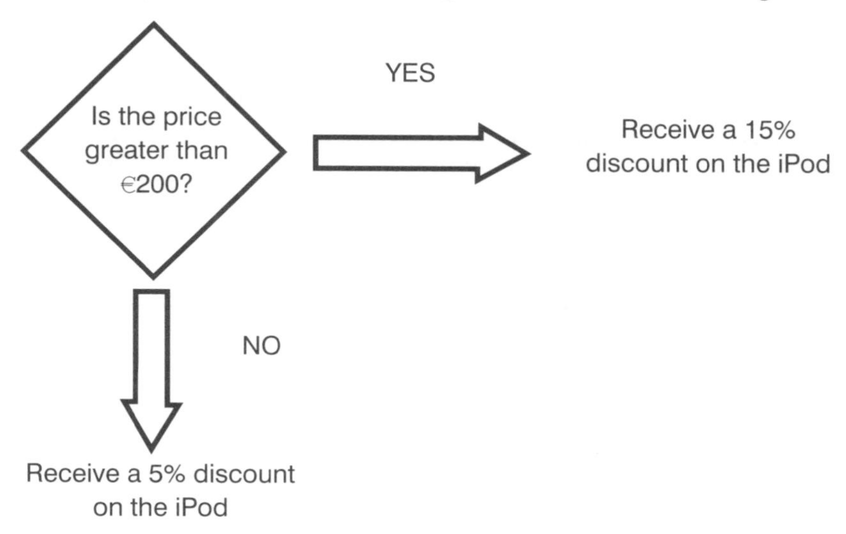

Figure 7.2 A flow chart tells the story of a decision using symbols

An IF function, in its simplest form, consists of three sections; a Condition, a True Action and a False Action. Writing the IF function in English would give something like this:

=IF(condition , True action , False action)

Commas are used to separate the sections of the IF function. Each of the three sections of the IF function has a specific job to do.

1. The Condition

This is the first section of the IF function. Its purpose is to carry out a test, which is similar to asking a question. Here we need to ask, 'Is the price greater than €200?' to see if we qualify for a 15% discount on the Apple iPod. Of course, this has to be put into a format that Excel understands, using cell references and what are called logical operators. Logical operators that can be used in a condition are displayed in Table 7.2.

Logical Operator	Meaning
=	Equal to
<	Less than
<=	Less than or equal to
>	Greater than
>=	Greater than or equal to
<>	Not equal to

Table 7.2

Logical operators are combined with cell references to form conditions. Each condition tests data in a specific cell. In Excel, there are five different condition types. Examples of each of the five condition types are shown in Table 7.3.

Condition Type	Example	Meaning
1. Numeric	A2<100	Is the number in A2 less than 100?
2. Text	B6="Yes"	Is *Yes* stored in B6?
3. Cell reference	D11<>E11	Is the data in D11 not equal to the data in E11?
4. Formula	F8>B8*C8	Is the number in F8 greater than the number resulting from multiplying B8 by C8?
5. Function	G5<=sum(E2:E4)	Is the number in G5 less than or equal to the sum of the numbers in E2 to E4?

Table 7.3 Condition Types used in IF Functions

Using the information displayed in Table 7.3, we can complete the first section of our IF function. We must check to see if the price of the iPod *(stored in cell C3 of Table 7.1)* is greater than €200. This is done as follows:

=IF(C3>200

This simply means, 'Is the price of the iPod greater than 200?'

Never type a euro sign in an IF function. ***=IF(C3>€200*** is incorrect and would cause an error in the completed IF function.

2. The True Action

The second section of the IF function is called the True Action. The true action tells Excel what to do when the condition is satisfied. Here, we must tell Excel what to do when the price of the iPod is greater than €200. There are five different types of true action. Unlike a condition, the true action must never include a logical operator. Examples of true actions are displayed in Table 7.4.

True Action Type	Example	Meaning
1. Numeric	150	Enter 150 in the current cell
2. Text	"Yes"	Enter *Yes* in the current cell
3. Cell reference	B9	Copy the data from B9 into the current cell
4. Formula	A2-A3	Subtract the number in A3 from the number in A2 and display the result in the current cell
5. Function	Average(C2:C10)	Calculate the average of the numbers in cells C2 to C10 inclusive, and display the result in the current cell

Table 7.4 True action types used in IF Functions

N A true action will never start with = because the IF function has already started with =.

We know that we will get a 15% discount on the iPod if the price *(stored in cell C3 of Table 7.1)* is greater than €200. Using the information displayed in Table 7.4, we can complete the second section of our IF function, as follows:

=IF(c3>200,c3*15%

This simply means, 'IF the price of the iPod is greater than €200, calculate the discount by multiplying the price by 15%.'

3. The False Action

The third section of the IF function is called the False Action. The false action tells Excel what to do when the condition is not satisfied. Here we must tell Excel what to do when the price is not greater than €200. Just like the true action, there are five different types of false action, examples of which are displayed in Table 7.4.

We know that we will receive only a 5% discount when the price *(stored in cell C3 of Table 7.1)* is €200 or less. Using the information displayed in Table 7.4, we can complete our IF function, as follows:

=IF(c3>200,c3*15%,c3*5%)

This simply means "IF the price of the iPod is greater than €200, calculate the discount by multiplying the price by 15%. If the price is not greater than €200, calculate the discount by multiplying the price by 5%.

The IF function can only implement either the true action or the false action. It can never implement both simultaneously. Which action is implemented depends on the result of the conditional test. In the example, the condition is satisfied as the price of the iPod is greater than €200. Because of this, the IF function implements the true action and ignores the false action.

SIMPLE IF FUNCTION

The purpose of an IF function is to reduce your workload by automating the decision-making process. A simple IF function is used when the IF function must decide to take one of two possible courses of action and where this decision is based on a single condition. As we have already seen, each simple IF function consists of three sections, which are called the Condition, the True Action and the False Action.

Using the *OnLine Insurance Company* example, we will see how the Simple IF function works.

	A	B	C	D
1	OnLine Insurance		Your Policy is just a click away!	
2				
3			Basic Premium	€ 300.00
4			Total Premium	
5				
6	Policy Holder	Jim Collins	Gender Premium	
7	Gender	Male	Age Premium	
8	Age	27	Sports Car Premium	
9	Full Drivers licence	Yes	Claims Bonus	
10	Engine cc	1800	Licence Bonus	
11	Sports model	Yes		
12	Claims to date	0		
13				

Figure 7.3

OnLine Insurance Example: Calculating the Gender Premium

In Figure 7.3, we must calculate the gender premium for Jim Collins. This is calculated on the following basis.

OnLine Insurance Gender Premium Guidelines

For male drivers there is an extra charge of 20% of the basic premium.

A Simple IF function will be used to calculate the gender premium. This IF function must decide to take one of the following courses of action:

1. Charge 20% extra
2. Charge nothing extra.

The IF function will make its decision based on a single condition – the gender of the driver.

Represented graphically, this would look like Figure 7.4.

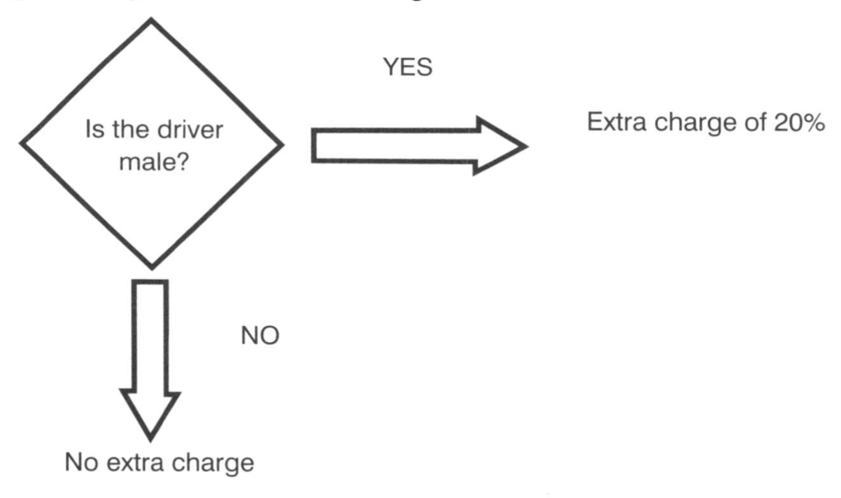

Figure 7.4: The IF function calculates the extra charge based on the gender of the driver

Before writing a Simple IF function, it is important to have a clear idea of its three sections; the condition, the true action and the false action. These are summarised in Table 7.5.

Condition	Is the driver male?
True Action	20% of the basic premium extra charge
False Action	No extra charge

Table 7.5 The three sections of the IF function

If we were to write this IF function in English, it would look something like this.

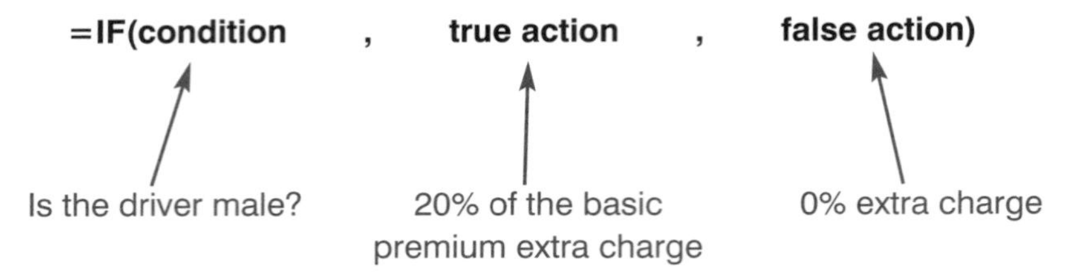

Notice how commas are used to separate the different sections of the IF function.

	A	B	C	D	E
1	OnLine Insurance		Your Policy is just a click away!		
2					
3			Basic Premium	€ 300.00	
4			Total Premium		
5					
6	Policy Holder	Jim Collins	Gender Premium	=IF(B7="Male",D3*20%,0)	
7	Gender	Male			
8	Age	27			
9	Full Drivers licence	Yes			
10	Engine cc	1800			
11	Sports model	Yes			
12	Claims to date	0			
13					

Figure 7.5 Calculating the gender premium with a Simple IF function

From Figure 7.5, it can be seen that the gender of the driver is in B7 and that the basic premium is in D3. When we feed this data into the IF function, we get the following:

=IF(B7="Male",D3*20%,0)

This IF function is entered in D6, as shown in Figure 7.5. The IF function will charge 20% only when it finds that 'Male' has been entered in B7. Where 'Male' has not been entered in B7, the IF function will not add on an extra charge. As Jim is male, the IF function calculates an extra charge of €60.00.

An IF function cannot refer to itself. If we were to type the function ***=IF(B7="Male",D3*20%,D6=0)*** in D6, it would be incorrect because the function is stored in D6 and also refers to D6.

Circular References: D6

This would cause a circular reference and would be indicated in the Status Bar, in the bottom left-hand corner of the screen.

Try it Yourself!

1. Create a new spreadsheet and enter the data shown in Figure 7.5.
2. Enter the Simple IF function in D6 as shown in Figure 7.5. As Jim is male, the gender premium calculated by the IF function should be €60.00.

3. Test the IF function by entering *Female* in B7. The gender premium should now be €0.00.
4. Change the gender back to *Male*.
5. Save the spreadsheet as **OnLine Insurance**

Points to Note

1. The condition and the true action are followed by commas. The first comma represents the word *then* and the second comma represents the word *otherwise*. Expressing the IF function in English, we would get the following: *If B7 is equal to Male* ***then*** *multiply D3 by 20%,* ***otherwise*** *enter zero in D6.*
2. When an IF function is dealing with text (here we are testing to see if B7 contains the text *Male*), the text must be enclosed in double quotes.

IF Functions Rule One: When referring to text in an IF function, the text must be enclosed in double quotes. This rule applies to all types of IF functions.

Set up Styles for Chapter 7

Before entering data for Assignment One, we will set up the Cell Styles that will be used to format all the spreadsheets in Chapter 7.

1. Create a new spreadsheet workbook.
2. In the Home section of the Ribbon, click the Cell Styles button.
3. Right click *Heading 4* and then select Modify from the pop-up menu.
4. In the Style dialog box, click the Format button.
5. In the Format Cells dialog box, select the formatting characteristics listed in Table 7.6.

Style Name	Heading 4
Font	Georgia
Font Style	Bold
Size	20
Font Colour	Purple, Accent4

Table 7.6

6. Click OK twice to apply these formatting characteristics to the *Heading 4* style.
7. Modify the *20% – Accent4* style to include the formatting characteristics listed in Table 7.7.

Style Name	20% – Accent4
Font	Calibri
Size	11
Border	Outline
Font Colour	Purple, Accent4, Darker 50%

Table 7.7

8. Modify the *Accent4* style to include the formatting characteristics listed in Table 7.8.

Style Name	Accent4
Font	Calibri
Size	12
Font Style	Bold
Font Colour	White, Background1

Table 7.8

9. Save the spreadsheet as **Toms Hardware**

Simple IF Assignment One

Open the *Toms Hardware* spreadsheet if it is not already open. Enter the data shown in Table 7.9. Enter formulas and functions in the shaded cells to complete the spreadsheet.

	A	B	C	D	E	F
1	Tom's Hardware Store					
2						
3	Product	Unit Price	Quantity	Total	Discount	Discounted Price
4	Card Index Cabinet	47.43	3			
5	Fortress Cash Box	192	1			
6	Junior Manual Typist Chair	67.23	10			
7	Computer Stand	284.80	10			
8	Keyboard Desk	40.41	5			
9	PC Desk	156.80	2			
10	Mobile Work Station	239.94	3			
11	Extension Shelves	96.62	2			
12	Low Level Printer Stand	54.70	4			
13	General Purpose Trolley	163.64	1			

Table 7.9

If you forget to include the False action in your IF function, Excel will display the text *FALSE* when the condition of the IF function is not satisfied.

1. Calculate the total for each product.
2. Create a Simple IF function to calculate the discount.
   - There is a discount of 10% of the total when the total is greater than 300.
   - There is no discount when the total is 300 or less.

When you copy the completed IF function, some of the answers will be €–. This doesn't mean that the IF function is incorrect. The IF function is simply implementing the false action of zero.

3. Test the IF function by changing the quantity of PC Desks to *1*. The discount on PC Desks should now be €0.00.
4. Change the quantity of PC Desks back to 2.
5. Calculate the discounted price.
6. Format all money amounts to currency.
7. Format the data using the styles listed in Table 7.10.

Range of Cells	Cell Style
A1	Heading 4
A3:F3	Accent4
A4:F13	20% - Accent4

Table 7.10

8. Sort the data in descending order of discounted price.
9. Create a Filter so that only products where the quantity is greater than 3 are displayed.
10. Save the spreadsheet.

CONDITIONAL FORMATTING

Conditional formatting is a dynamic type of formatting that adjusts as the data in your spreadsheet is updated. It is based on rules that tell Excel whether to apply formatting or not. Conditional formatting is intelligent in that it will decide itself whether to apply a formatting rule.

	A	B	C	D	E	F	G
1				VAT	21%		
2							
3	**Car Type**	**Daily Rate**	**Days**	**Discount**	**Subtotal**	**VAT**	**TOTAL**
4	Fiesta	€ 50.00	5	€ 10.00	€ 240.00	€ 50.40	€ 290.40
5	Primera	€ 55.50	2	€ 5.00	€ 106.00	€ 22.26	€ 128.26
6	Sunny	€ 52.00	1	€ 2.50	€ 49.50	€ 10.40	€ 59.90
7	Escort	€ 52.00	3	€ 7.50	€ 148.50	€ 31.19	€ 179.69
8	Corsa	€ 49.50	7	€ 15.00	€ 331.50	€ 69.62	€ 401.12
9	Tigra	€ 60.00	10	€ 25.00	€ 575.00	€ 120.75	€ 695.75
10	Corolla	€ 52.00	14	€ 30.00	€ 698.00	€ 146.58	€ 844.58
11	Focus	€ 52.00	7	€ 16.50	€ 347.50	€ 72.98	€ 420.48
12	Ibiza	€ 50.00	5	€ 10.00	€ 240.00	€ 50.40	€ 290.40
13							

Figure 7.6 Conditional formatting has been applied to discount amounts greater than €10

In Figure 7.6, discount amounts greater than €10 have been emphasised using a conditional formatting rule. In Figure 7.7, the discount amount for the Fiesta has changed as a result of changing the days hired from 5 to 8.

	A	B	C	D	E	F	G
1				VAT	21%		
2							
3	**Car Type**	**Daily Rate**	**Days**	**Discount**	**Subtotal**	**VAT**	**TOTAL**
4	Fiesta	€ 50.00	8	€ 16.00	€ 384.00	€ 80.64	€ 464.64
5	Primera	€ 55.50	2	€ 5.00	€ 106.00	€ 22.26	€ 128.26
6	Sunny	€ 52.00	1	€ 2.50	€ 49.50	€ 10.40	€ 59.90
7	Escort	€ 52.00	3	€ 7.50	€ 148.50	€ 31.19	€ 179.69
8	Corsa	€ 49.50	7	€ 15.00	€ 331.50	€ 69.62	€ 401.12
9	Tigra	€ 60.00	10	€ 25.00	€ 575.00	€ 120.75	€ 695.75
10	Corolla	€ 52.00	14	€ 30.00	€ 698.00	€ 146.58	€ 844.58
11	Focus	€ 52.00	7	€ 16.50	€ 347.50	€ 72.98	€ 420.48
12	Ibiza	€ 50.00	5	€ 10.00	€ 240.00	€ 50.40	€ 290.40
13							

Figure 7.7 Conditional formatting is automatically applied when data changes

The new discount amount of €16.00 is emphasised as it is now greater than €10 – satisfying the conditional formatting rule. This formatting happens automatically when the data is updated. Conditional formatting can be used to draw attention to specific data in a spreadsheet or to alert the spreadsheet user to important changes in the data.

Using Conditional Formatting – Worked Example

In the following example, we will use conditional formatting to emphasise discount amounts.

1. Open the *Toms Hardware* spreadsheet.
2. Highlight the range containing discount amounts *(E4:E13)*.

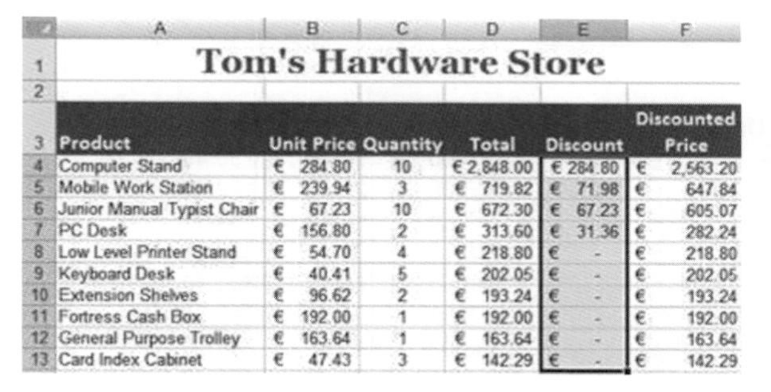

	A	B	C	D	E	F
1	Tom's Hardware Store					
2						
3	Product	Unit Price	Quantity	Total	Discount	Discounted Price
4	Computer Stand	€ 284.80	10	€ 2,848.00	€ 284.80	€ 2,563.20
5	Mobile Work Station	€ 239.94	3	€ 719.82	€ 71.98	€ 647.84
6	Junior Manual Typist Chair	€ 67.23	10	€ 672.30	€ 67.23	€ 605.07
7	PC Desk	€ 156.80	2	€ 313.60	€ 31.36	€ 282.24
8	Low Level Printer Stand	€ 54.70	4	€ 218.80	€ -	€ 218.80
9	Keyboard Desk	€ 40.41	5	€ 202.05	€ -	€ 202.05
10	Extension Shelves	€ 96.62	2	€ 193.24	€ -	€ 193.24
11	Fortress Cash Box	€ 192.00	1	€ 192.00	€ -	€ 192.00
12	General Purpose Trolley	€ 163.64	1	€ 163.64	€ -	€ 163.64
13	Card Index Cabinet	€ 47.43	3	€ 142.29	€ -	€ 142.29

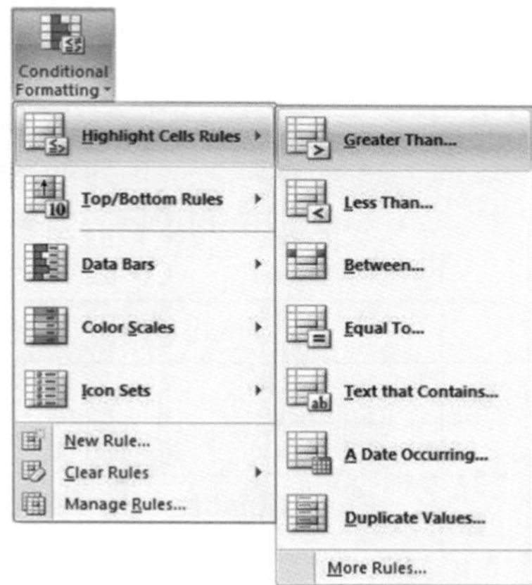

Figure 7.8 Creating a conditional formatting rule for the discount amounts

3. In the Home section of the Ribbon, click the Conditional Formatting button and select *Highlight Cells Rules*, as shown in Figure 7.8. Now select *Greater Than*.
4. In the Greater Than dialog box, shown in Figure 7.9, we must isolate the cells we want to format *(the discount amounts)*. What distinguishes the discount amounts from the other values in the highlighted range is that they are greater than zero.

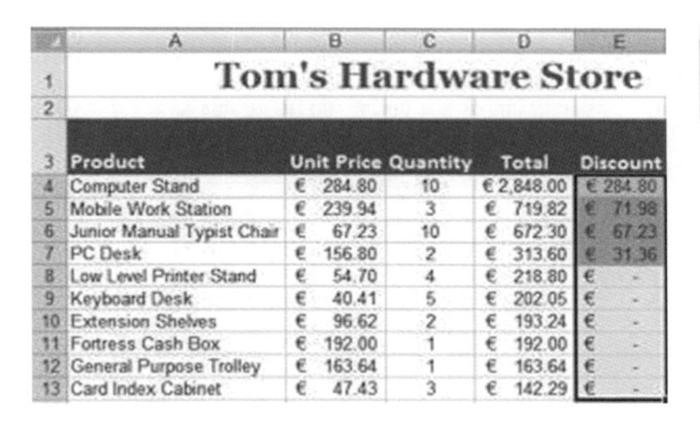

	A	B	C	D	E
1	Tom's Hardware Store				
2					
3	Product	Unit Price	Quantity	Total	Discount
4	Computer Stand	€ 284.80	10	€ 2,848.00	€ 284.80
5	Mobile Work Station	€ 239.94	3	€ 719.82	€ 71.98
6	Junior Manual Typist Chair	€ 67.23	10	€ 672.30	€ 67.23
7	PC Desk	€ 156.80	2	€ 313.60	€ 31.36
8	Low Level Printer Stand	€ 54.70	4	€ 218.80	€ -
9	Keyboard Desk	€ 40.41	5	€ 202.05	€ -
10	Extension Shelves	€ 96.62	2	€ 193.24	€ -
11	Fortress Cash Box	€ 192.00	1	€ 192.00	€ -
12	General Purpose Trolley	€ 163.64	1	€ 163.64	€ -
13	Card Index Cabinet	€ 47.43	3	€ 142.29	€ -

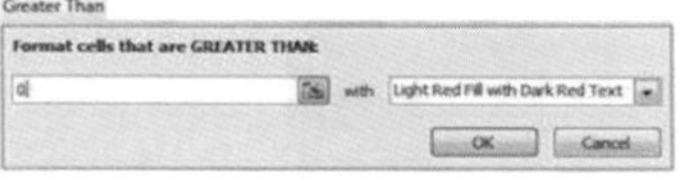

Figure 7.9 Isolating discount amounts with a Formatting Rule

5. In the Greater Than dialog box, enter ***0*** as shown in Figure 7.9. This isolates discount amounts in the highlighted range that are greater than zero.
6. Having identified the cells that we want to format, we must now define how we want those cells to be formatted. In the Greater Than dialog box, select *Light Red Fill with Dark Red Text* as shown in Figure 7.9. This formatting will be applied only to numbers in the highlighted range that are greater than zero.
7. Click OK to apply the Formatting.
8. In C10, change the quantity of extension shelves from 2 to 4. The IF function in the discount column calculates a discount of €38.65 as the total is now above €300. As this discount amount is now greater than zero, it is automatically formatted in red.
9. Save the *Toms Hardware* spreadsheet.

Simple IF Assignment Two

Part 1: Spreadsheet Setup

1. Create a new spreadsheet workbook and enter the data shown in Table 7.11 in Sheet1.

	A	B	C	D
1	**Summer Exam Results**			
2				
3	**Exam Number**	**Student Name**	**Marks out of 100**	**Result**
4	990101	Mark O Neill	46	
5	990102	Tony Meehan	70	
6	990103	Evelien Urbain	58	
7	990104	Eileen O Sullivan	61	
8	990105	Peter Greene	83	
9	990106	Heinrike Wolf	31	
10	990107	Evelyn Andrews	58	
11	990108	Aidan Jackson	76	
12	990109	Mike Jennings	60	
13	990110	Tanya Ryan	59	
14	990111	Richard Byrne	90	

Table 7.11

2. Create a simple IF function to display the text *Pass* or *Fail*. The pass mark is 60 out of 100.

Always use double quotes when referring to text in an IF function. Two single quotes are not the same as double quotes and will cause an error.

3. Test the IF function by changing Mark O Neill's mark to 60. His result should now be *Pass*.
4. Change Mark O Neill's mark back to 46.
5. Sort the data in descending order of marks out of 100.
6. Save the spreadsheet as **Summer Exam Results**

Part 2: Formatting, Filters and Spreadsheet Protection

1. Open the *Toms Hardware* spreadsheet.
2. In the *Summer Exam Results* spreadsheet, click the Cell Styles button in the Home section of the Ribbon.

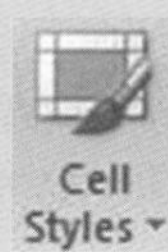

3. Click the Merge Styles button. Merge Styles...
4. In the Merge Styles dialog box, select *Toms Hardware.xlsx*. This copies the styles from the *Toms Hardware* spreadsheet to the *Summer Exam Results* spreadsheet. Merge styles from: Toms Hardware.xlsx
5. Click *Yes* to confirm that you want to merge styles that have the same names.
6. Format data in the *Summer Exam Results* spreadsheet using the styles listed in Table 7.12.

Range of Cells	Cell Style
A1	Heading 4
A3:D3	Accent4
A4:D14	20% – Accent4

Table 7.12

7. Use conditional formatting to emphasise the marks out of 100 of students who failed in *Light Red Fill with Dark Red Text*.
8. Test the conditional formatting by changing Richard Byrne's mark to 59. His mark should now be formatted in red.
9. Change Richard Byrne's mark back to 90.
10. Create a Filter that displays only students who scored above average in the exam.

    Change the Filter to display students who scored below average in the exam.
11. Rename Sheet1 as *Exam Data*
12. Delete all unused worksheets.

To delete multiple worksheets, hold down the *CTRL* key and click the worksheet tab of each worksheet you want to delete. Once the worksheets are selected, right click any selected worksheet and choose *Delete* from the pop-up menu. Click OK to confirm that you want to delete the selected worksheets.

13. Clear the filter and implement spreadsheet protection so that:
    - data can only be entered in the range A4:C14
    - the spreadsheet user cannot select locked cells.
14. Protect the workbook for structure only.
15. Print the *Exam Data* worksheet with gridlines and row and column headings displayed.
16. Save the *Summer Exam Results* spreadsheet.

Simple IF Assignment Three

Part 1: Spreadsheet Setup

1. Create a new spreadsheet workbook and enter the data shown in Table 7.13 in Sheet1.

	A	B	C	D	E	F
1	Environmental Waste Charges					
2						
3	Collection Number	Bin Type (Litres)	Lift Charge	Charge per Kg	Bin Weight (Kg)	Total Charge
4	1	240		0.25	15.0	
5	2	1100		0.25	28.7	
6	3	240		0.25	10.5	
7	4	240		0.25	12.2	
8	5	1100		0.25	23.4	
9	6	240		0.25	14.6	
10	7	1100		0.25	30.2	
11	8	1100		0.25	27.7	
12	9	1100		0.25	25.8	
13	10	240		0.25	8.1	

Table 7.13

2. Calculate the Lift Charge using an IF function.
   - 240-litre bins are charged at €4.00 per lift.
   - 1100-litre bins are charged at €18.00 per lift.

If Excel displays the text *False* as the result of some of the IF functions, it means that you have left out the false action.

3. Test the IF function by changing the bin type for collection number 1 to 1100. The lift charge should now be €18.00.
4. Change the bin type for collection number 1 back to 240.
5. Calculate the Total Charge incorporating the Lift Charge and the charge per kilo of Bin Weight.
6. Sort the data in descending order of total charge.

Part 2: Formatting, Filters and Spreadsheet Protection

1. Merge styles from the *Toms Hardware* spreadsheet.
2. Format data in the *Environmental Waste Charges* spreadsheet using the styles listed in Table 7.14.

Merge styles from:
Toms Hardware.xlsx

Range of Cells	Cell Style
A1	Heading 4
A3:F3	Accent4
A4:F13	20% – Accent4

Table 7.14

3. Using conditional formatting, emphasise all total charges under €20.00 in *Green Fill with Dark Green Text*.
4. Test the conditional formatting by changing the bin type for collection number 5 to *240*. The total charge should now be formatted in green.
5. Change the bin type for collection number 5 back to *1100*.
6. Using a Filter, display data for bins weighing more than 15kg.
7. Clear the Filter and display data where the total charge is above average.
8. Rename sheet1 as *Collection Details*
9. Delete all unused worksheets.
10. Clear the filter and implement spreadsheet protection so that:
    - data can only be entered in the ranges A4:B13 and E4:E13
    - formulas and functions are no longer displayed in the formula bar.
11. Protect the workbook for structure only.
12. Save the spreadsheet as **Environmental Waste Charges**

Simple IF Assignment Four

Part 1: Spreadsheet Setup

1. Create a new spreadsheet workbook and enter the data shown in Table 7.15 in Sheet1.

	A	B	C	D	E	F	G	H	I	J
1	DigiLite Payroll System									
2										
3	Employee Name	Annual Salary	Marital Status	Annual TFA	Weekly Pay	Weekly TFA	Weekly Taxable Pay	Weekly Tax	Income Levy	Net Pay
4	Paul Sheehan	63700	Single							
5	Mike Everett	57000	Married							
6	Tina Lovett	94720	Single							
7	Barry Walsh	89880	Single							
8	Karl Burke	42940	Married							
9	Andrea Livingston	91000	Married							
10	Cathy Dunne	45500	Single							
11	Adrian Looney	75500	Single							
12	Liam Nocton	50300	Married							
13	Niall Donnelly	82000	Married							

Table 7.15

2. Calculate annual TFA (tax-free allowance) using an IF function. This is €9400 for married people and €4700 for single people.
3. Test the IF function by changing Paul Sheehan's marital status to *Married*. His annual tax-free allowance should now be €9400.
4. Change Paul's marital status back to *Single*.

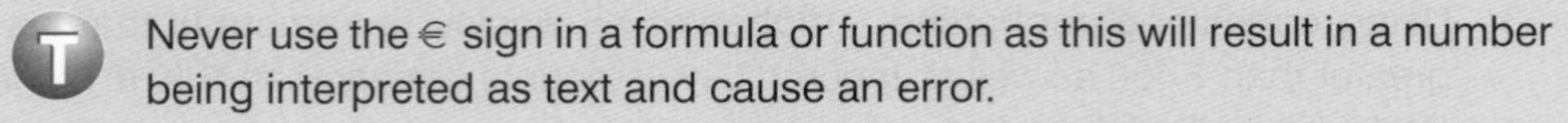

Never use the € sign in a formula or function as this will result in a number being interpreted as text and cause an error.

5. Calculate weekly pay, weekly TFA and weekly taxable pay.
6. Calculate the weekly tax using an IF function.
   - Employees whose weekly pay is €1100 or less pay tax of 25% on their weekly taxable pay.

- Employees who earn more than €1100 pay tax of 25% on the first €1100 of their weekly taxable pay and 40% on any amount above €1100.

7. Test the IF function by changing Mike Everett's annual salary to *€65000*. His weekly pay should now be *€1250.00*, pushing him over the €1100 threshold. His new weekly tax is *€262.69.*
8. Change Mike Everett's annual salary back to *€57000*.
9. Calculate Income Levy.
   - Employees whose weekly pay is €1443 or less pay a levy of 2% on their weekly pay (before deduction of the tax-free allowance).
   - Employees who earn more than €1443 pay 2% on the first €1443 of their weekly pay and 4% on the amount above €1443.
10. Test the IF function by changing Liam Nocton's pay to *€75500*. His weekly pay should now be *€1451.92*, pushing him over the €1443 threshold. His new income levy is *€29.22*.
11. Change Liam's annual salary back to *€50300*.
12. Calculate net pay.
13. Format all money amounts to currency.
14. Sort the data first in descending order of marital status and then in ascending order of annual salary.

Part 2: Formatting, Filters and Spreadsheet Protection

Merge styles from:
Toms Hardware.xlsx

1. Merge styles from the *Toms Hardware* spreadsheet.
2. Format data in the *Employee Payroll* spreadsheet using the styles listed in Table 7.16.

Range of Cells	Cell Style
A1	Heading 4
A3:J3	Accent4
A4:J13	20% – Accent4

Table 7.16

3. Using conditional formatting, emphasise all weekly tax amounts that are greater than €400 as well as Income Levy amounts greater than €40 in *Light Red Fill with Dark Red Text.*
4. Test the conditional formatting by changing Niall Donnelly's annual salary to *€89550*. Both his weekly tax and income levy should now be formatted in red.
5. Change Niall Donnelly's annual salary back to *€82000*.

6. Using a Filter, display single employees earning more than €50,000.
7. Rename Sheet1 as *Wages Data*
8. Delete all unused worksheets in the workbook.
9. Clear the filter and implement spreadsheet protection so that:
   - data can only be entered in the range A4:C13
   - the spreadsheet user cannot select locked cells.
10. Save the spreadsheet as **Digilite Payroll System**

MORE ABOUT CONDITIONAL FORMATTING

We have already looked at conditional formatting where the formatting depends on values that are *inside* the range of highlighted cells. An example of this is shown in Figure 7.10, where conditional formatting is used to format discount amounts in the *Toms Hardware* spreadsheet.

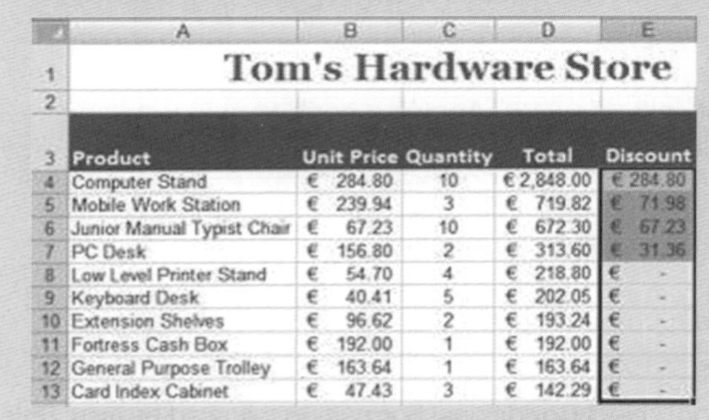

	A	B	C	D	E
1	Tom's Hardware Store				
2					
3	Product	Unit Price	Quantity	Total	Discount
4	Computer Stand	€ 284.80	10	€ 2,848.00	€ 284.80
5	Mobile Work Station	€ 239.94	3	€ 719.82	€ 71.98
6	Junior Manual Typist Chair	€ 67.23	10	€ 672.30	€ 67.23
7	PC Desk	€ 156.80	2	€ 313.60	€ 31.36
8	Low Level Printer Stand	€ 54.70	4	€ 218.80	€ -
9	Keyboard Desk	€ 40.41	5	€ 202.05	€ -
10	Extension Shelves	€ 96.62	2	€ 193.24	€ -
11	Fortress Cash Box	€ 192.00	1	€ 192.00	€ -
12	General Purpose Trolley	€ 163.64	1	€ 163.64	€ -
13	Card Index Cabinet	€ 47.43	3	€ 142.29	€ -

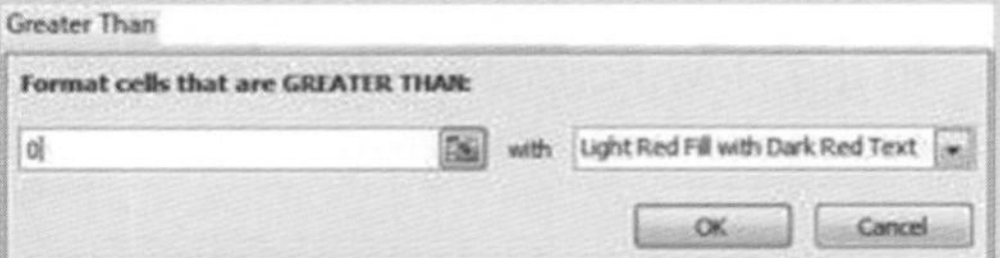

Figure 7.10 Values inside the highlighted range which are greater than zero are formatted in red

In Figure 7.10, *E4:E13* is highlighted. As the discount amounts are inside this highlighted range, applying conditional formatting is relatively straightforward. Having highlighted *E4:E13*, simply select Conditional Formatting in the Home section of the Ribbon. Now select Highlight Cells Rules and specify a logical rule in the Greater Than dialog box (Figure 7.10). Here, all discount amounts have been formatted in *Light Red Fill with Dark Red Text* using the *Greater Than 0* rule.

In some cases the conditional formatting may depend on values that are *outside* the range of highlighted cells. In the *DigiLite Payroll System* spreadsheet (Figure 7.11), we will use conditional formatting to emphasise the names of employees who pay more than €400 weekly tax.

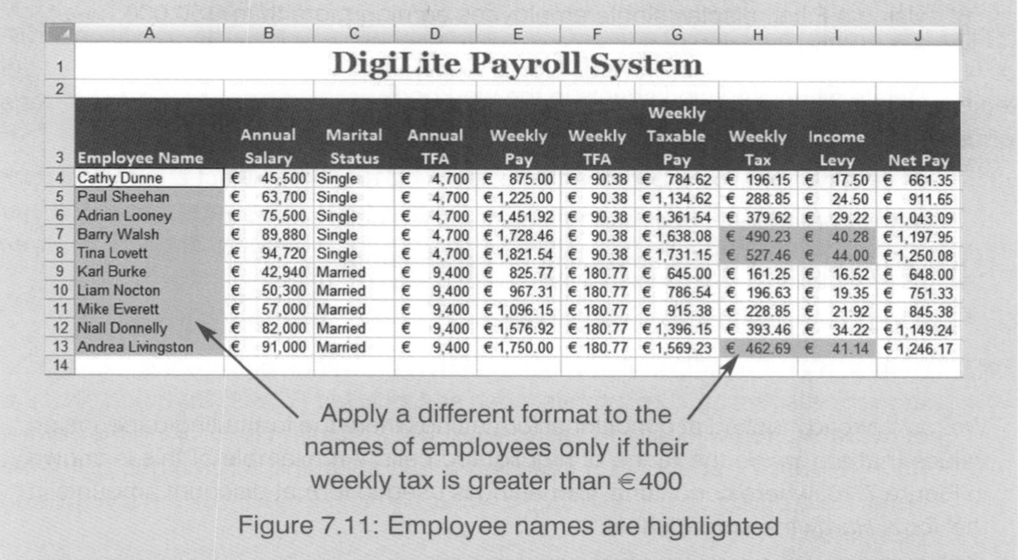

	A	B	C	D	E	F	G	H	I	J
1	**DigiLite Payroll System**									
2										
3	Employee Name	Annual Salary	Marital Status	Annual TFA	Weekly Pay	Weekly TFA	Weekly Taxable Pay	Weekly Tax	Income Levy	Net Pay
4	Cathy Dunne	€ 45,500	Single	€ 4,700	€ 875.00	€ 90.38	€ 784.62	€ 196.15	€ 17.50	€ 661.35
5	Paul Sheehan	€ 63,700	Single	€ 4,700	€ 1,225.00	€ 90.38	€ 1,134.62	€ 288.85	€ 24.50	€ 911.65
6	Adrian Looney	€ 75,500	Single	€ 4,700	€ 1,451.92	€ 90.38	€ 1,361.54	€ 379.62	€ 29.22	€ 1,043.09
7	Barry Walsh	€ 89,880	Single	€ 4,700	€ 1,728.46	€ 90.38	€ 1,638.08	€ 490.23	€ 40.28	€ 1,197.95
8	Tina Lovett	€ 94,720	Single	€ 4,700	€ 1,821.54	€ 90.38	€ 1,731.15	€ 527.46	€ 44.00	€ 1,250.08
9	Karl Burke	€ 42,940	Married	€ 9,400	€ 825.77	€ 180.77	€ 645.00	€ 161.25	€ 16.52	€ 648.00
10	Liam Nocton	€ 50,300	Married	€ 9,400	€ 967.31	€ 180.77	€ 786.54	€ 196.63	€ 19.35	€ 751.33
11	Mike Everett	€ 57,000	Married	€ 9,400	€ 1,096.15	€ 180.77	€ 915.38	€ 228.85	€ 21.92	€ 845.38
12	Niall Donnelly	€ 82,000	Married	€ 9,400	€ 1,576.92	€ 180.77	€ 1,396.15	€ 393.46	€ 34.22	€ 1,149.24
13	Andrea Livingston	€ 91,000	Married	€ 9,400	€ 1,750.00	€ 180.77	€ 1,569.23	€ 462.69	€ 41.14	€ 1,246.17
14										

Figure 7.11: Employee names are highlighted

From Figure 7.11, we can see that formatting the highlighted employee names depends on values in the weekly tax column. These weekly tax amounts are outside the highlighted range of cells *(A4:A13)*. Applying conditional formatting in this case is slightly more complex.

Conditional Formatting – Worked Example

1. Open the *DigiLite Payroll System* spreadsheet.
2. Highlight the employee names *(A4:A13)*.
3. In the Home section of the Ribbon, select Conditional Formatting followed by *New Rule.*
4. In the New Formatting Rule dialog box, select *Use a Formula to determine which cells to format*, as shown in Figure 7.12.

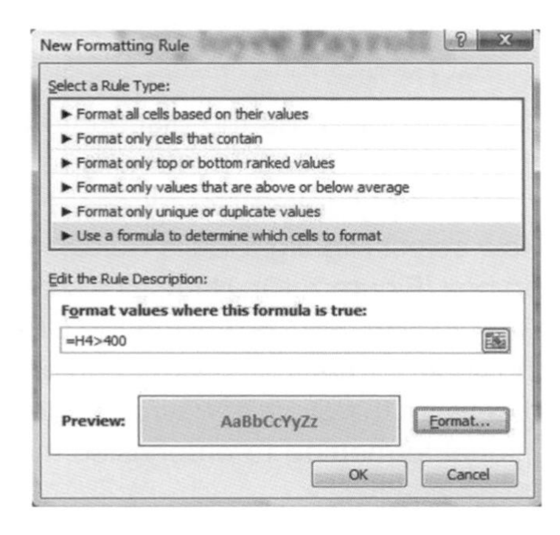

Figure 7.12 Using a conditional rule to isolate employees whose weekly tax is greater than €400

To isolate employees whose weekly tax is greater than €400, we need only specify a rule for the first employee, Cathy Dunne. Cathy's weekly tax is in H4. The conditional rule *=H4>400* checks Cathy's weekly tax. Conditional formatting of dark red text on a light red background will automatically be applied to any employees in the highlighted range whose weekly tax is greater than €400.

5. Type the conditional rule displayed in Figure 7.12 and then select a format of dark red bold text on a light red background. As Cathy's tax is not greater than €400, her name is not formatted in red. The conditional formatting is applied to three employees: Barry Walsh, Tina Lovett and Andrea Livingston.
6. Save the *Employee Payroll* spreadsheet.

When applying conditional formatting based on values outside the highlighted range of cells, the custom formats, such as *Light Red Fill with Dark Red Text*, are not available. You will need to set up your own formatting by clicking the *Format* button (Figure 7.12) and then selecting a font style and a fill colour, using the Format Cells dialog box. It is difficult to exactly match Excel's custom styles using this method.

Simple IF Assignment Five

Part 1: Create the Employee List

1. Create a new spreadsheet workbook and enter the data shown in Table 7.17 in Sheet1.

	A	B	C
1	**Employee No**	**Employee Name**	**Due In At**
2	1	Paul Sheehan	09:00
3	2	Mike Everett	10:00
4	3	Tina Lovett	11:00
5	4	Barry Walsh	09:00
6	5	Karl Burke	09:00
7	6	Ursel Vanderbilt	10:00
8	7	Cathy Dunne	10:00
9	8	Adrian Looney	09:00
10	9	Liam Nocton	09:00
11	10	Niall Donnelly	10:00

Table 7.17

2. Rename Sheet1 as *Employee List*

3. Merge styles from the *Toms Hardware* spreadsheet.

Merge styles from:
Toms Hardware.xlsx

4. Format data in the *Employee List* worksheet using the styles listed in Table 7.18.

Range of Cells	Cell Style
A1:C1	Accent4
A2:C11	20% – Accent4

Table 7.18

5. Implement spreadsheet protection so that data cannot be entered in this worksheet.

Part 2: Create Monday's Timesheet

1. Rename Sheet2 as *Monday*
2. Enter the data displayed in Table 7.19 in the worksheet named *Monday*. Formulas and functions will be entered in the shaded cells.

Hours and minutes must be separated by a colon in order for Excel to interpret the value entered in a cell as a time. Using a decimal point instead of a colon will cause Excel to interpret the value as a number.

	A	B	C	D	E
1	Monday Timesheet				
2					
3	Employee No	Employee Name	Clock-In Time	Due In At	Status
4			08:57		
5			09:50		
6			11:15		
7			09:03		
8			08:32		
9			09:47		
10			10:30		
11			09:21		
12			08:50		
13			08:56		

Table 7.19

3. Use linking formulas to read the employee numbers, employee names and due in at times from the *Employee List* worksheet. A4 links to employee 1, A5 links to employee 2 and so on.

N Refer to Chapter 3 for an explanation of linking formulas.

4. Use an IF function to display the status of each employee, which is either late or on time.
5. Format data in the *Monday* worksheet using the styles listed in Table 7.20.

Range of Cells	Cell Style
A1	Heading 4
A3:E3	Accent4
A4:E13	20% – Accent4

Table 7.20

6. Use conditional formatting to emphasise both the names of employees who were late and their status in *Yellow Fill with Dark Yellow Text*.

When referring to text with a conditional formatting rule, always ensure that the text is enclosed in double quotes.

7. Test both the IF function and the conditional formatting by changing Paul Sheehan's clock-in time to *9:05*. His status should change to *Late*. Both his name and his clock-in time should be formatted in yellow.
8. Change Paul's clock-in time back to *08:57*.
9. Implement spreadsheet protection so that:
   - data can only be entered in the range C4:C13
   - formulas and functions are no longer displayed in the formula bar.

Part 3: Create Tuesday's timesheet

1. Copy the worksheet named *Monday* and rename the copy as *Tuesday*

N The copy will initially be named Monday(2)

2. Unprotect the worksheet named *Tuesday*. Change the title to *Tuesday Timesheet* and then re-protect the worksheet.
3. Delete the existing clock-in times and enter the new times shown in bold print in Table 7.21.

	A	B	C	D	E
1	Tuesday Timesheet				
2					
3	Employee No	Employee Name	Clock-In Time	Due In At	Status
4			08:50		
5			09:59		
6			11:01		
7			08:50		
8			08:30		
9			09:53		
10			09:50		
11			09:03		
12			08:33		
13			08:41		

Table 7.21

Part 4: Create Wednesday's Timesheet

1. Copy the worksheet named *Tuesday* and rename the copy as *Wednesday*
2. Unprotect the worksheet named *Wednesday*. Change the title to *Wednesday Timesheet* and then re-protect the worksheet.
3. Delete the existing clock-in times and enter the new times shown in bold print in Table 7.22.

	A	B	C	D	E
1	Wednesday Timesheet				
2					
3	Employee No	Employee Name	Clock-In Time	Due In At	Status
4			08:50		
5			09:56		
6			11:07		
7			08:49		
8			08:40		
9			09:58		
10			10:30		
11			08:57		
12			09:00		
13			08:55		

Table 7.22

Part 5: Create Thursday's Timesheet

1. Copy the worksheet named *Wednesday* and rename the copy as *Thursday*
2. Unprotect the worksheet named *Thursday*. Change the title to *Thursday Timesheet* and then re-protect the worksheet.
3. Delete the existing clock-in times and enter the new times shown in bold print in Table 7.23.

	A	B	C	D	E
1			**Thursday Timesheet**		
2					
3	**Employee No**	**Employee Name**	**Clock-In Time**	**Due In At**	**Status**
4			**08:58**		
5			**09:23**		
6			**11:45**		
7			**08:50**		
8			**08:53**		
9			**09:55**		
10			**09:21**		
11			**08:59**		
12			**08:57**		
13			**08:56**		

Table 7.23

Part 6: Create Friday's Timesheet

1. Copy the worksheet named *Thursday* and rename the copy as *Friday*
2. Unprotect the worksheet named *Friday*. Change the title to *Friday Timesheet* and then re-protect the worksheet.
3 Delete the existing clock-in times and enter the new times shown in bold print in Table 7.24.

	A	B	C	D	E
1	Friday Timesheet				
2					
3	Employee No	Employee Name	Clock-In Time	Due In At	Status
4			08:48		
5			09:45		
6			11:01		
7			08:45		
8			08:55		
9			09:44		
10			09:55		
11			09:00		
12			09:03		
13			09:01		

Table 7.24

Part 7: Create the Weekly Attendance Summary

1. Enter the data in Table 7.25 in an unused worksheet within the same workbook, or insert a new worksheet if necessary. Formulas and functions will be entered in the shaded cells.

	A	B	C	D	E	F	G
1	Weekly Attendance Summary						
2							
3	Employee Name	Monday	Tuesday	Wednesday	Thursday	Friday	Number of Lates
4							
5							
6							
7							
8							
9							
10							
11							
12							
13							

Table 7.25

2. Rename this worksheet as *Summary*
3. Use linking formulas to read the employee names from the *Employee List* worksheet.
4. In columns B, C, D, E and F use linking formulas to read the daily status of each employee.
5. Use the COUNTIF function to calculate the number of lates for each employee.
6. Format data in the *Summary* worksheet using the styles listed in Table 7.26.

Range of Cells	Cell Style
A1	Heading 4
A3:G3	Accent4
A4:G13	20% – Accent4

Table 7.26

7. Use conditional formatting to emphasise the names of all employees who were late and the number of times they were late in *Yellow Fill with Dark Yellow Text*.
8. Test the conditional formatting by changing Mike Everett's clock-in time to *10:01* in the *Monday* worksheet. In the *Summary* worksheet, both Mike's name and number of times he was late should now be formatted in yellow.
9. In the *Monday* worksheet, change Mike's clock-in time back to 09:50.
10. Using a Filter, display employees who were late on two or more days. 
11. Clear the filter and implement spreadsheet protection so that:
    - data cannot be entered in the *Summary* worksheet
    - formulas and functions no longer appear in the formula bar.
12. Delete all unused worksheets in the workbook.
13. If necessary, rearrange worksheets so that they appear in the order displayed in Figure 7.13.

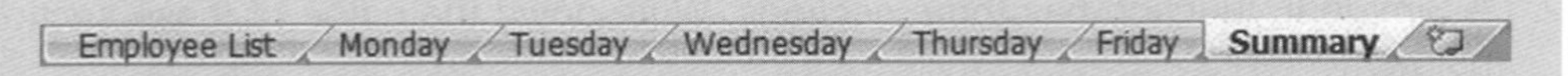

Figure 7.13 Sheet tabs in the correct order

14. Protect the workbook for Structure only.

Part 8: Create a Macro

1. Select cell A1 in the *Summary* worksheet.
2. Record a new macro named *clearweek* that performs the following tasks.
   - Deletes the contents of C4:C13 in the worksheet named *Monday*
   - Deletes the contents of C4:C13 in the worksheet named *Tuesday*
   - Deletes the contents of C4:C13 in the worksheet named *Wednesday*
   - Deletes the contents of C4:C13 in the worksheet named *Thursday*
   - Deletes the contents of C4:C13 in the worksheet named *Friday*
   - Selects C4 in the worksheet named *Monday*
3. Select the *Summary* worksheet and turn off worksheet protection.
4. Using the Insert section of the Ribbon, draw a rounded rectangle to the right of the data. Format the rectangle using the *Subtle Effect Dark 1* shape style. Type the text *Clear All* inside the rectangle. Link the rounded rectangle to the *clearweek* macro.

Clear All

You can quickly access the list of shapes using the *ALT+N+SH* keyboard combination.

5 Re-protect the *Summary* worksheet.

6 Test your macro by entering dummy times in each of the five worksheets. Run the macro by clicking the *Clear All* button.

7. Save the spreadsheet as **Employee Timesheet,** using the *Excel Macro-Enabled Workbook* file type.

SIMPLE IF REVIEW QUESTIONS

Answers to the review questions are available on www.gillmacmillan.ie

Test your knowledge of Simple IFs by answering the following questions.

1. IF functions are used to automate the ______________ making process.
2. A Simple IF function has three sections. Write down the name of these sections below:

   Section 1: ________________

   Section 2: ________________

   Section 3: ________________
3. In the condition of an IF function, ___________ operators are used to test data in a spreadsheet cell.

4.

	A	B	C
1		**Project Marks**	**Project Grade**
2	Erika Sommer	25	
3			

Table 7.27

Table 7.27 displays the marks scored by Erika Sommer in a project. Students who score less than 20 will be given a Fail. Students who score 20 or more will be given a Pass. Write down the IF function that will calculate Erika's grade.

____

5. Write down the names of the logical operators in Table 7.28.

Logical Operator	Meaning
<	
<=	
=	
>	
>=	
<>	

Table 7.28

6.

	A	B
1		**Total Spent**
2	John O Neill	€123.81
3	Clubcard Points	
4		

Table 7.29

Table 7.29 displays the total amount spent by John O Neill on his weekly shopping. Customers who spend €100 or less receive 25 clubcard points. Customers who spend more than €100 receive 80 clubcard points. Write down the IF function that will calculate John's clubcard points.

____

7.

	A	B
1		**Calls (minutes)**
2	Kate Byrne	109
3	Free Minutes	
4		

Table 7.30

Table 7.30 displays the total amount of talk time that Kate used on her mobile phone. Customers with 100 minutes or more talk time receive 40 free minutes. Customers with less than 100 minutes of talk time receive 10 free minutes. Write down the IF function that will calculate Kate's free minutes.

____

8.

	A	B	C	D
1		**Kilowatts**	**Total Bill**	**Discount**
2	Pascal Fournier	55	€189.55	
3				

Table 7.31

Table 7.31 displays the kilowatts used to calculate Pascal Fournier's electricity bill. Electricity customers who use 50 or more kilowatts are entitled to a 5% discount. Write down the IF function that will calculate Pascal's discount.

____

9.

	A	B	C
1		**Yellow Cards**	**Matches Missed**
2	Patrick Connolly	8	
3			

Table 7.32

Table 7.32 displays the number of yellow cards received by Patrick Connolly. Players with 4 yellow cards or less automatically miss 1 match. Players with 5 or more yellow cards miss 3 matches. Write down the IF function that will calculate the number of matches missed by Patrick.

____

10.

	A	B	C
1		**Tries Scored**	**Bonus Points**
2	Ireland	5	
3			

Table 7.33

Table 7.33 displays the number of tries scored by Ireland in an international rugby match. Teams that score 4 or more tries receive 1 bonus point. Write down the IF function that will calculate the number of bonus points.

____

NESTED SIMPLE IF FUNCTION

Not all decisions are limited to a choice between two alternative courses of action. For example, if you are buying a PC, it may come in five different colours. In choosing a colour, you must decide to take one of five possible courses of action. IF functions that allow you to choose between *three or more* possible courses of action are called Nested IF Functions. In a Nested Simple IF, *Nested* refers to the fact that one IF function is written inside another IF function. *Simple* refers to the fact that each decision made by the IF function is based on a single condition *(in this case the colour of the PC)*.

Using the *OnLine Insurance Company* example, we will see how a Nested Simple IF function works.

	A	B	C	D
1	**OnLine Insurance**		*Your Policy is just a click away!*	
2				
3			Basic Premium	€ 300.00
4			Total Premium	
5				
6	Policy Holder	Jim Collins	Gender Premium	€ 60.00
7	Gender	Male	Age Premium	
8	Age	27	Performance Premium	
9	Full Drivers licence	Yes	Claims Bonus	
10	Engine cc	1800	Licence Bonus	
11	Sports model	Yes		
12	Claims to date	0		
13				

Figure 7.14

OnLine Insurance Example: Calculating the Age Premium

In Figure 7.14, a Nested Simple IF function will be used to calculate the age premium for Jim Collins.

OnLine Insurance calculates the age premium on the following basis.

OnLine Insurance Age Premium Guidelines

- For drivers aged 18 or under there's an extra charge of 60% of the basic premium.
- For drivers aged between 19 and 21 inclusive there's an extra charge of 40% of the basic premium.
- For drivers aged between 22 and 25 inclusive there's an extra charge of 20% of the basic premium.
- For drivers older than 25 there's an extra charge of 10% of the basic premium.

As there are four possible courses of action, each of which depends on a single condition *(the age of the driver)*, a Nested Simple IF will be used to calculate the Age Premium. This Nested Simple IF function will calculate the Age Premium by taking one of the following courses of action:

1. Charge 60% extra.
2. Charge 40% extra.
3. Charge 20% extra.
4. Charge 10% extra.

The Nested Simple IF function makes its decision based on the age of the driver. Represented graphically, this would look like Figure 7.15.

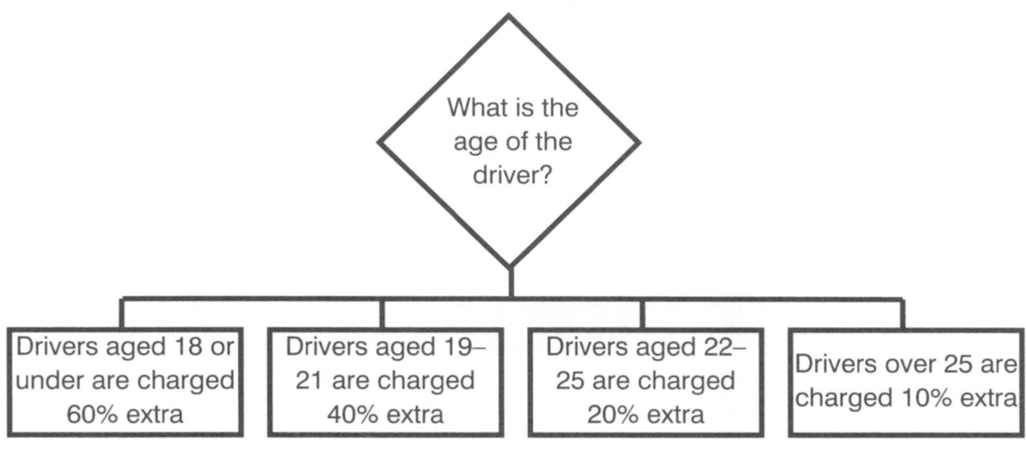

Figure 7.15 The Nested Simple IF function must calculate one of four different premiums, depending on the age of the driver

Before writing a Nested Simple IF function, it is important to have a clear idea of all of its sections. These are summarised in Table 7.34.

Condition 1	Is the driver under 18?
Action 1	60% of the basic premium extra charge
Condition 2	Is the driver aged 19–21?
Action 2	40% of the basic premium extra charge
Condition 3	Is the driver aged 22–25?
Action 3	20% of the basic premium extra charge
False Action	10% of the basic premium extra charge

Table 7.34 The sections of the Nested Simple IF function

N The false action is implemented only when the age of the driver does not satisfy any of the conditions tested by the IF function.

If we were to write this IF function in English, it would look something like this.

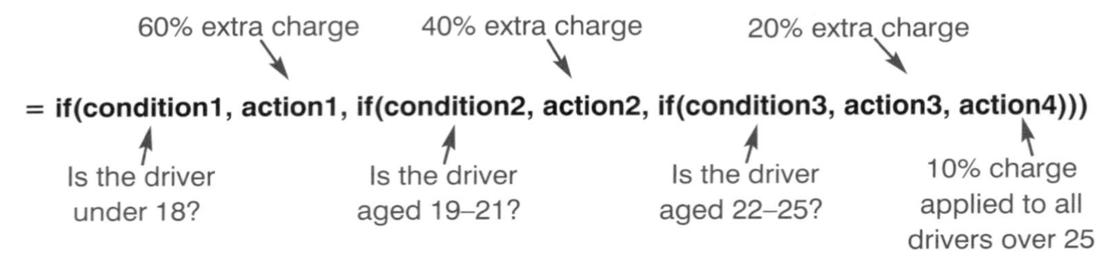

Notice how the second IF function is *inside* the first IF function. The third IF function is *inside* the second IF function. This is why this type of IF function is called a *Nested* Simple IF.

N The number of conditions in a Nested Simple IF function will vary according to the number of possible courses of action. Excel allows a maximum of 64 IFs in each Nested Simple IF function.

	A	B	C	D	E	F
1	OnLine Insurance		Your Policy is just a click away!			
2						
3			Basic Premium	€ 300.00		
4			Total Premium			
5						
6	Policy Holder	Jim Collins	Gender Premium	€ 60.00		
7	Gender	Male	Age Premium	=IF(B8<=18,D3*60%,IF(B8<=21,D3*40%, IF(B8<=25,D3*20%,D3*10%)))		
8	Age	27				
9	Full Drivers licence	Yes				
10	Engine cc	1800				
11	Sports model	Yes				
12	Claims to date	0				
13						

Figure 7.16 Calculating the age premium with a Nested Simple IF function

From Figure 7.16, it can be seen that the age of the driver is in B8 and that the basic premium is in D3. When we combine this information with the age premium guidelines and feed it all into an IF function, we get the following:

=if(B8<=18,D3*60%,if(B8<=21,D3*40%,if(B8<=25,D3*20%,D3*10%)))

This IF function is entered in D7, as shown in Figure 7.16. The conditions and associated actions of this IF function are summarised in Table 7.35.

	Condition (Age)	**Resulting Action (Calculation of Age Premium)**
1	<=18	60% of basic premium
2	19–21 inclusive	40% of basic premium
3	22–25 inclusive	20% of basic premium
4	>25	0% of basic premium

Table 7.35 Conditions and associated actions of the Nested Simple IF function

As Jim's age is 27, the IF function calculates his age premium by multiplying the basic premium in D3 by 10%, giving €30.

Try It Yourself!

1. Open the *OnLine Insurance* spreadsheet.
2. Enter the Nested Simple IF function in D7 as shown in Figure 7.16. As Jim is 27, the age premium calculated by the Nested Simple IF function should be €30.00.
3. Test the IF function by entering ages in B8 as follows:

Age	**Resulting Age Premium**
17	€180.00
20	€120.00
24	€60.00

4. Change Jim's age back to *27*.
5. Save the *OnLine Insurance* spreadsheet.

Points to Note

Although the second condition reads as *B8<=21*, Excel interprets this as meaning *between 19 and 21 inclusive*. This is because at this point the IF function has already established that the number in B8 is not less than or equal to 18. The same is true of the third condition, which Excel interprets as *between 22 and 25 inclusive*.

Interpreted as'19 to 21' by Excel — Interpreted as '22 to 25' by Excel — Applies to customers over 25

=if(B8<=18,D3*60%,if(B8<=21,D3*40%, if(B8<=25,D3*20%,D3*10%)))

IF functions rule two: When testing for numbers in different ranges, either start at the highest number and work downwards or start at the lowest number and work upwards. In the example, we have started at 18 and worked our way up to 25.

IF functions rule three: When testing for numbers in different ranges, all the signs should be pointing in the same direction, e.g. all greater than (>) signs or all less than (<) signs. In the example, < is used throughout.

IF functions rule four: The number of IFs is always one less than the number of actions, e.g. three actions means two IFs are required, four actions means three IFs are required, five actions means four IFs are required, and so on.

IF functions rule five: The last action never requires a conditional test.

IF functions rule six: The number of IFs determines how many brackets should be closed at the end of a Nested Simple IF function, e.g. two IFs means two brackets should be closed, three IFs means three brackets should be closed, four IFs means four brackets should be closed, and so on.

Nested Simple IF Assignment One

Part 1: Spreadsheet Setup

1. Create a new spreadsheet workbook and enter the data shown in Table 7.36 in Sheet1.
2. Calculate the total for each driver.
3. Calculate the discount using an IF function.
   - There is no discount on cars hired for five days or less.
   - There is a discount of 5% of the total on cars hired for six to ten days.
   - There is a discount of 10% of the total on cars hired for more than ten days.

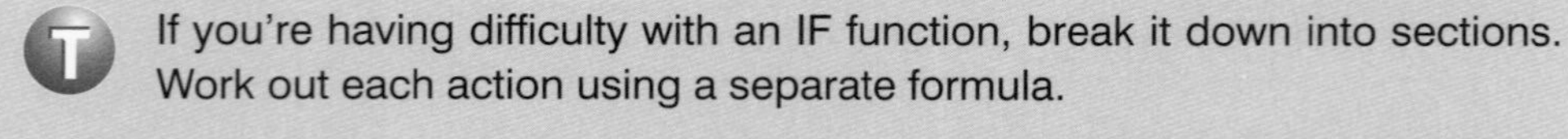

If you're having difficulty with an IF function, break it down into sections. Work out each action using a separate formula.

4. Test the IF function by entering the following days hired values for Frank Dunne. The IF function should calculate discounts as shown.

Days Hired	Discount
6	€19.50
12	€78.00

	A	B	C	D	E	F	G
1	Budget Car Rentals						
2							
3	Customer Name	Model Name	Days Hired	Cost per Day	Total	Discount	Amount Due
4	Frank Dunne	Fiesta	2	65			
5	Oliver O Shea	Mondeo	6	75			
6	Pat Murphy	Ka	1	55			
7	Michael O Neill	Focus	8	70			
8	Hanna Onderdonk	Clio	14	60			
9	Alex Evans	Megane	5	70			
10	Kevin Fanning	Prius	14	70			
11	Ciaran Molloy	Auris	14	60			

Table 7.36

5. Change Frank's days hired back to 2.
6. Calculate the amount due.
7. Format all money amounts to currency.
8. Sort the data in descending order of amount due.
9. Rename Sheet1 as *Customer Records*

Part 2: Formatting, Filters and Spreadsheet Protection

1. Merge styles from the *Toms Hardware* spreadsheet.
2. Format data in the *Customer Records* worksheet using the styles listed in Table 7.37.

Range of Cells	Cell Style
A1	Heading4
A3:G3	Accent4
A4:G11	20% – Accent4

Table 7.37

3. Delete all unused worksheets in the workbook.
4. Using a Filter, display all cars hired where the amount due is above average.
5. Clear the filter and implement spreadsheet protection so that:
   - data can only be entered in the range A4:D11
   - formulas and functions are no longer displayed in the formula bar.

6. Protect the workbook for structure only.
7. Print the *Customer Records* worksheet.
8. Save the spreadsheet as **Budget Car Rentals**

Nested Simple IF Assignment Two

Part 1: Spreadsheet Setup

1. Create a new spreadsheet workbook and enter the data shown in Table 7.38 in Sheet1.

	A	B	C	D	E
1	**Direct 2U Couriers**				
2					
3	**Job Description**	**Status**	**Basic Price**	**Additional Charge**	**Total**
4	Deliver goods to Clondalkin	Urgent	65		
5	Pick up package in Swords	Normal	55		
6	Collect documents at Four Courts	Normal	50		
7	Deliver package to Dun Laoghaire	Priority	65		
8	Pick up computers at airport	Urgent	70		
9	Deliver stationery to Blackrock	Normal	55		
10	Collect faulty PC at Sandyford	Urgent	60		
11	Courier airline ticket to Bray	Urgent	80		
12	Deliver exam papers to Athlone	Priority	170		
13	Deliver important documents to Sandymount	Urgent	50		

Table 7.38

2. Calculate the additional charge using an IF function as follows.
   - There is no additional charge for deliveries with a status of normal.
   - There is an additional charge of 20% of the basic price for deliveries with a status of urgent.
   - There is an additional charge of 50% of the basic price for deliveries with a status of priority.
3. Test the IF function by entering the following status values for the Four Courts collection. The IF function should calculate additional charges as shown.

Status	Additional Charge
Urgent	€10.00
Priority	€25.00

4. Change the status of the Four Courts collection back to *Normal*.
5. Calculate the total.
6. Format all money amounts to currency.
7. Rename Sheet1 as *Delivery List*
8. Delete all unused worksheets in the workbook.
9. Create a custom sort order as follows: *Normal, Urgent, Priority*. Using the custom sort order, sort the data in descending order of status.

Part 2: Formatting, Filters and Spreadsheet Protection

1. Merge styles from the *Toms Hardware* spreadsheet.
2. Format data in the *Delivery List* worksheet using the styles listed in Table 7.39.

Merge styles from:
Toms Hardware.xlsx

Range of Cells	Cell Style
A1	Heading4
A3:E3	Accent4
A4:E13	20% – Accent4

Table 7.39

3. Use conditional formatting to display the status of priority deliveries with a *Light Red Fill*.
4. Test the conditional formatting by changing the status of the *Clondalkin* delivery to *Priority*. The status of this delivery should now be formatted in red.
5. Change the status of the *Clondalkin* delivery back to *Urgent*.
6. Using a Filter, display urgent and priority deliveries where the total is greater than €50.
7. Clear the filter and implement spreadsheet protection so that:
   - data can only be entered in the range A4:C13
   - the spreadsheet user cannot select locked cells.
8. Protect the workbook for structure and windows.
9. Save the spreadsheet as **Direct 2U Couriers**

Nested Simple IF Assignment Three

Part 1: Create the Household Policies Worksheet

1. Create a new spreadsheet workbook and enter the data shown in Table 7.40 in Sheet1.

	A	B	C	D	E	F	G	H	I
1	**Don't Riskit Insurance**								
2	**Household Policies**								
3									
4	**Client Name**	**House Value**	**Contents Value**	**Payment Option**	**House Premium**	**Contents Premium**	**Total Payment**	**Initial Instalment**	**Monthly Instalment**
5	Joe Murphy	465000	18500	B					
6	Karol Macialek	480000	21250	B					
7	Peter Lynch	525000	35000	A					
8	Dave Power	478000	25000	C					
9	Margaret O'Neill	420000	23500	B					
10	Paul Hewitt	700000	27000	A					
11	Colin O'Sullivan	415000	17000	C					
12	Eddy Jones	650000	35000	A					
13	Gerry Thompson	675000	18500	C					

Table 7.40

2. Calculate the house premium using the information in Table 7.41.

House Value	Premium
<=€450000	0.1% of house value
€450001–€600000	0.2% of house value
>€600000	0.3% of house value

Table 7.41

3. Test the IF function by entering the following house values for *Colin O'Sullivan*. The IF function should calculate house premiums as shown.

House Value	**House Premium**
€460000	€920
€650000	€1950

4. Change Colin's house value back to *€415000*.
5. Calculate the contents premium using the information in Table 7.42.

Contents Value	Premium
<=€20000	0.5% of contents value
€20001–€25000	1.0% of contents value
€25001–€30000	1.5% of contents value
>€30000	2.0% of contents value

Table 7.42

6. Test the IF function by entering the following contents values for *Colin O'Sullivan*. The IF function should calculate contents premiums as shown.

Contents Value	Contents Premium
€22000	€220.00
€29500	€442.50
€33000	€660.00

7. Change Colin's contents value back to *€17000*.
8. Calculate the total premium.
9. Don't Riskit Insurance offers three methods of payment, as follows.
   - Payment option A: payment in full at time of purchase.
   - Payment option B: 50% initial payment + remainder paid in 12 monthly instalments.
   - Payment option C: 12 monthly instalments, no payment up front.
10. Calculate the initial payment and monthly instalment for each client using separate IF functions.

H If a client chooses payment option A, there would be no monthly instalments.

11. Test the IF functions by entering the following payment options for *Joe Murphy*. The IF functions should calculate initial payments and monthly installments as shown.

Payment Option	Initial Payment	Monthly Instalment
A	€1022.50	€0.00
C	€0.00	€85.21

12. Change Joe's payment option back to *B*.
13. Format all money amounts to currency.
14. Rename Sheet1 as *Household Policies*

15. Merge styles from the *Toms Hardware* spreadsheet.

Merge styles from:
Toms Hardware.xlsx

16. Format data in the *Household Policies* worksheet using the styles listed in Table 7.43.

Range of Cells	Cell Style
A1	Heading4
A2, A4:I4	Accent4
A5:I13	20% – Accent4

Table 7.43

17. Using a Filter, display clients who selected payment option B or C and whose total premium is greater than €700.
18. Clear all Filters from the worksheet.
19. Implement spreadsheet protection so that:
    - data can only be entered in the range A5:D13
    - the spreadsheet user cannot select locked cells.

Part 2: Create the Motor Policies Worksheet

1. Each of the clients listed in the *Household Policies* worksheet has also applied for car insurance. Enter the data displayed in Table 7.44 in Sheet2 of the same workbook.

	A	B	C	D	E	F	G	H	I	J	K
1	Don't Riskit Insurance										
2	Motor Policies										
3											
4	Client Name	Age	Value of Car	Dublin Area	Payment Option	Age Premium	Value Premium	Dublin Weighting	Total Premium	Initial Payment	Monthly Instalment
5		19	14000	Yes	C						
6		35	11500	No	A						
7		28	17500	Yes	A						
8		44	24000	Yes	C						
9		21	14500	Yes	B						
10		37	39000	Yes	B						
11		55	21000	No	C						
12		27	50000	Yes	A						
13		18	18000	No	B						

Table 7.44

2. Enter linking formulas to read the client names from the *Household Policies* worksheet.
3. Calculate age premium using the information in Table 7.45.

Age of Client	Premium
<25	10% of car value
25–35	5% of car value
36–50	3% of car value
>50	2% of car value

Table 7.45

4. Test the IF function by entering the following age values for *Joe Murphy*. The IF function should calculate age premiums as shown.

Age	**Age Premium**
26	€700
41	€420
57	€280

5. Change Joe's age back to 19.
6. Calculate the value premium using the information in Table 7.46.

Value of Car	Premium
<=€15000	1.0% of car value
€15001–€20000	1.5% of car value
€20001–€25000	2.0% of car value
>€25000	2.5% of car value

Table 7.46

7. Test the IF function by entering the following car values for *Joe Murphy*. The IF function should calculate value premiums as shown.

Value of Car	**Value Premium**
€16000	€240
€24000	€480
€44000	€1100

8. Change Joe's car value back to €14000.
9. Cars insured in the Dublin area have an additional weighting of 0.5% of the car value. Calculate the Dublin weighting using an IF function.

10. Test the IF function by changing Dublin Area to *Yes* for *Karol Macialek*. This should give a Dublin Weighting of *€57.50*.
11. Change Dublin Area back to *No* for *Karol Macialek*.
12. Calculate the total premium using the *SUM* function.
13. Calculate the initial payment and monthly instalment using the payment options guidelines listed for household insurance.
14. Format all money amounts to currency.
15. Rename Sheet2 as *Motor Policies*
16. Format data in the *Motor Policies* worksheet using the styles listed in Table 7.47.

Range of Cells	Cell Style
A1	Heading4
A2, A4:K4	Accent4
A5:K13	20% – Accent4

Table 7.47

17. Using a Filter, display clients in the Dublin area who selected payment option A.
18. Clear all Filters from the worksheet. 
19. Implement spreadsheet protection so that:
    - data can only be entered in the range B5:E13
    - the spreadsheet user cannot select locked cells.

Part 3: Create the Summary Worksheet

1. Enter the data displayed in Table 7.48 in Sheet3 of the same workbook.
2. In column A enter linking formulas to read the client names from the *Household Policies* worksheet.
3. In B5 calculate the total premium by adding the total premium from the *Household Policies* worksheet to the total premium from the *Motor Policies* worksheet.
4. In C5 calculate the total initial payment by adding the total initial payment from the *Household Policies* worksheet to the total initial payment from the *Motor Policies* worksheet.
5. In D5 calculate the total monthly instalment by adding the total monthly instalment from the *Household Policies* worksheet to the total monthly instalment from the *Motor Policies* worksheet.
6. Copy the summary formulas using Fill Down.

	A	B	C	D
1	Don't Riskit Insurance			
2	Policy Report			
3				
4	**Client Name**	**Total Premium**	**Total Initial Payment**	**Total Monthly Instalment**
5				
6				
7				
8				
9				
10				
11				
12				
13				

Table 7.48

7. Format all money amounts to currency.
8. Rename Sheet3 as *Summary*
9. Format data in the *Summary* worksheet using the styles listed in Table 7.49.

Range of Cells	Cell Style
A1	Heading4
A2, A4:D4	Accent4
A5:D13	20% – Accent4

Table 7.49

10. Using a Filter, display clients whose total premium is between €1000 and €2000.
11. Clear the filter and set up spreadsheet protection so that the spreadsheet user cannot select locked cells.
12. Delete all unused worksheets in the workbook.
13. Protect the workbook for structure and windows.
14. Save the spreadsheet as **Don't Riskit Insurance**

NESTED SIMPLE IF REVIEW QUESTIONS

Answers to the review questions are available on www.gillmacmillan.ie

1. Nested Simple IFs are used where an IF function must choose between ____ or more possible courses of action.
2. The process that automatically formats cells satisfying a conditional rule is called ____________________
3. Identify the error in the following IF function:

   =if(B6<50,B6*1%,if(B6<100,B6*2%,if(B6<150,B6*3%,B6*4%))

4.

	A	B
1		**Exam Mark**
2	Tina Cahill	78
3	Grade	
4		

Table 7.50

Table 7.50 displays the total marks scored by Tina in an exam. The grades are awarded as follows:

Mark	Grade
<=49	Fail
50–64	Pass
65–79	Merit
>80	Distinction

Write down the IF function that will calculate Tina's grade.

____

5. Identify the error in the following IF function:

   =if(A9<100,5,if(A9<200,10,if(A9<300,15,if(A9<400,20))))

6.

	A	B
1		**Car Category**
2	Zhanna Pyasetska	C
3	Basic Charge	
4		

Table 7.51

Table 7.51 displays the details of a car hired by Zhanna Pyasetska. The car hire company calculates the basic charge using the following information:

Category	Charge
A	€95
B	€125
C	€150
D	€180

Write down the IF function that will calculate Zhanna's basic charge.

7.

	A	B
1		**CO_2 Emissions**
2	Opel Corsa	139
3	Road Tax	
4		

Table 7.52

Table 7.52 displays details of CO_2 emissions. Road tax is calculated using the following information:

CO_2 emissions	Road tax
0–120	€104
121–140	€156
141–155	€302
156–170	€447
>170	€1165

Write down the IF function that will calculate the road tax for the Opel Corsa.

____

8.

	A	B
1		**Units Sold**
2	Tina Nolan	1395
3	Christmas Bonus	
4		

Table 7.53

Table 7.53 displays the details of Tina Nolan's Christmas bonus. Tina's bonus is calculated using the following information:

Units sold	Bonus
<=500	€200
501–999	€350
1000–1499	€600
>1499	€1000

Write down the IF function that will calculate Tina's Christmas bonus.

____

9.

	A	B	C
1		**Department**	**Parking Zone**
2	Joe Byrne	Finance	
3			

Table 7.54

Table 7.54 displays the details of Joe Nolan's car parking arrangements. Parking zones are allocated to employees by department, as follows:

Department	Parking Zone
Engineering	A
Sales	B
Finance	C
IT	D
Research	E

Write down the IF function that will allocate Joe's parking zone.

____

10.

	A	B
1		**Shots on Goal**
2	Zozo Robaldo	8
3	Fantasy League Points	

Table 7.55

Table 7.55 displays the statistics relating to the match performance of a professional football player. Fantasy Football League points are allocated according to the number of shots on goal by a particular player. Calculate Zozo's fantasy league points using the following information:

Shots on goal	Points
0	0
1	1
2–3	2
4–6	5
>6	10

Write down the IF function that will calculate Zozo's fantasy league points.

____

COMPOUND IF FUNCTION

In the Simple IF and Nested Simple IF functions, each of the decisions made by the IF function depends on a single condition. Consider the following statement: *A 5% discount is given to all customers who spend more than €200.* Here the IF function must decide whether to give a 5% discount or not. The decision is based on a single condition – the amount spent by the customer. Imagine for a moment that the discount policy has been changed. The new policy is as follows: *A 5% discount is given to all customers who spend more than €200 on Mondays only.* The nature of the decision is the same – *Do we give a 5% discount or not?* However, under the new policy this decision now depends on two conditions; the amount spent and the day of the week.

A decision that depends on more than one condition is called a compound condition. IF functions that make decisions depending on more than one condition are called Compound IFs. This is summarised in Table 7.56.

	Condition 1	Condition 2	True Action	False Action
Simple IF	Total Spent > €200	-	5% discount	No discount
Compound IF	Total Spent > €200	Day = "Monday"	5% discount	No discount

Table 7.56 In a Compound IF, the decision depends on more than one condition

When an IF function needs to test more than one condition, a special function is used to do the testing. Depending on the nature of the conditions, either an AND function or an OR function is used to test the conditions. An AND function is used when *all* the conditions must be satisfied. An OR function is used when *at least one* of the conditions must be satisfied. AND functions and OR functions are positioned inside the IF function where we would normally write the condition.

AND FUNCTION

An AND function is used to test multiple conditions. When all the conditions it is testing are satisfied it will return the value *TRUE*. When one or more of the conditions is not satisfied, the AND function will return the value *FALSE*.

Structure of an AND Function

=AND(condition1, condition2, condition3, ...)

Worked Example

Continuing with our customer discount example, we will give a discount of 5% to anyone who spends more than €200 on Monday. This data has been entered in Table 7.57.

	A	B
1	Total Spent	€250
2	Day	Monday
3		
4	**Discount**	

Table 7.57

The conditions required to test the total spent and the day are shown in Table 7.58.

Condition	Meaning
B1>200	Is the amount spent greater than €200?
B2="Monday"	Was the amount spent on a Monday?

Table 7.58

These conditions are entered in the AND function, giving the following:

=AND(B1>200,B2="Monday")

As both conditions are satisfied, the AND function will return the value *TRUE* (Table 7.59).

	A	B
1	Total Spent	€250
2	Day	Monday
3		
4	**Discount**	**True**

Table 7.59

An AND function is limited to testing conditions. Combining the AND function in Table 7.59 with an IF function will allow the IF function to make a decision based on the two conditions tested by the AND function.

Remember the structure of the Simple IF function?

=IF(Condition , True action , False action)

Simply replace the condition with the AND function and you have a Compound IF function that tests two conditions!

=IF(AND(B1>200,B2="Monday"),B1*5%,0)

This combination of IF and AND functions is entered in B4 to calculate the discount (Table 7.60).

	A	B
1	Total Spent	€250
2	Day	Monday
3		
4	**Discount**	€12.50

Table 7.60

You only need to write = at the start of the IF function. You don't need a second = when you are starting the AND function.

An AND function can test a maximum of 255 conditions.

OnLine Insurance Example: Calculating the Performance Premium

A Compound IF is used when the decision made by an IF function depends on two or more conditions. In a Compound IF the conditions are tested by an AND function or an OR function. In the *OnLine Insurance Company* spreadsheet an IF function combined with an AND function will calculate the performance premium for Jim Collins.

	A	B	C	D
1	OnLine Insurance		Your Policy is just a click away!	
2				
3			Basic Premium	€ 300.00
4			Total Premium	
5				
6	Policy Holder	Jim Collins	Gender Premium	€ 60.00
7	Gender	Male	Age Premium	€ 30.00
8	Age	27	Performance Premium	
9	Full Drivers licence	Yes	Claims Bonus	
10	Engine cc	1800	Licence Bonus	
11	Sports model	Yes		
12	Claims to date	0		
13				

Figure 7.17

OnLine Insurance calculates the performance premium on the following basis.

Drivers with sports cars that have an engine capacity above 1600cc are charged 40% extra on the basic premium.

Here, the IF function must decide to do one of two things. Either:

1. Charge 40% extra

   or:

2. Charge nothing extra.

However, the decision now depends on two conditions – the classification of the car and the engine capacity. The 40% charge only applies when both conditions are satisfied. Represented graphically, this would look like Figure 7.18.

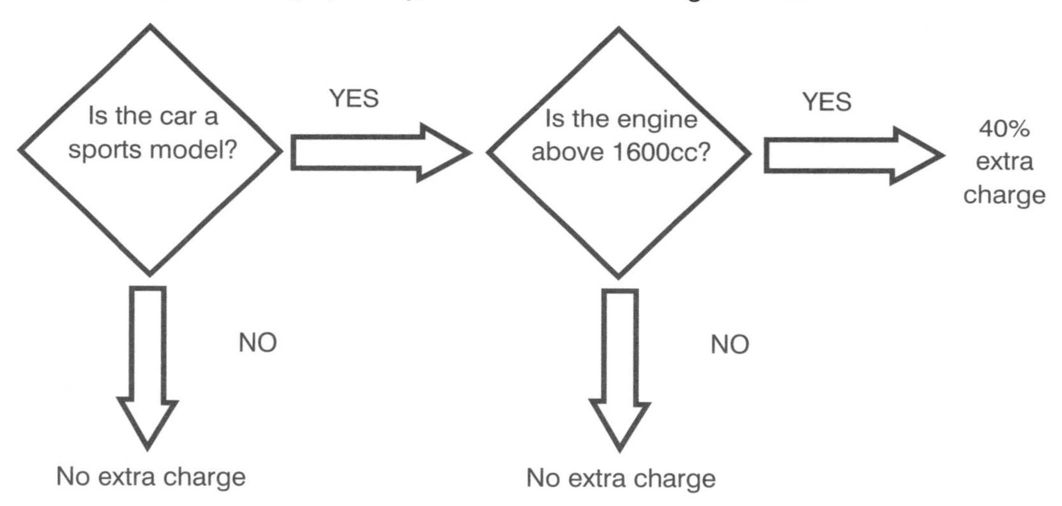

Figure 7.18 The IF function adds on the extra charge only when both conditions (sports and engine size) are satisfied. The extra charge doesn't apply when either one or both conditions are not satisfied.

Before writing the IF function, it is important to have a clear idea of its sections; the two conditions, the true action and the false action. These are summarised in Table 7.61.

Condition 1	Is the car a sports model?	Both conditions must be satisfied
Condition 2	Is the engine size above 1600cc?	
True Action	40% extra charge	
False Action	No extra charge	

Table 7.61 The sections of the Compound IF function

If we were to write the IF function in English, it would look something like this.

=IF(AND(condition 1, condition 2) , true action , false action)

- condition 1: Is it a sports car?
- condition 2: Is the engine size bigger than 1600cc?
- true action: 40% extra charge
- false action: No extra charge

Because there are two conditions, both of which must be satisfied, these conditions are tested by an AND function. Remember that the AND function is positioned inside the IF function. Notice how commas are used to separate the different sections of the IF function. A comma is also required to separate the conditions inside the AND function.

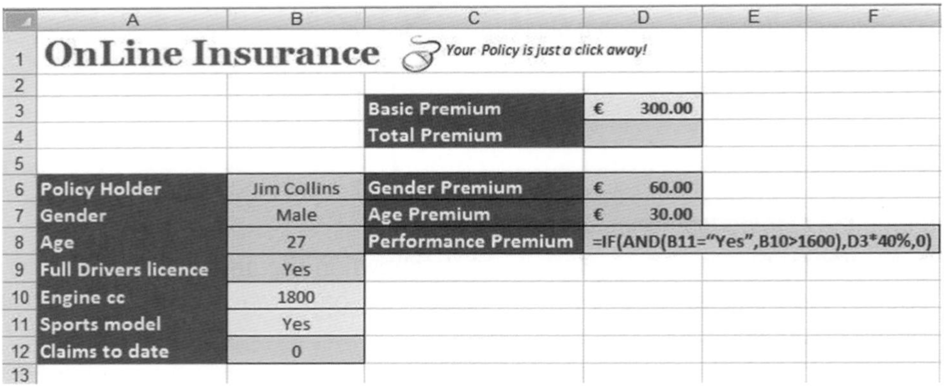

	A	B	C	D	E	F
1	OnLine Insurance		Your Policy is just a click away!			
2						
3			Basic Premium	€ 300.00		
4			Total Premium			
5						
6	Policy Holder	Jim Collins	Gender Premium	€ 60.00		
7	Gender	Male	Age Premium	€ 30.00		
8	Age	27	Performance Premium	=IF(AND(B11="Yes",B10>1600),D3*40%,0)		
9	Full Drivers licence	Yes				
10	Engine cc	1800				
11	Sports model	Yes				
12	Claims to date	0				
13						

Figure 7.19 Calculating the performance premium with a Compound IF function

From Figure 7.19, it can be seen that the information regarding the sports model is in B11 and the engine size is in B10. The basic premium is in D3. When we feed all of this data into the IF function, we get the following:

=IF(AND(B11="Yes",B10>1600),D3*40%,0)

This IF function is entered in D8, as shown in Figure 7.19. The IF function will charge 40% only where both *Yes* has been entered in B11 and the number in B10 is greater than

1600. When one or both of these conditions is not satisfied, the IF function will calculate a performance premium of €0.00. In the example, both conditions are satisfied. Jim's car is a sports model with an engine bigger than 1600cc, so the performance premium is calculated by multiplying D3 by 40%, giving €120.

The possible combinations of conditions and associated actions of this IF function are summarised in Table 7.62.

	Conditions		Resulting Action (Calculation of the Performance Premium)
Scenario 1	Engine cc	**>1600**	40% of basic premium
Both Conditions Satisfied	Sports Model	**Yes**	
Scenario 2	Engine cc	**>1600**	0
First Condition Satisfied	Sports Model	No	
Scenario 3	Engine cc	<=1600	0
Second Condition Satisfied	Sports Model	**Yes**	
Scenario 4	Engine cc	<=1600	0
No Conditions Satisfied	Sports Model	No	

Table 7.62

Try It Yourself!

1. Open the *OnLine Insurance* spreadsheet.
2. Enter the Compound IF function in D8 as shown in Figure 7.19. As Jim's car is a sports model with an engine size of 1800cc, the performance premium calculated by the IF function should be €120.00.
3. Test the IF function by entering different values for engine cc and sports model as follows:

Engine cc	Sports Model	Resulting Performance Premium
1800	No	€0.00
1400	No	€0.00
1400	Yes	€0.00

4. Change the Engine cc back to *1800*.
5. Save the *OnLine Insurance* spreadsheet.

Points to Note

The AND function is *inside* the IF function and is used to carry out the two conditional tests on which payment of the sports car premium depends. The bracket of the AND function must be closed off before completing the condition section of the IF function.

IF functions rule seven: Less than (<), less than or equal to (<=), equal to (=), greater than (>), greater than or equal to (>=) and not equal to (<>) should only be used in the condition section of the IF function. They *should not* be used in the true action or false action sections.

IF functions rule eight: Use of arithmetic operators + - * / within an AND/OR function is not recommended. It's best to do all of your calculations in separate cells and then refer to these cells using the AND/OR function.

OR FUNCTION

We have already seen how a Compound IF tests multiple conditions using an AND function. The AND function is used because *all* the conditions must be satisfied before the IF function implements the true action. This is a sort of 'all or nothing' approach. Unless every single condition is satisfied, the AND function will not allow the IF function to implement the true action. Sometimes you may want to allow the true action to be implemented when *some* but not all of the conditions are satisfied. This is a less strict approach and an OR function should be used in this case.

Just like the AND function, an OR function is used to test conditions. When one or more of the conditions it is testing is satisfied, it will return the value *TRUE*. When all the conditions are not satisfied, the OR function will return the value *FALSE*.

Structure of an OR Function

=OR(condition1, condition2, condition3, ...)

Worked Example

Consider the example in Table 7.63. Students who score 50 or higher in the exam or complete the thesis will be given a Pass certificate. Students who score less than 50 in the exam and don't complete the thesis will be given a Partial certificate.

	A	B
1	Exam Mark	45
2	Thesis	Yes
3		
4	**Qualification**	

Table 7.63

The conditions required to carried out these tests are shown in Table 7.64.

Condition	Meaning
B1>=50	Is the exam mark greater than or equal to 50?
B2="Yes"	Has the student completed the thesis?

At least 1 condition must be satisfied

Table 7.64

These conditions are entered in the OR function, giving the following:

=OR(B1>=50,B2="Yes")

In Table 7.65, only the condition relating to completion of the thesis is satisfied. The OR function will still return a value of *TRUE* as its minimum requirement is one satisfied condition.

	A	B
1	Exam Mark	45
2	Thesis	Yes
3		
4	**Qualification**	TRUE

Table 7.65

Just like the AND function, an OR function can only test conditions. We must combine the OR function in Table 7.65 with an IF function. This will allow the IF function to make a decision based on the two conditions tested by the OR function. The OR function is positioned inside the IF function where the condition would normally be, giving the following:

=IF(OR(B1>=50,B2="Yes"),"Pass Certificate","Partial Certificate")

This combination of IF and OR functions is entered in B4 to determine the type of certificate (Table 7.66).

	A	B
1	Exam Mark	45
2	Thesis	Yes
3		
4	**Qualification**	Pass Certificate

Table 7.66

N This OR function will allow the IF function to award a Pass Certificate in three possible scenarios:

1. A student scores 50 or higher in the exam but doesn't complete the thesis.
2. A student completes the thesis and scores less than 50 in the exam.
3. A student scores 50 or higher in the exam and also completes the thesis.

The possible combinations of conditions and associated actions of this IF function are summarised in Table 7.67.

	Conditions		**Resulting Action (Awarding of Certificate)**
Scenario 1	Exam Mark	**>=50**	Pass Certificate
First Condition Satisfied	Thesis	No	
Scenario 2	Exam Mark	<50	Pass Certificate
Second Condition Satisfied	Thesis	**Yes**	
Scenario 3	Exam Mark	**>=50**	Pass Certificate
Both Conditions Satisfied	Thesis	**Yes**	
Scenario 4	Exam Mark	<50	Partial Certificate
No Conditions Satisfied	Thesis	No	

Table 7.67

OnLine Insurance Example: Calculating the Claims Bonus

Returning to our *OnLine Insurance Company* spreadsheet we'll see how a combination of an IF function and an OR function is used to calculate Jim's claims bonus. OR functions are used when a minimum of one of the conditions tested must be satisfied.

	A	B	C	D
1	OnLine Insurance		Your Policy is just a click away!	
2				
3			Basic Premium	€ 300.00
4			Total Premium	
5				
6	Policy Holder	Jim Collins	Gender Premium	€ 60.00
7	Gender	Male	Age Premium	€ 30.00
8	Age	27	Performance Premium	€ 120.00
9	Full Drivers licence	Yes	Claims Bonus	
10	Engine cc	1800	Licence Bonus	
11	Sports model	Yes		
12	Claims to date	0		
13				

Figure 7.20

OnLine Insurance calculates the claims bonus on the following basis.

Drivers who are either over 30 or who have no previous claims are entitled to a reduction of 5% of the basic premium.

The IF function must decide to do one of two things. Either:

1. Give a 5% reduction

   or:

2. Don't give a reduction.

This decision depends on two conditions – the age of the driver and the number of previous claims. To qualify for the 5% reduction a minimum of one of the conditions must be satisfied. Represented graphically, the decision would look like Figure 7.21.

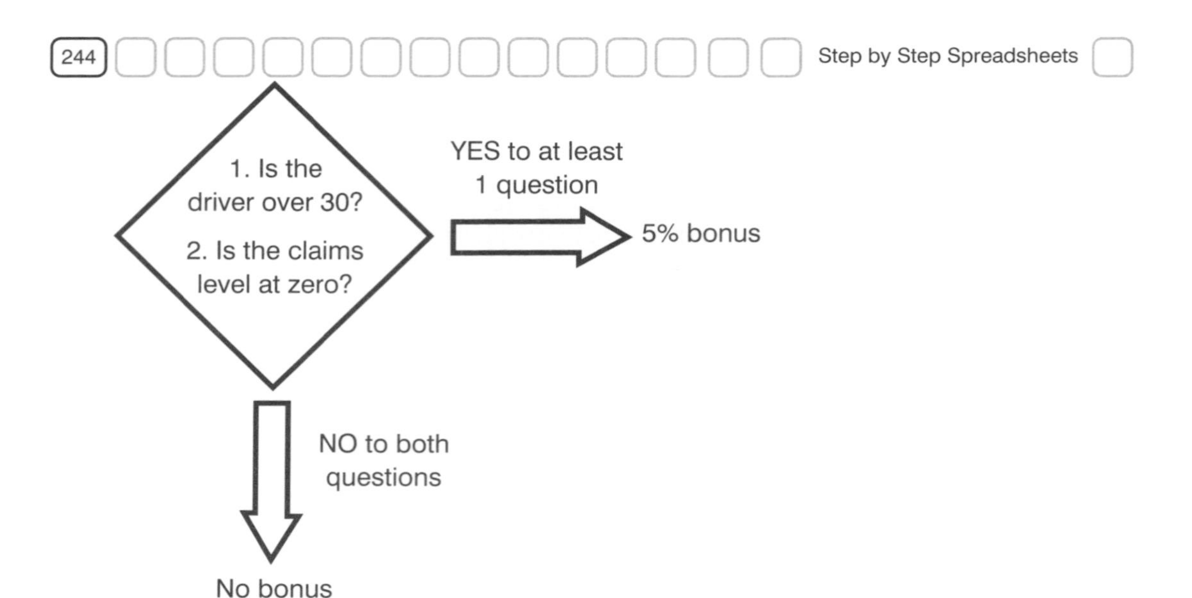

Figure 7.21 The IF function calculates the bonus when either one or both of the conditions is satisfied. Drivers who answered No to both questions do not qualify for the bonus.

Before writing the IF function, it is important to have a clear idea of its sections: the two conditions; the true action; and the false action. These are summarised in Table 7.68.

Condition 1	Is the driver over 30?	At least one condition must be satisfied
Condition 2	Is the claims level at zero?	
True Action	5% reduction	
False Action	No reduction	

Table 7.68 The sections of the Compound IF function

If we were to write this IF function in English, it would look something like this.

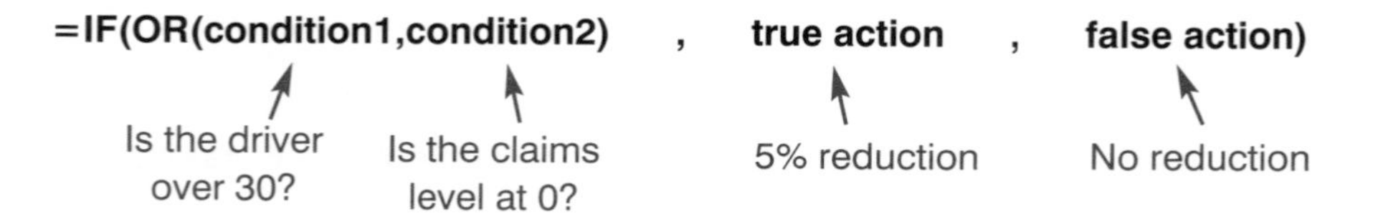

As there are two conditions, and the 5% reduction can be given when either one or both of these conditions are satisfied, the conditions are tested by an OR function. Remember that the OR function is positioned inside the IF function.

	A	B	C	D	E	F
1	OnLine Insurance		Your Policy is just a click away!			
2						
3			Basic Premium	€ 300.00		
4			Total Premium			
5						
6	Policy Holder	Jim Collins	Gender Premium	€ 60.00		
7	Gender	Male	Age Premium	€ 30.00		
8	Age	27	Performance Premium	€ 120.00		
9	Full Drivers licence	Yes	Claims Bonus	=IF(OR(B8>30,B12=0),D3*5%,0)		
10	Engine cc	1800				
11	Sports model	Yes				
12	Claims to date	0				
13						

Figure 7.22 Calculating the claims bonus with a Compound IF function

From Figure 7.22, it can be seen that the information regarding the driver age is in B8 and the claims to date is in B12. The basic premium is in D3. When we feed all this information into the IF function, we get the following:

=IF(OR(B8>30,B12=0),D3*5%,0)

This IF function is entered in D9, as shown in Figure 7.22. The IF function will give a 5% reduction in three possible scenarios:

1. When the driver is over 30 but has claimed previously.
2. When the driver has not claimed previously and is under 30.
3. When the driver is both over 30 and has not claimed previously.

When both of the conditions are not satisfied, the IF function will not calculate a reduction. In this case, Jim qualifies for the 5% reduction. Even though he is not over 30, he has no previous claims. As one of the two conditions is satisfied the IF function calculates a claims bonus of €15.

Table 7.69 summarises the circumstances in which AND and OR functions return *TRUE* or *FALSE* values.

	AND Function	OR Function
TRUE	Only when all conditions are satisfied	When one or more conditions are satisfied
FALSE	When one or more conditions are not satisfied	When all conditions are not satisfied

Table 7.69 Summary of AND/OR Functions

Try It Yourself!

1. Open the *OnLine Insurance* spreadsheet.
2. Enter the Compound IF function in D9 as shown in Figure 7.22. Jim's age is not over 30 but he has no claims to date. The claims bonus calculated by the IF function should be €15.00.
3. Test the IF function by entering different values for age and claims to date as follows:

Age	Claims to Date	Resulting Claims Bonus
27	1	€0.00
35	1	€15.00
35	0	€15.00

4. Change Jim's age back to *27*.
5. Save the *OnLine Insurance* spreadsheet.

Additional Points

1. Once you have created an IF function, always test it by entering different values in the cell or cells that the IF function refers to.
2. More complex IF functions should be planned before they are attempted. Use the checklist displayed in Table 7.70.

Number of actions?	
How many conditions does each action depend on?	
If there are multiple conditions, are conditions linked or independent of each other?	

Table 7.70 IF function checklist

The answers to these questions will determine the type of IF function required.

3. Finally, where the calculation executed by an IF function is very complex, break the calculation down into steps. A very complex calculation can often be carried out in two or more steps. Approaching complex calculations in this way will make your spreadsheets easier to use and understand in the long run.

Compound IF Assignment One

Part 1: Spreadsheet Setup

1. Create a new spreadsheet workbook and enter the data shown in Table 7.71 in Sheet1.

	A	B	C	D	E	F	G	H	I	J
1	Sales Team Bonuses									
2										
3	Name	Department	Salary	Weekly Pay	Week1 Hours	Week1 Bonus	Week1 Pay	Week2 Hours	Week2 Bonus	Week2 Pay
4	A Arnold	Finance	60900		35			35		
5	B Burke	Marketing	57000		40			35		
6	C Cotton	Sales	44614		45			30		
7	D Eastwood	Finance	38000		35			35		
8	G Hunt	Sales	38000		30			22		
9	P Byrne	Sales	39640		36			50		
10	R Madigan	Marketing	37960		35			35		
11	F Fox	Sales	38350		40			40		
12	J Costello	Sales	50300		24			33		
13	B Galway	Sales	47260		40			24		
14	S Troy	Marketing	48416		35			27		
15	L Keane	Sales	51780		30			18		

Table 7.71

2. Calculate weekly pay.
3. Employees in the sales department who work for more than 35 hours in any one week get a bonus of 20% of their weekly pay. Using this information, complete Table 7.72.

Number of actions?	
How many conditions does each action depend on?	
Must all conditions be satisfied?	

Table 7.72 Analysis of Week1 Bonus IF function

4. Calculate the bonuses for Week 1 and Week 2 using the information you entered in Table 7.72.
5. Test your IF function by changing *B Burke's* department to *Sales*. The IF function should calculate a bonus of *€219.23* for Week 1.
6. Change *B Burke's* department back to *Marketing*.
7. Week 1 pay is weekly pay plus Week 1 bonus. Create a similar formula to calculate Week 2 pay.
8. Rename Sheet1 as *Bonuses*
9. Delete all unused worksheets in the workbook.

Part 2: Formatting, Filters and Spreadsheet Protection

Merge styles from:
Toms Hardware.xlsx

1. Merge styles from the *Toms Hardware* spreadsheet.
2. Format data in the *Bonuses* worksheet using the styles listed in Table 7.73.

Range of Cells	Cell Style
A1	Heading 4
A3:J3	Accent4
A4:J15	20% – Accent4

Table 7.73

3. Use conditional formatting to emphasise all bonus amounts in *Green Fill with Dark Green Text.*

Conditional formatting for Week 1 bonuses can be copied to Week 2 using the Format Painter.

4. Test the conditional formatting by changing *G Hunt*'s Week 1 hours to *36*. The resulting Week 1 bonus should be formatted in green.
5. Change *G Hunt*'s hours back to *30*.
6. Format all money amounts to currency.
7. Using a Filter, display only employees who received a bonus in both weeks.
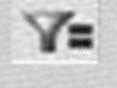
8. Clear the filter and implement spreadsheet protection so that:
   - data can only be entered in the ranges A4:C15, E4:E15 and H4:H15
   - formulas and functions are no longer displayed in the formula bar.

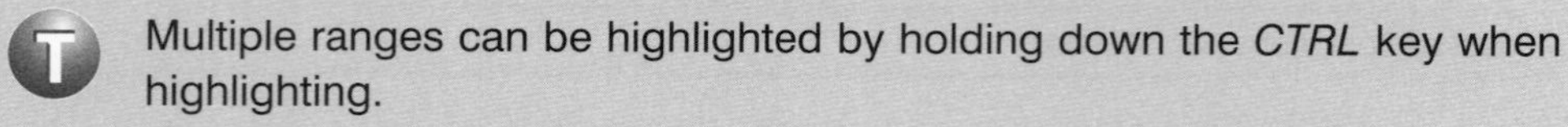
Multiple ranges can be highlighted by holding down the *CTRL* key when highlighting.

9. Print the *Bonuses* worksheet in landscape orientation with gridlines and row and column headings displayed.
10. Save the spreadsheet as **Sales Team Bonuses**

Compound IF Assignment Two

Part 1: Spreadsheet Setup

1. Create a new spreadsheet workbook and enter the data shown in Table 7.74 in Sheet1.

	A	B	C	D	E	F	G	H	I
1	**Totally Digital**								
2	***Blu ray and DVD Rentals***								
3									
4	**Film Title**	**Format**	**Day of Rental**	**Price per Night**	**Days Rented**	**Total**	**Special Offer**	**Blu-ray Offer**	**Amount Payable**
5	*Gran Torino*	DVD	Monday	6.5	1				
6	*Slumdog Millionaire*	Blu-ray	Monday	6.5	1				
7	*Seven Pounds*	DVD	Tuesday	5.5	1				
8	*The Pink Panther 2*	Blu-ray	Wednesday	5.5	1				
9	*The Wrestler*	DVD	Wednesday	6.5	2				
10	*Milk*	DVD	Thursday	6.5	1				
11	*Frost/Nixon*	Blu-ray	Thursday	5.5	2				
12	*The Reader*	DVD	Friday	6.5	2				
13	*Australia*	Blu-ray	Friday	5.5	1				
14	*Quantum of Solace*	DVD	Saturday	5.5	2				
15	*Bride Wars*	Blu-ray	Saturday	6.5	1				
16	*Valkyrie*	Blu-ray	Sunday	5.5	1				

Table 7.74

2. Calculate the total.
3. There is a reduction of 50% of the total on all films rented on Monday, Tuesday or Wednesday. Using this information, complete Table 7.75.

Number of actions?	
How many conditions does each action depend on?	
Must all conditions be satisfied?	

Table 7.75 Analysis of special offer IF function

4. Calculate the special offer using the information you entered in Table 7.75.
5. Test your IF function by changing the day of rental for *Frost/Nixon* to *Wednesday*. The special offer amount should now be *€5.50*.
6. Change the day of rental of *Frost/Nixon* back to *Thursday*.
7. There is a an additional reduction of €1.50 on all Blu-ray films rented on Monday. Using this information, complete Table 7.76.

Number of actions?	
How many conditions does each action depend on?	
Must all conditions be satisfied?	

Table 7.76 Analysis of Blu-ray offer IF function

8. Calculate Blu-ray offer using the information you entered in Table 7.76
9. Test this IF function by changing the format of *Gran Torino* to *Blu-ray*. The Blu-ray offer amount should now be *€1.50*.
10. Change the format of *Gran Torino* back to *DVD*.
11. Calculate the amount payable.
12. Format all money amounts to currency.
13. Rename Sheet1 as *Rentals*
14. Delete all other worksheets in the workbook.

Part 2: Formatting, Filters and Spreadsheet Protection

1. Merge styles from the *Toms Hardware* spreadsheet.
2. Format data in the *Rentals* worksheet using the styles listed in Table 7.77.

Merge styles from:
Toms Hardware.xlsx

Range of Cells	Cell Style
A1	Heading 4
A2, A4:I4	Accent4
A5:I16	20% – Accent4

Table 7.77

3. Use conditional formatting to display special offer and Blu-ray offer amounts *in Green Fill with Dark Green Text.*
4. Test the conditional formatting by changing the day of rental of *Australia* to *Monday*. Both special offer and Blu-ray offer should be highlighted in green.

5. Change the day of rental of *Australia* back to *Friday*.
6. Using a Filter, display only films rented on Friday, Saturday or Sunday for two days.
7. Clear the filter and implement spreadsheet protection so that:
   - data can only be entered in the range A5:E16
   - formulas and functions are no longer displayed in the formula bar
   - the spreadsheet user is allowed to format cells.
8. Save the spreadsheet as **Totally Digital**

Compound IF Assignment Three

Part 1: Spreadsheet Setup

1. Create a new spreadsheet workbook and enter the data shown in Table 7.78 in Sheet1.

	A	B	C	D	E	F
1	**PC Upgrade Plan**					
2						
3	**Model**	**Processor Speed (GHz)**	**Processor Type**	**RAM (Mb)**	**Hard Disk Size (Gb)**	**Upgrade?**
4	Dell Inspiron 546	1.8	Single Core	1024	250	
5	Dell Inspiron 530	2.33	Dual Core	2048	1024	
6	Acer Aspire R3600	3.1	Quad Core	2048	2048	
7	Packard Bell iMedia	1.9	Single Core	1024	160	
8	Acer X3200	2.2	Triple Core	3072	1024	
9	Advent AIO-101	1.55	Single Core	1536	320	
10	Sony Vaio	1.6	Single Core	1024	500	
11	HP Touchsmart	1.9	Dual Core	4096	320	

Table 7.78

2. All PCs satisfying the criteria listed in Table 7.79 are to be upgraded.

Processor Speed (GHz)	<2.0
Processor Type	Single Core
RAM (Mb)	<2048
Hard Disk (Gb)	<1024

Table 7.79

3. Using this information, complete Table 7.80.

Number of actions?	
How many conditions does each action depend on?	
Must all conditions be satisfied?	

Table 7.80 Analysis of Upgrade IF function

4. Create an IF function to determine which PCs should be upgraded using the information you entered in Table 7.80. The IF function should display *Yes* if the PC is to be upgraded and *No* if it isn't for upgrading.
5. Test your IF function by entering a Processor Speed of *1.3*, a processor type of *Single Core*, RAM of *1024* and a hard disk size of *640* for the *Dell Inspiron 530*. The IF function should now indicate that this PC is to be upgraded.
6. Change processor speed, processor type, RAM and hard disk size of the *Inspiron 530* back to their original values.

Holding down the *CTRL* key and typing *Z* repeatedly undoes your recent actions. Each time you type *Z* while holding down *CTRL*, a single action is undone.

7. Sort the data in ascending alphabetical order of model.
8. Rename Sheet1 as *List of PCs*
9. Delete all unused worksheets in the workbook.

Part 2: Formatting and Filters

1. Merge styles from the *Toms Hardware* spreadsheet.

Merge styles from:
Toms Hardware.xlsx

2. Format data in the *List of PCs* worksheet using the styles listed in Table 7.81.

Range of Cells	Cell Style
A1	Heading 4
A3:F3	Accent4
A4:F11	20% – Accent4

Table 7.81

3. Use conditional formatting to emphasise the cells containing the names of the models due for upgrade in *Light Red Fill with Dark Red Text*.
4. Test the conditional formatting by changing the processor type of the HP Touchsmart to *Single Core* and its RAM to *512*. HP Touchsmart should now be formatted in red. *Upgrade?* should now be *Yes*.
5. Change the processor type of the HP Touchsmart back to *Dual Core* and its RAM to *4096*.

 Use the *CTRL + Z* key combination.

6. In the Upgrade? column, use conditional formatting to emphasise all occurrences of the word *Yes* in *Light Red Fill with Dark Red Text*.
7. Using a Filter, display only PCs with dual, triple or quad core processors that have a processor speed greater than 2.0Ghz.
8. Clear all Filters from the worksheet. 

Part 3: Charts

1. Display the model names and processor speeds using a bar chart. Information relating to chart setup is displayed in Table 7.82.

Chart Type	Clustered Bar in 3-D
Chart Title	Comparison of Processor Speeds
Chart Location	Separate chart sheet named *Processor Speed*
Chart Style	Style 5

Table 7.82

2. Display the model names and RAM using a bar chart. Information relating to chart setup is displayed in Table 7.83.

Chart Type	Clustered Bar in 3-D
Chart Title	Comparison of RAM
Chart Location	Separate chart sheet named *RAM*
Chart Style	Style 2

Table 7.83

3. Display the model names and hard disk sizes using a bar chart. Information relating to chart setup is displayed in Table 7.84.

Chart Type	Clustered Bar in 3-D
Chart Title	Comparison of Hard Disk Sizes
Chart Location	Separate chart sheet named *Hard Disk*
Chart Style	Style 4

Table 7.84

Part 4: Spreadsheet Protection

1. Implement spreadsheet protection so that:
   - data can only be entered in the range A4:E11
   - the spreadsheet user cannot select locked cells.
2. Save the spreadsheet as **PC Upgrade Plan**

Compound IF Assignment Four

Part 1: Spreadsheet Setup

1. Create a new spreadsheet workbook and enter the data shown in Table 7.85 in Sheet1.

	A	B	C	D
1	**Passenger Manifest**			
2				
3	**Passenger Name**	**Age**	**Destination**	**Passenger Load Fee**
4	Tom Tiernan	25	Miami	
5	Alison Byrne	23	La Paz	
6	Cathy Burke	48	Atlanta	
7	Miriam Delaney	21	Boston	
8	Maeve Twomey	20	Boston	
9	Tomasz Fojtar	7	Boston	
10	Denis Langton	33	Brussels	
11	Conor Callaghan	52	Chicago	
12	Tim Mooney	16	Chicago	
13	Sue Dunne	19	London	
14	Nora Evans	15	London	
15	Mitko Dimitrovi	11	New York	

Table 7.85

2. The passenger load fee is €15.23 on the New York, Boston, Atlanta and Chicago routes. On all other routes the passenger load fee is €6.95. Using this information, complete Table 7.86.

Number of actions?	
How many conditions does each action depend on?	
Must all conditions be satisfied?	

Table 7.86 Analysis of passenger load fee IF function

3. Calculate the passenger load fee using the information you entered in Table 7.86.

When repeatedly testing the same cell in an IF function, make sure that you include its cell reference in each condition. Each condition must have three components: a cell reference, a logical operator and the data being tested.

4. Test the IF function by changing Cathy Burke's destination to Shannon. Her passenger load fee should change from €15.23 to €6.95.
5. Change Cathy Burke's destination back to Atlanta.
6. Format all money amounts to currency.
7. Sort the data in ascending alphabetical order of destination.
8. Rename Sheet1 as *Passenger Load Fees*
9. Delete all other worksheets in the workbook.

Part 2: Formatting, Filters and Spreadsheet Protection

Merge styles from:
Toms Hardware.xlsx

1. Merge styles from the *Toms Hardware* spreadsheet.
2. Format data in the *Passenger Load Fees* worksheet using the styles listed in Table 7.87.

Range of Cells	Cell Style
A1	Heading 4
A3:D3	Accent4
A4:D15	20% – Accent4

Table 7.87

3. Using a Filter, display passengers under 21 travelling to New York or Boston.

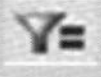

4. Clear the filter and implement spreadsheet protection so that:
   - data can only be entered in the range A4:C15
   - the spreadsheet user cannot select locked cells.
5. Save the spreadsheet as **Passenger Manifest**

COMPOUND IF REVIEW QUESTIONS

Answers to the review questions are available on www.gillmacmillan.ie

Test your knowledge of Compound IFs by answering the following questions.

1. When the outcome of a decision depends on two or more ____________ , an AND/OR function is required to test these ____________.

2. In a situation where all conditions must be satisfied before the IF function implements the true action, an _______ function must be used to test the conditions.

3. How many conditions must be satisfied for an OR function to return a TRUE value?
   (i) None
   (ii) 1 or more
   (iii) 2 or more
   (iv) All conditions must be satisfied.

4. How many conditions must be satisfied for an AND function to return a TRUE value?
   (i) None
   (ii) 1 or more
   (iii) 2 or more
   (iv) All conditions must be satisfied.

5. Identify the error in the following IF function:
   =if(AND(B2>100,C2="Yes",250,0))

6.

	A	B	C	D
1		**Communications**	**Work Experience**	**Other Modules**
2	Linda O Neill	Yes	Yes	6
3	FETAC Cert?			
4				

Table 7.88

Table 7.88 displays FETAC modules successfully completed by Linda O Neill to date. In order to qualify for a FETAC Certificate, Linda must complete Communications, Work Experience and 6 or more other modules.

Write down the IF function that will determine whether Linda qualifies for a full certificate. The IF function should display *Yes* or *No* depending on whether Linda qualifies for the certificate.

____

7. Identify the error in the following IF function:
   =if(OR(C4="No",<125),C6*10%,C6*20%)

8.

	A	B	C	D
1		**Tries Scored**	**Losing Margin**	**Bonus Points**
2	Munster	3	6	
3				

Table 7.89

Table 7.89 displays the number of tries scored by Munster in a rugby match, which they lost. When the losing team either scores 4 or more tries or loses by 7 points or less, they get a bonus point. Write down the IF function that will calculate the number of bonus points.

____

9.

	A	B	C	D
1		**Engine Size**	**Commercial**	**Road Tax**
2	Ford Transit	1.8	Yes	
3				

Table 7.90

Table 7.90 displays the details of a Transit van. The road tax for commercial vans with an engine size of 1.6 or greater is €250. The road tax for all other vehicles is €180. Write down the IF function that will calculate the road tax.

____

10.

	A	B	C	D
1		**NCT**	**Previous Claims**	**Insurance Premium**
2	Josef Grejc	Yes	0	
3				

Table 7.91

Table 7.91 displays the details of an application for car insurance. The insurance premium for customers who have a full NCT cert and who have no previous claims is €300. Customers who don't satisfy both of these criteria will pay an insurance premium of €450. Write down the IF function that will calculate Josef's insurance premium.

____

NESTED COMPOUND IF FUNCTION

We have seen that a Nested IF consists of two or more IF functions. The number of IFs that are required depends on the number of possible actions. A Compound IF, on the other hand, is used when the decision made by the IF function depends on more two or more conditions. In a Compound IF the conditions are tested by an AND function or an OR function.

We could summarise this by saying that *Nested* relates to the number of IFs and *Compound* relates to the number of conditions. The most difficult type of IF function is one that is both Nested and Compound. This is where there are three or more possible actions and each one of these actions depends on two or more conditions. A summary of IF functions is displayed in Table 7.92.

	Simple IF	Nested IF	Compound IF	Nested Compound IF
Conditions	1	1 per action	From 2 to a maximum of 255	From 2 to a maximum of 255
Actions	2	From 3 to a maximum of 64	2	From 3 to a maximum of 64

Table 7.92 A summary of IF functions

From Table 7.92 we can see that a nested compound IF can choose between a maximum of 64 alternative courses of action and that each course of action can depend on up to 255 conditions.

OnLine Insurance Example: Calculating the Licence Bonus

Returning to our *OnLine Insurance Company* spreadsheet we'll see how a Nested Compound IF function must decide whether Jim qualifies for one of four possible licence bonuses, each of which depends on two factors – full licence and age.

	A	B	C	D
1	**OnLine Insurance**		*Your Policy is just a click away!*	
2				
3			**Basic Premium**	€ 300.00
4			**Total Premium**	
5				
6	**Policy Holder**	Jim Collins	**Gender Premium**	€ 60.00
7	**Gender**	Male	**Age Premium**	€ 30.00
8	**Age**	27	**Performance Premium**	€ 120.00
9	**Full Drivers licence**	Yes	**Claims Bonus**	€ 15.00
10	**Engine cc**	1800	**Licence Bonus**	
11	**Sports model**	Yes		
12	**Claims to date**	0		
13				

Figure 7.23

OnLine Insurance calculates the licence bonus on the following basis.

	Full License	Age	Licence Bonus
1	Yes	<=18	1%
2	Yes	19–21	2%
3	Yes	22–25	3%
4	Yes	26–70	5%
5	*No bonus is given to drivers who don't hold a full licence or to drivers aged 71 or over*		

Table 7.93 OnLine Insurance licence bonus guidelines

As there are five possible courses of action, each of which depends on two conditions *(holding a full licence and the age of the driver)*, a Nested Compound IF will be used to calculate the licence bonus. The Nested Compound IF function must decide to take one of the following courses of action:

1. Give a 1% reduction
2. Give a 2% reduction
3. Give a 3% reduction
4. Give a 5% reduction
5. Don't give a reduction.

Each possible course of action depends on two conditions – the age of the driver and whether the driver has a full licence or not. As both conditions must be satisfied in each case, an AND function will be used to test these conditions. Four separate AND functions are required. The last action, which is the false action, doesn't require a conditional test.

Represented graphically, this would look like Figure 7.24.

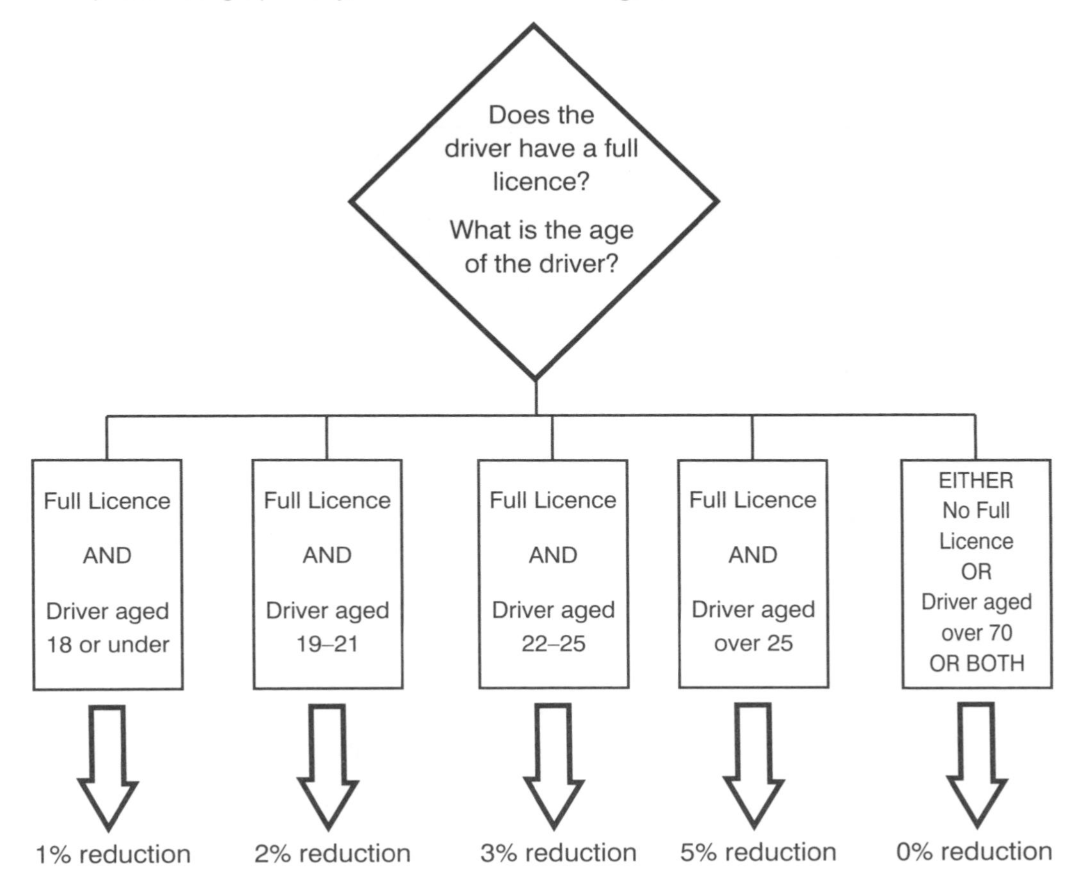

Figure 7.24 The IF function must calculate one of five different reductions, depending on the type of licence and the age of the driver

Before writing a Nested Compound IF function, it is important to have a clear idea of all of its sections. These are summarised in Table 7.94.

Condition 1	Does the driver hold a full licence?
Condition 2	Is the driver aged 18 or under?
Action 1	***1% Reduction***
Condition 3	Does the driver hold a full licence?
Condition 4	Is the driver aged 19–21?
Action 2	***2% Reduction***
Condition 5	Does the driver hold a full licence?
Condition 6	Is the driver aged 22–25?
Action 3	***3% Reduction***
Condition 7	Does the driver hold a full licence?
Condition 8	Is the driver aged 26–70?
Action 4	***5% Reduction***
False Action	***0% Reduction***

Table 7.94 The sections of the Nested Compound IF function

IF we were to write this IF function in English, it would look something like this.

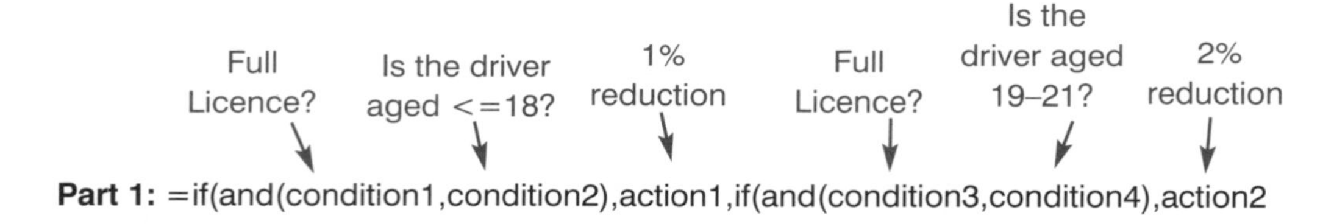

Part 1: =if(and(condition1,condition2),action1,if(and(condition3,condition4),action2

Part 2: ,if(and(condition5,condition6),action3,if(and(condition7,condition8),action4,action5))))

From Figure 7.25, it can be seen that the information regarding the full licence is in B9 and the driver age is in B8. The basic premium is in D3. When we feed all this information into the IF function, we get the following:

=IF(AND(B8<=18,B9="Yes"),D3*1%,IF(AND(B8<=21,B9="Yes"),D3*2%
,IF(AND(B8<=25,B9="Yes"),D3*3%,IF(AND(B8<=70,B9="Yes"),D3*5%,0))))

This IF function is entered in D10, as shown in Figure 7.25. As Jim is 27 and holds a full driver's licence he qualifies for a 5% reduction. The IF function calculates a licence bonus of €15.00.

The conditions and associated actions of this IF function are summarised in Table 7.95.

	A	B	C	D	E	F	G
1	**OnLine Insurance**		*Your Policy is just a click away!*				
2							
3			Basic Premium	€ 300.00			
4			Total Premium				
5							
6	Policy Holder	Jim Collins	Gender Premium	€ 60.00			
7	Gender	Male	Age Premium	€ 30.00			
8	Age	27	Performance Premium	€ 120.00			
9	Full Drivers licence	Yes	Claims Bonus	€ 15.00			
10	Engine cc	1800	Licence Bonus	=IF(AND(B8<=18,B9="Yes"),D3*1% ,IF(AND(B8<=21,B9="Yes"),D3*2% ,IF(AND(B8<=25,B9="Yes"),D3*3% ,IF(AND(B8<=70,B9="Yes"),D3*5%,0))))			
11	Sports model	Yes					
12	Claims to date	0					
13							
14							
15							

Figure 7.25 Calculating the licence bonus with a Nested Compound IF function

	Condition 1: Age	Condition 2: Full Licence	Resulting Action: Licence Bonus
1	<=18	Yes	*€3.00*
2	19–21	Yes	*€6.00*
3	22–25	Yes	*€9.00*
4	26–70	Yes	*€15.00*
False Action	–	–	*€0.00*

Table 7.95 Conditions and associated actions of the Nested Compound IF function

Conditions in a nested compound IF function may require AND functions, OR functions or a combination of both. The number of conditions will vary according to the number of possible courses of action. Excel allows a maximum of 64 IFs in a Nested Compound IF. Each AND or OR function can test up to 255 conditions.

Try It Yourself!

1. Open the *OnLine Insurance* spreadsheet.
2. Enter the Nested Compound IF function in D10 as shown in Figure 7.25. As Jim is 27 and holds a full licence, the licence bonus calculated by the IF function should be €15.00.
3. Test the IF function by entering different values for age and full licence as follows:

Age	Full Licence	Resulting Claims Bonus
17	Yes	€3.00
17	No	€0.00
21	No	€0.00
21	Yes	€6.00
23	Yes	€9.00
23	No	€0.00
27	No	€0.00
73	No	€0.00
73	Yes	€0.00

4. Change Jim's age back to *27*.
5. Complete the *OnLine Insurance* spreadsheet by entering a formula in D4 to calculate Jim's total premium as follows:

   =D3+D6+D7+D8-D9-D10

   This formula adds the Basic Premium, Gender Premium, Age Premium and Performance Premium and then subtracts the Claims Bonus and Licence Bonus. Jim's total premium is €480, which can be seen in Figure 7.26.

	A	B	C	D
1	OnLine Insurance		Your Policy is just a click away!	
2				
3			Basic Premium	€ 300.00
4			Total Premium	€ **480.00**
5				
6	Policy Holder	Jim Collins	Gender Premium	€ 60.00
7	Gender	Male	Age Premium	€ 30.00
8	Age	27	Performance Premium	€ 120.00
9	Full Drivers licence	Yes	Claims Bonus	€ 15.00
10	Engine cc	1800	Licence Bonus	€ 15.00
11	Sports model	Yes		
12	Claims to date	0		
13				

Figure 7.26 The completed OnLine Insurance spreadsheet

6. Save the *OnLine Insurance* spreadsheet.

Nested Compound IF Assignment One

Part 1: Spreadsheet Setup

1. Create a new spreadsheet workbook and enter the data shown in Table 7.96 in Sheet1.

	A	B	C	D	E	F	G	H
1	**Travel Expenses**							
2								
3	**Depart Date**	**Return Date**	**Name**	**Kilometres**	**Conference**	**Number of Nights**	**Hotel Expenses**	**Special Expenses**
4	01/05/2010	05/05/2010	Lisa Barrett	168	Yes			
5	04/05/2010	06/05/2010	Mark Smith	57	No			
6	12/05/2010	12/05/2010	Gerry Dunne	129	Yes			
7	13/05/2010	14/05/2010	Andriv Diyab	81	Yes			
8	13/05/2010	17/05/2010	Caroline Murphy	63	No			
9	14/05/2010	14/05/2010	Lucy O Neill	205	Yes			
10	18/05/2010	24/05/2010	Sam Hartnett	188	No			

Table 7.96

2. Calculate the number of nights for each trip.

When you refer to dates or times in a calculation, the result may be displayed in Date/Time format. Click the Comma Style button  to display the result as a number.

3. Hotel expenses are calculated on the following basis:
   - there are no hotel expenses for people who return on the same day
   - for people who stay overnight, hotel expenses are paid at €150 per night.
4. Using this information, complete Table 7.97.

Number of actions?	
How many conditions does each action depend on?	
Must all conditions be satisfied?	

Table 7.97 Analysis of hotel expenses IF function

5. Calculate hotel expenses using the information you entered in Table 7.97.
6. Test your IF function by changing Lucy O Neill's return date to *15/05/2010*. Hotel expenses should now be *€150*.
7. Change Lucy's return date back to *14/05/2010*.
8. Special expenses are paid on the following basis.
   - People who attend a conference and travel more than 200 kilometres are entitled to €150.
   - Those who attend a conference and travel between 150 and 200 kilometres inclusive are entitled to €100.
   - Those who attend a conference and travel less than 150 kilometres are entitled to €50.
   - People who don't attend a conference are not entitled to special expenses regardless of the distance they travelled.
9. Using this information, complete Table 7.98.

Number of actions?	
How many conditions does each action depend on?	
Must all conditions be satisfied?	

Table 7.98 Analysis of special expenses IF function

10. Calculate special expenses using the information you entered in Table 7.98.

AND functions are not required for all of the IFs.

11. Test your IF function by entering the following kilometre and conference values for Mark Smith. The IF function should calculate special expenses as shown.

Kilometres	Conference	Special Expenses
57	Yes	€50
175	Yes	€100
175	No	€0
225	No	€0
225	Yes	€150

12. Change Mark Smith's kilometres back to *57* and conference to *No*.
13. Format all money amounts to currency.
14. Sort the data in descending order of kilometres.

15. Rename Sheet1 as *Expense Claims*
16. Delete all other worksheets in the workbook.

Part 2: Formatting, Filters and Spreadsheet Protection

Merge styles from:
Toms Hardware.xlsx

1. Merge styles from the *Toms Hardware* spreadsheet.
2. Format data in the *Expense Claims* worksheet using the styles listed in Table 7.99.

Range of Cells	Cell Style
A1	Heading 4
A3:H3	Accent4
A4:H10	20% – Accent4

Table 7.99

3. Use conditional formatting to emphasise the names of those entitled to special expenses in *Green Fill with Dark Green Text*.
4. Test the conditional formatting by changing Conference to *Yes* for *Sam Hartnett*. Sam's name should now be formatted in green.
5. Change Conference back to *No* for *Sam Hartnett*.
6. Using a Filter, display those who stayed for more than two nights and attended a conference.
7. Clear the filter and implement spreadsheet protection so that:
   - data can only be entered in the range A4:E10
   - formulas and functions are no longer displayed in the formula bar.
8. Save the spreadsheet as **Travel Expenses**

Nested Compound IF Assignment Two

Part 1: Spreadsheet Setup

1. Create a new spreadsheet workbook and enter the data shown in Table 7.100 in Sheet1.

	A	B
1	**Colour Predictor**	
2		
3	Enter first colour	
4		
5	Enter second colour	
6		
7	Resulting colour	

Table 7.100

2. The following is a list of colour combinations used to determine the resulting colour in B7.
   - Red and white gives pink.
   - Red and yellow gives orange.
   - Red and blue gives purple.
   - Yellow and blue gives green.
   - Red and green gives brown.
3. Using this information, complete Table 7.101

Number of actions?	
How many conditions does each action depend on?	
Must all conditions be satisfied?	

Table 7.101 Analysis of resulting colour IF function

4. Using the information you entered in Table 7.101, create an IF function in B7 that will predict the colour when any of the five colour combinations listed above is entered in cells B3 and B5 respectively.
5. Edit the IF function so that it displays the text *Enter Colours* when no colours are entered.

6. Test the IF function by entering the following colour combinations. The IF function should calculate resulting colours as shown.

First Colour	Second Colour	Resulting Value
Red	White	Pink
Red	Yellow	Orange
Red	Blue	Purple
Yellow	Blue	Green
Red	Green	Brown
–	–	Enter Colours

7. Rename Sheet1 as *Mix Colours*
8. Delete all other worksheets in the workbook.

Part 2: Formatting and Spreadsheet Protection

Merge styles from:
Toms Hardware.xlsx

1. Merge styles from the *Toms Hardware* spreadsheet.
2. Format data in the *Mix Colours* worksheet using the styles listed in Table 7.102.

Range of Cells	Cell Style
A1	Heading 4
A3, A5, A7	Accent4
B3, B5, B7	20% – Accent4

Table 7.102

3. Implement spreadsheet protection so that:
   - data can only be entered in B3 and B5
   - the spreadsheet user cannot select locked cells.

Part 3: Macros

1. Select cell A1. Record a new macro (named *clearcolours*) that performs the following tasks:
   - Deletes the contents of B3
   - Deletes the contents of B5
   - Selects B3.
2. Turn off worksheet protection. Using the Insert section of the Ribbon, draw a rounded rectangle to the right of the data. Format the rectangle using the

Subtle Effect Dark 1 shape style. Type the text *Clear Colours* inside the rectangle. Link the rounded rectangle to the *clearcolours* macro.

Clear Colours

3. Re-protect the *Mix Colours* worksheet.
4. Test your macro by entering colour combinations and then clicking the *Clear Colours* button.
5. Save the spreadsheet as **Colour Predictor**

Nested Compound IF Assignment Three

Part 1: Spreadsheet Setup

1. Create a new spreadsheet workbook and enter the data shown in Table 7.103 in Sheet1.

	A	B	C	D	E	F
1	**Monthly Travel Report**					
2						
3	**Employee Name**	**Car**	**Engine Size**	**Distance**	**Rate**	**Total**
4	Stephen Aherne	Yaris	1.0	8350		
5	Jane Dineen	Colt	1.3	8200		
6	Maurice Ryan	Mondeo	1.6	15890		
7	Denis Kinsella	Fiesta	1.1	9850		
8	Avril Byrne	Mazda 626	1.8	10340		
9	Handi Kerkotti	Focus	1.4	7001		
10	Paul Walsh	Passat	1.8	2598		

Table 7.103

The rate is calculated using the data in Table 7.104.

Distance Travelled	Engine Size	Rate
<=10000	<=1.6	0.95
<=10000	>1.6	1.05
>10000	<=1.6	1.05
>10000	>1.6	1.15

Table 7.104

2. Using the information in Table 7.104, complete Table 7.105.

Number of actions?	
How many conditions does each action depend on?	
Must all conditions be satisfied?	

Table 7.105 Analysis of rate IF function

3. Calculate the rate using the information you entered in Table 7.105.
4. Test your IF function by entering the following distance travelled and engine size values for Stephen Aherne. The IF function should calculate the rate as shown.

Engine Size	Distance Travelled	Rate
1.8	8350	€1.05
1.8	15890	€1.15
1.6	15890	€1.05

5. Change Stephen Aherne's engine size back to 1.0 and his distance to 8350.
6. Calculate the total.
7. Format engine sizes to display one decimal place.
8. Format all money amounts to currency.
9. Sort the data in descending order of total.
10. Rename Sheet1 as *Travel Expenses*
11. Delete all unused worksheets in the workbook.

Part 2: Formatting

Merge styles from:
Toms Hardware.xlsx

1. Merge styles from the *Toms Hardware* spreadsheet.
2. Format data in the *Travel Expenses* worksheet using the styles listed in Table 7.106.

Range of Cells	Cell Style
A1	Heading 4
A3:F3	Accent4
A4:F10	20% – Accent4

Table 7.106

Part 3: Charts

1. Display the total claimed by all employees using a pie chart. Information relating to chart setup is displayed in Table 7.107.

 You'll have to highlight two separate ranges.

Chart Type	2-D Pie
Chart Title	Breakdown of Expenses
Data Labels	Category Name, Value and Percentage – Outside End position
Chart Location	Separate chart sheet named *Expense Chart*

Table 7.107

Part 4: Filters and Spreadsheet Protection

1. Using a Filter, display cars with engine sizes from 1.0 litre to 1.3 litres. 
2. Clear the filter and implement spreadsheet protection so that:
   - data can only be entered in the range A4:D10
   - the spreadsheet user cannot select locked cells.
3. Protect the workbook for structure only.
4. Save the spreadsheet as **Monthly Travel Report**

WORKING WITH TIME VALUES IN EXCEL

When working with times in Excel, it is important to understand that when you enter a time in a spreadsheet cell, Excel stores that time as a number between 0 and 0.9999999.

A2 fx 14:55:00

	A	B	C	D	E
1	Time of Call	Duration (minutes)			
2	14:55	0.5			
3					

Figure 7.27 The time 14:55 is stored in A2

In Figure 7.27, 14:55 has been entered in A2 as the time of a particular phone call. The value 14:55:00 appears in the Formula Bar. However, Excel does not actually store 14:55:00 in A2.

, Clicking the comma button reveals what's actually stored in A2.

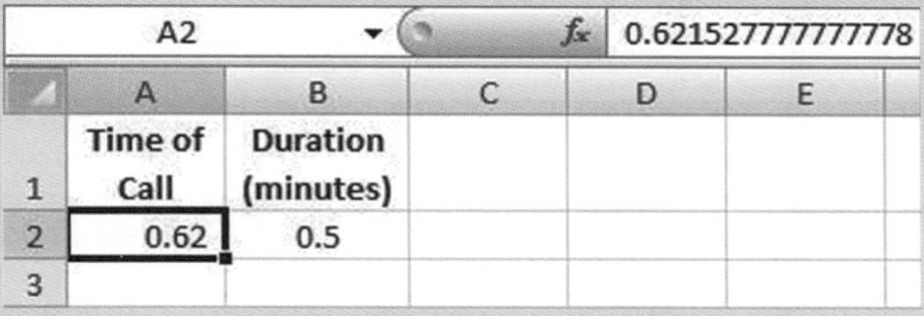

A2 fx 0.621527777777778

	A	B	C	D	E
1	Time of Call	Duration (minutes)			
2	0.62	0.5			
3					

Figure 7.28 Clicking the comma button reveals the decimal number associated with 14:55

In Figure 7.28, the number representing the time 14:55 has been revealed by clicking the comma button. It has been rounded to two places of decimals in A2. Notice from the Formula Bar that this number has much more than two places of decimals.

In Excel, each time entered in a cell is converted to a number between 0 and 0.9999999, representing the times from 0:00:00 to 23:59:59. Examples of times and their corresponding numeric values are displayed in Table 7.108.

Time entered in cell	Value stored in cell
00:01	0.000694444444444444
01:00	0.0416666666666667
02:00	0.0833333333333333
10:00	0.416666666666667
15:00	0.625
18:00	0.75
23:00	0.958333333333333
23:59	0.999305555555556

Table 7.108

The discrepancy between the cell display *(14:55)* and the cell contents *(0.621527777777778)* can cause problems when referring to cells containing times either with a formula or a function. For example, the spreadsheet displayed in Table

7.109 calculates the cost of mobile phone calls depending on the duration of the call and the time the call was made. Calls made before 18:00 cost €0.60 per minute. Calls made from 18:00 onwards cost €0.20 per minute.

	A	B	C	D
1	**Time of Call**	**Duration (minutes)**	**Cost per Minute**	**Total Cost**
2	14:55	0.5	***=IF(A2<18:00,0.6,0.2)*** is incorrect because it refers to a time instead of a number. The correct function is ***=IF(A2<0.75,0.6,0.2)***	
3	17:01	6.0		
4	18:20	21.2		
5	19:56	35.6		
6	21:09	12.0		

Table 7.109

The cost per minute is calculated using an IF function. This IF function needs to refer to the time 18:00 so that it can apply the higher rate to calls made before 18:00 and the lower rate to calls made from 18:00 onwards. However, Excel doesn't recognise 18:00 as a value.

Referring to a time in the IF function, e.g. *=IF(A2<18:00,0.6,0.2)*, results in an error message. Instead of referring to 18:00 we need to refer to the number corresponding to 18:00, which is 0.75. So the correct IF function is *=IF(A2<0.75,0.6,0.2)*.

There are two problems with using numbers representing times in formulas and functions.

1. Formulas and functions that contain numbers representing times are difficult to understand.
2. Because some of these numbers have up to 18 places of decimals, it's easy to make a mistake when entering them in formulas and functions.

The solution is to enter each time that a formula or function must refer to in a separate cell. Instead of referring to the number, refer to the cell containing the relevant time. Better still, assign a name to each cell containing a time.

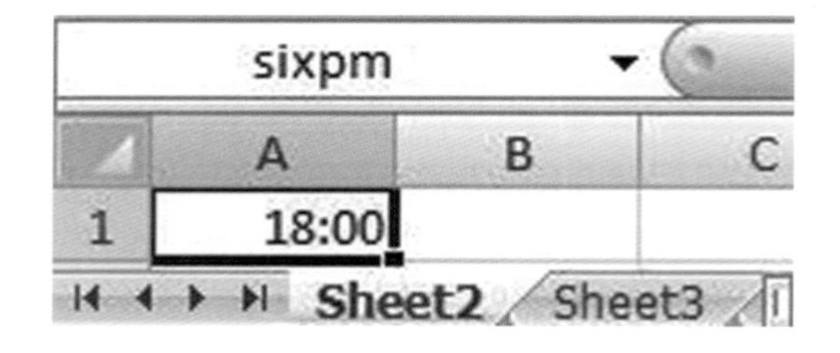

Figure 7.29

In Figure 7.29, *18:00* has been entered in A1 of *Sheet2* and this cell has been assigned the name *sixpm*. We can now rewrite our IF function as follows: *=IF(A2<sixpm,0.6,0.2)*. The function is much easier to understand and there is no need to use a number with lots of decimal places.

Exercise

1. Enter the data displayed in Table 7.109 in Sheet1 of a new spreadsheet workbook.
2. Enter 18:00 in cell A1 of *Sheet2*. Assign the name *sixpm* to this cell.
3. Create an IF function in cell C2 of *Sheet1* to calculate the unit cost *(calls made before 18:00 cost €0.60 per minute, calls made from 18:00 onwards cost €0.20 per minute)*. The function should refer to the cell named *sixpm*.
4. Calculate total cost.
5. Format all money amounts to currency.
6. Rename Sheet1 as *Call Analysis*
7. Merge styles from the *Toms Hardware* spreadsheet.
8. Format data in the *Call Analysis* worksheet using the styles listed in Table 7.110.

Merge styles from:
Toms Hardware.xlsx

Range of Cells	Cell Style
A1:D1	Accent4
A2:D6	20% – Accent4

Table 7.110

9. Save the spreadsheet as **Mobile Phone Bill**

Nested Compound IF Assignment Four

Part 1: Spreadsheet Setup

1. Create a new spreadsheet workbook and enter the data shown in Table 7.111 in Sheet1.
2. Assign cell names in *Sheet2* as follows:
   - Enter 15:00 in A1. Assign the name *threepm* to this cell.
   - Enter 17:30 in A2. Assign the name *fivethirty* to this cell.
   - Enter 18:00 in A3. Assign the name *sixpm* to this cell.
3. The price is €5.00 for films shown before 15:00, €7.00 for films shown between 15:00 and 18:00 and €8.50 for films shown after 18:00. Using this information, complete Table 7.112.

	A	B	C	D	E	F	G	H	I
1	Scene Cinema								
2									
3	Screen Number	Film Title	Date	Time	Price	Group Size	Total	Group Discount	Amount Due
4	1	*Angels and Demons*	26/09/2010	14:00		10			
5	2	*Hannah Montana*	26/09/2010	14:00		25			
6	3	*Star Trek*	26/09/2010	14:00		12			
7	1	*Angels and Demons*	26/09/2010	17:30		18			
8	2	*Hannah Montana*	26/09/2010	17:30		30			
9	3	*Star Trek*	26/09/2010	17:30		20			
10	1	*Angels and Demons*	26/09/2010	20:45		16			
11	2	*Hannah Montana*	26/09/2010	20:45		35			
12	3	*Star Trek*	26/09/2010	20:45		12			

Table 7.111

Number of actions?	
How many conditions does each action depend on?	
Must all conditions be satisfied?	

Table 7.112 Analysis of price IF function

4. Calculate price using the information you entered in Table 7.112. Refer to the cells named *threepm* and *sixpm* in the function.

Pressing the F3 key while writing a formula or function displays a list of all cell and range names stored in your spreadsheet. Instead of typing the cell name, you can paste it into your function.

Don't enclose cell names in double quotes when referring to them in formulas or functions as this causes Excel to treat them as text instead of references to specific cells.

5. Test your IF function by changing the time for the first showing of *Angels and Demons* from 14:00 to 17:30. The price should now be €7.00. Now change the time of *Angels and Demons* to 20:30. This should give a price of €8.50.
6. Change the time of *Angels and Demons* back to 14:00.
7. Calculate the total.

8. A 10% discount is given to groups of 15 or more in screens one and two for the 17:30 show.
9. Using this information, complete Table 7.113.

Number of actions?	
How many conditions does each action depend on?	
Must all conditions be satisfied?	

Table 7.113 Analysis of group discount IF function

10. Calculate the discount using the information you entered in Table 7.113, referring to the cell name *fivethirty.*
11. Test your IF function by entering the following screen number, time and group size values for the first showing of *Angels and Demons*. The IF function should calculate discounts as shown.

Screen Number	Time	Group Size	Discount
1	17:30	16	€11.20
1	17:30	14	€0.00
1	14:00	16	€0.00
2	17:30	25	€17.50
2	17:30	10	€0.00
2	20:45	21	€0.00

12. Change the screen number to *1*, the time to *14:00* and the group size to *10* for the first showing of *Angels and Demons*.
13. Calculate the amount due.
14. Format all money amounts to currency.
15. Rename Sheet1 as *Group Discounts*

Part 2: Formatting, Filters and Spreadsheet Protection

1. Merge styles from the *Toms Hardware* spreadsheet.
2. Format data in the *Group Discounts* worksheet using the styles listed in Table 7.114.

Merge styles from:
Toms Hardware.xlsx

Range of Cells	Cell Style
A1	Heading 4
A3:I3	Accent4
A4:I12	20% – Accent4

Table 7.114

3. Rename Sheet2 as *Cell Names*
4. Delete all unused worksheets in the workbook.
5. Use conditional formatting to emphasise the film names and group discount amounts in *Red Text* for all films where the group discount applies.
6. Test the conditional formatting by changing the time of the first showing of *Hannah Montana* to *17:30*. *Hannah Montana* should be formatted in red. The IF function should calculate a discount of €17.50 formatted in red.
7. Change the time of the first showing of *Hannah Montana* back to *14:00*.
8. Using a Filter, display only group sizes from 20 to 30 inclusive where the group discount applies.
9. Clear the filter and implement spreadsheet protection in the *Group Discounts* worksheet so that:
   - data can only be entered in the ranges A4:D12 and F4:F12
   - formulas and functions aren't displayed in the formula bar
   - the spreadsheet user is allowed to format cells.
10. Set up spreadsheet protection in the *Cell Names* worksheet so that no data can be entered.
11. Print the *Group Discounts* worksheet.
12. Save the spreadsheet as **Scene Cinema**

CHAPTER 7 SUMMARY

1. Basic Concepts

IF functions are used to automate the decision-making process. In doing so, they reduce our workload. There are four different types of IF function:

1. Simple IF
2. Nested Simple IF
3. Compound IF
4. Nested Compound IF

The type of IF function that you will need to use depends on two factors:

1. The number of conditions that must be satisfied before deciding to take a particular course of action.
2. The number of possible actions.

A summary of IF functions is displayed in Table 7.115.

	Simple IF	Nested IF	Compound IF	Nested Compound IF
Conditions	1	1 per action	From 2 to a maximum of 255	From 2 to a maximum of 255
Actions	2	From 3 to a maximum of 64	2	From 3 to a maximum of 64

Table 7.115 A comparison of IF functions

Each time you create an IF function you must provide Excel with all the information it needs to make the decision independently.

IF Function Types

Simple IF
A Simple IF is used where an IF function must decide to take one of *two possible courses of action* and where the decision depends on only *one condition*.

Example:
In Table 7.116, the IF function automatically calculates Anna Murphy's exam result. There are two possible outcomes; pass or fail. Which outcome is chosen depends on a single condition; the exam mark.

	A	B
1		**Exam Mark**
2	Anna Murphy	55
3	Result	=IF(B2>=50,"Pass","Fail")

Table 7.116

Nested Simple IF

A Nested Simple IF is used where an IF function must choose one of *three or more possible courses of action* and where the decision to take a particular course of action depends on a single condition.

Example:

In Table 7.117, the IF function automatically calculates the price of a Ford Fiesta depending on the engine size selected. There are four possible prices and each price depends on a single factor; the engine size. As there are four different prices, three separate IFs are required. The decision to charge €19990 occurs when none of the other prices apply. Because of this, a separate IF is not required for this action, which is referred to as the false action. Both the second and third IFs are nested inside the first IF. All three opening brackets must be closed at the end of this nested IF function.

	A	B	C	D	E
1		**Engine Size**			
2	Ford Fiesta	1.1			
3	Price	=IF(B2=1.1,16070,IF(B2=1.3,17050,IF(B2=1.4,18500,19990)))			

Table 7.117

Compound IF

A Compound IF is used where an IF function must choose one of two possible courses of action and where the decision depends on *two or more conditions*.

Example:

In Table 7.118, the IF function automatically determines whether a lottery ticket is a winning ticket. It does this by evaluating three conditions, each of which must be satisfied. The number revealed in each of the three panels must be €25. When all three conditions are satisfied, the IF function displays the text, 'You are a winner!' When one or more of the three conditions is not satisfied, the IF function displays the text, 'Try again'.

	A	B	C	D	E	F
1	**Qwik Lottery**					
2						
3		**Panel 1**	**Panel 2**	**Panel 3**		
4	Amount Revealed	€25	€25	€25		
5						
6	Result	=IF(AND(B4=25,C4=25,D4=25),"You are a winner!","Try again")				

Table 7.118

Nested Compound IF

A Nested Compound IF is used where an IF function must decide to take one of *three or more possible courses of action* and where each decision depends on *two or more conditions*.

Example:

In Table 7.119, the IF function automatically determines the price per night in a caravan and camping park.

	A	B	C
1	**LakeView Caravan and Camping**		
2			
3		**Pitch Type**	**Adults**
4	Orla Brown	Camper	2
5			
6	Price per Night	=IF(AND(B4="Caravan",C4<=2),35	
7		,IF(AND(B4="Caravan",C4>2),40	
8		,IF(AND(B4="Camper",C4<=2),25	
9		,IF(AND(B4="Camper",C4>2),30	
10		,IF(AND(B4="Tent",C4<=2),15,20)))))	

Table 7.119

The information that the IF function needs to make this decision is diplayed in Table 7.120.

Pitch Type	Adults	Price per Night
Caravan	2 or less	35
Caravan	More than 2	40
Camper	2 or less	25
Camper	More than 2	30
Tent	2 or less	15
Tent	More than 2	20

Table 7.120

Because there are six possible prices, five IFs are required. As each price depends on two conditions – pitch type and number of adults – an AND function is used to evaluate each set of conditions. When writing this type of IF function, you need to be careful when closing brackets. The bracket for each AND function is closed as the AND function is completed. The brackets for the IF functions are all closed at the very end of the function.

2. Formatting

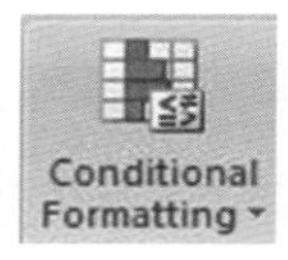

Conditional formatting is used to emphasise specific cells. For example, we could use conditional formatting to display all amounts owed of €100 or more in red. Conditional formatting is dynamic and updates automatically when data in your spreadsheet changes.

3. Potential Pitfalls

- For each IF, make sure you close a bracket at the end of the IF function.
- The closing brackets of AND/OR functions are never positioned at the end of the IF function.
- A conditional test should not be used for the last action implemented by the IF function.
- Never use = in the true action or false action of an IF function. = should be typed at the beginning of the IF function. = can also be used in the condition.
- Don't use a mixture of > and < in a Nested Simple IF function. It is okay to do this in a Nested Compound IF in the AND/OR functions.
- When referring to numbers in an IF function, never enclose the numbers in double quotes.
- When referring to cell names in an IF function, never enclose the cell names in double quotes.

- When referring to text in an IF function, always enclose the text in double quotes.
- A formula or function cannot refer to a time, such as 12:51.

4. Useful Shortcuts

Keyboard Combination	Effect
CTRL + Z	Undoes last action
ALT+N+SH	Accesses the list of shapes in the Insert group

Table 7.121

IF FUNCTIONS REVIEW QUESTIONS

Answers to the review questions are available on www.gillmacmillan.ie

The following questions contain a mixture of the different types of IF functions. See if you can figure out which IF to use!

1.

	A	B	C	D
1		**Vehicle Type**	**Vehicle Height (metres)**	**Fare**
2	Shuyan Wang	MPV	2.5	
3				

Table 7.122

Table 7.122 displays the details of a ferry booking to Holyhead made by Shuyan Wang. The fare is calculated using the following information:

Vehicle Type	Height	Fare
Car	Up to 2.4m	€250
MPV	Up to 2.4m	€285
MPV	Over 2.4m	€320
All other vehicles	–	€450

Write down the IF function that will calculate Shuyan's fare in the space below.

2. Identify the errors in the following IF function.

```
=if(and(F2>sum(E2:E6,G2<average(D2:D6),A2,A2*5)
```

3.

	A	B	C	D
1		**Baggage Weight (Kg)**	**Weight Limit (Kg)**	**Excess Charge**
2	Anna Murphy	27	20	
3				

Table 7.123

Table 7.123 displays the details of Anna Murphy's checked-in baggage on a flight to London. There is an excess charge when the total weight is over 20 kilograms. Excess charges are calculated using the following information:

Weight	**Charge per Excess Kilo**	**Note**
21-25	€5	*Charged on each kilo above 20kg*
26-30	€8	*Charged on each kilo above 20kg*
31-35	€12	*Charged on each kilo above 20kg*
>35	€15	*Charged on each kilo above 20kg*

Write down the IF function that will calculate Anna's excess charge.

____

4.

	A	B	C
1	**Diarmuid Murphy – Race Results**		
2			
3	**Race**	**Position**	
4	Maulin	12	
5	Three Rock	7	
6	Scalp	–	
7	Bray Head	6	
8	Howth	15	
9	Sugarloaf	19	
10	Tirbradden	7	
11			
12	**League Status**		

Table 7.124

Table 7.124 displays Diarmuid Murphy's finishing positions in the summer league of mountain races. Calculate Diarmuid's league status using the following information.

- Runners who have completed five or more races have a status of Complete
- Runners who have completed fewer than five races have a status of Incomplete.

Write down the IF function that will determine Diarmuid's league status in the space below.

____

5.

	A	B	C	D
1	**Customer**	**Season**	**Group Size**	**Total Charge**
2	Tim Fahey	High	25	
3				

Table 7.125

Table 7.125 displays the details of a booking made by Tim Fahey for a tour bus. The total charge is calculated using the following information:

Season	Group Size	Total Charge
Low	35 or less	€150
Low	More than 35	€200
High	35 or less	€220
High	More than 35	€300

Write down the IF function that will calculate the total charge in the space below.

____

6.

Table 7.126 displays Vanessa Walsh's ECDL results. Students must obtain a Pass in all seven modules before they qualify for a certificate.

Write down the IF function that will determine whether Vanessa has qualified for the ECDL certificate in the space below. The IF function should display the text *Yes* for students who qualify for the certificate and *No* for all other students.

____

	A	B	C
1	ECDL Results: Vanessa Walsh		
2			
3	**Module**	**Result**	
4	1	Pass	
5	2	Pass	
6	3	Pass	
7	4	Pass	
8	5	Fail	
9	6	Pass	
10	7	Pass	
11			
12	**ECDL Cert?**		

Table 7.126

7.

	A	B	C	E	F
1	London Marathon				
2					
3	**Competitor**	**Previous Bookings**	**Club Membership**	**Standard Price**	**Discounted Price**
4	Andreas Linko	3	Yes	€550	
5					

Table 7.127

Table 7.127 displays details of entrants to the London marathon who have booked an all-inclusive travel package. Discounts are available to runners on the following basis:

Previous Bookings	Club Membership	Discount
<=2	No	0%
<=2	Yes	5%
>2	No	5%
>2	Yes	10%

Write down the IF function that will calculate Andreas Linko's discounted price in the space below.

____

8.

	A	B
1		**Traffic Light**
2	Colour	Amber
3	Driver Behaviour	

Table 7.128

Table 7.128 displays the colour of a traffic light. Depending on the colour of the traffic light, there are three possible driver behaviours.

Colour	Behaviour
Green	Go
Amber	Slow down
Red	Stop

Write down the IF function that will determine the appropriate driver behaviour.

____

9.

	A	B	C	D	E
1	**Be Sure Insurance**				
2					
3	**Customer Name**	**House Alarm**	**Previous Claims**	**Standard Premium**	**Discounted Premium**
4	Carl Kinsella	Yes	1	€350	
5					

Table 7.129

Table 7.129 displays details of Carl Kinsella's house insurance policy renewal. Be Sure Insurance customers are entitled to a discount on the standard premium on the following basis:

Alarm	Previous Claims	Discount %
No	0	5%
Yes	0	15%
No	>0	0%
Yes	>0	3%

Write down the IF function that will calculate Carl's discounted premium in the space below.

____

10.

	A	B	C	D	E
1	Hi-Tech College Entrance Exam				
2					
3	Student Name	English	Maths	General Knowledge	Accepted
4	Robert Morgan	78	85	92	
5					

Table 7.130

Table 7.130 displays details of Robert Morgan's entrance exam results. Hi-Tech college accepts students on the following basis:

	English	Maths	General Knowledge
Pass Mark	60	75	65

Students must pass all three exams before being accepted by Hi-Tech college.

Write down the IF function that will determine whether Robert has been accepted. The IF function should display *Yes* if Robert is successful and *No* if he is unsuccessful.

____

8 Lookup Functions

In Chapter 8, you will learn how to:

- Create a vertical lookup table
- Create a horizontal lookup table
- Use lookup functions to access data stored in a lookup table

WHAT IS A LOOKUP FUNCTION?

Imagine you work in a company that supplies office equipment and stationery. The company has a total of 1000 items in stock. Details of the items are kept in a price list. Each item has a number, e.g. item no. 1, item no. 2, item no. 3 and so on. Table 8.1 displays the first ten of the 1000 items in the price list.

Office Supplies Price List		
Item Number	**Description**	**Price**
1	Appointments Book	€18.93
2	Telephone Calls Book	€14.66
3	Postages Book	€13.33
4	Time Book	€9.56
5	Petty Cash Book	€21.60
6	A4 Analysis Pads(5)	€4.22
7	Twinlock Accounts Book	€19.75
8	Post-It Notes	€7.50
9	Crocodile Clip Badge(25)	€28.10
10	Universal Name Badge(5)	€4.21

Table 8.1

In your capacity as accounts executive, other members of staff frequently ask you questions such as 'What's the price of item 10?' Each time you're asked a question like this, you get out the price list and look down the first column until you find the number (in this case 10). Looking across to the next column, you see that item 10 is Universal Name Badge(5). Then you look across to the next column to find the price, which is €4.21.

In any process where data is stored in a list and that list is frequently referred to, lookup functions can be used to speed up the process of retrieving data from the list. The lookup function works in a way that is very similar to the process of manually looking up a list, as described above. First, the information about products and prices must be stored in a special area in the spreadsheet, known as a lookup table. The first column (item number) is used as a reference to locate specific items in the table. Once an item is located, the spreadsheet can access all the information relating to that item.

In a real-life scenario, this table would contain hundreds or even thousands of rows. Consider your local Tesco store. Each time a product bar code is scanned at a checkout desk, the resulting product code entered in the system is used to find the product price and description in a table similar to Table 8.1. The only difference is that the table used by Tesco contains thousands of products and is updated daily.

There are two types of lookup tables: vertical lookup tables and horizontal lookup tables.

VERTICAL LOOKUP TABLES

In a vertical lookup table the information is set up in columns. When looking for the price of item 10 in Table 8.2, *you must look down* the first column to find 10 *and then across* to the third column to find the price.

Item Number	Description	Price
1	Appointments Book	€18.93
2	Telephone Calls Book	€14.66
3	Postages Book	€13.33
4	Time Book	€9.56
5	Petty Cash Book	€21.60
6	A4 Analysis Pads(5)	€4.22
7	Twinlock Accounts Book	€19.75
8	Post-It Notes	€7.50
9	Crocodile Clip Badge(25)	€28.10
10	Universal Name Badge(5)	€4.21

Table 8.2

The first column of a vertical table must contain data that uniquely identifies each item stored in the lookup table. Here, each product has a unique item number.

For vertical lookup tables, the first column must be in ascending alphabetical or ascending numerical order.

HORIZONTAL LOOKUP TABLES

In a horizontal lookup table the information is set up in rows. When looking for the price of item 10 in Table 8.3, *you must look across* the first row to find 10 *and then down* to the third row to find the price.

Item Number	1	2	3	4	→	10
Description	Appointments Book	Telephone Calls Book	Postages Book	Time Book	→	Universal Name Badge (5)
Price	€18.93	€14.66	€13.33	€9.56	→	€4.21

Table 8.3

The top row of a horizontal table must contain data that uniquely identifies each item stored in the lookup table.

For horizontal lookup tables, the top row must be in ascending alphabetical or ascending numerical order.

Horizontal and vertical lookup tables work in the same way and will give the same answer when used correctly. Which one you use depends on the layout of your spreadsheet, the data you're storing and your own personal preference.

Lookup tables save time and reduce errors. They eliminate the need to look through paper-based lists to find information relating to a particular item. Instead, this work is done by the lookup function. Second, updates or changes made to data stored in the lookup table are automatically recognised by the lookup function. In a retail spreadsheet application this would greatly reduce the chance of a customer being charged the wrong price. Sales staff wouldn't have to remember price changes. The prices can be stored in a lookup table. Once the bar code for a particular product is entered in the spreadsheet, the lookup function can find the price relating to that bar code. Usually, one member of staff would be given the responsibility for updating prices in the lookup table. As long as the sales staff enter the correct bar code at the point of sale, the up-to-date price for a particular product will be found by the lookup function.

Vertical Lookup Tables – Worked Example

In this example we will use a vertical lookup table to store product descriptions and prices.

Step One – Set Up the Lookup Table

The lookup table will store product and price information. This product and price information will be referred to each time a sale is made. When creating a lookup table, the best method is to set it up in a separate worksheet. This makes the spreadsheet less cluttered and easier to work with.

1. Enter the product and price information in Sheet1 of a new spreadsheet workbook, as shown in Table 8.4.

	A	B	C
1	**Item Number**	**Description**	**Price**
2	1	Appointments Book	€18.93
3	2	Telephone Calls Book	€14.66
4	3	Postages Book	€13.33
5	4	Time Book	€9.56
6	5	Petty Cash Book	€21.60
7	6	A4 Analysis Pads(5)	€4.22
8	7	Twinlock Accounts Book	€19.75
9	8	Post-It Notes	€7.50
10	9	Crocodile Clip Badge(25)	€28.10
11	10	Universal Name Badge(5)	€4.21

Table 8.4

2. Rename Sheet1 as *Stock* and format the prices to currency.

Step Two – Name the Lookup Table

We will assign the name *pricelist* to the lookup table.

1. Highlight everything except the first row *(A2:C11)*, as shown in Figure 8.1.

	A	B	C	D
1	Item Number	Description	Price	
2	1	Appointments Book	€ 18.93	
3	2	Telephone Calls Book	€ 14.66	
4	3	Postages Book	€ 13.33	
5	4	Time Book	€ 9.56	
6	5	Petty Cash Book	€ 21.60	
7	6	A4 Analysis Pads(5)	€ 4.22	
8	7	Twinlock Accounts Book	€ 19.75	
9	8	Post-It Notes	€ 7.50	
10	9	Crocodile Clip Badge(25)	€ 28.10	
11	10	Universal Name Badge(5)	€ 4.21	
12				

Figure 8.1 The highlighted data for the lookup table

2. Assign the name *pricelist* to this range, as shown in Figure 8.2.

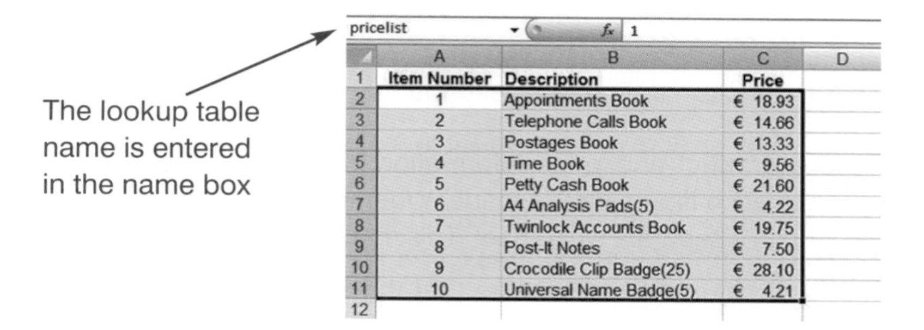

	A	B	C	D
1	Item Number	Description	Price	
2	1	Appointments Book	€ 18.93	
3	2	Telephone Calls Book	€ 14.66	
4	3	Postages Book	€ 13.33	
5	4	Time Book	€ 9.56	
6	5	Petty Cash Book	€ 21.60	
7	6	A4 Analysis Pads(5)	€ 4.22	
8	7	Twinlock Accounts Book	€ 19.75	
9	8	Post-It Notes	€ 7.50	
10	9	Crocodile Clip Badge(25)	€ 28.10	
11	10	Universal Name Badge(5)	€ 4.21	
12				

Figure 8.2 Naming a lookup table using the name box

Excel will now recognise the range named *pricelist* as a vertical lookup table. We can refer to this lookup table for product and price information.

N Excel does not allow spaces in range names.

N The row containing the headings isn't included in the lookup table as the headings will not be referred to by the lookup functions.

N For the purposes of the lookup function, Excel numbers the columns in the lookup table from left to right. Item Number is column 1, Description is column 2 and Price is column 3. It is important to remember this as these numbers will be used in the lookup function later on.

Step Three – Enter Sales Data in a Separate Worksheet

1. Enter the data displayed in Table 8.5 in Sheet2.

	A	B	C	D	E
1			**Sales Records**		
2					
3	**Item Number**	**Quantity**	**Description**	**Price**	**Total**
4	9	5			
5					

Table 8.5

2. Rename Sheet2 as *Sales*

Details of items sold are stored in the *Sales* worksheet (Table 8.5). For each item number entered in the *Sales* worksheet, two lookup functions will automatically display the description and the price relating to that item number. In Table 8.5, *9* refers to *Crocodile Clip Badge(25)* in the lookup table.

Step Four – Create Lookup Function to find the Description

Each product sold is identified by an item number. In Table 8.5, item number 9 has been entered in the spreadsheet.

We will use two lookup functions to find the information relating to item number 9 in the lookup table. The first lookup function will tell us that item 9 is a *Crocodile Clip Badge(25)*. The second lookup function will tell us that the price of this product is *€28.10*. This is similar to what happens when a bar code is scanned at a supermarket checkout.

Because we have organised the data in the lookup table in columns, Excel recognises it as a vertical lookup table. We must use a VLOOKUP function to access data from this lookup table.

The first lookup function will be entered in C4 in the worksheet named *Sales*. It will find the description relating to item number 9. Each lookup function contains three sections, separated by commas.

=VLOOKUP(1, 2, 3)

"1" In Table 8.5, item number 9 has been entered in A4. This item number is used to retrieve data from the lookup table. Once the lookup function finds 9 in the first column of the lookup table, it can read all the associated data in that row. We can complete the first section of the lookup function as follows**: =vlookup(A4,**

"2" This is where we refer to the lookup table itself. We have already assigned the name *pricelist* to the lookup table. We can complete the second section of the lookup function as follows: **=vlookup(A4,pricelist,**

"3" This is where we identify the column of the lookup table containing the information we require. We're using a vertical lookup table that has three columns. Column one stores the item number, column two stores the description and column three stores the price. As we're looking for the description, which is in column 2, we must enter the number 2 in the third section of the lookup function.

We can now complete the lookup function as follows:

=vlookup(A4,pricelist,2)

What you are looking for → A4
Name of the lookup table → pricelist
The column the data is in → 2

1. In the *Sales* worksheet, select C4 and type *=vlookup(A4,pricelist,2)*. The text *Crocodile Clip Badge(25)*, which is the description of item 9, is displayed.
2. Enter the additional item numbers displayed in Table 8.6.
3. Copy the lookup function using Fill Down.

	A	B	C	D	E	F
1	Sales Records					
2						
3	Item Number	Quantity	Description	Price	Total	
4	9	5	**=vlookup(a4,pricelist,2)** finds *Crocodile Clip Badge (25)*			
5	4	100	**=vlookup(a5,pricelist,2)** finds *Time Book*			
6	6	25	**=vlookup(a6,pricelist,2)** finds *A4 Analysis Pads(5)*			
7	8	10	**=vlookup(a7,pricelist,2)** finds *Post-It Notes*			

Table 8.6

Create a Lookup Function to Find the Price

This lookup function is very similar to the first one except that in this case the information we require is in column three instead of column two.

- *Step one* (set up the lookup table): *already complete*
- *Step two* (name the lookup table): *already complete*
- *Step three* (enter data in the *Sales* worksheet): *already complete*
- *Step four:* create a lookup function to find the price, which is stored in column 3 of the lookup table.

This gives the following lookup function: *=vlookup(a4,pricelist,3)* which is entered in D4, as shown in Table 8.7.

4. Select D4 and type *=vlookup(a4,pricelist,3).*
5. Copy this lookup function using Fill Down.

	A	B	C	D	E	F
1	Sales Records					
2						
3	Item Number	Quantity	Description	Price		
4	9	5	Crocodile Clip Badge(25)	**=vlookup(a4, pricelist,3)** finds *€28.10*		
5	4	100	Time Book	**=vlookup(a5, pricelist,3)** finds *€9.56*		
6	6	25	A4 Analysis Pads(5)	**=vlookup(a6, pricelist,3)** finds *€4.22*		
7	8	10	Post-It Notes	**=vlookup(a7, pricelist,3)** finds *€7.50*		

Table 8.7

We can complete the exercise by entering a simple formula to calculate the total, as shown in Table 8.8.

	A	B	C	D	E
1	**Sales Records**				
2					
3	**Item No**	**Quantity**	**Description**	**Price**	**Total**
4	998	5	Crocodile Clip Badge(25)	€28.10	**=b4*d4**
5	4	100	Time Book	€9.56	**=b5*d5**
6	6	25	A4 Analysis Pads(5)	€4.22	**=b6*d6**
7	256	10	Post-It Notes	€7.50	**=b7*d7**

Table 8.8

6. In E4, enter the multiplication formula shown in Table 8.8
7. Copy this formula using Fill Down.
8. Save the spreadsheet as **Office Supplies**

You can also write a lookup function without naming the lookup table. However, this isn't recommended as it makes the lookup function more difficult to interpret. If we didn't name the lookup table, the lookup function to find the description would be *=vlookup(A4,Stock!A2:C11,2)*. It is also more difficult to copy a lookup function using this method.

LOOKUP FUNCTION ERRORS

The most common errors that occur in lookup functions are listed below.

1. Number referred to by lookup function doesn't exist in the lookup table.
In our example, we used the Vlookup function to find the description and price relating to a particular item number. For example, by entering item number 4, one lookup function finds the description *Time Book* and a second lookup function finds the price *€9.56*.

A lookup function will return an incorrect answer when the item number doesn't exist in the lookup table.

	A	B	C	D	E	F
1	**Sales Records**					
2						
3	**Item No**	**Quantity**	**Description**	**Price**	**Total**	
4	18	5	**=vlookup(a4,pricelist,2)** finds *Universal Name Badge(5)*			
5						

Table 8.9: A lookup function can give an incorrect answer

In the example shown in Table 8.9, an item number of 18 has been entered in A4. This item number doesn't exist in the first column of the lookup table. The lookup function finds the item number immediately before 18 (item number 10) and incorrectly returns the value *Universal Name Badge(5)*. This error can be prevented by adding the false argument to the lookup function. The false argument causes the lookup function to display the **#N/A** error message when the value referenced by the lookup function doesn't exist in the first column or row of the lookup table. This is shown in Table 8.10.

	A	B	C	D	E	F
1	**Sales Records**					
2						
3	**Item No**	**Quantity**	**Description**	**Price**	**Total**	
4	18	5	**=vlookup(a4,pricelist,2,false)** returns the value *#N/A*			
5						

Table 8.10: Adding the false argument to the lookup function prevents errors

It is good practice always to include the false argument in your lookup functions. This will prevent the lookup function from displaying incorrect data.

2. First column of the lookup table not in ascending order.

The first column of a vertical lookup table contains data that uniquely identifies each item. In Figure 8.3, each item stored in the lookup table has a unique code. To work correctly, the first column of a lookup table must be in ascending order.

	A	B
1	**Code**	**Colour**
2	5	Red
3	3	Green
4	1	Blue
5	4	Yellow
6	6	Black
7	2	White

Figure 8.3 Incorrectly set up lookup table

As you can see from Table 8.3, the first column of the lookup table is not in ascending order. This will cause some errors when lookup functions are used to access data from this lookup table (displayed in Table 8.11).

	A	B	C	D	E	F
1	**Code**	**Colour**				
2	1	**=vlookup(a4,colours,2)** finds *Blue*				✔
3	2	**=vlookup(a5,colours,2)** finds *Blue*				✘
4	3	**=vlookup(a6,colours,2)** finds *Blue*				✘
5	4	**=vlookup(a7,colours,2)** finds *Yellow*				✔
6	5	**=vlookup(a8,colours,2)** finds *Yellow*				✘
7	6	**=vlookup(a9,colours,2)** finds *Black*				✔

Table 8.11 Some lookup functions give incorrect answers

In the example, the range name *colours* has been assigned to the lookup table. Lookup functions incorrectly report items 2 and 3 as being blue in colour and item 5 as being yellow in colour. This is because the first column of the lookup table is not in ascending order of code. Always ensure that the first column of your lookup table is in ascending order. In horizontal lookup tables, the first row of the table must be in ascending order.

3. Incorrect column number in the lookup function.

The number of columns in your lookup table determines the numbers that can be used inside the lookup function when referring to the lookup table. In Figure 8.4, the lookup table has three columns.

	A	B	C
1	**Employee Number**	**Vehicle Registration Number**	**Driver Name**
2	3298	08D2395	Owen Roberts
3	9837	09KE19872	Paul Thomas
4	12857	07D55601	Stuart Aston
5	76963	06KY50771	Adrian Renshaw

Figure 8.4 A lookup table with three columns

Excel assigns the number *1* to the first column of the lookup table, *2* to the second column and *3* to the third column (Figure 8.4).

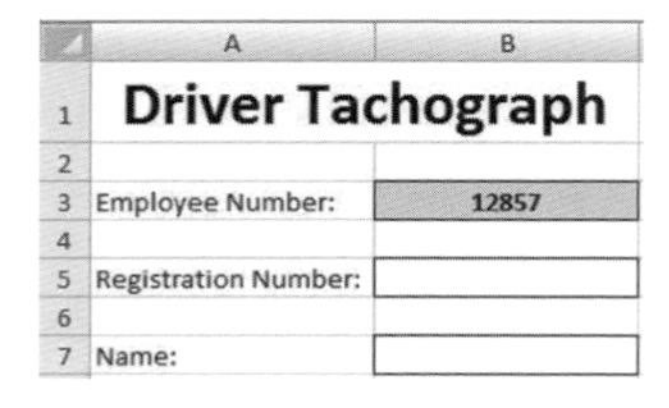

Figure 8.5 Accessing data from the lookup table

Assuming that the lookup table has been assigned the name *drivers*, in Figure 8.5 we can access data from the lookup table using the following lookup functions:

=vlookup(b3,drivers,2) finds 07D55601
=vlookup(b3,drivers,3) finds Stuart Aston

Because there are three columns in the lookup table, using a number less than 1 or greater than 3 in the lookup function will return an error.

=vlookup(b3,drivers,0) returns a **#VALUE!** error
=vlookup(b3,drivers,4) returns a **#REF!** error

Using column reference *1* in the lookup function, e.g. *=vlookup(b3,drivers,1)*, doesn't provide any meaningful information as this will simply return the value stored in B3, i.e. *12857*.

Horizontal Lookup Tables – Worked Example

In this example we'll use a horizontal lookup table to store contact information for a sales representative.

Step One – Set Up the Lookup Table

This lookup table will contain information about sales contacts and distances that will be frequently referred to.

1. Create a new spreadsheet workbook.
2. Rename Sheet1 as *Clients*
3. Enter the data shown in Table 8.12 in the *Clients* worksheet.

	A	B	C	D	E	F
1	**Location**	Gort	Headford	Loughrea	Oughterard	Tuam
2	**Contact**	Mark O Shea	Peter Flynn	Sue Barrett	Tina Moore	John Lynch
3	**Distance (km)**	40	27	39	26	35

Table 8.12

Step Two – Name the Lookup Table

In the *Clients* worksheet, assign the name *distances* to the range B1:F3. Excel automatically assigns numbers to the rows in the lookup table. Location is in row 1, contact is in row 2 and distance is in row 3.

Never include row or column headings when naming a lookup table.

The row or column numbers that Excel assigns to a lookup table are not actually displayed anywhere in the spreadsheet.

Step Three – Enter Sales Data in a Separate Worksheet

1. Enter the data displayed in Table 8.13 in Sheet2.

	A	B	C	D	E
1	**Travel Expenses Calculator**				
2					
3	**Rate per Kilometre:**	0.75			
4					
5	**Date**	**Location**	**Contact**	**Distance**	**Expenses**
6	04/08/2010	Tuam			
7	04/08/2010	Headford			
8	05/08/2010	Loughrea			
9	05/08/2010	Gort			
10	05/08/2010	Oughterard			

Table 8.13

2. Rename Sheet2 as *Sales Trips*

Details of sales trips are displayed in Table 8.13. Each location name refers back to data stored in the *distances* lookup table. e.g. John Lynch is the contact in Tuam and the distance is 35 kilometres. In step four, we'll create a lookup function that will find the contact relating to each location.

Step Four – Create the Lookup Function

Each contact is identified by the location name. As the data in the *distances* lookup table is set up in rows, we must use an HLOOKUP function to find the contact for each location.

The first lookup function is entered in C6 of the *Sales Trips* worksheet. It will find the contact name relating to Tuam.

Each horizontal lookup function contains three sections, separated by commas.

=HLOOKUP(1, 2, 3)

"1" In Table 8.13, *Tuam* has been entered in B6. This is used to retrieve data from the lookup table. Once the lookup function finds *Tuam* in the lookup table, it can read all the associated data in that column. We can complete the first section of the lookup function as follows: **=hlookup(B6,**

"2" This is where we refer to the lookup table itself. We've already given the name *distances* to the lookup table. We can complete the second section of the lookup function as follows: **=hlookup(B6,distances,**

"3" This is where we identify the row of the lookup table containing the information we require. We are using a horizontal lookup table that has three rows. Row 1 stores the location, row 2 stores the contact and row 3 stores the distance. In this case we are looking for the contact so we use the number *2* to identify row 2. We can now complete the lookup function as follows: **=hlookup(B6,distances,2)**

1. Enter *=hlookup(B6,distances,2)* in cell C6 of the *Sales Trips* worksheet. The text *John Lynch*, who is the contact in Tuam, is displayed, as shown in Table 8.14.

	A	B	C	D	E
1	**Travel Expenses Calculator**				
2					
3	**Rate per Kilometre:**	0.75			
4					
5	**Date**	**Location**	**Contact**	**Distance**	**Expenses**
6	04/08/2010	Tuam	**=hlookup(B6,distances,2)** finds *John Lynch*		
7	04/08/2010	Headford	**=hlookup(B7,distances,2)** finds *Peter Flynn*		
8	05/08/2010	Loughrea	**=hlookup(B8,distances,2)** finds *Sue Barrett*		
9	05/08/2010	Gort	**=hlookup(B9,distances,2)** finds *Mark O Shea*		
10	05/08/2010	Oughterard	**=hlookup(B10,distances,2)** finds *Tina Moore*		

Table 8.14

2. Copy the lookup function using Fill Down.
3. In D6, create a lookup function to find the distance to Tuam.
4. Copy this lookup function using Fill Down.
5. Format B3 as currency.
6. Calculate expenses.

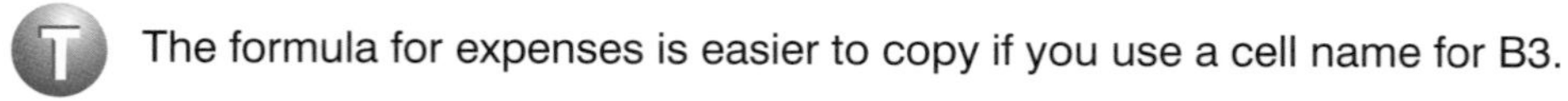
The formula for expenses is easier to copy if you use a cell name for B3.

7. Save the spreadsheet as **Record of Sales Trips**

EDITING A LOOKUP TABLE

If you add data to or remove data from your lookup table, you will need to edit the range name defining the range of cells contained in the lookup table. Follow these steps to adjust your lookup table.

1. In the Formulas section of the Ribbon, click the Name Manager button. The Name Manager dialog box is displayed.

You can quickly access the Name Manager using the *ALT+M+N* keyboard combination.

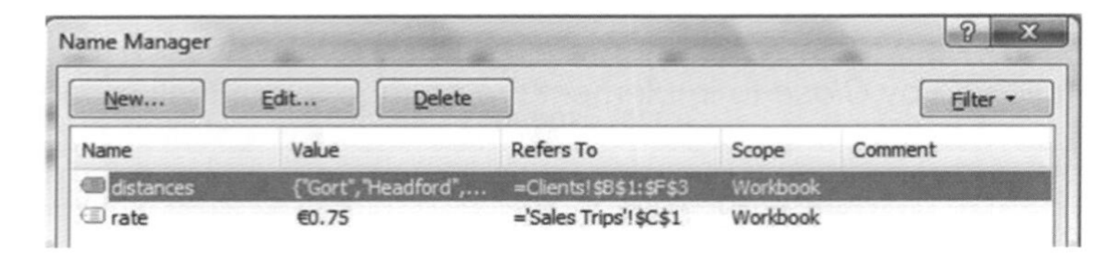

Figure 8.6 Two names have been defined in this workbook

The Name Manager dialog box shows the names defined in the *Record of Sales Trips* workbook (Figure 8.6). The name *distances* has been assigned to the lookup table and this includes cells B1 to F3 inclusive.

2. In the Name Manager dialog box, select the lookup table name. Click the *Edit* button to change the range of cells included in the lookup table. The Edit Name dialog box is displayed (Figure 8.7).

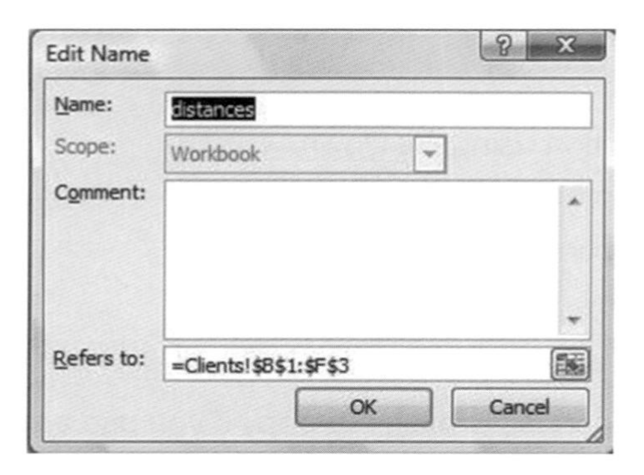

Figure 8.7 The Edit Name dialog box is used to adjust the range of cells included in a lookup table

To adjust the range of cells included in the lookup table, click in the *Refers to* box. A new row can be included in the lookup table by changing F3 to F4, as shown in Figure 8.8.

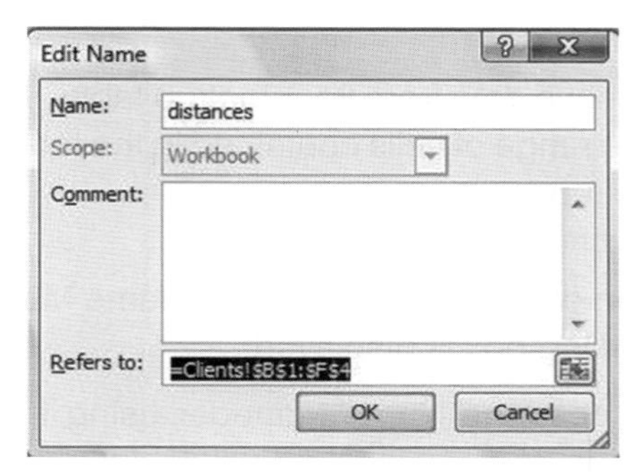

Figure 8.8

3. Click *OK* followed by *Close* to implement the change to the lookup table.

Set up Styles for Chapter 8

Before entering data for assignment one, we will set up the Cell Styles that will be used to format all the spreadsheets in Chapter 8.

1. Create a new spreadsheet workbook.
2. In the Home section of the Ribbon, click the Cell Styles button.
3. Right click *Title* and then select Modify from the pop-up menu
4. In the Style dialog box, click the Format button.
5. In the Format Cells dialog box, select the formatting characteristics listed in Table 8.15.

Style Name	Title
Font	Georgia
Font Style	Bold
Size	20
Border	None
Font Colour	Aqua, Accent5, Darker 50%

Table 8.15

6. Click OK twice to apply these formatting characteristics to the *Title* style.
7. Modify the *20% – Accent5* style to include the formatting characteristics listed in Table 8.16.

Style Name	20% – Accent5
Font	Calibri
Size	11
Border	Outline
Font Colour	Aqua, Accent5, Darker 50%

Table 8.16

8. Modify the *Accent5* style to include the formatting characteristics listed in Table 8.17.

Style Name	Accent5
Font	Calibri
Size	12
Font Style	Bold
Font Colour	White, Background1

Table 8.17

9. Save the spreadsheet as **Miles of Tiles**

Lookup Functions Assignment One

Part 1: Create the Tiles Lookup Table

	A	B	C	D	E	F	G
1	**Product Code**	**Manufacturer**	**Tile Name**	**Colour**	**Height (metres)**	**Width (metres)**	**Unit Price**
2	1	Tiles International	Fleurette	Navy	0.1	0.1	0.85
3	2	Tile Designs	Malibu	Light Blue	0.5	0.5	3.50
4	3	Tiles International	Textile	Light Brown	0.2	0.2	1.20
5	4	Northern Tiles	Florence	Purple	0.1	0.1	0.85
6	5	Northern Tiles	Paisley	Mixed	0.05	0.05	0.27
7	6	Tiles International	Serenity	Green	0.5	0.5	3.50
8	7	Tiles International	Opal	Indigo	0.1	0.1	0.90
9	8	Tile Designs	Marble	Grey	0.1	0.1	0.85
10	9	Tile Designs	Stone	Charcoal	0.2	0.2	1.15
11	10	Northern Tiles	Stone	Grey	0.1	0.1	0.80

Table 8.18

1. Open the *Miles of Tiles* spreadsheet if it is not already open.
2. Rename Sheet1 as *Tile Details*
3. Enter the data shown in Table 8.18 in the worksheet named *Tile Details*
4. Assign the name *tiles* to an appropriate range of cells.
5. Format unit prices to currency.
6. Format data using the styles listed in Table 8.19.

Range of Cells	Cell Style
A1:G1	Accent5
A2:G11	20% – Accent5

Table 8.19

Part 2: Record Customer Orders

1. Rename Sheet2 as *Customer Requirements*
2. Enter the data shown in Table 8.20 in the worksheet named *Customer Requirements*. Formulas and functions will be entered in the shaded cells.

	A	B	C	D	E	F	G	H	I	J	K	L
1	Miles of Tiles											
2												
3	Customer	Product Code	Manu-facturer	Tile Name	Colour	Height (metres)	Width (metres)	Tile Area (sq. metres)	Area to Cover (sq. metres)	No. of Tiles Required	Unit Price	Total
4	Paul O Shea	8							5.4			
5	Bob Finnegan	2							7.2			
6	Jakek Wielgosz	10							6.0			
7	Regina Irwin	3							10.5			
8	Ger Mullins	2							8.5			
9	Roy Byrne	5							2.5			
10	Matt Evans	8							4.1			
11	Betty Moore	9							4.9			
12	Maura Quinn	10							7.8			

Table 8.20

Type the heading in column C without the hyphen, i.e manufacturer.

3. Create lookup functions to display the manufacturer, tile name, colour, height (metres) and width (metres) for each product code entered.

Instead of typing the name *tiles* when creating the lookup function, press *F3* and then select *tiles* from the Paste Name dialog box. This eliminates the possibility of making a spelling mistake when referring to a range name.

4. Calculate tile area (square metres).
5. Calculate the number of tiles required.
6. Display the number of tiles with zero decimal places.

N Using the Decrease Decimals button will cause an error in the Total. Regina Irwin requires 262.5 tiles. If we round this to zero decimal places using the decrease decimals button, 263 is displayed in J7. However, 262.5 is actually stored in J7. The formula =J7*K7, where the number of tiles is multiplied by the unit price, uses 262.5 as the number of tiles. The resulting total of €315.00 is based on 262.5 tiles and not 263 tiles. The correct total is €315.60. To get the correct total, the number of tiles must be rounded up, using the ROUND function.

7. Display the number of tiles with one decimal place.
8. Edit the formula in J4 to read as follows: *=ROUND(I4/H4,0)*. This rounds the result of the formula *=I4/H4* to zero decimal places.
9. Copy the ROUND function using Fill Down. Regina Irwin's number of tiles is rounded up from 262.5 to 263. Betty Moore's number of tiles is rounded up from 122.5 to 123. The ROUND function has rounded these numbers ***up*** as the number after the decimal place is 5.
10. Display the number of tiles with zero decimal places.
11. Display unit price using a lookup function.
12. Calculate the total.
13. Format data in the *Customer Requirements* worksheet using the styles listed in Table 8.21.

Range of Cells	Cell Style
A1	Title
A3:L3	Accent5
A4:L12	20% – Accent5

Table 8.21

14. Using a Filter, display data for customers where the total is above average.
15. Clear the Filter and display data where the number of tiles is *greater than 500* and the total is *greater than €300*.

16. Clear all filters in the *Customer Requirements* worksheet.

Part 3: Analyse Sales Data

1. Rename Sheet3 as *Sales Analysis*
2. Enter the data displayed in Table 8.22 in the worksheet named *Sales Analysis*

	A	B	C
1		**Sales Analysis**	
2			
3	**Manufacturer**	**Number of Tiles Sold**	**Sales Revenue**
4	Tiles International		
5	Tile Designs		
6	Northern Tiles		

Table 8.22

3. Calculate the total number of tiles sold by each manufacturer using the SUMIF function.
4. Display tiles sold with no decimal places.
5. Calculate the total sales revenue for each manufacturer using the SUMIF function.
6. Format data in the *Sales Analysis* worksheet using the styles listed in Table 8.23.

Range of Cells	Cell Style
A1	Title
A3:C3	Accent5
A4:C6	20% – Accent5

Table 8.23

7. Display the number of tiles sold by each manufacturer using a pie chart. Information relating to chart setup is displayed in Table 8.24.

Chart Type	Pie in 3-D
Chart Title	Units Sold by Manufacturer
Data Labels	Value and Percentage – Inside End position
Chart Location	*Sales Analysis* worksheet, below the data

Table 8.24

- Apply the *Subtle Effect – Dark 1* shape style to the chart background.
- Apply the *Subtle Effect – Accent 1* shape style to the chart title.

8. Display the total sales revenue by manufacturer using a pie chart. Information relating to chart setup is displayed in Table 8.25.

Chart Type	Pie in 3-D
Chart Title	Sales Revenue by Manufacturer
Data Labels	Value and Percentage – Inside End position
Chart Location	*Sales Analysis* worksheet, below the Units Sold by Manufacturer pie chart

Table 8.25

- Apply the *Subtle Effect – Dark 1* shape style to the chart background.
- Apply the *Subtle Effect – Accent 1* shape style to the chart title.

9. Delete all unused worksheets in the workbook.
10. Rearrange the sheet tabs so that they appear in the order shown in Figure 8.9.

Figure 8.9

11. In the *Tile Details* and *Sales Analysis* worksheets, implement spreadsheet protection so that data cannot be entered in any cells.
12. In the *Customer Requirements* worksheet, implement spreadsheet protection so that:
    - data can only be entered in the ranges A4:B12 and I4:I12
    - the spreadsheet user cannot select locked cells.
13. Protect the workbook for structure only.
14. Print the *Customer Requirements* and *Sales Analysis* worksheets.

Part 4: Create a Macro

1. Save the spreadsheet as **Miles of Tiles**, using the *Excel Macro-Enabled Workbook* file type.
2. Turn off worksheet protection in the *Customer Requirements* worksheet.
3. Select any cell in the *Tile Details* worksheet.
4. Record a new macro (named *clearsales*) that performs the following tasks:
   - selects the *Customer Requirements* worksheet
   - deletes the contents of A4:B12 and I4:I12
   - positions the cell pointer in A4.
5. Draw a rounded rectangle in column L, above the heading *Total*. Format the rectangle using the *Subtle Effect Dark 1* shape style. Type the text *Clear All* inside the rectangle. Link the rounded rectangle to the *clearsales* macro.

   Clear All

6. Re-protect the *Customer Requirements* worksheet.
7. Test your macro by entering dummy sales data. Run the macro by clicking the *Clear All* button.
8. Save the **Miles of Tiles** spreadsheet.

Lookup Functions Assignment Two

Part 1: Create the PCs Lookup Table

1. Create a new spreadsheet workbook and rename Sheet1 as *List of PCs*
2. Enter the data shown in Table 8.26 in the worksheet named *List of PCs*.
3. Assign the name *computers* to an appropriate range of cells.
4. Merge styles from the *Miles of Tiles* spreadsheet.

	A	B	C	D	E	F	G	H	I	J
1	**PC Number:**	1	2	3	4	5	6	7	8	9
2	**Model :**	Dell Vostro 220	Sony Vaio	Compaq Pavilion 6100	Dell Optiplex 760	Compaq Touchsmart IQ800t	Dell Optiplex 940	Dell Vostro 220	Dell Optiplex 940	Compaq Pavilion 6100
3	**Year of Purchase:**	2008	2010	2009	2010	2010	2008	2009	2009	2010
4	**Location:**	Marketing	Marketing	Sales	Accounts	Administration	Accounts	Engineering	Engineering	Accounts

Table 8.26

5. Format data in the *List of PCs* worksheet using the styles listed in Table 8.27.

Range of Cells	Cell Style
A1:A4	Accent5
B1:J4	20% – Accent5

Table 8.27

Part 2: Create the Spare Parts Lookup Table

1. Rename Sheet2 as *Spare Parts*
2. Enter the data shown in Table 8.28 in the worksheet named *Spare Parts*.

	A	B	C
1	**Part No**	**Description**	**Cost**
2	1	Mouse	13.97
3	2	2 Tb Hard Disk	149.17
4	3	1.0 GHz Motherboard	135.13
5	4	1.5 GHz Motherboard	159.54
6	5	15" Monitor	153.35
7	6	17" Monitor	230.22
8	7	Network Card	32.55
9	8	Broadband Router	52.85
10	9	DVD Drive	60.25
11	10	Power Supply Unit	24.37
12	11	Sound Card	32.17
13	12	Keyboard	8.55

Table 8.28

3. Assign the name *pcparts* to an appropriate range of cells.
4. Format all costs to currency.
5. Format data using the styles listed in Table 8.29.

Range of Cells	Cell Style
A1:C1	Accent5
A2:C13	20% – Accent5

Table 8.29

Part 3: Record PC faults

1. Rename Sheet3 as *Job Sheet*
2. Enter the data shown in Table 8.30 in the worksheet named *Job Sheet*. Formulas and functions will be entered in the shaded cells.

	A	B	C	D	E	F	G	H	I
1	**PC Repair Workshop**								
2									
3	PC Number	Model	Year Purchased	Location	Problem Description	Date Referred	Part No Used	Description	Price
4	8				Faulty mouse	02/07/2010	1		
5	1				Broken monitor	04/07/2010	5		
6	5				Not starting up	07/07/2010	3		
7	7				Failed hard drive	10/07/2010	2		
8	9				Won't connect to Internet	10/07/2010	7		
9	3				Keyboard stuck	14/07/2010	12		
10	1				Can't install new software	18/07/2010	12		
11	6				Won't connect to network	23/07/2010	7		
12	2				Mouse pointer jumping	25/07/2010	1		
13	8				Blank screen	29/07/2010	6		
14	2				Not powering up	01/08/2010	10		
15	7				Crashes frequently	06/08/2010	4		

Table 8.30

3. Format data using the styles listed in Table 8.31.

Range of Cells	Cell Style
A1	Title
A3:I3	Accent5
A4:I15	20% – Accent5

Table 8.31

4. Create lookup functions to display the model, year purchased and location for each PC number entered.
5. Create lookup functions to display the description and price for each part number entered.

6. Format all prices to currency.
7. Using a Filter, display records of repairs where a *mouse* was used as a replacement part.
8. Clear the Filter and display records of repairs for *Compaq PCs* only.
9. Clear all filters in the *Job Sheet* worksheet.

Part 4: Analyse Repair Data

1. Insert a new worksheet and rename this worksheet as *Job Analysis*
2. Enter the data shown in Table 8.32 in the worksheet named *Job Analysis*

	A	B	C
1		**Analysis by Department**	
2			
3	**Department**	**Number of Referrals**	**Total Cost**
4	Accounts		
5	Administration		
6	Engineering		
7	Marketing		
8	Sales		

Table 8.32

3. Calculate the total number of referrals made by each department.
4. Calculate the total cost of repairs for each department.
5. Format data using the styles listed in Table 8.33.

Range of Cells	Cell Style
A1	Title
A3:C3	Accent5
A4:C8	20% – Accent5

Table 8.33

6. Adjust column widths so that the title *Analysis by Department* fits across columns A, B and C.
7. Display the number of referrals by department using a pie chart. Information relating to chart setup is displayed in Table 8.34.

Chart Type	Pie in 3-D
Chart Title	Referrals by Department
Data Labels	Percentage – Outside End position
Chart Location	*Job Analysis* worksheet

Table 8.34

- Apply the *Coloured Outline – Accent2* shape style to the chart background.
- Apply the *Coloured Fill – Accent2* shape style to the chart title.

8. Display the total cost by department using a pie chart. Information relating to chart setup is displayed in Table 8.35.

Chart Type	Pie in 3-D
Chart Title	Total Cost by Department
Data Labels	Percentage – Outside End position
Chart Location	*Job Analysis* worksheet, to the right of the Referrals by Department pie chart

Table 8.35

- Apply the *Coloured Outline – Accent2* shape style to the chart background.
- Apply the *Coloured Fill – Accent2* shape style to the chart title.

9. Delete any unused worksheets in the workbook.
10. Rearrange the sheet tabs so that they appear in the order shown in Figure 8.10.

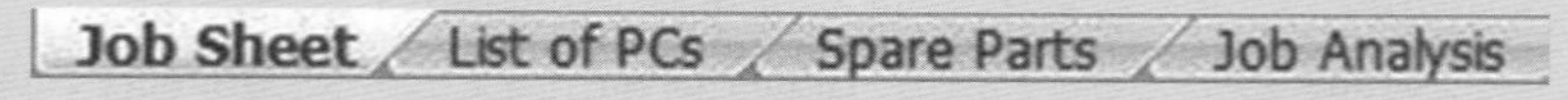

Figure 8.10

11. In the *List of PCs*, *Spare Parts* and *Job Analysis* worksheets, implement spreadsheet protection so that data cannot be entered in any cells.
12. In the worksheet named *Job Sheet*, implement spreadsheet protection so that:
    - data can only be entered in the ranges A4:A15 and E4:G15
    - formulas and functions are no longer displayed in the formula bar.
13. Protect the workbook for structure only.

Part 5: Create a Macro

1. Save the spreadsheet as **PC Repair Workshop**, using the *Excel Macro-Enabled Workbook* file type.
2. Turn off worksheet protection in the *Job Sheet* worksheet.
3. Select any cell in the *Spare Parts* worksheet.
4. Record a new macro (named *cleardata*) that performs the following tasks:
   - selects the *Job Sheet* worksheet
   - deletes the contents of A4:A15 and E4:G15
   - positions the cell pointer in A4.
5. Draw a rounded rectangle in column I, to the right of the heading *PC Repair Workshop*. Format the rectangle using the *Subtle Effect Dark 1* shape style. Type the text *Clear All* inside the rectangle. Link the rounded rectangle to the *cleardata* macro.

   Clear All
6. Re-protect the *Job Sheet* worksheet.
7. Test your macro by entering dummy repair data. Run the macro by clicking the *Clear All* button.
8. Save the **PC Repair Workshop** spreadsheet.

Lookup Functions Assignment Three

Part 1: Create the Grades Lookup Table

1. Create a new spreadsheet workbook and rename Sheet1 as *CAO Points*
2. Enter the data shown in Table 8.36 in the *CAO Points* worksheet.

	A	B	C
1	Grade	Higher Level	Ordinary Level
2	A1	100	60
3	A2	90	50
4	B1	85	45
5	B2	80	40
6	B3	75	35
7	C1	70	30
8	C2	65	25
9	C3	60	20
10	D1	55	15
11	D2	50	10
12	D3	45	5

Table 8.36

3. Assign the name *grades* to an appropriate range of cells in the *CAO Points* worksheet.
4. Merge styles from the *Miles of Tiles* spreadsheet.
5. Format data in the *CAO Points* worksheet using the styles listed in Table 8.37.

Range of Cells	Cell Style
A1:C1	Accent5
A2:C12	20% – Accent5

Table 8.37

Part 2: Create the Points Lookup Table

1. Rename Sheet2 as *Choices*
2. Enter the data shown in Table 8.38 in the *Choices* worksheet.

	A	B	C
1	**Preference**	**Course Title**	**Minimum Points**
2	1	Mathematics	510
3	2	Theoretical Physics and Maths	485
4	3	Astrophysics	425
5	4	Biotechnology	340
6	5	Computer Science	325

Table 8.38

3. Assign the name *coursepref* to an appropriate range of cells in the *Choices* worksheet.
4. Format data in the *Choices* worksheet using the styles listed in Table 8.39.

Range of Cells	Cell Style
A1:C1	Accent5
A2:C6	20% – Accent5

Table 8.39

Part 3: Analyse Student Results

1. Rename Sheet3 as *Results*
2. Enter the data shown in Table 8.40 in the *Results* worksheet.

	A	B	C	D
1	Susan O Neill			
2	Leaving Cert Results			
3				
4	**Subject**	**Grade**	**Level**	**Points**
5	Irish	B3	Ordinary	
6	English	B1	Higher	
7	Maths	A2	Higher	
8	French	C1	Ordinary	
9	Chemistry	B2	Ordinary	
10	Biology	A2	Higher	
11	Physics	A1	Higher	
12				
13			**Total Points**	
14				
15	**Enter Preference (1–5):**			1
16				
17	**Course Title:**			
18				
19	**Points Required:**			
20				
21	**Admit to this course?**			

Table 8.40

3. Calculate the points for each subject using a lookup function.

H You will also need an IF function for this calculation.

4. Test the function you have just created by entering the following grades and levels:

Grade	Level	Points
A1	Lower	60
B1	Lower	45
C1	Lower	30
D1	Lower	15

Contd.

A2	Higher	90
B2	Higher	80
C3	Higher	60
D2	Higher	50

5. Calculate total points.
6. Display the *course title* using an appropriate function.
7. Test the function created in question 6 by entering different course preferences.
8. Display the *points required* using an appropriate function.
9. In cell D21, display the text *Yes* or *No* depending on whether the total points are equal to/greater than or less than the points required.
10. Format data using the styles listed in Table 8.41.

Range of Cells	Cell Style
A1	Title
A2, A4:D4, C13, A15, A17, A19, A21	Accent5
A5:D11, D13, D15, D19, D21	20% – Accent5
C17	Input

Table 8.41

11. Use conditional formatting to format grades A1 and A2 in *Light Red Fill with Dark Red Text*.

You may need two separate conditional formatting rules to do this.

12. Test the conditional formatting by changing Susan's Irish result to A2. The result should now be formatted in red.
13. Change Susan's Irish result back to B3.
14. Delete any unused worksheets in the workbook.
15. In the *CAO Points* and *Choices* worksheets, implement spreadsheet protection so that data cannot be entered in any cells.
16. In the *Results* worksheet, implement spreadsheet protection so that:
    - data can only be entered in A1, in the range A5:C11 and in D15
    - the spreadsheet user cannot select locked cells.
17. Protect the workbook for structure only.

Part 4: Create a Macro

1. Before recording this macro, select any cell in the *CAO Points* worksheet.
2. Record a new macro (named *cleargrades*) that performs the following tasks:
   - selects the *Results* worksheet
   - deletes the contents of A1, A5:C11 and D15
   - positions the cell pointer in A1.
3. Turn off worksheet protection in the *Results* worksheet.
4. Draw a rounded rectangle in column E to the right of the text *Leaving Cert Results*. Format the rectangle using the *Subtle Effect Dark 1* shape style. Type the text *Clear Grades* inside the rectangle. Link the rounded rectangle to the *cleargrades* macro.

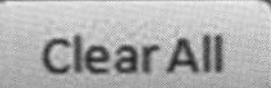

5. Re-protect the *Results* worksheet.
6. Save the **CAO Points Calculator** spreadsheet as an *Excel Macro-Enabled Workbook*.

Part 5: Enter New Data

1. In the *Results* worksheet, delete the data relating to Susan O Neill. Enter new data shown in Table 8.42.

Nataliya Shevelova		
Preference	**2**	
Subject	**Grade**	**Level**
Irish	B3	Higher
English	B2	Higher
Maths	A1	Higher
French	C1	Ordinary
Applied Maths	A1	Higher
Physics	A1	Higher
Technical Drawing	A1	Higher

Table 8.42

2. Check your answers: Nataliya's course preference is *Theoretical Physics and Maths*. She will be admitted to this course as her points total of 585 is greater than the entry requirement of 485 points.
3. Save the *CAO Points Calculator* spreadsheet.

CHAPTER 8 SUMMARY

1. Basic Concepts

Vertical Lookup Table Data is stored in columns and is retrieved using a Vlookup function. The first column is the key column. The lookup table must be in ascending order of the first column.

Horizontal Lookup Table Data is stored in rows and is retrieved using an Hlookup function. The first row is the key row. Data must be in ascending order as you move across the first row of the lookup table.

Vlookup Function The Vlookup function is used to access data from a vertical lookup table. Example: *=vlookup(a2,products,4,false)*. This Vlookup function will take the data from a2 and then search for a match in the first column of the lookup table named *products*. This isolates a specific row in the lookup table. The data in the fourth column of this row will then be extracted by the lookup function. The false argument prevents the lookup function from returning an incorrect answer for a number that doesn't exist in the lookup table.

Hlookup Function Used to access data from a horizontal lookup table. Example: *=hlookup(b7,accounts,3,false)*. Hlookup functions work with horizontal lookup tables where the data is organised in rows. The function will seek a match for b7 in the first row of the *accounts* lookup table. This isolates a specific column in the lookup table. The function will then extract data from the third row of this column. The false argument works in the same way as it does for the Vlookup function.

2. Potential Pitfalls

- The column or row headings should not be included when naming a lookup table.
- If the data referred to by the lookup function doesn't exist in the first column or row of the lookup table, an incorrect answer will be returned by the lookup function unless you include the *false* argument in the lookup function.
- If the first column or row of the lookup table is not in ascending order, some lookup functions will give incorrect answers.
- The column or row number referred to by the lookup function must not be zero and cannot be greater than the number of rows or columns contained in the lookup table.
- Excel does not allow spaces in range names.

3. Useful Shortcuts

Keystroke	Action
F3	Displays a list of cell and range names in your spreadsheet workbook. Can be used when writing a Vlookup or Hlookup function instead of typing the range name.
ALT+M+N	Accesses the Name Manager in the Formulas group.

Table 8.43

LOOKUP FUNCTIONS REVIEW QUESTIONS

Answers to the review questions are available on www.gillmacmillan.ie

1. When a lookup table is arranged in columns, you should use a ____________ function.

   When a lookup table is arranged in rows, you should use a ____________ function.

2. Figure 8.11 displays customer data for a jewellery wholesaler.

	A	B
1	Customer Code	Customer Name
2	1001	Diamond House
3	1002	House of Gold
4	1003	Macks Jewellers
5	1004	Precious Stones
6	1005	Rubies Ireland
7		

Figure 8.11

   (i) What range of cells should be highlighted to set this data up as a lookup table?

   (ii) Assuming that the name *customers* has been correctly assigned to the lookup table, write down the function required to display the customer name in Figure 8.12.

   ____

	A	B
1	Customer Code	1004
2		
3	Customer Name	
4		

Figure 8.12

3. The data in Figure 8.13 has been set up as a lookup table.

	A	B
1	Product Number	Product Name
2	3	Hub
3	6	Rim
4	1	Spoke
5	4	Brake pads
6	2	Disk rotor
7	5	Cross Country Tyre
8		

Figure 8.13

(i) What is wrong with the way this lookup table has been set up?

___

(ii) What errors will occur when lookup functions are used to access product names from the lookup table?

___

4. Figure 8.14 displays customer data relating to company drivers.

	A	B	C
1	Employee Number	Vehicle Registration Number	Driver Name
2	3298	08D2395	Owen Roberts
3	9837	09KE19872	Paul Thomas
4	12857	07D55601	Stuart Aston
5	76963	06KY50771	Adrian Renshaw
6	83395	05KK349	Mike Lloyd
7	89423	09D61224	Mathew Rider
8	97591	10LH4099	John Smith
9	117929	09WW449	Andrew Reid
10	118896	08WX1182	Joan Reid
11	118899	10D7601	Jimmy Mac Donald
12	135926	09KE2223	Andrew Smith
13	144535	10D8312	Wayne Rogers
14			

Figure 8.14

(i) What range of cells should be highlighted to set this data up as a lookup table?

(ii) Assuming that the name *drivers* has been correctly assigned to the lookup table, write down the function required to display the vehicle registration number in Figure 8.15.

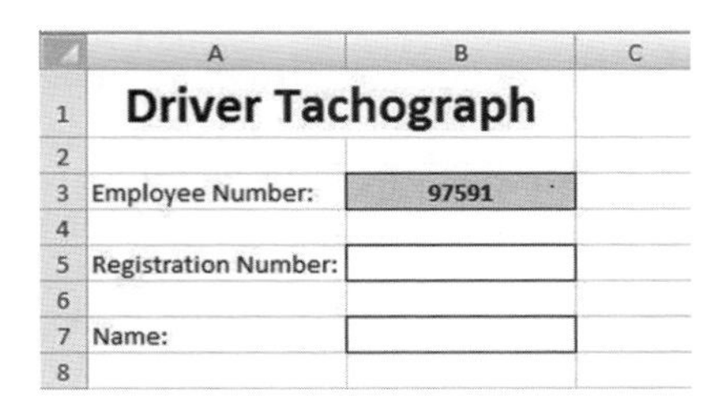

Figure 8.15

(iii) Write down the function that will display the driver name in Figure 8.15.

(iv) If the number 85000 is entered in A3 in Figure 8.15, which employee name will be displayed by the lookup function? __________

(v) What should be included in the lookup function to prevent this error occurring?

5. Figure 8.16 displays a lookup table which stores data relating to computer components.

	A	B	C	D
1	Product Code	Description	Amount in Stock	Unit Price
2	B1001	512 Mb Graphics Card	2	€ 58.99
3	B1002	1GHz Motherboard	5	€ 75.99
4	B1003	Quad core processor	10	€ 85.99
5	B1004	1Gb DDR RAM Module	12	€ 24.99
6	C1001	2Tb Hard Disk	3	€ 57.99
7	C1002	Blu Ray Drive	5	€ 45.99
8				

Figure 8.16

The lookup table has been assigned the name *stock*. Figure 8.17 displays an invoice which uses lookup functions to access data from the *stock* lookup table.

	A	B	C	D
1			Invoice	
2				
3	Item Number	Product Code	Description	Unit Price
4	1	C1001	=VLOOKUP(,stock,)	=VLOOKUP(,stock,)
5	2	B1004	=VLOOKUP(,stock,)	=VLOOKUP(,stock,)
6				
7				
8			Total:	€82.98
9				

Figure 8.17

Using the information in Figure 8.17, complete the lookup functions in Table 8.44.

(i)	Display description for product C1001	=vlookup(,stock ,)
(ii)	Display unit price for product C1001	=vlookup(,stock ,)
(iii)	Display description for product B1004	=vlookup(,stock ,)
(iv)	Display unit price for product B1004	=vlookup(,stock ,)

Table 8.44

6. In Table 8.45, the name *parts* has been assigned to the lookup table.

	A	B	C
1	**Part Number**	**Type**	**Location**
2	12855	A	Area 1
3	12856	B	Area 3
4	12857	A	Area 1
5	12858	C	Area 2
6	12859	C	Area 2
7	12860	B	Area 1
8			

Table 8.45

In Figure 8.18, a lookup function has been entered to access data from the *parts* lookup table.

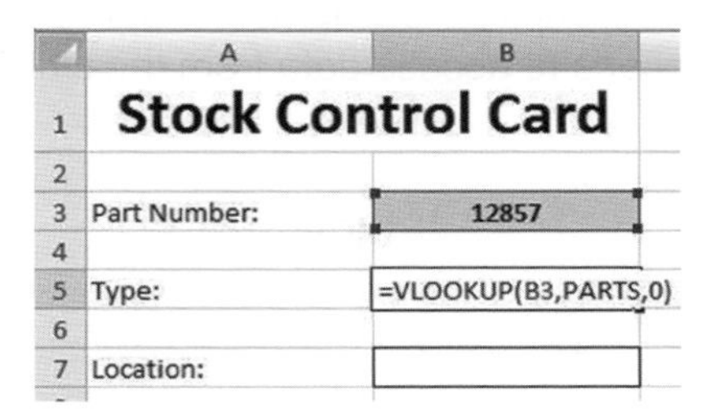

Figure 8.18

(i) What is wrong with the lookup function in Figure 8.18? ______________

____

(ii) What error will be returned by this lookup function? ______________

7. Table 8.46 displays data relating to a courier company.

	A	B	C	D	E	F	G	H
1	**Code:**	106	128	207	225	246	341	357
2	**Name:**	P. Daly	A. Doyle	H. Jones	P. Coyle	J. Murphy	R. Dunne	W. Wise
3	**Collection Charge:**	2.0%	1.5%	3.0%	2.5%	1.5%	0.5%	3.5%

Table 8.46

(i) What range of cells should be highlighted to set this up as a lookup table?

____

	A	B	C
15	**Code**	**Name**	**Collection Charge**
16	225		
17			

Table 8.47

(ii) A customer code has been entered in A16 in Table 8.47. Assuming the name *charges* has been assigned to the correct range in Table 8.46, write down the lookup function to display the customer name.

____

(iii) Write down the lookup function to display the collection charge.

____

8. In Table 8.48, the name *members* has been assigned to the lookup table.

	A	B	C
1	**Membership Number**	**Member Name**	**Membership Type**
2	1	John Burke	Full
3	2	Kapinga Mukendi	Full
4	3	Ruth Burchall	Associate
5	4	Frank Stewart	Full
6	5	Paul Murphy	Associate
7	6	Eva Bursekas	Associate
8			

Table 8.48

In Figure 8.19, a lookup function has been entered to access data from the *members* lookup table.

	A	B	C
1	**Membership Card**		
2			
3	Membership Number:	2	
4			
5	Name:	=VLOOKUP(B3,MEMBERS,4)	
6			
7	Membership Type:		

Figure 8.19

(i) What is wrong with the lookup function in Figure 8.19?

____

(ii) What error will be returned by this lookup function?

____

9. Table 8.49 displays data relating to factory production.

	A	B	C	D	E	F
1	**Factory Number:**	1	2	3	4	5
2	**Manager:**	J. Doyle	H. Lee	S. Byrne	A. Smith	T. Jones
3	**Capacity:**	4500	4000	3000	6000	6500

Table 8.49

(i) What range of cells should be highlighted to set this up as a lookup table?

____

	A	B	C
12	**Factory Number**	**Manager**	**Capacity**
13	2		
14			

Table 8.50

(ii) A factory number has been entered in A13 in Table 8.50. Assuming the name *factories* has been assigned to the correct range in Table 8.49, write down the lookup function to display the manager's name.

____

(iii) Write down the lookup function to display the factory capacity.

____

10. Figure 8.20 displays a lookup table which stores data relating to customer accounts.

	A	B	C	D
1	Account Number	Client Name	Account Total	Credit Period (days)
2	205798	Murphy and Son	€ 1,009.27	30
3	301442	Dunne Haulage	€ 2,058.00	60
4	321567	O Sullivan Ltd	€ 519.45	14
5	325770	Tullymore Concrete	€ 2,017.11	60
6	349608	Bob the Builder	€ 1,542.39	30
7	400012	Murrays Movers	€ 285.55	7
8				

Figure 8.20

The lookup table has been assigned the name *accounts*. Figure 8.21 displays a summary which accesses data from the *accounts* lookup table.

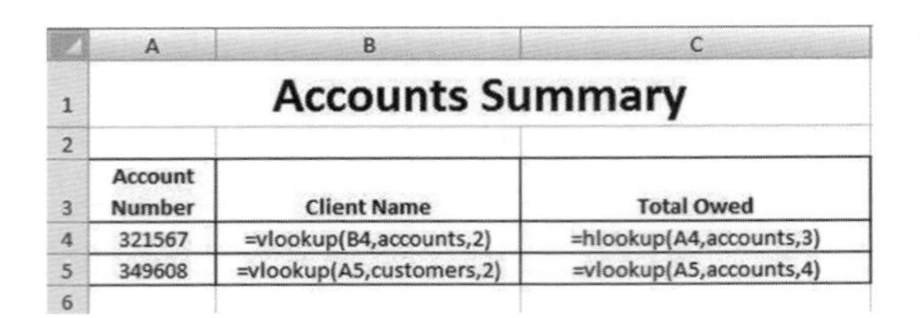

	A	B	C
1	Accounts Summary		
2			
3	Account Number	Client Name	Total Owed
4	321567	=vlookup(B4,accounts,2)	=hlookup(A4,accounts,3)
5	349608	=vlookup(A5,customers,2)	=vlookup(A5,accounts,4)
6			

Figure 8.21

Each of the lookup functions displayed in Figure 8.21 contains an error. Write down the correct lookup functions in Table 8.51.

	Incorrect Lookup Function	Correct Lookup Function
(i)	=vlookup(B4,accounts,2)	
(ii)	=hlookup(A4,accounts,3)	
(iii)	=vlookup(A5,customers,2)	
(iv)	=vlookup(A5,accounts,4)	

Table 8.51

SECTION 3

Project Guidelines and Sample Exams

9 Project Guidelines and Sample Exams

SPREADSHEETS PROJECT

As part of the FETAC Level 5 Spreadsheet Methods Module you are required to complete a spreadsheet project. The project tests whether you can apply what you have learned about spreadsheets to a fictitious problem and then design and create a spreadsheet to solve the problem. The problem may be in a business context, such as the need to computerise the payroll of a small business, or it may be in relation to an interest or hobby, such as creating a spreadsheet to maintain the league table of a local football league.

The spreadsheet project must be completed in three distinct phases.

- Phase one: Design (40%)
- Phase two: Implementation (40%)
- Phase three: Proposed Modifications (20%).

The project must be completed in this order. You must design your spreadsheet on paper before you set it up in Excel. It's worth noting that there are more marks for designing your spreadsheet and for suggesting modifications than for creating the spreadsheet in Excel. Many students spend too much time on setting up the spreadsheet and not enough time on design and modifications.

PHASE ONE – DESIGN (40%)

1. Describe the aims of your project.
2. Specify input and output data.
3. Design a data capture form.
4. Specify formulas and functions used for processing.

Describe the Aims of Your Project

1. Provide some background information to set the scene for your project.

Example

Widget Engineering Ltd is a small engineering firm that employs 12 people. Payment of wages in the company is done weekly and is calculated using a manual payroll system. This system is very complicated and above all very time-consuming. It's also prone to error.

The aim of this project is to computerise the payroll system using a spreadsheet. The new system will ensure that all calculations and weekly wages slips will be processed quickly and efficiently with the minimum amount of problems.

2. Identify problems that exist in the current system. For each problem that you identify, describe in detail how the spreadsheet will solve the problem.

Example

Problem: With the manual payroll system each employee's weekly tax and tax to date are worked out by the accounts clerk, using a calculator. As many of the employees work overtime, the amount of tax varies from week to week. Due to the number of calculations required, the clerk sometimes makes a mistake and is unavailable for other work while the wages are being calculated.

Solution: In the spreadsheet system, each employee's tax rate will be worked out using an IF function. The clerk will no longer have to decide when an employee moves on to the higher rate of tax because the spreadsheet will make this decision in the future. The calculation of weekly tax will also be carried out by the IF function. Tax to date will be calculated using a formula. The clerk will only have to input the hours worked. The reduction in workload will free the clerk up for other duties.

Specify Input and Output Data

Input data is any data that is entered in the spreadsheet after the spreadsheet has been set up. For example, *Hours Worked* is input data and would be entered for each employee. Output data is anything that is worked out by formula or function. For example, *Net Pay* is output data.

1. Input and output data should be identified and specified using the following headings: Variable Name; Data Type; Format; Example.

Input Data Example

Variable Name	Data Type	Format	Example
Employee Name	Text	Arial, 14	Tom Jenkins
Annual Salary	Numeric	Currency, 0 decimals	€62,560

Table 9.1

Output Data Example

Variable Name	Data Type	Format	Example
Weekly Gross Pay	Numeric	Currency, 2 decimals	€1203.07
Weekly PRSI	Numeric	Currency, 2 decimals	€25.08

Table 9.2

3. Identify which areas of the spreadsheet are protected and can only be accessed by entering a password. The spreadsheet user should only have access to cells where data is input. All other cells should be protected. In some cases an entire worksheet, such as a worksheet containing a lookup table, may be hidden. Formulas and functions should be hidden and should require a password to view them. Alternatively, the spreadsheet user may be prevented from selecting locked cells.

Design a Data Capture Form

A data capture form is a printed form that is used to collect data on paper before it is entered in a spreadsheet. It should be designed to capture all of the input data. We have all filled in data capture forms at one time or another. Club membership forms, an application for a bank account and job application forms are examples of data capture forms. It's a good idea to look at how data capture forms are designed in practice before you create your own. A well-designed data capture form will:

- be easy to complete
- contain instructions on how to complete the form
- indicate to whom the form is to be returned or where the form is to be sent once it is completed
- be well laid out on the page using appropriate fonts, colours, tick boxes and lines (for writing names and addresses).

A sample data capture form for Widget Engineering is displayed below.

Widget Engineering

Weekly Timesheet

Employee Name ______________________________

PPS Number | | | | | | | | |

	Monday	Tuesday	Wednesday	Thursday	Friday	Saturday	Sunday
Clock-In							
Clock-Out							

Completed timesheets should be returned to your supervisor no later than 4:00 p.m. the following Monday.

Specify Formulas and Functions Used for Processing

List each formula or function by name and give a brief explanation of how it works. Include all the formulas and functions that will be used in your spreadsheet.

Example

Weekly gross pay is annual salary divided by 52.
PRSI is calculated using an IF function: If PRSI Code = "AO" or "AX" then gross pay for tax purposes is multiplied by 8.5%, otherwise gross pay for tax purposes is multiplied by 12%.

PHASE TWO – IMPLEMENTATION (40%)

1. Spreadsheet well designed.
2. Cell formats appropriately applied.
3. Formulas and functions accurately applied.
4. Change of variable.
5. Spreadsheets saved and printed out.

Spreadsheet Well Designed

In general your spreadsheet will contain at least three worksheets, as follows.

1. *The Input Worksheet:* This is where the user will enter the input data. The layout of this worksheet should reflect the layout of the data capture form and both should include the same items of input data.
2. *The Processing Worksheet:* This worksheet contains all the formulas and functions. All of the data processing is carried out in the processing worksheet.
3. *The Output Worksheet:* This worksheet displays the results of the data processing, e.g. a wages slip.

Depending on the nature of your project you may require more than three worksheets. If you're using a lookup table, this should be stored in a separate worksheet.

Cell Formats Appropriately Applied

- Headings and data should be aligned as appropriate.
- Correct formats should be used for currency, percentages and decimal places. The spreadsheet should be formatted in a way that makes it attractive and easy to use.
- Colour should be used appropriately. Use of a particular colour to identify cells where data is input often makes a spreadsheet easier to use.

Formulas and Functions Accurately Applied

- The spreadsheet should at least contain an IF function or a Lookup function.
- The results of calculations performed by the spreadsheet should be correct. Formulas and functions should be tested by working out the calculations on paper and then checking to see if the results are the same as those produced by the spreadsheet.
- A printout of all formulas and functions contained in your spreadsheet must be produced (formulas and functions can be displayed by selecting the Formulas tab in the Ribbon and then clicking *Show Formulas*). Save this version of your spreadsheet workbook under a different name, such as *Spreadsheet Project Formulas*.

Change of Variable

If the worksheets are linked correctly, changing a number in the input worksheet will cause data to change in the output worksheet, e.g. changing hours worked in the input worksheet will result in changes to gross pay, tax and net pay in the output worksheet, as long as your formulas and functions are linked correctly.

This must be demonstrated by changing an item of input data, printing this altered input worksheet and also printing out the resulting output worksheet. Save this version of the spreadsheet under a different name, such as *Project Variable Change*.

Spreadsheets Saved and Printed Out

When you have completed the project you should have three saved versions of your spreadsheet (each with a different name) together with a printout of each.

Saved Spreadsheets	
Version	**Example**
Original spreadsheet workbook	Spreadsheet Project.xlsx
Spreadsheet with formulas and functions displayed	Spreadsheet Project Formulas.xlsx
Spreadsheet with input variable changed	Project Variable Change.xlsx

Table 9.3

PHASE THREE – PROPOSED MODIFICATIONS (20%)

1. List the aspects of your project that you are particularly pleased with.
2. Suggest at least three ways in which your spreadsheet could be improved if you had more time. Students working on a spreadsheet project will often notice limitations in the design of the spreadsheet. These should be noted and used as potential modifications. Because this section of the project is worth 20%, an in-depth

description of each modification is required. Modifications should be illustrated using examples and diagrams where appropriate.

Example

Currently Widget Engineering Ltd employs 12 people. In the spreadsheet all of the formulas and functions are set up to process the earnings of these 12 people.

In the event of a new employee joining the company, a new worksheet would have to be set up together with an additional row being added to the processing sheet to do the wages calculations for the new employee. At the moment the set-up of the spreadsheet doesn't allow this to be done automatically. Either an existing worksheet would have to be copied and then amended or a completely new worksheet would have to be set up from scratch. Apart from this being very time-consuming, it can be a difficult task for anyone who is unfamiliar with the spreadsheet system.

Given more time, I would create a macro to solve this problem. Each time the macro is run it would add a new worksheet to the spreadsheet and adjust the processing sheet to accommodate the new employee. The accounts clerk would no longer have to go through the painstaking process of setting up a new input sheet and creating new formulas and functions in the processing sheet, as this would be done automatically when the macro is run. The macro could be run from a button, making it easy to use.

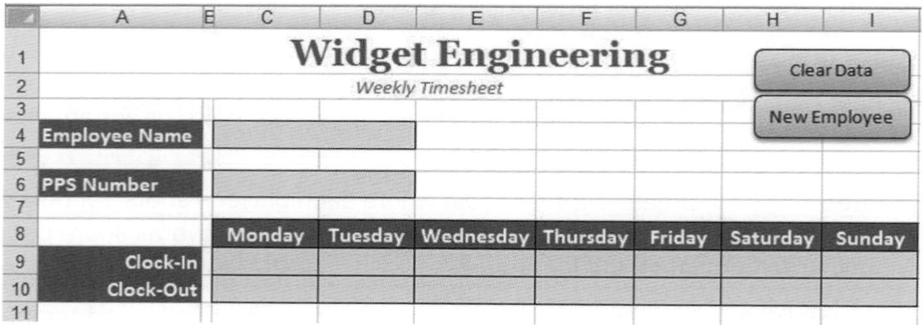

Figure 9.1: The Clear Data and New Employee buttons make the spreadsheet easier to use

Figure 9.1 is an example of what this might look like. When the clerk clicks the *New Employee* button, he or she would be prompted for the new employee's name and PPS number. The macro would automatically set this information up in a new worksheet and then add the new data to the processing sheet. I would also include a *Clear Data* button to make it easier to enter the next employee's clock-in and clock-out times.

POSSIBLE SPREADSHEET PROJECT TOPICS

Foreign exchange: Create a spreadsheet that converts amounts entered in euros to an equivalent amount for a selection of currencies outside the euro zone.

Home decoration estimates: Set up a spreadsheet that will produce a quote for decorating a room where dimensions of the room can be entered and the type of paint, wallpaper or tiles can be selected from a list.

Travel allowances: Produce a weekly travel expense report for sales reps who claim for travel and overnight accommodation allowances.

Exam grades: Create a spreadsheet that allows a teacher to enter student marks per subject and which will then produce a sorted report of students and grades.

Car rentals: Create a spreadsheet that calculates the daily rental fee depending on the type of car. Special offers might be applied to off-peak times.

Fantasy football league: Set up a spreadsheet that allocates points to teams in a league where the total points per game depend on the actions of each player in the team. For example, five points could be awarded to a player for scoring a goal.

Cash flow analysis: Record the income and expenditure of a company over a twelve-month period using a spreadsheet. The spreadsheet should alert the user when creditors must be paid or when customer payments are late.

Golf scores: Create a spreadsheet where each player's shots per hole can be entered and which will then produce an overall score per player and a leader board.

Weather statistics: Produce monthly weather statistics for rainfall and temperature using a spreadsheet. Use charts to show trends in rainfall and temperatures over a particular period.

Opinion poll results: Create a spreadsheet to analyse the results of election opinion polls. Use charts to show how voter preferences are changing over time.

For more ideas have a look through the examples and spreadsheet assignments in *Step by Step Spreadsheets*. The topics listed above are only suggestions and the list of possible spreadsheet projects is endless. What works best is if you can do your spreadsheet project on a topic that interests you, e.g. a hobby or an area that you have worked in before.

FETAC LEVEL 5 SPREADSHEET METHODS

SAMPLE EXAM ONE

Rapid Repair Services Ltd are involved in the servicing and repair of specialist equipment. They have an expert group of service engineers who travel around the country. Each service engineer is paid travel and overnight expenses. You are required to set up a spreadsheet to calculate the expenses for the engineers. All monetary data should be displayed in currency format with two decimal places.

	A	B	C	D	E	F
1	**Rapid Repair Services Ltd**					
2	*Travel and Overnight Expenses*					
3					**Date:**	
4						
5	**Depart Date**	**Return Date**	**Name**	**Kilometres**	**Rate per Kilometre**	**Travel Expenses**
6	01/05/2010	05/05/2010	Kelso Lorna	245		
7	04/05/2010	06/05/2010	Donnelly Helen	76		
8	12/05/2010	12/05/2010	Murphy James	124		
9	13/05/2010	14/05/2010	O Brien Mary	65		
10	13/05/2010	17/05/2010	Regan Thomas	258		
11	14/05/2010	14/05/2010	Tynan Patrick	158		
12	18/05/2010	24/05/2010	Dunne Siobhan	248		
13						
14					**Total:**	
15					**Average:**	

Table 9.4

Part 1

1. Create a new spreadsheet and rename Sheet1 as *Weekly Travel Report*
2. Input the data shown in Table 9.4 in the *Weekly Travel Report* worksheet, with alignments as shown and appropriate column widths.
3. Insert today's date using an appropriate function next to the heading *Date:*
4. Use an IF function to calculate the **rate per kilometre** based on the following information:

- If the kilometres are less than 100, then the rate per kilometre is €0.60.
- If the kilometres are 100 or greater, then the rate per kilometre is €0.50.

5. Calculate the **travel expenses** as the **kilometres** multiplied by the **rate per kilometre.**
6. Use the SUM function to calculate the total travel expenses, and display in the cell beside the side heading *Total:*
7. Use the AVERAGE function to calculate the average travel expenses, and display in the cell beside the side heading *Average:*
8. Save the spreadsheet under the file name **Travel Expenses**, for printing now or later.
9. Produce a printout of the entire spreadsheet **Travel Expenses**, excluding the main heading, and showing row/column identifiers.
10. Produce a printout of the spreadsheet **Travel Expenses** showing all formulas with cell references and row/column identifiers.

Part 2

1. Setup the lookup table displayed in Table 9.5 in Sheet2 of the workbook.

	A	B
1	Code	Rate
2	A	0.95
3	B	1.05
4	C	1.15
5	D	1.20
6	E	1.25
7	F	1.30
8		

Table 9.5

2. Assign the name *rates* to an appropriate range of cells.
3. In the *Weekly Travel Report* worksheet, delete the record for Thomas Regan from the spreadsheet.
4. In the *Weekly Travel Report* worksheet, input the additional information shown in the shaded cells in Table 9.6.
5. Move the side heading *Date:* and today's date to their new positions.

	A	B	C	D	E	F	G	H	I	J
1						Rapid Repair Services Ltd				
2						*Travel and Overnight Expenses*				
3									Date:	
4										
5	Depart Date	Return Date	Name	Kilometres	Code	Rate per Kilometre	Travel Expenses	Overnight Expenses	Special Expenses	Total Payment
6	01/05/2010	05/05/2010	Kelso Lorna	245	A					
7	04/05/2010	06/05/2010	Donnelly Helen	76	C					
8	12/05/2010	12/05/2010	Murphy James	124	A					
9	13/05/2010	14/05/2010	O'Brien Mary	65	B					
10	14/05/2010	14/05/2010	Tynan Patrick	158	B					
11	18/05/2010	24/05/2010	Dunne Siobhan	248	C					
12	22/05/2010	24/05/2010	Donnelly Mary	86	C					
13										
14						Total:				
15						Average:				

Table 9.6

6. Delete the contents in the Rate per Kilometre column.
7. Use a Lookup function to insert the rate from the *rates* lookup table into the *Rate per Kilometre* column.
8. Use an IF function to calculate the overnight expenses based on the following information:
   - If the return date is equal to the depart date then there are no overnight expenses.
   - If the return date is greater than the depart date then the overnight expenses are paid at €50.75 per night.
9. Use an IF function to calculate the special expenses based on the following information:
   - If the travel expenses are greater than €100.00 and the overnight expenses are €200.00 or more, then the special expenses are €53.80.
   - If the travel expenses are greater than €50.00 and the overnight expenses are €100.00 or more, then the special expenses are €29.60.
   - Otherwise no special expenses are paid.
10. Calculate the *total payment* for each engineer as the sum of travel expenses, overnight expenses and special expenses.
11. Use the SUM function to calculate the totals for the travel expenses, overnight expenses, special expenses and total payment columns, and place in the row beside the side heading *Total*.
12. Use the AVERAGE function to calculate the average for travel expenses, overnight expenses, special expenses and total payment and place in the row beside the side heading *Average:* under the appropriate column.
13. Sort the spreadsheet in ascending order on the *Name* column.
14. Save the spreadsheet under the file name **Updated Travel Expenses** for printing now or later.
15. Produce a printout of the *Weekly Travel Report* worksheet in landscape orientation showing row/column identifiers.
16. Produce a printout of the *Weekly Travel Report* worksheet showing all formulas with cell references and row/column identifiers.

Part 3

1. Display the total payment made to each engineer using a column chart.
2. Information relating to chart setup is displayed in Table 9.7.

Chart Type	3-D Clustered Column
Chart Title	Travel and Overnight Payments
Vertical Axis Title	Total Payment
Chart Location	Separate chart sheet named *Engineer Payments*

Table 9.7

3. Print the chart.

SAMPLE EXAM TWO

Discount Spares Ltd is a specialist company involved in the production and distribution of spare parts for a limited range of products. You're required to produce a quotation and subsequently convert it into an order and an invoice. Finally, you're required to produce a macro that will clear the invoice.

All monetary data should be displayed in currency format with two decimal places.

Part 1

1. Create a new spreadsheet and rename Sheet1 as *Quotation Details*.
2. Input the data shown in Table 9.8 in the *Quotation Details* worksheet, with alignments as shown and appropriate column widths.

	A	B	C	D	E	F
1	**Discount Spares Ltd**					
2	*Quotation*					
3	**Name:**	Doyle Bros			**Date:**	16/05/10
4		Main Street				
5		Dunboyne				
6						
7	**Part No.**	**Description**	**Qty**	**Unit Price**	**Discount**	**Line Total**
8	564	Valve Body	6	56.87		
9	624	Piston	3	36.43		
10	574	Chest Assembly	4	124.67		
11	865	Gasket Set	5	24.32		
12	735	Bolt	25	1.20		
13						
14					**Net:**	
15					**VAT:**	
16					**Total:**	

Table 9.8

3. The *discount* should be calculated per unit at 10% of the *unit price.*
4. Calculate the *line total* as the *unit price* minus *discount* multiplied by the *quantity.*
5. Use the SUM function to calculate the *net* value as the sum of the line totals and display it in the cell beside the side heading *Net.*
6. Calculate the *VAT* at 21% of the net value and display it in the cell beside the side heading *VAT.*
7. Calculate the *total* as the *net* plus the *VAT* and display it in the cell beside the side heading *Total.*
8. Save the spreadsheet under the file name **Quote** for printing now or later.

Part 2

1. Setup the lookup table displayed in Table 9.9 in Sheet2 of the workbook.

	A	B
1	**Part Number**	**Type**
2	564	A
3	574	B
4	624	A
5	735	C
6	865	D
7		

Table 9.9

2. Assign the name *parts* to an appropriate range of cells.
3. In the *Quotation Details* worksheet, input the additional information input shown in the shaded cells in Table 9.10.

	A	B	C	D	E	F	G	H
1	**Discount Spares Ltd**							
2	*Order*							
3	**Name:**	Doyle Bros					**Order Date:**	16/05/10
4		Main Street						
5		Dunboyne						
6								
7	**Part No.**	**Description**	**Type**	**Qty**	**Unit Price**	**Disc %**	**Discount**	**Line Total**
8	564	Valve Body		6	56.87			
9	624	Piston		3	36.43			
10	574	Chest Assembly		4	124.67			
11	865	Gasket Set		5	24.32			
12	735	Bolt		25	1.20			
13								
14							**Net:**	
15							**VAT:**	
16							**Total:**	

Table 9.10

4. Change the heading in row 2 to *Order*.
5. Use a lookup function to insert the type from the *parts* lookup table in column C.
6. Use an IF function to display the correct value in the Disc % column based on the following information:
   - If the type is A then the discount is 10%.
   - If the type is B then the discount is 5%.
   - All other types have a 0% discount.
7. Display the figures in the Disc % column in percentage format.
8. Delete the values in the discount column and calculate the new discount as the disc % multiplied by the unit price.
9. Save the spreadsheet under the file name **Order.**
10. Print the Quotation Details worksheet, showing gridlines and row and column headings.

Part 3

1. Setup the lookup table displayed in Table 9.11 in Sheet3 of the workbook.

	A	B
1	VAT Code	VAT Rate
2	1	21%
3	2	15%
4	3	12.5%
5	4	10%
6		

Table 9.11

2. Assign the name *vatrates* to an appropriate range of cells.
3. Input the additional information shown in the shaded cells in Table 9.12.
4. Change the heading in row 2 to *Invoice*. Move side headings as required.
5. Use an IF function to insert the VAT codes in the VAT Code column using the following criteria:
   - If the type is A then the VAT code is 1.
   - If the type is B then the VAT code is 2.
   - If the type is C then the VAT code is 3.
   - All other types have a VAT code of 4.
6. Use a lookup function to insert the correct VAT rate into the VAT Rate column.
7. Display the VAT rate in percentage format with one decimal place.
8. Use a formula to calculate the number of days between the order date and the invoice date and place in the cell beside the *Days – Order to Invoice:* side heading.
9. Calculate the penalty using the *Days – Order to Invoice* value and place in the cell beside the side heading *Penalty*. The calculation should be based on the following criteria:
   - If the number of days is five or more then the penalty is 2% of the total.
   - If the number of days is three or four then the penalty is 1% of the total.
   - If the number of days is less than three, there is no penalty.

	A	B	C	D	E	F	G	H	I	J
1					Discount Spares Ltd					
2					*Invoice*					
3	**Name:**	Doyle Bros							**Order Date:**	16/05/10
4		Main Street							**Invoice Date:**	21/05/10
5		Dunboyne								
6										
7	**Part No.**	**Description**	**Type**	**Qty**	**Unit Price**	**Disc %**	**Discount**	**VAT Code**	**VAT Rate**	**Line Total**
8	564	Valve Body		6	56.87					
9	624	Piston		3	36.43					
10	574	Chest Assembly		4	124.67					
11	865	Gasket Set		5	24.32					
12	735	Bolt		25	1.20					
13										
14	**Days – Order to Invoice:**								**Net:**	
15		**Penalty:**							**VAT:**	
16									**Total:**	

Table 9.12

10. Display the penalty in currency format.
11. Recalculate the *VAT* using the appropriate VAT rates and line totals.
12. Sort the spreadsheet in ascending order on the *description* column.
13. Save the spreadsheet under the file name **Invoice** for printing now or later.
14. Produce two printouts, in landscape orientation, of the *Quotation Details* worksheet to show (i) values and (ii) formulas and cell references.

Part 4

1. Save the spreadsheet as **Macro**, using the *Excel Macro-Enabled Workbook* option.
2. Produce a macro named *cleardata* that will perform the following tasks:
   - Delete the order date and the invoice date.
   - Delete the name and address.
   - Delete the values from the *Part Number* and *Description* columns.
   - Delete the values from the *Quantity* and *Unit Price* columns.
   - Insert the date from the computer clock in cell headed *Invoice Date*
   - Select cell B3.

Glossary of Spreadsheet Terms

Absolute Cell Reference

An absolute cell reference may be used in a formula or a function. Absolute cell references don't change when the formula or function is copied. A cell reference can be made absolute by inserting $ on either side of the reference to the column letter. Example: *A1* is relative, *A1* is absolute.

Cell Name

A name can be assigned to an individual cell by selecting the cell and then entering a name in the name box, which is part of the formula bar. Once a cell has been given a name this name can be used in formulas, e.g. *=B2*taxrate*. Cell names are absolute.

Chart

A method of representing data graphically so that trends and exceptional values can be quickly recognised. In a chart, numbers can be represented by vertical columns, horizontal bars, slices of a pie or dots that are joined up to form a series of lines.

Chart Sheet

A sheet within a workbook that displays a chart separately from the numbers that the chart is representing. Data cannot be entered in a chart sheet.

Condition

A test carried out by an IF function, an AND function or an OR function using a logical operator.

Conditional Formatting

A method of emphasising specific cells in a worksheet. Formatting can be applied to cells that match a certain condition or multiple conditions. For example, amounts that are greater than €100 could be displayed in red. Conditional formatting is dynamic and automatically adjusts to reflect changes in the data.

Custom Sort

Custom sorts are used to sort data by two or more columns or rows. When the required order doesn't follow an alphabetical pattern, Excel's pre-programmed custom sorts can be used. For example, if weekdays were sorted alphabetically the result would be Friday, Monday, Saturday, Sunday, Thursday, Tuesday, Wednesday. A custom sort is required to display days in sequential order (Monday, Tuesday, Wednesday, Thursday, Friday, Saturday, Sunday).

False Action

The section of an IF function that is implemented when the condition is not satisfied.

Formula

A method of calculation using a combination of cell references together with the arithmetic operators + - * /. Brackets can be used to change the natural order of calculation in a formula. In any formula that doesn't contain brackets, multiplication and division are always done first.

Formula Bar

This appears above the column headings. It tells us which cell the cell pointer is currently in. It also displays the contents of the current cell, which may be a number, text, a formula or a function.

Function

A function is a calculation tool designed to carry out a specific task, e.g. calculating the average of a set of numbers. Using functions reduces the workload of the spreadsheet user.

Logical Operator

Logical operators are used in the condition of an IF function. They are also used in AND functions and OR functions. They are combined with cell references, values and/or text to form logical expressions.

Logical Operator	Meaning
=	Equal to
<	Less than
<=	Less than or equal to
>	Greater than
>=	Greater than or equal to
<>	Not equal to

Table 1

Lookup Table

A lookup table stores data that can be referenced by a lookup function. Lookup tables are very useful where there's a large amount of data to be referenced. For example, a lookup table could store all the bar codes, product descriptions and prices of products in a hardware store.

Macro

A method of automating repetitive spreadsheet tasks. A series of spreadsheet commands are recorded and stored in the macro. When the macro is played back, all of the recorded commands are executed at high speed.

Office Button

In Excel 2007 the File menu has been replaced by the Office button, which appears in the top left-hand corner of the screen. The *New*, *Open*, *Save*, *Save As* and *Print* commands are accessed by clicking the Office button. Clicking the Office button also displays a list of recently used spreadsheet workbooks. In Office 2010, the Office button has been replaced by the File menu.

Quick Access Toolbar

The Quick Access Toolbar contains frequently used commands. It appears to the right of the Office button in the top left-hand corner of the screen and can be used to open or save a spreadsheet file as well as creating new spreadsheet files. The Undo and Redo buttons also appear in the Quick Access Toolbar.

Range

Two or more cells that can be highlighted in a worksheet. Multiple ranges can be highlighted by holding down the *CTRL* key as you highlight cells with the mouse. Ranges are used in functions, e.g. *=SUM(b6:h6)*

Range Name

A name can be assigned to a range of cells by highlighting the cells and then entering a name in the name box, which is part of the formula bar. Once a range has been given a name, this name can be used in functions, e.g. *=SUM(sales)*.

Relative Cell Reference

Relative cell references are used in formulas and functions. Relative cell references change when a formula or function is copied, depending on the direction in which the formula or function is copied.
Example: The formula *=B6*C6* contains relative cell references. It becomes =B7*C7 when copied down to the next row.

Ribbon

In Excel 2007, menus and toolbars have been replaced by the Ribbon. In the Ribbon, command buttons and drop-down menu lists are collected together under tabs. There are seven tabs in the Ribbon representing seven different groups of commands. Each tab relates to a particular activity. For example, the Home tab primarily consists of commands related to formatting data.

Sort

Data stored in a spreadsheet can be rearranged into ascending or descending alphabetical or numerical order by clicking the *Sort & Filter* button and then selecting either *Sort A to Z* or *Sort Z to A* when sorting text. When sorting numbers, the options are *Sort Smallest to Largest* and *Sort Largest to Smallest*.

Spreadsheet Window

This is the section of the spreadsheet that you can see on the screen at any given time. The entire spreadsheet is too big to fit on the computer screen.

True Action

The section of an IF function that is implemented when the condition is satisfied.

Workbook

A collection of worksheets that are saved as a spreadsheet file.

Workbook Protection

Protecting a workbook for *Structure* prevents the spreadsheet user from deleting, moving or renaming worksheets contained in a workbook. Protecting a workbook for *Windows* prevents the spreadsheet user from resizing, moving or closing windows within the workbook.

Worksheet

An individual sheet in a workbook. In Excel 2007, each new workbook consists of three worksheets. The maximum number of worksheets in a workbook depends on your PC's available memory. Data entered in multiple worksheets can be linked using formulas.

Worksheet Protection

A method of restricting access to specific cells in a worksheet. When a worksheet is protected, data can only be entered in cells that have been unlocked by the spreadsheet designer. In a protected worksheet, formulas and functions will no longer be displayed in cells where the Hidden property has been turned on.

Worksheet Tabs

The worksheet tabs display the names of the worksheets in the workbook. Each worksheet can be displayed by clicking its worksheet tab.

List of Excel Keyboard Shortcuts

Keyboard Combination	Action
F3	Pressing F3 while writing a function displays a list of cell and range names in your workbook. Select the appropriate name and click OK to paste it into the function.
F4	Converts highlighted cell reference in a formula from relative to absolute.
F11	Creates a column chart in a separate chart sheet based on the selected cells.
SHIFT+F11	Inserts a new worksheet.
ALT+L	Displays the Developer group in the Ribbon.
ALT+N	Displays the Insert group in the Ribbon.
ALT+R	Displays the Review group in the Ribbon.
ALT+W	Displays the View group in the Ribbon.
ALT+JA	Displays the Layout group in the Ribbon.
ALT+JC	Displays the Design group in the Ribbon.
ALT+L+AS	Displays the *Macro Security* settings.
ALT+M+N	Accesses the *Name Manager* in the Formulas group.
ALT+N+G+A	Displays the *Add Signature Services* options.
ALT+N+SH	Accesses the list of shapes in the Insert group.
ALT+R+S	Checks spelling and grammar.
ALT+R+PW+W	Displays the *Protect Structure and Windows* settings.
ALT+W+M+R	Displays the *Record Macro* dialog box.
ALT+F8	Displays a list of macros in the current workbook.
CTRL+C	Copy.
CTRL+N	Create a new Excel workbook.
CTRL+S	Save the current workbook.
CTRL+V	Paste.
CTRL+X	Cut.
CTRL+F2	Print Preview.